Lecture Notes in Artificial Intelligence   8386

Subseries of Lecture Notes in Computer Science

For further volumes:
http://www.springer.com/series/1244

Tina Balke · Frank Dignum
M. Birna van Riemsdijk · Amit K. Chopra (Eds.)

Coordination, Organizations, Institutions, and Norms in Agent Systems IX

COIN 2013 International Workshops
COIN@AAMAS, St. Paul, MN, USA, May 6, 2013
COIN@PRIMA, Dunedin, New Zealand,
December 3, 2013
Revised Selected Papers

 Springer

Editors
Tina Balke
University of Surrey
Guildford
UK

Frank Dignum
Utrecht University
Utrecht
The Netherlands

M. Birna van Riemsdijk
Delft University of Technology
Delft
The Netherlands

Amit K. Chopra
Lancaster University
Lancaster
UK

ISSN 0302-9743   ISSN 1611-3349   (electronic)
ISBN 978-3-319-07313-2   ISBN 978-3-319-07314-9   (eBook)
DOI 10.1007/978-3-319-07314-9
Springer Cham Heidelberg New York Dordrecht London

Library of Congress Control Number: 2014941078

LNCS Sublibrary: SL7 – Artificial Intelligence

Printed on acid-free paper

Springer is part of Springer Science+Business Media (www.springer.com)

Preface

This volume is the ninth in the COIN (Coordination, Organizations, Institutions and Norms in Agent Systems) workshop series, which has its roots in 2005. The volume contains revised versions of 20 selected papers presented at COIN workshops in 2013. The first of these workshops was co-located with AAMAS 2013 and took place on May 6 in St. Paul, Minnesota, while the second was co-located with PRIMA and was held on December 3 in Dunedin, New Zealand.

The papers in this collection have undergone a substantial process of refinement. As in previous editions, at least three Program Committee members reviewed each submitted paper and revised versions of the accepted papers were presented in the workshop sessions. After their presentation, some papers were selected to be part of this volume. We selected 18 papers and two invited papers out of the 28 submissions. These selected papers had to be revised again to take into account both the reviewers' remarks in light of the comments during the workshop and also the issues sparked by the oral presentations. All revised papers from the two workshops underwent a second stage of review before producing the final version that is included in this volume.

COIN strives to fulfill its workshop role of stimulating discussion, facilitating convergence and synergy of approaches, and weaving a community. Authors and reviewers were encouraged to contribute to a workshop program that welcomes the presentation of unconventional approaches perhaps stemming from other disciplines as well as reports about ongoing work and testimonials of the application of the ideas of this community. The papers in this collection correspond to that invitation while adhering to the high standard of the formal proceedings of COIN.

In keeping with the aim of the COIN workshops, the collected papers share the basic premise of looking into coordination, organizations, institutions, and norms as governance elements for the regulation of open multi-agent systems. While this basic focus is shared, the papers contained in this volume exhibit a healthy diversity of approaches. We have grouped them in six sections.

Four of the sections fell exactly along the lines of the four elements of the workshop title; coordination, organizations, institutions, and norms. However, this year it appeared that we had quite a substantial number of submissions centered around norms and thus we decided to make three norms sections, with one general section on norms and two more specific clusters on norm conflicts and norm-aware agents.

We would like to end this brief preface with a note of gratitude. Thus, as workshop chairs and as editors of this volume, we want to express our sincere thanks to the reviewers of the COIN 2013 editions. Everyone knows that reviewing is not an easy task: it demands generosity to allocate time and energy that is taken away from other duties; good sense and optimism to provide constructive criticism; plus a balanced use of confidence, altruism, and courage to recommend the acceptance or rejection of papers. The names of this year's Program Committee members are listed for everyone to see in the front matter of this volume, but their contribution is subtly present in the many suggestions that were taken up by the authors to enrich the final version of their papers. Of course, we would also like to thank the authors for submitting and seriously revising their papers such that we can present a high-quality COIN volume again.

February 2014

Tina Balke
Amit K. Chopra
Frank Dignum
M. Birna van Riemsdijk

Organization

Program Committee

Huib Aldewereld	Delft University of Technology, The Netherlands
Sergio Alvarez-Napagao	Universitat Politècnica de Catalunya, Spain
Tina Balke	University of Surrey, UK
Guido Boella	University of Turin, Italy
Olivier Boissier	ENS Mines Saint-Etienne, France
Patrice Caire	University of Luxembourg, Luxembourg
Cristiano Castelfranchi	Institute of Cognitive Sciences and Technologies, Italy
Amit K. Chopra	Lancaster University, UK
Antonio Costa	Universidade Federal do Rio Grande, Brazil
Luciano Coutinho	Universidade Federal do Maranhão (UFMA), Brazil
Nuno David	Instituto Universitário de Lisboa, Portugal
Marina De Vos	University of Bath, UK
Gennaro Di Tosto	Utrecht University, The Netherlands
Frank Dignum	Utrecht University, The Netherlands
Virginia Dignum	Delft University of Technology, The Netherlands
Nicoletta Fornara	Università della Svizzera Italiana, Switzerland
Armando Geller	George Mason University, USA
Amineh Ghorbani	Delft University of Technology, The Netherlands
Aditya Ghose	University of Wollongong, Australia
Nigel Gilbert	University of Surrey, UK
Chris Haynes	King's College London, UK
Jomi Fred Hubner	Federal University of Santa Catarina, Brazil
Joris Hulstijn	Delft University of Technology, The Netherlands
Eric Matson	Purdue University, USA
John-Jules Meyer	Utrecht University, The Netherlands
Simon Miles	King's College London, UK
Daniel Moldt	University of Hamburg, Germany
Pablo Noriega	IIIA-CSIC, Spain
Eugénio Oliveira	Universidade do Porto – LIACC, Portugal
Andrea Omicini	University of Bologna, Italy
Nir Oren	University of Aberdeen, UK
Sascha Ossowski	Rey Juan Carlos University, Spain
Julian Padget	University of Bath, UK
Alessandro Ricci	University of Bologna, Italy
Juan Antonio Rodriguez Aguilar	IIIA-CSIC, Spain

Contents

Coordination

A Detailed Analysis of a Multi-agent Diverse Team

Leandro Soriano Marcolino[✉], Chao Zhang, Albert Xin Jiang,
and Milind Tambe

University of Southern California, Los Angeles, CA 90089, USA
{sorianom,zhan661,jiangx,tambe}@usc.edu

Abstract. In an open system we can have many different kinds of
agents. However, it is a challenge to decide which agents to pick when
forming multi-agent teams. In some scenarios, agents coordinate by voting continuously. When forming such teams, should we focus on the diversity of the team or on the strength of each member? Can a team of diverse
(and weak) agents outperform a uniform team of strong agents? We propose a new model to address these questions. Our key contributions
include: (i) we show that a diverse team can overcome a uniform team
and we give the necessary conditions for it to happen; (ii) we present
optimal voting rules for a diverse team; (iii) we perform synthetic experiments that demonstrate that both diversity and strength contribute to
the performance of a team; (iv) we show experiments that demonstrate
the usefulness of our model in one of the most difficult challenges for
Artificial Intelligence: Computer Go.

Keywords: Multi-agent systems · Coordination and collaboration
· Distributed AI

1 Introduction

It is well known that teams can often outperform individual agents. However,
different combinations of agents have different performances, and it is even possible for a team to perform worse than its members. In an open system, we can
have a variety of agents available. How can we pick a limited number of them in
order to form strong teams?

This paper is an extended version of [1]. We include here more empirical results:
while in [1] there are results only for white, here we also study in Sect. 4.2 teams
playing as black, hence showing a more general result. Moreover, in [1] we analyze the
agents only using our proposed model, but here (again in Sect. 4.2) we also analyze
them using classical voting models, emphasizing the importance of our new model.
In addition, we present in Sect. 5 a new study by a human expert of some games
from our experiments, in order to better understand why a team of diverse agents is
able to overcome a uniform team of strong agents. Finally, we have new discussions
in the Conclusion.

T. Balke et al. (Eds.): COIN 2013, LNAI 8386, pp. 3–24, 2014.
DOI: 10.1007/978-3-319-07314-9_1, © Springer International Publishing Switzerland 2014

After forming a team, their members must work together. Voting is an important coordination mechanism for a multi-agent team. By voting, we can use agents that were not originally designed to work together, and there are theoretical guarantees that a team of voting agents can get closer to finding the best possible decision in a given situation [2]. Sometimes the agents must vote continuously in many different scenarios. Consider, for example, agents that are cooperating in a board game [3], deciding together stock purchases across different economic scenarios, or even picking items to recommend to a large number of users [4]. This situation imposes a conflict for team formation: should we focus on the diversity of the team or on the strength of each individual member? Previous works do not address this issue. Diversity is proposed as an important concept for team formation in the field of Economics and Social Science [5,6]. However, [5,6] assume a model where each agent brings more information, and the system converges to one of the best options known by the group. When a team votes to decide its final opinion, their model and theorems do not hold anymore. In the current literature on voting it is assumed a model where agents have a fixed probability to take the best action [2,7–10], and under that model it is not possible to show any advantage in having a diverse team of agents. Our experiments show, however, that a diverse team can outperform a uniform team of stronger agents. It is necessary to develop, therefore, a new model to analyze a team of voting agents.

We present a new model of diversity and strength for a team of voting agents. The fundamental novelty of our model is to consider a setting with multiple world states, and each agent having different performance levels across world states. Under this model, we can show that a team of diverse agents can perform better than a uniform team composed by strong agents. We present the necessary conditions for a diverse team to play better than a uniform team, and study optimal voting rules for a diverse team. We show synthetic experiments with a large number of teams that demonstrate that both diversity and strength are important to the performance of a team. We also show results in one of the main challenges for Artificial Intelligence: Computer Go. Go is an iterative game, and the possible board states can represent a great variety of different situations, in such a way that the relative strength of different Go playing software changes according to the board state. Therefore, we can use our model to study a team of agents voting to play Computer Go. By using a diverse team we were able to increase the winning rate against Fuego (one of the strongest Go software) by 18.7 %, and we could play 11 % better than a team of copies of Fuego. Moreover, we could play 15.8 % better than one of the versions of parallelized Fuego. We could also improve the performance of the diverse team by 12.7 % using one of our proposed voting rules. Therefore, we effectively show that a team of diverse agents can have competitive strength, and even play better, than a uniform team composed by stronger agents. Our new model provides a theoretical explanation for our results.

2   Related Work

This work is related mainly to the study of team formation, diversity and voting. We will first introduce general works on team formation, then we will talk about diversity, and finally we will discuss voting.

Team formation is the problem of selecting the best possible team to accomplish a certain goal, given limited resources. In the traditional model, certain skills are necessary to accomplish a task, and we must select a team that has all the necessary skills with the minimum cost [11,12]. More recent work go beyond a simple sum of skills and also models the synergy of a group [13], how to lead a group to the optimal joint action with a new ad-hoc agent [14] or how to automatically configure a network of agents [15]. In [16], a team formation procedure is presented for a class of online football prediction games, and the system is able to play successfully against a large number of human players. However, the existing models do not cover the situation where we must select a team to vote together at each step of a complex problem. In this work, we present a new perspective to team formation, and we also introduce a new problem: in the pursuit of the best possible team of voting agents should we focus on the diversity of the team or on the strength of each individual member?

Hong and Page presented a contribution to team formation in the Social Science literature by showing the importance of diversity [5]. They proposed a model for agents, and proved that a team of diverse agents can perform better than a team of high-ability agents. In their model, each agent has a set of local minima that they reach while trying to maximize an objective function. The agents can improve the solution from the local minima of their team members, therefore the search of a team stops only in the intersection of the local minima of all agents. By using a large number of diverse agents the system is able to converge to the optimal solution. Many papers followed their work [17–19], showing the importance of diversity in different settings. Their model, however, does not cover situations where agents are unable to improve the solution from their team members local minima. This can happen, for example, when we use existing software, that were not architectured to collaborate in this way or when there are time constraints. Therefore, there are many situations where the agents have to collaborate in other ways, such as voting. If a team of agents votes, the system will not necessarily converge to an option in the intersection of their local minima. However, as we will show, it is still possible for a diverse team to play better than a uniform strong team.

A more recent model to analyze diversity was proposed in [6]. It is an equivalent model to Page's and still do not overcome the limitations previously described. In [20], the authors show the benefits of diverse agents voting to estimate the optimum of a single peaked function. In our work we are dealing with a harder problem, as the function to be optimized changes at every iteration. Another work that uses voting to study diversity is [21], but they assumed that Page's model would work in a voting context, and do not propose a new model.

Concerning voting, the field has two possible views: voting for aggregating different preferences, and voting to estimate the best possible decision. Our work is related to the second view. The classical work in this line is the Condorcet's Jury Theorem [7]. According to the theorem, when facing a binary decision, as long as the average of the probability of each individual being correct is higher than $\frac{1}{2}$, a group of independent individuals doing plurality voting will have a higher probability of being correct than the individuals alone. This theorem is extended to the k options case in [2], where it is shown that if each of the individuals have a probability of choosing the best answer higher than choosing any other answer, the group performing plurality voting will be stronger than the individuals alone. These theorems, however, do not present any benefits in having diverse agents. Researchers in Artificial Intelligence contributed to this view of voting by using a maximum likelihood approach to find the optimal voting rule. The idea is that given the votes, we can find which option has the highest probability of being the best, if we have a model of the probability distribution of the agents [8–10]. However, they still do not address the issue of diversity and team formation in the context of voting, as they assume that all agents follow the same probability distribution. As all agents are essentially the same, team formation is not yet an issue in their work.

3   Methodology

Let $\mathbf{\Phi}$ be a set of agents ϕ_i voting to decide an action a in the set of possible actions $\mathbf{A}$ and $\mathbf{\Omega}$ be a set of world states ω_j. We assume that we can rank the actions from best to worst and $\mathbf{U_j}$ is the vector of expected utilities of the actions in world state ω_j, ordered by rank. The agents do not know the ranking of the actions, and will vote according to some decision procedure, characterized by a probability distribution function (pdf) over action ranks. Hence, each agent ϕ_i has a pdf $\mathbf{V_{i,j}}$ for deciding which action to vote for in state ω_j. Agents that have the same $\mathbf{V_{i,j}}$ in all world states will be referred as copies of the same agent.

Let α_j be the likelihood of world state ω_j. If we expect the world states to be equally frequent, we can use $\alpha_j = 1/|\mathbf{\Omega}|$. We define strength as the weighted average of the expected utility of an agent or a team. It is given by the following dot product: $s = \sum_{\omega_j \in \Omega} \alpha_j \mathbf{V_j} \cdot \mathbf{U_j}$, where $\mathbf{V_j}$ is the pdf of the agent/team in world state ω_j. $\mathbf{V_j}$ can be calculated given a team of agents and a voting rule. A voting rule is a function that given the (single) votes of a team of agents, outputs an action.

We define the team formation problem as selecting from the space of all possible agents $\mathbf{\Psi}$ a set of n agents $\mathbf{\Phi}$ that has the maximum strength in the set of world states $\mathbf{\Omega}$. An application does not necessarily know $\mathbf{V_{i,j}}$ for all agents and for all world states. In this work, we will focus on showing that the naïve solution of forming a team by selecting the strongest agents (or copies of the best agent) is not necessarily the optimal solution. Therefore, we are introducing a new problem to the study of team formation.

We define diversity as how different are the probability distributions of agents in $\mathbf{\Phi}$ in the set of world states $\mathbf{\Omega}$: $d = \frac{1}{|\Phi|^2} \sum_{\omega_j \in \Omega} \sum_{\phi_i \in \Phi} \sum_{\phi_k \in \Phi} \alpha_j H(\mathbf{V_{i,j}}, \mathbf{V_{k,j}})$, where H is a distance measure between two pdfs. In this paper, we used the Hellinger Distance [22], given by: $H(\mathbf{V_{i,j}}, \mathbf{V_{k,j}}) = \frac{1}{\sqrt{2}} \sqrt{\sum_{a \in \mathbf{A}} (\sqrt{V_{i,j}(a)} - \sqrt{V_{k,j}(a)})^2}$.

Table 1. A team of deterministic agents that can reach perfect play under simple voting. "1" indicates agent plays perfect action.

Agent	State 1	State 2	State 3	State 4	Strength
Agent 1	1	0	1	1	0.75
Agent 2	0	1	1	0	0.5
Agent 3	1	1	0	0	0.5
Agent 4	1	1	0	1	0.75
Agent 5	0	0	1	1	0.5

At each iteration, each agent will examine the current world state and submit its (single) opinion about which one should be the next action. The opinions are then combined using plurality voting, that picks as a winner the option that received the most votes. We consider in this paper three different voting rules: *simple* - break ties randomly, *static* - break ties in favor of the strongest agent overall, *optimal* - break ties in favor of the strongest agent of each world state. We consider the *static* voting rule because in some applications we might have a clear idea of which is the strongest agent overall, but the information of which is the strongest agent for a given world state might not be available. We will encounter this situation in the Computer Go domain, as will be clear in Sect. 4.2. This voting procedure will repeat at every iteration, until the end, when the system can obtain a reward.

We present examples to demonstrate that a diverse team can play better than a uniform team. First, let's consider the simplest case, when all agents are deterministic. The team made of copies of the strongest agent will play as well as the strongest agent, no matter how many members we add in the team. However, a team of diverse agents can overcome the strongest agent, and even reach perfect play, as we increase the number of agents. Consider, for example, the team in Table 1. This diverse team of 5 agents will reach perfect play under simple voting, while copies of the best agent (Agent 1 or Agent 4) will be able to play well only in 3 out of 4 world states, no matter how many agents we use in the team.

We can easily change the example to non-deterministic agents, by decreasing slightly the probability of them playing their deterministic action. A detailed description of the agents used in this example is available in the Appendix (in http://teamcore.usc.edu/people/sorianom/coin2013Book-appendix.pdf). The resulting strength of the teams is very similar to the deterministic case. Assuming all world states are equally likely, the strength of the diverse team is 0.9907, while copies of the best agent have strength 0.7499. Therefore, it is possible for a team of weak diverse agents to overcome a uniform team of stronger agents, when in certain states the individual agents are stronger than the overall strongest agent.

Even if we make the number of agents go to infinity, copies of the best agent will still be unable to perform the best action in one world state, and will play worse than the diverse team with only five agents. This situation is not considered in the Condorcet's Jury Theorem, neither in the classical nor in the extended version, because they assume independent agents with a fixed pdf. Therefore, in the previous models, we would not be able to show the importance of diversity.

We present a formal proof of the conditions necessary for a diverse team to play better than copies of the best agent, under the simple voting rule. If the conditions of the theorem are not met, we can simply use copies of the best agent as the optimal team. To simplify the presentation of the proof, we will consider a utility function with a value of 1 for the optimal action and 0 for the other actions. That is, we will consider the optimal team in a fixed world state as the team that has the highest probability of performing the optimal action. Let ψ_{best} be the strongest agent in Ψ, and a_{best} be the best action in a given world state.

Theorem 1. *For a diverse team to be the optimal team under the simple voting rule it is necessary that at least one agent in Ψ has a higher probability of taking the best action than ψ_{best} in at least one world state, or a lower probability of taking a suboptimal action than ψ_{best} in at least one world state.*

Proof. We develop the proof by showing that copies of the best agent of a given world state will be the optimal team in that world state. Therefore, it is necessary that the agents in the diverse team play better than the best agent overall in at least one world state. Let $\psi_{best,j}$ be the strongest agent in world state ω_j. Let's define the pdf of this agent as $<p_1, \ldots, p_k>$, where p_1 is the probability of taking the best action. We will show that a team of n copies of $\psi_{best,j}$ doing simple voting will have a higher probability of taking the best action than a team of n agents composed of x copies of $\psi_{best,j}$ and m agents ψ_i doing simple voting, where the probabilities of each ψ_i are given by $<p_1 - \epsilon_i, p_2 + \gamma_{i2}, \ldots, p_k + \gamma_{ik}>$, $\gamma_{il} \geq 0 \ \forall l \in (2, k)$ and $\sum_{l=2}^{k} \gamma_{il} = \epsilon_i$.

Given a team of agents, let them all vote. We will start with a team of x copies of agent $\psi_{best,j}$. We will perform m iterations, and at each one we will add either another agent $\psi_{best,j}$ or agent ψ_i, where i is the current iteration. Let v_{i-1} be the current vote result. The result of v_{i-1} is either: (i) victory for a_{best}, (ii) tie between a_{best} and other options, (iii) defeat for a_{best}.

(i) If v_{i-1} is a victory for a_{best}, the new agent can change the result only when it votes in another option. Suppose a_l is an option that upon receiving one more vote will change a victory for a_{best} into a tie between a_{best} and a_l. Agent $\psi_{best,j}$ will vote in option a_l with probability p_l, while agent ψ_i will vote in option a_l with probability $p_l + \gamma_{il}$. Therefore, if v_{i-1} is such that one vote can change a victory for a_{best} into a tie between a_{best} and other options, agent ψ_i will have a higher probability of changing a victory for a_{best} into a tie between a_{best} and other options.

(ii) If v_{i-1} is a tie between a_{best} and other options, agent $\psi_{best,j}$ will break the tie in favor of a_{best} with probability p_1 while agent ψ_i with probability $p_1 - \epsilon_i$. Therefore, agent $\psi_{best,j}$ will have a higher probability of breaking the tie in favor of a_{best}. Moreover, if a_l is an option that is currently tied with a_{best}, agent $\psi_{best,j}$ will vote for a_l with probability p_l, while agent ψ_i

with probability $p_l + \gamma_{il}$. Therefore, agent ψ_i will have a higher probability of changing a tie between a_{best} and other options into a defeat for a_{best}.

(iii) If v_{i-1} is a defeat for a_{best}, agent $\psi_{best,j}$ will vote for a_{best} with probability p_1 while agent ψ_i will vote for a_{best} with probability $p_1 - \epsilon_i$. Therefore, if v_{i-1} is such that one vote can change a defeat for a_{best} into a tie between a_{best} and other options, agent $\psi_{best,j}$ will have a higher probability of changing a defeat for a_{best} into a tie between a_{best} and other options.

In all three cases, agent $\psi_{best,j}$ leads to a higher increase in the probability of picking a_{best} than agent ψ_i. Therefore, up to any iteration i, copies of $\psi_{best,j}$ will have a higher probability of playing the best action than a diverse team. Hence, if $\psi_{best,j} = \psi_{best} \forall j$, then copies of the best agent ψ_{best} will be the best team in all world states, and therefore it will be the optimal team. Therefore, for a diverse team to perform better, at least one agent must have either a higher probability of taking the best action or a lower probability of taking a suboptimal action than ψ_{best} in at least one world state. ∎

This theorem, however, only gives the necessary conditions for a diverse team to be stronger than a non-diverse team. The sufficient conditions will depend on which specific game the agents are playing. Basically, given the pdf of the agents for a set of world states, we can calculate the pdf of both the diverse team, and the team made of copies of the best agent. If the diverse team has a higher probability of taking the best action in a subset of the world states that is enough for it to play better, considering that it will have a lower probability of taking the best action in the complementary subset, then the diverse team will play better than copies of the best agent.

Now we study optimal voting rules. Given the result of a voting iteration, and the pdf of all agents in a world state, we can calculate which action has the highest probability of being the best. Formally, let $<p_1^i, \ldots, p_k^i>$ be the pdf of agent ϕ_i in world state ω_j, where p_l^i is the probability of playing the action with rank l. The optimal voting rule is the one that given a voting pattern, selects the action a_x that has the highest probability of being the best. Let $\mathbf{Y}$ be the set of all other possible rank combinations for all other actions. We write an element of $\mathbf{Y}$ as a sequence $y_1 \ldots y_{k'-1}$, where y_l is a position in the ranking, and k' is the number of actions in the given voting pattern. We also define $\mathbf{\Phi_{a_l}}$ as the set of agents in $\mathbf{\Phi}$ that voted for an action a_l, and $\mathbf{A_\gamma}$ as the set of all actions in the given voting pattern. Assuming a uniform prior probability for the ranking of all actions, we can calculate the probability of a_x being the best action by:

$$\sum_{y_1 \ldots y_{k'-1} \in \mathbf{Y}} \prod_{\phi_{i_x} \in \mathbf{\Phi_{a_x}}} p_1^{i_x} \prod_{a_l \in \mathbf{A_\gamma} - \{a_x\}} \prod_{\phi_{i_l} \in \mathbf{\Phi_{a_l}}} p_{y_l}^{i_l}$$

The derivation of the expression is available in the Appendix. We can extend this definition to picking the option with maximum expected utility by calculating the probability of each possible rank (instead of only the best one) and multiplying the resulting probability vector by a utility vector to obtain the expected utility of an option a_x.

However, it is possible to use a simpler voting rule. In our next theorem, we show that given some conditions, the optimal voting rule for a diverse team is to consider plurality voting, but break ties in favor of the strongest agent that participates in the tie. Basically, we have to assume that all agents are strong enough to contribute to the team, so no agent should be ignored. If there are harmful agents in the team, we can try to remove them until the conditions of the theorem are satisfied. Again, we consider a utility function with a value of 1 for the optimal action and 0 for the other actions. Given a team Φ with size n, our conditions are:

Assumption 1. *Weak agents do not harm.*

For any subset of Φ with an even number of agents n', and for a fixed world state ω_j, let $\phi'_{best,j}$ be the best agent of the subset. We divide the agents in 2 sets: *Weak* containing the $n'/2 - 1$ agents that have the lowest probability of taking the best action and the highest probability of taking a suboptimal action, and *Strong* containing the $n'/2$ agents that have the highest probability of playing the best action and the lowest probability of taking a suboptimal action (except for the best agent $\phi'_{best,j}$, that is in neither one of the sets). We assume that when all agents in *Weak* and $\phi'_{best,j}$ vote together in an option a_x, and all agents in *Strong* vote together in another option a_y, the probability of a_x being the best action is higher than the probability of a_y being the best action.

Assumption 2. *Strong agents are not overly strong.*

Given a fixed world state ω_j, we assume that if m_1 agents voted in an action a_x and m_2 agents voted in an action a_y, the probability of a_x being the best action is higher than a_y being the best action, if $m_1 > m_2$. If there is a situation where the opinion of a set of agents always dominates the opinion of another set, we can try to remove the dominated agents until the assumption holds true.

Theorem 2. *The optimal voting rule for a team is to consider the vote of all agents, but break ties in favor of the strongest agent if the above assumptions are satisfied.*

Proof Sketch. Our detailed proof is available in the Appendix. We present here a proof sketch. By *Assumption 2* we know that we are looking for a tie-breaking rule, as the action chosen by most of the votes should always be taken. By *Assumption 1* we know that in the worst possible case, we should still break ties in favor of the strongest agent. If in the worst case, the group with the strongest agent still has a higher probability of selecting the best action than the group without the strongest agent, for any other case the group with the strongest agent will still have a higher probability. ∎

An application may not have the knowledge of the pdf of the agents in individual world states. Therefore, we also study an approximation of the optimal voting rule, that break ties in favor of the strongest agent overall, instead of breaking ties in favor of the strongest agent in a given world state. In the next section we will see that both the optimal voting rule and our approximation improves the performance of a diverse team.

4 Results

4.1 Synthetic

We perform synthetic experiments using the quantal response (QR) model for the agents [23]. The quantal response model is a pdf from behavioral game theory to approximate how human beings (or non-rational players) behave while playing a game. It states that the probability of playing the best action is the highest, and it decays exponentially as the utility of the action gets worse. We use the QR model in our experiment, because it is a convenient way to represent non-rational agents with different strengths playing a game with a great number of options.

The pdf depends on a parameter, λ, that defines how rational (i.e., strong) is the agent. As λ gets higher, the agent provides a closer approximation to a perfect player. We define a λ_{ij} for each agent i and world state j.

We generated 1200 random teams of 4 agents, playing in 10 world states, and with 82 possible actions. We define each λ_{ij} as a random number in the interval $(0, 7)$, according to a uniform distribution. For each team, we can calculate the diversity and the average strength of the agents, according to the equations defined earlier. In Fig. 1, we can see the performance of each team, as a function of diversity and the strength of its members. The strength of a team can be calculated after we generate the pdf of the team, by calculating the probability of all possible situations where the system would pick a particular ranking position. We assume that all world states are equally likely, hence the strength of a team is the average over all world states. We used a utility vector that gives a value close to 1 to the best action, and a low value to the other actions.

We performed a multiple linear regression for each voting rule. The following models were found: $simple{:}z = -0.09 + 1.48s + 0.45d$; $static{:}z = -0.03 + 1.36s + 0.55d$; $optimal{:}z = 0.09 + 0.92s + 1.29d$. The variable s is the average strength of the team members, d is the diversity of the team, and z is the strength of the team. The coefficient of multiple determination (R^2) of the models are 0.96, 0.81, 0.88, respectively.

As can be seen, both diversity and strength had a positive weight. This shows that groups with more diversity are stronger, given a fixed strength for

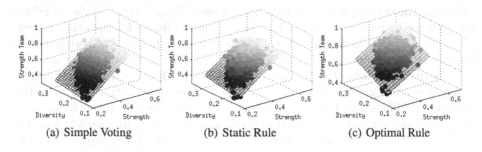

(a) Simple Voting   (b) Static Rule   (c) Optimal Rule

Fig. 1. 1200 random teams of 4 agents.

their members. It is interesting to note that the impact of diversity increases as we change the voting rule from *simple* to *static*, and from *static* to *optimal*. The mean strength of all teams are $0.56(\pm0.08)$, $0.61(\pm0.08)$, $0.74(\pm0.06)$, respectively. We can note that, as expected, *simple* had the lowest strength, followed by *static*, and *optimal* had the highest strength. The *optimal* voting rule is 30 % stronger than *simple* voting in average.

4.2   Experiments in Computer Go

We also perform experiments with four Go software: Fuego 1.1, GnuGo 3.8, Pachi 9.01, MoGo 3, and two (weaker) variants of Fuego (FuegoΔ and FuegoΘ), in a total of 6 different agents. These are all publicly available Go software. Fuego is known to be the strongest Go software among all of them. Fuego, Pachi and MoGo follow a UCT Monte Carlo Go algorithm [24]. The description of FuegoΔ and FuegoΘ is available at the Appendix. All results presented are obtained by playing 1000 9x9 Go games, in a HP dl165 with dual dodeca core, 2.33 GHz processors and 48 GB of RAM. We first present results when our system plays as white, against the original Fuego playing as black with opening database. Then, we present results of our system playing as black, against the original Fuego playing as white with opening database. We will compare the winning rate of different agents and teams when playing against the same opponent. When we say that a result is significantly better than another, we use a *t-test* with 1 % significance level ($\alpha = 0.01$).

We call a team composed by different Go software as "Diverse" or by the name of the voting rule that they use ("Simple" or "Static"). The team of copies of the strongest agent (Fuego) will be called "Copies". The copies are initialized with different random seeds, therefore due to the nature of the search algorithms, they will not always choose the same movement. When we want to be explicit about the number of agents in a team we will add a number after the name of the team. "Diverse" is composed by Fuego, GnuGo, Pachi and MoGo when executed with 4 agents, and is composed by all agents when executed with 6 agents. We also work with a parallelized version of Fuego ("Parallel"), and we will add a number after its name to indicate the number of threads.

Before introducing our results, we first analyze the agents under the classical voting theory and under our proposed theory. To simplify the analysis, we consider here the probability of playing the best move (P_{best}); therefore, we consider a utility vector with a value of 1 for the best move, and 0 for the other moves. We start by the classical voting theories. In order to estimate P_{best}, we use 1000 board states from our experiments. In 1000 games, we randomly choose a board state between the first and the last movement. We then ask Fuego to perform a movement in that state, but we give Fuego a time limit 50x higher than the default one. Therefore, Fuego is approximating how a perfect (or at least much stronger) player would play. To avoid confusion with the names we will call this agent Perfect. We then obtain Perfect's evaluation for all the positions of the board, and organize them into a ranking.

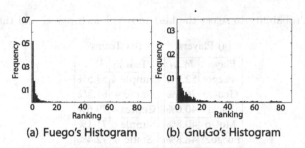

(a) Fuego's Histogram   (b) GnuGo's Histogram

Fig. 2. Histogram of the agents, using real data.

We ran all agents in the selected 1000 board states and for each state we verify in which position of the ranking each agent would play. If, instead of playing, the agent resigns, we randomly pick a different board state and regenerate the data for all agents, including Perfect's evaluation. Based on that, we can generate a histogram for all agents. Some examples can be seen in Fig. 2. Although we do not have enough space to show here all histograms, they have similar shapes, giving a high frequency for the best possible move and lower frequencies for the subsequent moves, with the stronger agents having a higher frequency of playing the best move. The interested reader can see all the generated histograms in the Appendix.

Assuming that the agents are independent, and that each one will choose a move according to the probability distribution corresponding to its histogram, we can calculate P_{best} of any group and voting rule that we want. Basically we have to calculate the probability of all the possible situations where the system would pick the best move. For a team of k agents we have to calculate $O(n^{k-1})$ probabilities, where n is the number of possible options. While for a team of 4 agents we are able to calculate the precise value, for a team of 6 agents we are going to show approximations.

In Table 2 we can see P_{best} of each individual player and of all teams. The P_{best} of the teams is higher than the P_{best} of each one of the agents, and is higher for a team of 6 agents than for a team of 4 agents. This result is expected when we consider the extended version of the Condorcet's Jury Theorem [2], at least for a uniform team. According to the theorem P_{best} approaches 1 when the number of agents goes to infinity. However, we would also expect Copies to perform better than Diverse. Would it be possible, then, for a diverse team to perform better than a uniform team?

Intuitively, we would expect that a uniform team would agree on certain moves much more often than a diverse team. And indeed, when we look at the graph of the frequency of the size of the set of agents that voted for the winning move (Fig. 3), we can see that they are very different. In the x-axis we show the number of agents that agreed in the selected movement, and in the y-axis the frequency of each number considering all moves in the 1000 games. The expected size of the set for Diverse is 3.50, while for Copies is 4.43. Therefore, if Fuego plays badly in a certain board state, all copies of Fuego would also tend

Table 2. Probability to select the best move of each player and the teams.

(a) Players

Player	P_{best}
Fuego	52.3%
GnuGo	26.4%
Pachi	40.6%
MoGo	40.8%
FuegoΔ	48.8%
FuegoΘ	47.7%

(b) Teams

Team	P_{best}
Simple 4	57.5%
Static 4	61.8%
Copies 4	79.6%
Simple 6	71.1%
Static 6	72.4%
Copies 6	86.6%

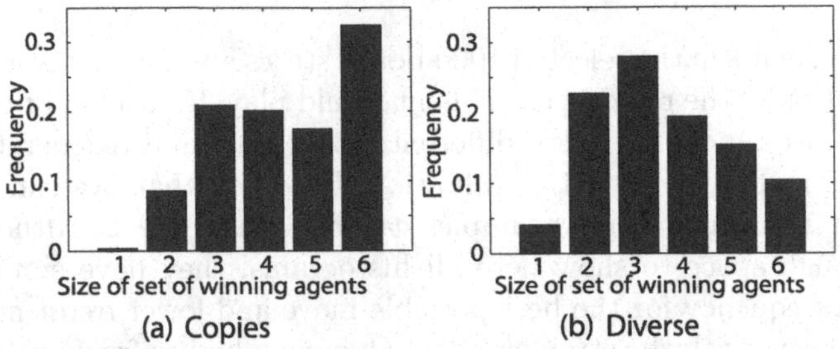

(a) Copies   (b) Diverse

Fig. 3. Expected size of the set of agents that vote for the winning move, with 6 agents and no opening database.

to vote for the same bad moves. In a diverse team, however, some agents could be able to play better in that particular situation. The extended Condorcet's Jury Theorem assumes that agents are independent, but in fact their relative performances might change according to the state of the board.

Now we analyze the agents according to our proposed theory. We will use Theorem 1 to justify that it is worth it to explore a diverse team. If Fuego, the strongest agent, is always stronger in all board positions, then we can just use copies of Fuego as the optimal team. Therefore, we will test if all agents are able to play better than Fuego in some board positions. We selected 100 board states, and we played all agents 50 times for each board state. Based on our estimate of the best move (obtained from Perfect), we can calculate P_{best} for each agent and for each board state. In Table 3, we can see in how many board states the agents have a higher P_{best} than Fuego (in its default time limit). As can be observed, all agents are able to play better than Fuego in some board positions, therefore it is possible for a diverse team to play better than copies of the best agent. As the number of board states where an agent plays better is not small, we can expect that a diverse team should be able to overcome the uniform team.

According to Theorem 2, if we assume that the weak agents (like GnuGo) are not weak enough to harm the system, and the strong agents (like Fuego and its variants) are not strong enough to dominate a subset of the agents, then the optimal voting rule is to break ties in favor of the strongest agent.

Table 3. Weak agents can play better in some board states. In parentheses, we show when the difference in P_{best} is 99 % significant.

Player	# Higher P_{best}
GnuGo	17 % (12 %)
Pachi	21 % (11 %)
MoGo	20 % (7 %)
FuegoΔ	25 % (6 %)
FuegoΘ	26 % (6 %)

However, during a game the system does not have access to the pdf of the agents, and has no way to identify which is the strongest agent. Therefore, we present results using the *static* voting rule, that break ties in favor of the strongest agent overall. Based on our synthetic results, we can predict that *static* should perform better than *simple*. We also tried a weighted voting rule, which allowed us to empirically learn the best weights by a hill climbing algorithm. The resulting rule was equivalent to the *static* voting rule.

We can see our results for white in Fig. 4(a,b). Diverse plays significantly better than Fuego, with 6 agents or with the *static* voting rule. When we keep the opening database, Diverse plays significantly better than Copies and Parallel with 6 agents. Without the opening database, Diverse still plays significantly better than Parallel with 6 agents, but the difference between Diverse and Copies is not significant. Static is either significantly better than Simple, or the difference between them is not significant.

In Fig. 4(c,d) we can see the results for black. Again, Diverse plays significantly better than Fuego when using the *static* voting rule. This time, however, Diverse (with 6 agents or using the *static* voting rule) is able to play significantly better than Copies without the opening database, but with the opening database the difference between them is not significant. Again, Static is either significantly better than Simple, or the difference between them is not significant. Static is always significantly better than Parallel.

To verify the generality of improving the results by the *static* voting rule and by adding more agents, we also played our system as white against Pachi as black, without opening database. Simple 4 won 56.2 % of the games, Static 4 won 65.5 % and Simple 6 won 66.8 %. Therefore, these techniques can improve the results in other situations.

By the classical view of voting, our experimental result is not expected. If we view each agent as having a fixed pdf, we would predict that copies of the best agent would perform much better than a diverse team with weaker agents. However, in our results we showed that the diverse team has a competitive strength, and is able to play even better than copies of the best agent in some situations. Our new model provides a theoretical explanation for our experimental results.

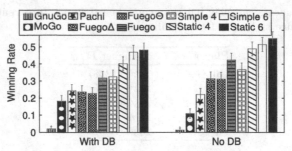

(a) Results for white. Single agents and the diverse team (Simple/Static).

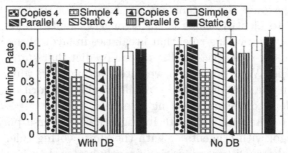

(b) Results for white. The uniform team (Copies), the diverse team (Simple/Static), and a parallelized agent (Parallel).

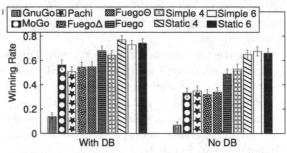

(c) Results for black. Single agents and the diverse team (Simple/Static).

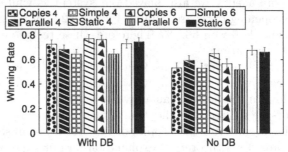

(d) Results for black. The uniform team (Copies), the diverse team (Simple/Static), and a parallelized agent (Parallel).

Fig. 4. Results in the Computer Go domain. The error bars show the confidence interval, with 99 % of significance.

5 Detailed Study: Why a Team of Diverse Agents Perform Better?

We study in detail three games from our experiments, in order to better understand why a team of weak players can perform as well, or better than a team made of copies of the best player. We study games with 6 agents, using the *simple* voting rule. According to our theoretical work, at least one agent must play better than the strongest agent in at least one world state for a diverse team to overcome a uniform team. These are only necessary conditions, for a diverse team to effectively play better this must happen in many world states, specially in critical situations that can decide the game. Here we show that this really happens in Computer Go, based on an analysis by an expert human player. As Go is a complex game, we note that some expert readers might not agree completely with all points of our analysis. Although we present results in the Computer Go domain, this phenomenon should also occur in other complex domains, where the relative strength of the agents change according to the world state.

These games are analyzed by Chao Zhang, a 4-dan amateur Go player. In order to show that the weak agents are not playing better simply by chance, we estimate the probability of all agents playing all analyzed moves by repeatedly playing them 100 times in the board state under consideration. Based on these probabilities, we calculate the probabilities of the diverse team and the uniform team, to show that the diverse team would perform better in these board states. An important point to note is that it is not the case that a certain subset of the agents always vote for a better move; the set of agents that can find a better move than Fuego changes according to each board state.

This analysis requires some Go knowledge to be fully understood. Go is a turn-based game between two players: black and white. At each turn, the players must place a stone in an empty intersection of the board. If a group of stones is surrounded by the opponent's stones they are removed from the board (i.e. they are "killed"). The stones that surround an area form a territory, whose value is counted by the number of empty intersections inside. In the end of the game, the score is defined by the amount of territory minus the number of captured stones, and the player with the highest score wins. A detailed description of the rules can be found in [25].

We first analyze the Go game in Fig. 5. In some positions, the weak agents vote for better moves than Fuego, the strongest agent. Move 11 is a very interesting situation. Here, Fuego, Pachi and MoGo vote for move D4, while GnuGo votes for E8 (X). Even though GnuGo is the weakest agent, in this situation it is able to find a better move than all other agents. E8 is better because it allows white to get the territory in the upper left corner. Besides, white can aim at G7 to kill the black group in the upper right. If white plays D4, black can play E8 to kill white aiming at the upper left corner. Unfortunately, GnuGo loses the vote in this situation. In all other positions, we show situations where the weak agents vote together for a better move than Fuego. For example, in move 23, Fuego votes for B4 (Δ) while Pachi, MoGo, FuegoΔ and FuegoΘ vote for B7. If white chooses B7, white can kill C7&D7 or B5&C5&D5&E5. If black saves

C7&D7, white can use B4 to kill the other group; If black saves B5&C5&D5&E5, white can use C8 to kill C7&D7. If white chooses B4, black will use B7 to kill the white group in the upper left. Fuego's mistake is critical in this situation, and would lead to losing the game. In move 45, Fuego would make another mistake. Fuego votes for B9 (Δ), while GnuGo and Pachi vote for H3. B9 wastes a move: it cannot affect the final result and wastes a chance for further developments. H3, on the other hand, is aiming at killing black in the right bottom. In this case FuegoΔ also votes for B9, so the *static* voting rule would choose a worse move. In move 63, Fuego would play E3, while GnuGo, Pachi, FuegoΔ and FuegoΘ vote for G2. If white plays G2, the black group in the right bottom dies, while if white plays E3, white cannot kill them. This is another critical mistake, that would make white lose the game. Finally, in move 75, Fuego votes for A7, while Pachi and FuegoΘ vote for G2. G2 is better than A7, as it allows white to have a larger territory. As can be seen, there are many situations where the weaker agents vote together for a better move than Fuego. The probabilities of each agent playing the analyzed moves can be seen in Table 4. It is clear that Fuego did not choose the worse move by accident: in many cases it has a lower probability than the other agents of playing the best move between the two options. Consequently, the uniform team is still not able to perform well in these situations, it still has a low probability of playing the best move, and it is always outperformed by the

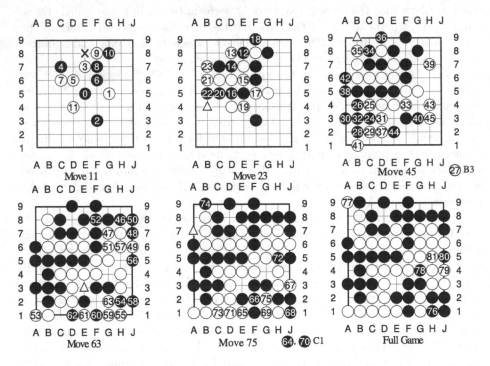

Fig. 5. First example, the diverse team plays as white without the opening database against Fuego. White wins by resignation.

Table 4. Probability of playing the moves in the first example. * indicates the better move.

Agent	Move 11		Move 23		Move 45		Move 63		Move 75	
	E8* (%)	D4 (%)	B7* (%)	B4 (%)	H3* (%)	B9 (%)	G2* (%)	E3 (%)	G2* (%)	A7 (%)
Fuego	2	51	83	14	1	76	53	29	22	16
GnuGo	100	0	0	0	100	0	100	0	0	0
Pachi	6	75	30	70	46	0	78	1	35	1
MoGo	2	61	100	0	0	0	0	84	53	0
FuegoΔ	24	19	100	0	16	19	76	13	24	7
FuegoΘ	35	9	99	0	12	30	78	10	31	11
Diverse	15	57	99	0	20	28	88	7	45	5
Copies	0	73	95	4	0	98	63	26	23	21

diverse team. In some situations, the probability of playing the worst move even increases by using multiple copies of Fuego.

We now analyze the game in Fig. 6. In move number 4, FuegoΔ and Pachi vote for C7, while Fuego votes for move G3 (Δ). G3 is a bad opening for white, because the two white groups would be split by black. Another example is in move 7, when GnuGo, Pachi and FuegoΔ vote for B6, while Fuego votes for G7 (Δ). Black and white are fighting in the upper left corner. If white plays G7, it waives the fight and plays in a place that is not immediately important. White should choose B6 to continue the fight in order to win. Even GnuGo, the weakest agent, knows that B6 is a better move. In move 25, GnuGo and Mogo choose A8, while Fuego chooses F2 (Δ). If white does not play A8, black will play A5 to kill the white group in the left side. White has to kill with A8. This time Fuego's mistake is critical, and could lead to losing the whole game. In this situation GnuGo helps avoid a critical mistake, because FuegoΘ also votes for F2. Moreover, it is an example of a case where the *static* voting rule fails, as it would break the tie in favor of Fuego. We expect that significant improvements in game play would be possible if we learn which is the strongest agent in a given situation, and better approximate the *optimal* voting rule. Another interesting move is 37. Fuego and FuegoΔ vote for D2, while MoGo and FuegoΘ vote for E3. Both moves are equally good, as they get the same territory. However, GnuGo might have a better move: F6. If white plays F6, it can aim at both G6 and F4 for the next moves, which will cause great harm to black's territory. This is another example of a situation where the weakest agent has a better move than all other agents. The probabilities of each agent playing the analyzed moves can be seen in Table 5. Again, we can see that the diverse team would have a higher probability of finding the better moves than the uniform team.

In the games with the opening database, an interesting one is in Fig. 7. In move 29, GnuGo, Pachi and MoGo choose D2, while Fuego votes for B8 (Δ). D2 can protect the lower left, while B8 cannot kill the black group in the upper left, and ends up making it more solid. In move 31, Pachi and MoGo vote for B3, and

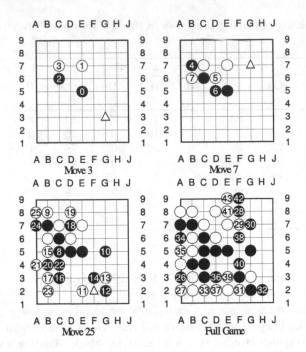

Fig. 6. Second example, the diverse team plays as white without the opening database against Fuego. White wins by resignation.

Table 5. Probability of playing the moves in the second example. Some results are unavailable due to lack of memory. * indicates the better move.

Agent	Move 3		Move 7		Move 25		Move 37		
	C7* (%)	G3 (%)	B6* (%)	G7 (%)	A8* (%)	F2 (%)	F6* (%)	D2 (%)	E3 (%)
Fuego	20	2	7	41	11	30	1	53	19
GnuGo	0	0	100	0	100	0	100	0	0
Pachi	27	14	99	1	28	19	26	27	0
MoGo	0	8	1	0	89	0	0	41	45
Fuego△	20	0	34	20	28	10	0	83	7
FuegoΘ	25	4	50	7	37	11	0	80	12
Diverse	–	–	77	0	70	1	1	90	5
Copies	19	0	2	30	7	27	0	84	8

Fuego votes for B1 (△). Even if both moves might be able to kill the black stone in B2, B3 can kill it for sure. If white plays B1, black can play B3 and would lead to complications. This mistake could make white lose the game. If black survives, it can kill the white group in the lower left. In move 45, Pachi, MoGo and Fuego△ vote for F4, while Fuego votes for A4 (△). F4 splits black into two groups and can make use of this division in the future. A4 just wastes a move and gives black more territory. In move 51, Pachi and MoGo choose E9, and Fuego chooses H6 (△). E9 makes the white group on the left survive, while H6 wastes a move and will lead to the death of the white group. This is a critical mistake,

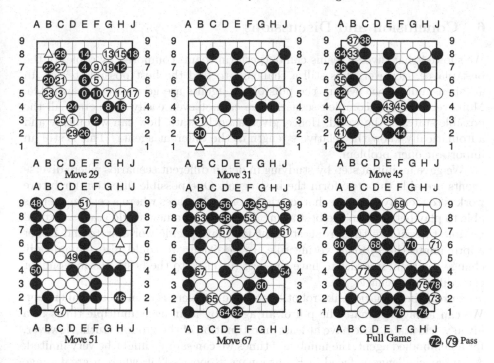

Fig. 7. Third example, the diverse team plays as white with the opening database against Fuego. White wins by resignation.

Table 6. Probability of playing the moves in the third example. * indicates the better move.

Agent	Move 29		Move 31		Move 45		Move 51		Move 67	
	D2* (%)	B8 (%)	B3* (%)	B1 (%)	F4* (%)	A4 (%)	E9* (%)	H6 (%)	B4* (%)	G2 (%)
Fuego	3	16	44	26	17	40	0	35	0	12
GnuGo	100	0	0	0	0	0	0	0	100	0
Pachi	77	18	64	0	78	17	90	0	3	0
MoGo	91	0	98	0	92	0	51	0	46	4
Fuego△	6	4	11	1	51	12	0	1	0	9
FuegoΘ	5	7	13	0	50	21	0	2	0	5
Diverse	82	3	75	0	54	12	37	0	9	1
Copies	0	12	56	32	5	53	0	44	0	4

that would make white lose the game. In move 67, GnuGo and MoGo vote for B4, while Fuego votes for G2 (△). B4 is better, as it can get more territory. G2 just wastes a move. The probabilities of each agent playing the analyzed moves can be seen in Table 6. Again, in all these situations the diverse team has a higher probability of playing the better move than the uniform team. In some cases, the probability of playing the worse move even increases with multiple copies of Fuego.

6   Conclusion and Discussions

We showed that diverse teams can outperform teams composed by copies of the best player. However, it is still a challenge to find the best possible teams. In an open multi-agent system the pdfs of the agents are generally not available. Moreover, in many complex scenarios we cannot even easily enumerate all the possible states of the world. Hence, given a world state, how can we quickly and automatically know the relative strength of the different agents? This is still an important open problem.

We gave an initial step by studying in detail different scenarios where diverse agents are able to outperform the best agent. One possible direction for future work is to identify common characteristics of world states where a certain agent is able to play better than the best agent. Hence, given a new world state we would be able to estimate the strongest agent for that specific world state and better approximate the *optimal* voting rule. In addition, we could also dynamically change the team in order to have the best (or close to the best) possible one for each different scenario.

In real-life scenarios, like robot teams, the problem is even more challenging. We can always estimate the pdf of an agent by running it multiple times in a given world state, if we have at least an estimation of the ground truth. However, for an embodied agent, the number of times we can sample might be very limited. A similar challenge is faced in Evolutionary Robotics [26], where a great range of robots/controllers must be constantly evaluated. One common approach is to perform the evaluation in simulation, and implement in real life the best performing solution. Likewise, we could sample the pdf of different robots in simulation, in order to estimate their pdfs in the real world. Of course, the accuracy of the pdf estimation would depend on the accuracy of the simulation environment.

In general, however, even without knowledge of the pdfs of the agents, this paper shows that a team composed by strong but very similar agents is not necessarily optimal. Hence, if a designer is not able to estimate the pdfs, she should at least evaluate the performance of diverse teams before picking only the strongest agents as the chosen team for a certain multi-agent application.

Acknowledgments. This research was supported by MURI grant W911NF-11-1-0332.

References

1. Marcolino, L.S., Jiang, A.X., Tambe, M.: Multi-agent team formation - diversity beats strength? In: Proceedings of the 23rd International Joint Conference on Artificial Intelligence (2013)
2. List, C., Goodin, R.E.: Epistemic democracy: generalizing the condorcet jury theorem. J. Polit. Philos. **9**, 277–306 (2001)

3. Obata, T., Sugiyama, T., Hoki, K., Ito, T.: Consultation algorithm for computer Shogi: move decisions by majority. In: van den Herik, H.J., Iida, H., Plaat, A. (eds.) CG 2010. LNCS, vol. 6515, pp. 156–165. Springer, Heidelberg (2011)
4. Burke, R.: Hybrid recommender systems: survey and experiments. User Model. User-Adap. Inter. **12**(4), 331–370 (2002)
5. Hong, L., Page, S.E., Baumol, W.J.: Groups of diverse problem solvers can outperform groups of high-ability problem solvers. Proc. Natl. Acad. Sci. U S A **101**(46), 16385–16389 (2004)
6. LiCalzi, M., Surucu, O.: The power of diversity over large solution spaces. Manage. Sci. **58**(7), 1408–1421 (2012)
7. Condorcet, M.: Essai sur l'application de l'analyse a la probabilite des decisions rendues a la pluralite des voix. L'Imprimerie Royale (1785)
8. Young, H.P.: Optimal voting rules. J. Econ. Perspect. **9**(1), 51–64 (1995)
9. Conitzer, V., Sandholm, T.: Common voting rules as maximum likelihood estimators. In: Uncertainty in Artificial Intelligence: Proceedings of the Twentieth Conference (UAI2005), pp. 145–152. Morgan Kaufmann Publishers (2005)
10. Xia, L.: Computational voting theory: game-theoretic and combinatorial aspects. Ph.D. thesis, Duke University, Durham (2011)
11. He, L., Ioerger, T.R.: A quantitative model of capabilities in multi-agent systems. In Arabnia, H.R., Joshua, R., Mun, Y., eds.: Proceedings of the International Conference on Artificial Intelligence, IC-AI 03, June 23–26, 2003, Las Vegas, Nevada, USA, vol. 2, pp. 730–736. CSREA Press (2003)
12. Guttmann, Ch.: Making allocations collectively: iterative group decision making under uncertainty. In: Bergmann, R., Lindemann, G., Kirn, S., Pěchouček, M. (eds.) MATES 2008. LNCS (LNAI), vol. 5244, pp. 73–85. Springer, Heidelberg (2008)
13. Liemhetcharat, S., Veloso, M.: Modeling and learning synergy for team formation with heterogeneous agents. In: Proceedings of the 11th International Conference on Autonomous Agents and Multiagent Systems - Volume 1. AAMAS '12, Richland, SC, pp. 365–374. International Foundation for Autonomous Agents and Multiagent Systems (2012)
14. Agmon, N., Stone, P.: Leading ad hoc agents in joint action settings with multiple teammates. In: Proceedings of the 11th International Conference on Autonomous Agents and Multiagent Systems - Volume 1. AAMAS '12, Richland, SC, pp. 341–348. International Foundation for Autonomous Agents and Multiagent Systems (2012)
15. Gaston, M.E., desJardins, M.: Agent-organized networks for dynamic team formation. In: Proceedings of the Fourth International Joint Conference on Autonomous Agents and Multiagent Systems. AAMAS '05, pp. 230–237. ACM, New York (2005)
16. Matthews, T., Ramchurn, S.D., Chalkiadakis, G.: Competing with humans at fantasy football: team formation in large partially-observable domains. In: Hoffmann, J., Selman, B., (eds.) Proceedings of the 26th AAAI. AAAI Press (2012)
17. Luan, S., Katsikopoulos, K., Reimer, T.: When does diversity trump ability (and vice versa) in group decision making? a simulation study. PLoS One **7**(2), e31043 (2012)
18. Lakhani, K.R., Jeppesen, L.B., Lohse, P.A., Panetta, J.A.: The value of openness in scientific problem solving. HBS Working Paper (07-050) (2007)
19. Krause, S., James, R., Faria, J.J., Ruxton, G.D., Krause, J.: Swarm intelligence in humans: diversity can trump ability. Anim. Behav. **81**(5), 941–948 (2011)

20. Braouezec, Y.: Committee, expert advice, and the weighted majority algorithm: an application to the pricing decision of a monopolist. Comput. Econ. **35**(3), 245–267 (2010)
21. West, D., Dellana, S.: Diversity of ability and cognitive style for group decision processes. Inf. Sci. **179**(5), 542–558 (2009)
22. Hellinger, E.: Neue begrndung der theorie quadratischer formen von unendlichvielen vernderlichen. Journal fr die reine und angewandte Mathematik **136**, 210–271 (1909)
23. McKelvey, R.D., Mckelvey, R.D., Mckelvey, R.D., Palfrey, T.R., Palfrey, T.R., Palfrey, T.R.: Quantal response equilibria for normal form games. Games Econ. Behav. **10**, 6–38 (1996)
24. Gelly, S., Wang, Y., Munos, R., Teytaud, O.: Modification of UCT with patterns in Monte-Carlo Go. Technical report (2006)
25. Pandanet: Introduction to Go. http://www.pandanet.co.jp/English/introduction_of_go/
26. Nolfi, S., Floreano, D.: Evolutionary Robotics. The Biology Intelligence, and Technology of Self-organizing Machines. MIT Press, Cambridge (2001). (2001: 2nd print, 2000: 1st print)

Modelling the Effects of Personality and Temperament in Small Teams

Mehdi Farhangian[✉], Martin K. Purvis, Maryam Purvis,
and Bastin Tony Roy Savarimuthu

Information Science, University of Otago, Dunedin, New Zealand
mehdi.farhangian@otago.ac.nz

Abstract. We present an investigation into the effects that player personality can have on team performance in games that have been designed to have a social purpose ("serious games"), such as games intended to enhance more consideration for the environment and for sustainable energy usage. The work involves multi-agent-based model of team play, where individual player personalities are characterized by Myers-Briggs Type Indicator (MBTI), which specifies personality according to several psychological categories. This includes a fuzzy-logic-based MBTI parameterization of player personality. Experiments employing agent-based simulation are then presented that show the effects of various combinations of personality and temperament types on team performance in the context of competing team profiles. Modelling of this nature can generally be used by policy makers in connection with the recruitment of project teams that are likely to work together more effectively.

Keywords: Agent-based simulation · Myers-Briggs type indicator · MBTI · Fuzzy logic · Serious games · Performance · Team-work

1 Introduction

In many project tasks, teamwork plays a vital role for getting things done and the efficiency of the results. Effective teamwork is one of the predictors of organizational success, since it can cause rapid information exchange and increase responsiveness [1]. Interactions among members of a group can generate social support, sharing of work and cooperation [2].

Previous research considered various factors in teamwork such as skills, gender, leadership as well as knowledge, experiences, and age. Some of them emphasise specially the importance of personality as predictor of peoples' behaviour [3].

There are various mechanisms to analyze team performance. Some researchers suggest team members do not perform uniformly in team processes and they analyze how individuals contribute to teamwork. Nevertheless, they believe that such contributions to the team process can still be described by individual-level activities [4] and most of them consider team composition as a predictor of team performance. Team composition here refers to the configuration of members that have a significant influence on team process and outcomes [5]. In this paper, both level of analysis are

T. Balke et al. (Eds.): COIN 2013, LNAI 8386, pp. 25–41, 2014.
DOI: 10.1007/978-3-319-07314-9_2, © Springer International Publishing Switzerland 2014

taken into consideration and individual attribute of teams and team composition are both considered to affect team performance.

The empirical examination of how team composition affects performance would normally require large data samples collected over nontrivial time periods, and such data are not easily obtained [6]. In order to assist in this analysis, we believe that virtual worlds and computer-assisted game environments can provide platforms for analysing teamwork [7]. So our goal here is to demonstrate the usefulness of a simulation model that can be used to examine how various player performance profiles can influence overall team behaviour.

In fact our longer-term goal is to investigate how game procedures can encourage human behaviour that contributes to the common good, which is sometimes called "green behaviour". Games that can encourage such green behaviour are called "serious games".

Although, in general, some of the most popular games are those in which a single user tries to achieve a high score by playing against a machine, we believe that team-oriented games are more naturally suited to induce the desired collaborative and cooperative attitudes necessary for improved "green" behaviour. However, team games are more difficult to design so that they have the appropriate compelling gameplay and cannot be dominated by a single player. In this respect, one doesn't want a game that is dependent on the skill of the most talented player – rather, one wants a game that is likely to be won by the team that employs the most teamwork. So the individual game activities in this kind of game should not be particularly difficult or demanding. What should matter is the teamwork.

To assist the team-oriented game designer, we have constructed an agent-based model of a "serious game" in order to examine how various mechanisms affect game performance. In the work presented here we are particularly interested in the issue of teamwork and how the different player "personalities" can affect the team performance in the game. Although our focus here is on gameplay, our study of personality influence on team effectiveness applies to project teamwork in general. As such the work can be used to support improved policy-making in connection with project team composition.

2 Player Personality and Performance

Understanding human personality and its effect on performance is an enormous subject in itself, and we do not pretend to treat this subject in all its depth here. Nevertheless, there are some commonly held notions concerning variations of human temperament and personality that have been developed over the past century, and we take advantage of some of them. Carl Jung developed an initial scheme of psychological type, which included the notion of introversion and extroversion [8]. Myers added additional elements to this arrangement [9], and it has evolved into what is now referred to as the Myers-Briggs Type Indicator (MBTI) scheme [10].

According to the MBTI scheme, there are four "dimensions" of human personality:

- **Extraversion vs. Introversion** – the degree to which one faces the outer social world or keeps more to him or herself.
- **Sensing vs. iNtuition** – the degree to which one gathers information that is in concrete, objective form or is more abstract and understood according to one's inner compass.
- **Thinking vs. Feeling** – the degree to which one makes decisions based on logic and demonstrable rationality or is more empathic and attempts to see things from given perspectives.
- **Judgmental vs. Perceptive** – the degree to which one wants to come to quick, categorical decisions or is more inclined to withhold judgement for the time being.

An individual can then be indexed according to one of sixteen possible types. For example a person identified as INFP is introverted, intuitive, feeling, and perceptive.

Although the scientific accuracy of the MBTI scheme may be questioned, and there have been other alternative personality categorization schemes that partitioned people into a small set of types, such as "Big Five" (aka OCEAN) [11] and Temperament theory [12], the MBTI scheme is the most well-known. In addition, there are several accessible and publicly-available MBTI instruments for categorizing people according to this scheme, and we have found them to be relatively reproducible in connection with our own experiments. So we believe that the MBTI measure can be a potentially useful yardstick to distinguish game players in terms of their game personalities. And this is what we use to guide our initial agent-based game designs. We also employed Temperament theory that is related to the MBTI scheme, indeed a pared-down version of it. Temperaments can be considered to be aggregations of MBTI types into smaller groups according to Table 1.

Table 1. Temperament theory

Temperament	MBTI types
Duty seeker	ESFJ, ISFJ, ESTJ, ISTJ (JS)
Knowledge seeker	ENTP, INTP, ENTJ, INTJ (NT)
Action seeker	ESFP, ISFP, ESTP, ISTP (SP)
Ideal seeker	ENFP, INFP, ENFJ, INFJ (NF)

3 Structure of Environment

We constructed some games involving four-member teams that would engage in various tasks involving environment-enhancing activities. Teams would draw mission "cards" that stipulated the tasks to be performed, and then the team would have to go out and perform the tasks. All the tasks require group cooperation. The basic sequence of gameplay is shown as a flowchart in Fig. 1.

In our game environment we considered two types of tasks:

- **Structured tasks:** those are not complex. These tasks require individual team members to use less cognitive recourse and they have specific question and specific answers.

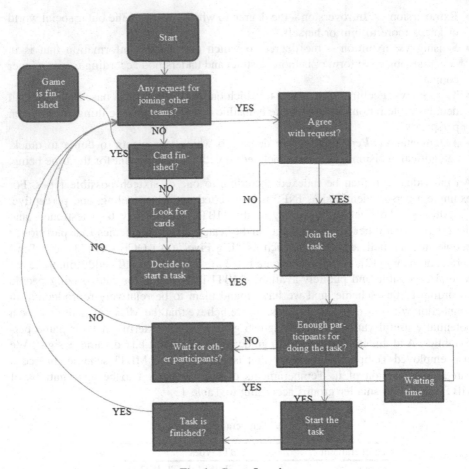

Fig. 1. Game flowchart

- **Open-ended:** or 'cognitive', tasks that require relatively more creativity and imagination.

Some examples of open-ended and structured tasks are shown in Table 2.

The effectiveness of a team's performance in these types of projects or games can be strongly influenced by the personality makeup of the team. In our work, we have developed a model that shows how team personality composition is related to team performance during serious games. The modelling approach outlined in this research can be of use for policy makers whose aim either is fostering sustainability via behaviour change or is simply discovering what is the most effective team composition. The model can also be used to recruit team members of certain personality in order to perform certain type of tasks.

Figure 1 illustrates how our game works. This is from one agent's point of view and describes how it starts a task or forms a group and performs the tasks during the game. In Sect. 3.1–3.4, we show how personality types, as indicated by MBTI measures, can collectively affect team performance.

Table 2. Tasks on mission cards

Open ended task	Structured task
Host and participate in an event for lunch and have a short tutorial about healthier food	Check different kind of bins (paper, compost, plastic and trash bins) and make sure waste goes to proper bins. Teams can compete together and gather as much waste as they can
Present survey results about sustainable issues	Fill assessment sheets to assess sustainability in different parts of the town
Start a recycling program	Tree-planting event
Express sustainability issues through arts and crafts	Teams put out some bins in the city for second hand clothes or other sharing items
Film current sustainable projects and activities and upload to Internet	Offering waste reduction tips for consumers
Run an event for swapping second hand clothes	Gathering donations for non-profit green organizations

3.1 Personality and Information

Intuitive people (MBTI: N, as opposed to S) focus on the big picture and look for overall patterns, rather than focussing on details. They are looking for something larger than just the current activities. In contrast, sensing people (S) prefer to collect all the immediate information around them. So they spend more time tracking than doing [10]. Therefore we assume that in games, intuitive (N) people are faster overall in making up their mind for doing a new task than sensing people (S), who may need more time to know all the information about that task.

3.2 Personality and Interaction

In connection with thinking and feeling (the F-T dimension of MBTI), feeling people are more likely to be concerned about the impacts of their decisions in connection with their social context. Thinkers follow their objective principles and standards that are less influenced by context [10]. Therefore T-people are logical, and F-people make decisions based on their heartfelt concerns.

Moreover, when it comes to joining up to make a team, the sociability of a person can be a factor. This is the I-T (introversion vs. extraversion) dimension of MBTI. Extraverts are energized by interacting with others, and so they prefer to work in groups. Introverts prefer to work alone to get things done. As a result, we assume having high feeling and extroverted personality has a positive effect on a player's decision to interact with others. These factors affect players' behaviour for asking others to join them and also replying others' request to join the task.

3.3 Personality and Flexibility

After players decide to start a task, they send requests to others to join them. In this stage, the judgmental vs. perceiving aspect of one's personality (the J-P dimension of the MBTI scheme) comes into play. Judgers (J-people) prefer to operate in a planned and settled fashion, while perceivers (P-people) can operate in a more flexible and spontaneous way – they prefer to remain open to new information that may come in at any time [10]. Therefore, we assume J-people are more likely to wait longer for others to join them, whereas P-people may leave a task in order to opportunistically pursue a new task.

3.4 Personality and Team Performance

During task activities, a team's personality composition strongly influences success in finishing a task. To model this aspect of team performance, we investigated the degree to which differing personalities can work together effectively as a team. So we examined (a) single team metrics that quantify certain aspects of team composition as well as (b) a more detailed examination of team composition with respect to a new individual team member parameter. In this connection, we introduce two additional indicators [13] that are used in conjunction with the MBTI measures:

- Team Personality Elevation (TPE): a team's mean level for a particular personality trait;
- Team Personality Diversity (TPD): the variance with respect to a particular personality trait among team members.

With respect to TPE, we make the following observations.

- A high TPE in sensing (S) is presumed to have a positive effect on structured tasks. Recall that MBTI Sensing and iNtuition concern how people gather information. Sensing people are fact-driven and prefer to develop a single idea fully [14].
- A high TPE in judging (J) is also taken to have a positive effect on structured tasks. People high in judging prefer to live according to plan, and avoid extended periods of doubt. Some research has confirmed the positive relationship between conscientiousness and team performance for pooled tasks [15].
- A high TPE in intuition (N), however, has a positive effect on open-ended tasks. Intuitive people are imaginative and creative. They tend to think about several things at the same time and make connections between them.
- A high TPE in feeling (F) has a positive effect on both open-ended and structured tasks. Feeling can lead to greater cohesion among team members. Some research has shown that 'agreeableness' from the Big Five model, which is correlated with feeling in the MBTI model, has a positive effect on team performance [16]. In the connection with 'green' activity, feeling is expected to play a significant role, because green actions support the activities of others; and F-people try to meet the needs of others, even at the expense of their own needs.
- A high TPE in thinking (T) can have a positive effect on structured tasks. Thinkers follow rationally-derived procedures, which conform well with structured tasks [17].

With respect to TPD, we make some further observations.

- A high TPD in the judgmental-perceiving (J-P) domain has a positive effect on open-ended tasks. A perceiver is flexible and often finds new ways to do things, but at the same time they sometimes dwell on the task work at the expense of reaching closure [18]. Overemphasis on judgment in complex tasks might lead premature completion of the project with limited achievement; while overemphasis on perceiving might lead to interim successes without final task completion. Therefore it might be good to have a team with a mixture of judgers and perceivers. Some research has shown that a variation in conscientiousness on a team can have positive effects in connection with the performance of intellectual and analytical tasks [19].
- Low TPD in the sensing and intuition (S-N) domain can have a positive effect on structured tasks. The literature suggests that homogeneity in this area tends to benefit teams in connection with tasks that are well-defined. Homogeneity in this area can have two main beneficial consequences: integration and conflict avoidance [20]. This is because highly intuitive (high N) people are self-directed and know what they want, which can make sensing people (high S) frustrated.
- However, a high TPD along the sensing-intuition (S-N) axis is believed to have a positive effect on open-ended tasks. Having a balance in this connection can be advantageous, because high intuition can see the big picture, and high sensing can then put the derived concept into action [21].
- A low TPD along the feeling-thinking (F-T) axis is expected to have a positive effect on both open-ended and structured task performance. A disparity on a team with respect to feeling and thinking can conflict with the decision-making process. In that case some of the team members are concerned with the longer-term impacts of their decisions, while others are focused on the immediate pros and cons of the decisions. Research with respect to the Big Five category of 'agreeableness', which is thought to correspond to the MBTI F-T axis, suggests that homogeneity with respect to agreeableness has a positive effect on team performance [22].
- A high TPD along the extraverted-introverted axis (E-I) is expected to have a positive effect on both structured and open-ended tasks. Extraverts increase team communication, but too many of them may be deleterious and lead to a decreased focus on getting the job done [13].

The rules for team performance are based on assumptions which were described earlier. Accordingly, some factors affect performance of structured tasks (we abbreviate the given effect by using the numbered letters shown in parentheses) – such as TPE in sensing (S1), TPE in judging (S2), TPE in feeling (S3), TPE in thinking (S4), TPD in sensing and intuition (S5), TPD in feeling and thinking (S6), and TPD in extraverted and introverted (S7). Factors affecting performance in open-ended tasks included TPE in intuition (O1), TPE in feeling (O2), TPD in judging and perceiving (O3), TPD in sensing and intuition (O4), TPD in feeling and thinking (O5) and TPD in the extraverted and introverted category (O6). These factors are crucial for agents to estimate the probability of performing the task successfully in each attempt.

Rules were then constructed for structured tasks and open-ended tasks. Two of them are exampled here:

IF the task is Open-ended AND O1 is high AND O2 is high AND O3 is high AND O4 is high AND O5 is high
THEN Performance is very high
IF the task is Structured AND S1 is high AND S2 is high AND S3 is high AND S4 is high AND S5 is high AND S6 is high
THEN Performance is high

Such fuzzy rules are executed for each team to show their performance in structured and open ended tasks.

3.5   Fuzzy Model

Because we are constructing an agent model of players who make decisions with respect to imprecisely-known information, the agents employ a fuzzy-reasoning decision model [23]. In this respect the agents deal with information that can have a fuzzy membership value with respect to their categorization. Thus, for example considering size, something could be considered to be both medium-sized (to a certain degree by having a fuzzy membership value between 0 and 1) and large (also with a fuzzy membership value between 0 and 1).

The fuzzy logic we employ is based on Takagi-Sugeno-Kang (TSK) fuzzy inferencing [24], which is similar to Mamdani fuzzy inferencing [25] but has advantages with respect to computational efficiency. The general form of TSK method which is employed in this work presented as follows:

$$\textbf{IF } x_1 \text{ is } A_{1,r} \text{ and } \ldots \text{ and } x_p \text{ is } A_{p,r} \textbf{ THEN } y_r = f_r(x_1, x_2, \ldots x_p) \qquad (1)$$

where

$A_{p,r}$ is a partitioned domain of the input variable x_p in the r_{th} If-Then rule,

p is the number of input variables, and

y_r is the output variable in the r_{th} If-Then rule.

It is assumed that there are $R_r (r = 1, 2, \ldots, n)$ and for each implication of R_r, we have

$$y_r = f_r(x_1, x_2, \ldots x_p) = b_{0,r} + b_{1,r} x_1 + \ldots, b_{p,r} x_p \qquad (2)$$

where $b_{0,r}, \ldots, b_{p,r}$ are consequents of the input variables that specify the variables involved in the r_{th} rule's premise.

The weight of input variables is calculated as following:

$$r_r = T(\mu_{A_{1,r}}(x_1), \ldots, \mu_{A_{p,r}}(x_p)) \qquad (3)$$

where T is the minimum *t-norm* which is recommended by Mamdani and called the Godel t-norm that can be presented as following.

$$r_r = \min\{\mu_{A_{1,r}}(x_1), \ldots, \mu_{A_{p,r}}(x_p)\} \qquad (4)$$

The final output y inferred from n implications is given as the average of all the weights r_r:

$$y = \frac{\sum_{r=1}^{n} r_r \times y_r}{\sum_{r=1}^{n} r_r} \tag{5}$$

To illustrate, in one stage of task activity, agents must decide to start a task or not, which will depend on the degree of extraversion and feeling in the personality. Here the input is the degree of one's extraversion and feeling, and the output is the level of confidence about starting a new task, which can be "quite interested", "interested" and "not interested". Membership function of feeling and extraverted is illustrated in Figs. 2 and 3. The sets related to the linguistic variable "feeling" and "extraverted" are those representing membership grades to fuzzy sets shown in Table 3:

The use of linguistic rules in combination with fuzzy inference can then serve as an effective knowledge base for analysis of action (see Figs. 4 and 5). Consider the nine fuzzy rules shown in Table 4.

The nine fuzzy rules for this activity are shown in Table 4:

In this example we assume crisp input data for the degrees of *feeling* and *extravertedness*. Let us consider a situation where Feeling = 70 and Extraversion = 45, According to Table 3 then the feeling will be considered to be *medium* with a degree $\mu_{feeling-medium}(70) = 0.6$; and it will be considered to be *high* with a degree $\mu_{feeling-high}(x) = 0.4$. Extraversion here is considered to be *low* with $\mu_{extraverted-low}(45) = 0.2$, and it is considered to be *medium* with $\mu_{extraverted-medium}(45) = 0.8$.

Four activated rules for these sets can be found in Table 4: R2, R3, R5, R6. We employ the zero-order TSK method, where the output of each fuzzy rule is constant, and all consequent membership functions are represented by a singleton spike. In this case each output is a constant number representing an agent's interest to start a task.

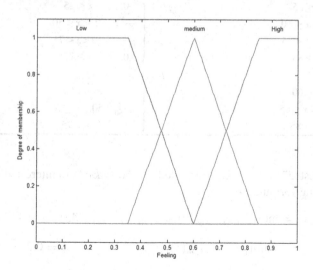

Fig. 2. Membership function for feeling

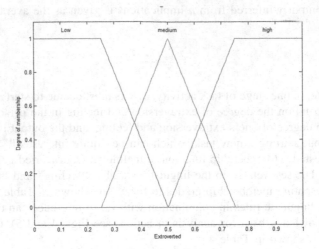

Fig. 3. Membership function for extraverted

Table 3. Membership grades

The characteristic functions of the sets reacted to linguistic variable *feeling* are:	The characteristic functions of the sets reacted to linguistic variable *extraverted* are:
$\mu_{feeling-low}(x)$ $$= \begin{cases} 0 & x > 60 \\ \frac{60-x}{60-35} & 35 \le x \le 60 \\ 1 & x < 35 \end{cases}$$	$\mu_{extroverted-low}(x)$ $$= \begin{cases} 0 & x > 50 \\ \frac{50-x}{50-25} & 25 \le x \le 50 \\ 1 & x < 25 \end{cases}$$
$\mu_{feeling-medium}(x)$ $$= \begin{cases} 0 & x \le 35 \\ \frac{x-35}{60-35} & 35 < x \le 60 \\ \frac{85-x}{85-60} & 60 < x < 85 \\ 0 & x \ge 85 \end{cases}$$	$\mu_{extroverted-medium}(x)$ $$= \begin{cases} 0 & x \le 25 \\ \frac{x-25}{50-25} & 25 < x \le 50 \\ \frac{75-x}{75-50} & 50 < x < 75 \\ 0 & x \ge 75 \end{cases}$$
$\mu_{feeling-high}(x)$ $$= \begin{cases} 0 & x < 60 \\ \frac{x-60}{85-60} & 60 \le x \le 85 \\ 1 & x > 85 \end{cases}$$	$\mu_{extroverted-high}(x)$ $$= \begin{cases} 0 & x < 50 \\ \frac{x-50}{75-50} & 50 \le x \le 75 \\ 1 & x > 75 \end{cases}$$

"quite interested" $= 75 = k_1$; "interested" $= 50 = k_2$; "not interested" $= 10 = k_3$
And by using formula (4):

$$r_2 = \min\{\mu_{feeling-high}(x), \mu_{extroverted-medium}(45)\} = 0.4 \tag{6}$$

$$r_3 = \min\{\mu_{feeling-high}(x), \mu_{extroverted-low}(45)\} = 0.2 \tag{7}$$

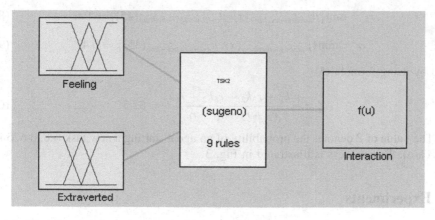

Fig. 4. The fuzzy inference system estimates the probability of interaction with other teammates.

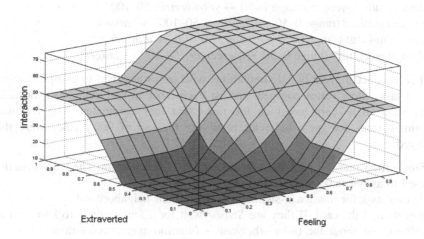

Fig. 5. Fuzzy surface *Feeling*, *Extraverted* and *Interaction*.

Table 4. Fuzzy rules about interaction

IF	*Feeling*	AND	*Extraverted*	THEN	*Interaction*
R1	High		High		Quite Interested
R2	High		Medium		Quite Interested
R3	High		Low		Interested
R4	Medium		High		Quite Interested
R5	Medium		Medium		Interested
R6	Medium		Low		Not Interested
R7	Low		High		Interested
R8	Low		Medium		Not Interested
R9	Low		Low		Not Interested

$$r_5 = \min\{\mu_{feeling-medium}(x), \mu_{extroverted-medium}(45)\} = 0.6 \tag{8}$$

$$r_6 = \min\{\mu_{feeling-medium}(x), \mu_{extroverted-low}(45)\} = 0.4 \tag{9}$$

And by using formula (5)

$$Z = \frac{r_2 k_1 + r_3 k_2 + r_5 k_2 + r_6 k_3}{r_2 + r_3 + r_5 + r_6} = 62.5 \tag{10}$$

The value of Z denotes the probability of an agent starting a new task (i.e. 0.625 in this case). This process is illustrated in Fig. 3.

4   Experiments

Experiments have been implemented in NetLogo [14]. We assigned a random number between 0 and 100 for each personality as follows:

- Extraverted/introverted: (range 0–50 → *introverted*; 50–100 → *extraverted*).
- Sensing/intuitive: (range 0–50 → *intuitive;* 50–100 → *sensor*),
- Feeling/thinking: (range 0–50 → *feeler;* 50–100 → *thinker*),
- Judging/perceiving: (range 0–50 → *perceiver;* 50–100 → *judger*).

We then conducted agent-based simulations with teams assigned to complete green-oriented tasks. Four teams compete against each other to find and finish the tasks. Teams received a score based on the tasks that they completed. The following algorithmic steps for agent behavior involving the use of fuzzy rules were then employed:

1. Stochastic values for personality were assigned to each agent. The values are then used to assign fuzzy membership.
2. Agents look for mission assignment cards in their neighborhood.
3. Agents find the card. If they are *Sensor* wait for a few seconds to know all the information about the tasks otherwise – *intuition* agents-make their mind very fast.
4. Agents make their decisions whether start the task. The alacrity of this decision is influenced by the degree to which have *feeling* and an *extraverted* personality.
5. When an agent finds a task, it invites other teammates to join it. At least two agents are needed for starting a task. (Again they accept or decline a request according to their (fuzzified) interests in starting a task as determined by feeling/thinking and extraverted/introverted personalities).The score desponds on the number of agents in a team. If four members of team do a task successfully they score one. In the cases that fewer agents finish a task successfully, the scores for two and three agents are 0.5 and 0.75 respectively.
6. If the minimum number of teammates is not achieved, then the recruiting agent waits for a short time and repeats its request. (The duration that they wait for others is limited and depends on its *judging/perceiving* personality - Judgers wait longer.)

7. After the agents start a task, we use personality composition measurements to see how they perform during the task. *TPE* and *TPD* of the group members who are working on a task are computed. TPE is the mean of each personality and TPD is the standard deviation of each personality. After fuzzification and applying the rules the performance of teams are determined. Diffuzification determines the probability of finishing the tasks.

5 Results

The simulation study examined all 3876 (all the possible combinations of four personalities among 16 personalities for four team members) MBTI team combinations in a four-team competition. The average scores in terms of number of tasks completed for the various MBTI types are shown in the Tables 4 and 5. With respect to the results and the computed scores, we note the following:

- An individual experimental run involved teams whose members had randomly selected MBTI personalities working on the completion of 200 tasks (100 open-ended and 100 structured), which usually took about 10,000 time steps. These runs were repeated 65,000 times with different randomly selected team-personality makeups in order to ensure that all possible personality combinations occurred. The score for each team combination was calculated based on the average number of tasks that that team completed successfully.
- All the 3876 possible combinations are ranked for structured and open-ended tasks based on their average scores.
- The aggregated average performance for each individual personality in the overall team scores is shown in Tables 5 and 6.
- For the purposes of further demonstrating the aggregated results, the teams were also classified according to their temperament makeups based on the MBTI classifications of temperaments presented in Table 1. The average scores of the 35 possible temperament combinations for teams are presented in Table 7.

Table 5 shows that flexibility has some merit for open-ended tasks. Since most of them with personality with P (Perceivers) generally did better than those with J (Judgers). In structured tasks Judgers did slightly better than Perceivers because of their positive role during performance of tasks. In Fig. 6 performance of each personality for open ended and structured tasks are compared.

Table 5. Personality ranking for open ended tasks

Personality	ENFP	INFJ	INFP	ENFJ	ISFP	ESFJ	ENTP	ESFP	ESTP	ENTJ	INTP	ISFJ	ISTP	ISTJ	ESTJ	INTJ
Score	35	34	34	34	31	30	30	28	28	27	23	22	19	19	15	14

Table 6. Personality ranking for Structured tasks

Personality	ESFJ	ENFP	ISFJ	ESFP	ENFJ	ENTJ	INFJ	ESTJ	ESTP	ENTP	ISFP	INFP	ISTJ	INTJ	INTP	ISTP
Score	46	41	40	39	39	35	34	31	30	27	26	25	25	23	18	17

Table 7. Ranking of combinations in structured task and open-ended tasks

Rank	Structured				Score	Rank	Open-ended				Score
1	Ideal	Ideal	Ideal	Ideal	21.86	1	Ideal	Ideal	Act	Act	17.14
2	Duty	Duty	Duty	Duty	21.81	2	Ideal	Ideal	Act	Duty	17.12
3	Duty	Duty	Duty	Act	19.67	3	Duty	Ideal	Act	Knw	17.07
4	Act	Duty	Duty	Act	18.65	4	Ideal	Act	Act	Knw	16.72
5	Ideal	Ideal	Ideal	Knw	17.73	5	Knw	Knw	Act	Duty	16.7
6	Act	Duty	Act	Act	17.35	6	Knw	Knw	Act	Act	16.37
7	Ideal	Duty	Duty	Duty	17.34	7	Duty	Duty	Ideal	Ideal	16.13
8	Ideal	Duty	Ideal	Ideal	17.24	8	Duty	Ideal	Duty	Knw	15.97
9	Act	Act	Act	Act	16.51	9	Duty	Ideal	Act	Act	15.66
10	Ideal	Ideal	Ideal	Act	16.02	10	Knw	Knw	Duty	Duty	15.56
11	Act	Duty	Duty	Ideal	15.78	11	Ideal	Duty	Duty	Act	15.24
12	Ideal	Ideal	Duty	Duty	15.73	12	Duty	Act	Act	Knw	15.04
13	Duty	Duty	Duty	Knw	15.2	13	Ideal	Act	Act	Act	14.57
14	Ideal	Ideal	Duty	Act	14.48	14	Knw	Act	Duty	Duty	14.52
15	Ideal	Act	Duty	Act	14.37	15	Act	Ideal	Ideal	Ideal	14.27
16	Ideal	Ideal	Knw	Knw	14.16	16	Duty	Ideal	Ideal	Ideal	14.2
17	Duty	Duty	Act	Knw	13.74	17	Act	Knw	Knw	Knw	14.16
18	Ideal	Ideal	Knw	Duty	13.62	18	Ideal	Ideal	Knw	Act	14.08
19	Ideal	Ideal	Act	Act	13.35	19	Ideal	Knw	Knw	Act	14.06
20	Duty	Duty	Ideal	Knw	13.12	20	Duty	Knw	Knw	Knw	13.95
21	Act	Ideal	Act	Act	13.11	21	Act	Act	Act	Knw	13.83
22	Ideal	Ideal	Knw	Act	12.46	22	Ideal	Knw	Knw	Duty	13.77
23	Act	Act	Knw	Duty	12.44	23	Ideal	Ideal	Knw	Duty	13.77
24	Ideal	Knw	Knw	Knw	12.41	24	Duty	Duty	Duty	Ideal	13.48
25	Knw	Knw	Knw	Knw	11.71	25	Duty	Duty	Duty	Knw	12.48
26	Act	Duty	Ideal	Knw	11.67	26	Duty	Duty	Act	Act	9.184
27	Act	Act	Act	Knw	11.23	27	Act	Duty	Act	Act	8.729
28	Knw	Knw	Duty	Duty	11.1	28	Act	Duty	Duty	Duty	8.322
29	Ideal	Knw	Duty	Knw	11.01	29	Ideal	Ideal	Ideal	Ideal	7.341
30	Act	Ideal	Act	Knw	10.52	30	Act	Act	Act	Act	6.579
31	Act	Knw	Duty	Knw	9.946	31	Duty	Duty	Duty	Duty	5.728
32	Ideal	Knw	Act	Knw	9.891	32	Ideal	Ideal	Ideal	Knw	5.662
33	Knw	Knw	Duty	Knw	9.561	33	Knw	Knw	Knw	Knw	4.703
34	Act	Knw	Act	Knw	8.772	34	Ideal	Ideal	Knw	Knw	4.63
35	Knw	Knw	Knw	Act	8.468	35	Ideal	Knw	Knw	Knw	4.336

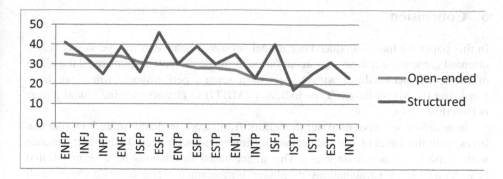

Fig. 6. Comparing the performance of personalities in open-ended and structured tasks

5.1 Temperament as a Factor in Effective Performance

To examine the impact of team composition in a more detail, we grouped agent-based simulation results with respect to temperament that is represented in Table 1, which is a generalization of the MBTI scheme [10]. There are then 35 possible combinations of teams according to temperament, and the team performances of these various combinations are shown for open-ended tasks, and for structured tasks in Table 7 – where "Duty" represents duty seekers, "Knw" represents knowledge seekers, "Act" represents action seekers and "Ideal" represents ideal seekers.

For structured tasks, there appeared to be an advantage in having homogeneity across duty seekers and ideal seekers (top two results). In contrast, homogeneous teams of action seekers and knowledge seekers did not perform well (ranked 9 and 25). In addition, combinations of duty seekers and action seekers tended to do well (ranked 3 and 4), while combinations of action seekers and ideal seekers were less successful. Although knowledge seekers did not generally perform well in this task category, their performance was relatively better when they teamed with ideal seekers. For example when a knowledge seeker teamed with three ideal seekers, it ranked fifth overall.

For open-ended tasks the best combination was two ideal seekers with two action seekers. In addition the combination of duty seekers and action seekers teamed with either knowledge seekers or ideal seekers did well. In general, heterogeneous teams had good performance for these tasks. Homogeneous teams were relatively less successful, and even the best homogeneous team (all ideal seekers) was only ranked 29th out of the 35 teams. Overall, the relative success of the combination of ideal seekers and action seekers was presumably due the fact that the team combined situational openness with active performance. Knowledge seekers fared poorly; but the combination of knowledge seekers with duty seekers performed better than the combination of ideal seekers with duty seekers, and the combination of knowledge seekers with action seekers did better than the combination of duty seekers and action seekers.

6 Conclusion

In this paper we have introduced our model for agent behaviour in a pervasive team-oriented game environment. Our agent-based simulations have demonstrated the effect of individual personalities with respect to a team's performance, where we have employed the Myers-Briggs Type Indicator (MBTI) to characterize individual player personality.

In addition, we have used our modelling framework to demonstrate how one can investigate the effect of various personality interactions on overall team performance with respect to four-person teams. Our agent-based simulations have demonstrated how some player combinations of player temperaments can enhance the overall efficiency of a team, while other combinations can prove to be detrimental. The demonstration of these effects, we believe, can prove to be useful both to designers of serious games and to policy makers in general: by employing this framework, designers and policy makers can examine the degree to which cooperative teamwork is a key influence in overall team performance.

In the future we intend to extend our investigations in connection with this agent-based gameplay framework in several ways. Up to now we have kept player personality separate from individual skill level, but future work will examine connections between personality traits and difficulty (for example, response to frustrations and recovery from setbacks), as well as the connection between personality traits and exploratory activity (a form of creativity). In addition, we will be examining how competitive teams or a given collective personality composition may alter their behaviour in response to the presence of competing teams of differing personality compositions. We have also so far considered personality to be essentially static, but in the future, we will also develop a dynamic player personality model that affords some shifts in attitude and social trust in response to activities during games.

References

1. Cohen, S.G.: What makes teams work: group effectiveness research from the shop floor to the executive suite. J. Manage. **23**(3), 239–290 (1997)
2. Campion, M.A., Papper, E.M., Medsker, G.J.: Relations between work team characteristics and effectiveness: a replication and extension. Pers. Psychol. **49**(2), 429–452 (1996)
3. LePine, J.A., Buckman, B.R., Crawford, E.R., Methot, J.R.: A review of research on personality in teams: accounting for pathways spanning levels of theory and analysis. Hum. Resour. Manag. Rev. **21**(4), 311–330 (2011)
4. Sonnentag, S., Volmer, J.: Individual-level predictors of task-related teamwork processes: the role of expertise and self-efficacy in team meetings. Gr. Organ. Manag. **34**(1), 37–66 (2009)
5. Kozlowski, S., Bell, B.: Work Groups and Teams in Organizations (2001)
6. Agneessens, F., Everett, M.G., Zhu, M., Huang, Y., Contractor, N.S.: Motivations for self-assembling into project teams. Soc. Netw. **35**(2), 251–264 (2013)
7. Reeves, B., et al.: Leadership in Games and at Work: Implications for the Enterprise of Massively Multiplayer Online Role-Playing Games. Palo Alto, CA (2007)

8. Jung, C.G.: Psychological Types: or the Psychology of Individuation. Harcourt, Brace, New York (1921)
9. Myers, I.: The Myers-Briggs Type Indicator. Consulting Psychologists Press, Palo Alto (1962)
10. Myers, I.B., McCaulley, M.H.: Manual: A guide to the development and use of the Myers-Briggs Type Indicator. Consulting Psychologists Press, Palo Alto (1985)
11. Costa, P.T., McCrae, R.R.: Professional Manual: Revised NEO Personality Inventory (NEO-PI-R) and NEO Five-Factor Inventory (NEO-FFI). Psychological Assessment Resources Inc., Odessa (1992)
12. Keirsey, D.: Please Understand Me II: Temperament, Character Intelligence, p. 350. Prometheus Nemesis, Del Mar (1998)
13. Neuman, G.A., Wagner, S.H., Christiansen, N.D.: The relationship between work-team personality composition and the job performance of teams. Gr. Organ. Manag. 24(1), 28–45 (1999)
14. Herden, R., Lyles, M.: Individual attributes and the problem conceptualization process. In: Human Systems Management, vol. 2, no. 4, pp. 275–284. IOS Press, Amsterdam (1981)
15. Driskell, J.E., Hogan, R., Salas, E.: Personality and group performance. In: Hendrick, C. (ed.) Group Processes and Intergroup Relations: Review of Personality and Social Psychology, pp. 91–112. Sage Publications, Beverly Hills (1987)
16. Driskell, J.E., Goodwin, G.F., Salas, E., O'Shea, P.G.: What makes a good team player? personality and team effectiveness. Gr. Dyn. Theory Res. Pract. 10(4), 249–271 (2006)
17. Culp, G., Smith, A.: Understanding psychological type to improve project team performance. J. Manag. Eng. 17(1), 24–33 (2001)
18. Bradley, J.H., Hebert, F.J.: The effect of personality type on team performance. J. Manag. Dev. 16(5), 337–353 (1997)
19. Barrick, M.R., Mount, M.K.: THE big five personality dimensions and job performance: a meta-analysis. Pers. Psychol. 44(1), 1–26 (1991)
20. Bowers, C.A., Pharmer, J.A., Salas, E.: When member homogeneity is needed in work teams: a meta-analysis. Small Gr. Res. 31(3), 305–327 (2000)
21. Mansoor, H.S., Ali, H., Ali, N., Ali, H.: Cognitive diversity and team performance : a review. J. Basic Appl. Sci. Res. 3(6), 9–13 (2013)
22. Mohammed, S., Angell, L.C.: Personality heterogeneity in teams: which differences make a difference for team performance? Small Gr. Res. 34(6), 651–677 (2003)
23. Zadeh, L.A.: Fuzzy sets. Inf. Control 8(3), 338–353 (1965)
24. Takagi, T., Sugeno, M.: Fuzzy identification of systems and its applications to modeling and control. IEEE Trans. Syst. Man. Cybern. SMC-15(1), 116–132 (1985)
25. Mamdani, E.H.: Application of fuzzy algorithms for control of simple dynamic plant. Proc. Inst. Electr. Eng. 121(12), 1585 (1974)

Multiagent Socio-Technical Systems: An Ontological Approach

Daniele Porello[1]([✉]), Francesco Setti[1], Roberta Ferrario[1], and Marco Cristani[2]

[1] Institute of Cognitive Sciences and Technologies, CNR, Trento, Italy
[2] University of Verona, Verona, Italy
{daniele.porello,francesco.setti,roberta.ferrario}@loa.istc.cnr.it,
marco.cristani@univr.it

Abstract. Socio-technical systems constitute a challenge for multiagent systems as they are complex scenarios in which human and artificial agents share information, interact and make decisions. For example, the design of an airport requires to interface information coming from automatic apparatuses as security cameras, conceptual information coming from agents, and normative information which agents' behavior must comply with. Thus, in order to design systems that are capable of assisting human agents in organizing and managing socio-technical systems, we need fine grained tools to handle several types of information. The aim of this paper is to discuss a general framework to describe socio-technical systems as cases of complex multiagent systems. In particular, we use a foundational ontology to address the problems of interoperability and conceptual analysis, we discuss how to interface conceptual information with low level information obtained by computer vision or perception, and we discuss how to integrate information coming from heterogeneous agents.

1 Introduction

This work concentrates on the mutual influence of vision, cognition and social interaction in socio-technical systems, i.e. technologically dense contexts, such as, for instance, airports, hospitals, schools, public offices [9]. The process of seeing a scene, forming a belief or an expectation and engaging in interaction with other agents are essential features of agents' (both human and artificial) behavior in such systems. The entanglement of several layers of information (e.g. individual vs collective, visual vs inferential, human vs artificial) poses a challenge to the modeling of such complex environments. The overall aim of the work initiated with this paper is to build a rich model of agents' interaction that is capable of providing guidance and possibly performance evaluation of real socio-technical systems. We believe that the multiagent systems paradigm [27,28] is a valuable

Supported by the VisCoSo project grant, financed by the Autonomous Province of Trento through the "Team 2011" funding programme.
We would like to thank the anonymous reviewers and the participants of the COIN workshop for their useful comments and suggestions.

T. Balke et al. (Eds.): COIN 2013, LNAI 8386, pp. 42–62, 2014.
DOI: 10.1007/978-3-319-07314-9_3, © Springer International Publishing Switzerland 2014

framework to set up the construction of such complex models, as what is at stake is not only how autonomous agents form beliefs and expectations, communicate and act within a norm-governed system, but also their interaction with decisions that must be taken at systemic level. Our claim is that all these layers that are required in order to describe agents' information in socio-technical systems can be represented and reasoned about by using a rich ontological model, that is capable of specifying our conceptual hierarchy in a way that is general enough to describe a complex categorization including physical and social objects, events, roles and organisations. In order to be effectively connected with the visual systems of artificial agents, such ontological models must contain information about the external context, both in its physical and institutional aspects, and information about the agents that inhabit it, in their physical, perceptual, cognitive and social aspects.

In this paper we address three research challenges: (1) providing a rich and structured description of the domain in all its aspects that is usable and interoperable among agents, both human and artificial; (2) integrating visual information with knowledge representation and reasoning and (3) defining and describing the concept of systemic information as information coming from heterogeneous agents.

Our present contribution is restricted to a conceptual analysis of what are the fundamental elements in order to set up an ontological model of socio-technical systems, thus we shall not focus on possible implementations. The ontological model we propose to use is DOLCE [21], and such choice is motivated by a series of reasons. First, the ontological perspective allows us to specify the properties of the concepts that we deploy and the relations holding among them. Such properties and relations are obtained through a foundational analysis and are expressed as formal axioms [21]. Second, one of DOLCE's basic assumptions is its "cognitive bias", in the sense that it is meant to express the perspective of a cognitive agent on a given domain, rather than "how things really are in the world". Finally, given that DOLCE comprises a social [3,22] and a cognitive module [13], it is capable of dealing with several layers of information.

Regarding the visual information, we rely on a probabilistic methodology based on graphical models such as Bayesian Networks (BN) [19]; essentially, they allow to process low-level information, such as video sequences, audio streams and multisensorial input through graph-based inferential mechanisms in a robust and formal way. In our framework, BNs capture the finer grained knowledge under the form of action detection (run, sit, drink) and social signals recognition (visual focus of attention, facial expressions) [12], all expressed under the form of posterior distributions; this way, the uncertainty associated to the noise of the sensors and the accuracy of the modeling can be delegated to and managed within the ontological multiagent engine. Even though information is processed with probabilistic means in BNs, we assume that these will give as output, via a mechanism based on thresholds, a discrete proposition, that will then be available to be reasoned upon with logical and ontological tools.

The relationship between individual and systemic information will be approached by means of techniques developed in multiagent systems, in particular in social choice theory, judgment aggregation, and belief merging [4,20].

Ontologies for multiagent systems have been developed in particular in order to provide agents' communication languages [14,16]. Moreover, models of socio-technical systems based on goal models have been recently introduced in [6]. The aim of this paper is to provide a general multiagent model based on DOLCE to represent the entanglement of several layers of information in socio-technical systems. The systematic treatment of these aspects of socio-technical systems is, up to our knowledge, the most original contribution of this paper.

The guiding examples of this paper are taken from the organization of an airport. This is motivated by the fact that, although an airport is certainly a very complex scenario and it is very difficult to provide an exhaustive model that captures all its aspects, it is a type of system that exhibits all the difficult features that our modeling aims at least to formally grasp. Thus, airports provide the right examples and counterexamples to the project that we pursue. Such socio-technical system involves several types of agents, surveillance cameras, security officers, customers, who interact and share information of different kinds, for example information coming from cameras, procedural information concerning rules, information that can only be indirectly inferred.

The remainder of this paper is organized as follows. In Sect. 2, we discuss the connection between low-level information coming from vision and high-level information contained in agents' knowledge bases. Section 3 presents our ontological modeling of socio-technical systems. In Sect. 4 we deal with the issue of how to integrate the information coming from different agents and we propose procedures that define systemic information. Section 5 concludes and points at the required steps in order to develop the conceptual analysis that we have presented.

2 Linking Computer Vision and Propositional Information

Modeling the connection between propositional information and visual information is a difficult task to approach. This problem is related to some of the classical problems in AI that are known by a number of keywords, such as the symbol grounding problem [17] and symbol anchoring [5] and it is in general connected in computer vision to the problem of interfacing statistical and discrete information [8]. In computer vision, a label denoting a scene (e.g. "the plane has landed") is associated to a process that models the interaction of several features usually expressed by a graphical model [19]. More specifically, Bayesian Networks (BN) have been widely adopted in vision systems as they are applicable to all levels of processing, from the extraction of low-level actions (e.g., running, walking) to more complex high-level reasoning (e.g., Mark runs *and then* walks); essentially, they embed a mapping into a graph structure so that the nodes represent concepts or parameters of interest and dependencies are given by edges. Their diffused use is due to fast numerical updating in singly connected trees and to the availability of techniques to decompose complex models into simpler ones, adopting heterogeneous learning techniques [24]. Bayesian networks can be learned and model dependencies for either static (BBN) or dynamic (DBN) domains. A simple DBN with single conditional dependencies over time, the Hidden Markov Model, is often used for speech analysis [26] and has been extensively adapted for heterogeneous applications in the Computer Vision realm [23]. Bayesian Networks are the workhorses for the automated surveillance community: in most cases, different activities correspond to different BNs; they are trained in advance, and employed afterwards in classification tasks, aimed at discovering usual or abnormal activities. One of the main limitations of this philosophy, i.e., describing high-level activities employing BNs, is their scarce expressivity: the usual architecture of a surveillance system builds upon a low-level layer in which simple actions are recognized (run, walk, sit); these outputs, expressed in the form of posterior probabilities, are fed into a mid-level layer of the network which connects them considering spatio-temporal relations: an individual can walk for a minute, and in the meantime he/she can talk with another guy, or he/she can make a phone call. In practice, this layer gives as output a set of BNs, one for each activity; in turn, each BN generates a posterior probability, depending on how well the structural knowledge embedded in the network fits the visual data. The high-level layer of the surveillance system performs the final classification, recognizing as ongoing activity the one which corresponds to the BN with the highest posterior probability. As a matter of fact, the kind of understanding provided by this architecture is limited: in one sense, it is fixed, enclosed in a graphical model which describes conditional dependencies among random variables, whose structure is decided a priori, drawn by hand from the researcher. In another sense, it is limited, since it is restricted to a set of available activities that have to be recognized. In order to interface visual and propositional information, we want to associate the set of BNs that describes the activity of a camera with a knowledge base consisting of formulas that are defined by means of the predicates specified in our ontology. The knowledge base contains a set of low-level propositions that are directly connected with the BNs as well as higher level propositions that can be inferred by means of the ontological definitions. For example, "there is a queue at gate 8" is a perceptual proposition that is triggered by the BN, whereas "the boarding at gate 8 has started" is a proposition that can be inferred on the basis of the previous visual proposition. This methodology aims to extend the limitation of the BN approach by integrating information that can be inferred by means of a knowledge base. One of the challenges of this work is to understand how the information coming from a BN, which is probabilistic, entails the assumption that a certain proposition holds in the knowledge base. In particular, a BN provides a degree of probability that the proposition that describes a scene is true or false (e.g. "an aircraft is landing on runway 4 with a probability of 75 %"). Our approach is the following. As we are interested in providing human agents with a tool that assists their activity in monitoring the system, propositional information that becomes available to human agents should be as simple as possible. Thus, we associate probabilistic BNs with discrete information (true or false) concerning the corresponding propositions, by defining a threshold of the degree of reliability provided by the BN that is sufficient to accept the proposition. The thresholding mechanism is also well founded under a Bayesian point of view, since it corresponds to the cost associated to a particular classification output [7]. Moreover, the reliability of the information coming from vision shall be discussed at systemic level as a problem of aggregating possibly divergent sources of information. For example, the reliability provided by the BN corresponding to a particular camera has to be confronted with others pointing at the same object and to other agents in the system. That is, the thresholding problem has to be dealt with at a systemic level. We shall discuss how to integrate possibly divergent information in Sect. 4.

3 Ontological Analysis: DOLCE

In order to describe agents' information in socio-technical systems, we need to integrate visual, conceptual, factual and procedural information. We propose to use the DOLCE ontology as integrating framework. The methodology employed in the construction of the DOLCE ontology is the following. Firstly, we define basic properties and relations, that are generic enough so to be common to all specific domains, like being an endurant (more simply, an object), being a perdurant (an event), being a quality or being an abstract (entity), one entity being part of another, an object participating to an event or having a certain quality... Then, we specify different modules, like the mental or the social module, that are composed by entities that share some characterizing features. For example, mental entities are characterized by being ascribable to intentional agents and social entities are characterized by the dependence on collectives of agents. These conceptual relations specify the definitions of the basic entities in our ontology, e.g. roles are properties of a certain kind that are ascribable to objects. Finally, we introduce domain specific concepts that specify more general concepts belonging to all these modules (like "an aircraft is a physical object").

We begin by presenting the general *ground* ontology; this is meant to be not context sensitive and to provide a shared language to talk about some fundamental properties of concepts and entities. In this sense, the ontology provides a general language to exchange heterogeneous information and may be used as vocabulary to define communication languages for agents[1]. We are here interested in presenting the descriptive features of DOLCE rather than in

---

[1] Ideally, this is not the case, as in multiagent systems agents can be heterogeneous under many respects, including the adoption of different languages and also of different ontologies. The strong requirement should be that their ontologies are well founded, so that their underlying assumptions are explicit enough as to enable communication and exchange of information via "connecting axioms". In the current paper, for the sake of simplicity, we will assume that all agents in the system share the same ontology, DOLCE.

complexity or implementability issues. Notice that in [21] an appendix may be found with more implementable but less expressive versions of DOLCE, that are called DOLCE-Lite.

3.1 Foundational Ontology

We present some features of DOLCE-CORE, the ground ontology, in order to show that they allow for keeping track of the rich structure of information in a socio-technical system. For an introduction to DOLCE-CORE, we refer to [2], here we simply point at the relevant features.

The ontology partitions the objects of discourse, labelled *particulars* PT into the following six basic categories: *objects* O, *events* E, individual qualities Q, *regions* R, *concepts* C, and *arbitrary sums* AS. The six categories are to be considered rigid, i.e. a particular cannot change category through time. For example, an object cannot become an event. In particular, we shall focus on the following categories.

Objects represent particulars that are mainly located in space, e.g. the aircraft 777, the gate 6, the queue at gate 6. On the other hand, events have properties that are mainly related to time, e.g. landing, the boarding of flight 717, the delay of flight 717. The relation that links objects and events is the *participation* relation: "an object x participates in event y at time t" $\mathsf{PC}(x, y, t)$.

Individual qualities shall play an important role in modeling information coming from perception, or from different agents of the system, thus we shall take a closer look at them in the next paragraphs. An individual quality is simply an entity that we can perceive and measure, which inheres to a particular (e.g. the length of runway A2 of Malpensa airport, the weight of Mark's luggage, the temperature inside waiting room 3. . .). The relationship between the individual quality and its (unique) bearer is the *inherence*: $\mathsf{I}(x, y)$ "the individual quality x inheres to the entity y". The category Q is partitioned into several *quality kinds* Q_i, for example, color, weight, temperature, the number of which may depend on the domain of application. Each quality kind Q_i is associated to (one or more) *quality spaces* $S_{i,j}$ that provides a measure for the given quality. We say that individual qualities are *located* at a certain point of a space S at time t: $\mathsf{L}(x, y, t)$: "x is the location of quality y at time t".

Spaces allow for evaluating relationships between objects from the point of view of a given quality. For example, "the temperature inside room 3 (q) is higher than the temperature inside room 4 (q')" is represented in the ontology by assuming spaces of values with order relations and by saying that the location of the individual property q is lower than the location of q'. Spaces may be more structured objects and they may be specified along several dimensions[2].

The axioms that define the relationships between individual qualities, locations, and spaces state for example that every individual quality must be located in some of its associated spaces and that the location in a particular space must be unique, cf. [2]. E.g. the color of an object may be associated to color quality kinds with their relevant spaces such as hue, saturation, brightness.

---

[2] Quality spaces are related to the famous treatment of concepts in [15].

The category of *regions* R includes subcategories for spatial locations and a single region for time, denoted T: T(x) means "x is a time location" (e.g. October 10, 2012, 12:31 PM). The relation PRE(x, t), where t is a time location, allows to specify that "x is present at time t". Note that in DOLCE-CORE we have that all entities exist in time:

$$\mathrm{PT}(x) \rightarrow \exists t \mathrm{PRE}(x, t)$$

The category of *concepts* shall be used in particular to model social objects. Concepts are reified properties that allow for viewing them as entities and to specify their attributes. In particular, concepts are used when the intensional aspects of a property are salient for the modeling purposes. The relationship between a concept and the object that instantiates it is called *classification* CF(x, y, t) "x is classified by concept y at time t".

If we represent the DOLCE taxonomy as a tree (cf. Table 1), more specific categories, such as physical objects, mental objects and so on, can be plugged into the tree as children of the relevant categories. Summing up, there are three ways of understanding properties in DOLCE-CORE and therefore there are three ways to deal with different levels of information [2]. We can understand properties as extensional classes, as individual qualities, or as concepts. We shall apply this distinction to our modeling task: extensional predicates are used to model robust information (e.g. "waiting room 3 is located at gate 3"), individual qualities are used to model information coming from human and artificial perception, e.g. computer vision, and concepts and roles are used to model information about norms, social objects and organizational properties.

3.2 Individual Qualities and Visual Information

In order to integrate the information coming from computer vision or from perceptions of observers in the system with other types of information, we proceed as follows. We assume that agents, both human agents and artificial agents such as surveillance cameras, provide observation points of the system. For example, take a surveillance camera that is trained in the sense of Sect. 2 for a specific task. We represent the features that the surveillance camera is supposed to detect by means of individual qualities of the object/action/event that it is focusing on. As the information coming from visual detection may be revisable and depends on the perception of the observer, we represent it as a specific subtype of "mental object" (MOB) (cf. Table 1), namely, we introduce a specific category VIS that includes visual objects[3]. Visual objects are representations of physical objects from the point of view of a given observer. Therefore, VIS may contain a visual copy for any physical object that we may assume to be recognizable by means of perception. We denote the elements of VIS by v_P where P is a predicate that expresses the property of the object: for example, $v_{airplane}$ denotes the visual representation of an instance of an airplane. The recognition of an object, the

---

[3] The cognitive module of DOLCE has been discussed in [13].

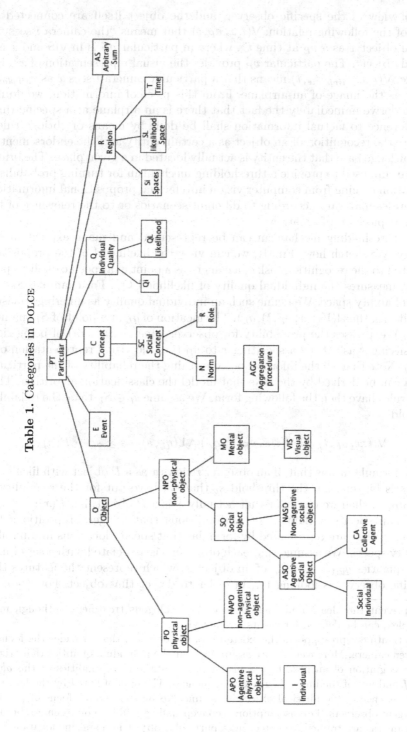

Table 1. Categories in DOLCE

point of view of the specific observer, and the object itself are connected by means of the following relation: $V(i, x, v_P, t)$ that means "the camera i sees the physical object x as a v_P at time t", where in particular v_P is in VIS and x is a physical object[4]. The particular v_P provides the visual representation of x[5]. For example, $V(i, x, v_{airplane}, t)$ means that a particular camera i sees x as $v_{airplane}$, namely as the image of an airplane. From this piece of information, we do not want to derive immediately the fact that there is an airplane at a specific time. The inference to factual information shall be done by means of "bridge rules" that link the recognition of an object as a certain entity and the endorsement in our knowledge base that the entity is actually located in a given place. The bridge rules are supposed to provide a thresholding mechanism for turning probabilistic information coming from computer vision into factual propositional information. Bridge rules may vary according to different scenarios or to the relevance of the particular piece of information.

The thresholding mechanism can be represented and made explicit in our ontology. We sketch how. Firstly, we can view the likelihood of the proposition associated to the recognition task of a camera as a point in a specific quality space S_L that measures the individual quality of likelihood Q_L. For example, S_L can be a probability space. We define such an individual quality as inhering to visual propositions, thus $I(V(i, x, v_P, t), q_L)$. The location of q_L at a point of S_L, namely $L(q_L, s_L)$, expresses the probability for observer i (e.g. a camera) of being right in classifying x as a P by associating x to v_P (i.e. the visual representation of x as a P). Note that all the information concerning the reliability of the particular camera can be derived by the BNs that model the classification algorithm. Thus bridge rules have then the following form. We assume $s_t \in S_L$ to be the reliability threshold.

$$V(i, x, v_P, t) \wedge I(V(i, x, v_P, t), q_L) \wedge L(q_L, s) \wedge s \geq s_t \rightarrow P(x)$$

The formula means that, if an observer i views x as a P object with likelihood s and s is bigger than the threshold s_t that we have put for the reliability of $V(i, x, v_P, t)$, then we can infer that actually x is a P object, i.e. $P(x)$.

We can specify a number of preconditions that trigger propositions like $V(i, x, v, t)$: they are represented by formulas that specify locations in a number of quality spaces. We assume that each observer i is associated with a set of individual qualities $q_{ix1}, \ldots, q_{ixm}$ of an object x, which represent the features that a specific observer is looking for, in order to detect that object. For example,

---

[4] We present the idea for physical object. An analogous treatment, although more complex, can be defined for events and activities.

[5] This treatment presupposes the existence of the object x that provides the focus of a given camera. Moreover, we are assuming that the individual qualities that trigger the recognition of an object as a visual representation are qualities of the *object itself* and not of the image (e.g. video sequence). This is motivated by the fact that the existence of the physical object is assumed to be the "same" focus of possibly divergent observers. This assumption is conceptually possible in our scenario because the cameras are trained for detecting a particular object in a specific location.

such individual qualities represent pieces of information such as "the dimension of the object x from the point of view of camera i". By locating such qualities in specific regions of quality spaces, we can specify a set of preconditions that trigger the recognition of x as v from the point of view of i.

$$L(q_{1x}, s_1, t_1) \wedge \cdots \wedge L(q_{nx}, s_n, t_n) \rightarrow V(i, x, v, t)$$

For example, such conditions state that, according to camera i, if the dimension has a certain value, and the shape is of a certain type, and the color is such and such, then camera i recognizes x as an airplane. Of course the information required in order to model the locations of the individual qualities and the relevant spaces shall be provided by integrating the ontological analysis with the properties of the algorithm used in computer vision. Moreover, note that the specific preconditions only express verbalizations of features that are cognitively relevant. It shall include the features that are relevant from the point of view of agents' communication and shall not list all the features that are actually used by the algorithm. Moreover, in case of human agents, we can represent the relevant cognitive aspects of vision by means of suitable qualities of objects and quality spaces.

The motivation for our treatment is that it allows for handling information coming from different observation points, or from a same observation point at different times, by spelling out the preconditions that trigger such information. An assumption we shall stick to is that the same camera cannot see an object in two ways at the same time:

$$V(i, x, v, t) \wedge V(i, x, v', t) \rightarrow v = v'$$

This amounts to assuming that the algorithm for visual detection is well-defined. However, at different times, the same camera can change the visual object that it provides, or it can even fail to recognize the object, thus we do not force more demanding constraints on visual propositions. Moreover, we do not presuppose that different observers of the same object in the same location and at the same time have to agree on the same recognition. Thus, for example, a camera can see an object as a person whereas another fails to recognize it or classifies it as something else. We believe that this forms of mismatches of information have to be made explicit in our modeling and represented accordingly, as they are an important aspect of the interaction in socio-technical systems. We shall discuss how to handle possible mismatches of information in the next section.

3.3   Social Objects and Norms

One predicate that is particularly important for modeling socio-technical systems is the classification predicate: $CF(x, y, t)$, meaning that "x is classified as y at time t"[6]. By using CF, we can define a special type of social object, namely the notion of *role*. Roles are supposed to be contextual properties, that are characterised

---

[6] For an axiomatic definition of the predicates that we introduce, we refer to [22].

by *anti-rigidity* (AR) and *foundational dependence* (FD): roles are concepts that classify entities at a certain point in time, but not necessarily classify them in each moment or each possible world in which they are present (AR) and that require a level of definitional dependence on another property (FD). In this sense, roles are social objects as they are grounded in a sort of *counts as*.

For instance, someone who is a student at a certain point, not necessarily will be a student all throughout his/her life and there are possible worlds in which he/she is not a student; in order for someone to be classified as an employee, we need someone else who is classified as an employer.

$$AR(x) \equiv \forall y, t(CF(y,x,t) \rightarrow \exists t'(PRE(y,t') \wedge \neg CF(y,x,t')))$$

$$FD(x) \equiv \exists y, d(DF(x,d) \wedge US(y,d) \wedge \forall z, t(CF(z,x,t)$$
$$\rightarrow \exists z'(CF(z',y,t) \wedge \neg P(z,z',t) \wedge \neg P(z',z,t))))$$

The anti-rigidity condition states that if something y is classified by the concept x at t, then there is a time t' such that y is present at t' ($PRE(y,t')$) but y is not classified as x at t'. The foundational dependence is somehow more complicated. It states that a concept x is foundationally dependent iff there is a definition of x, say d, and a concept y such that: d defines x ($DF(x,d)$), the definition x uses the concept y ($US(y,d)$) and, for any entity z also classified by x, there is another entity z' that is classified by y, which is external to z (this is expressed by means of the notion of "part": neither z is a part of z', nor z' is a part of z, ($\neg P(z,z',t) \wedge \neg P(z',z,t)$)). For example, the role of security officer depends on the concept of person.

Given these characteristics, roles are essential to model organizations, as they allow to talk about properties that one acquires in virtue of the fact that one is member of an organization or has some rights/duties connected with the role he/she is playing in that very moment. Take for instance a security officer, who is allowed to carry a gun inside the airport terminal, but just when he/she is playing (or is classified by) the role of security officer; if the same person enters the airport while playing the role of passenger, he/she is no more allowed to carry a gun. The same role can be played by many entities within the same domain (even entities of very different nature, like a human being and a software), the same entity can play more than one role, even simultaneously (like in airports with self-check-in stations, where the same person simultaneously plays the role of passenger and that of check-in operator).

Further developments of ontological analysis treat also norms and plans by means of DOLCE, cf. [1]. Here we just sketch some possible applications that show the entanglement of visual, factual and normative information. Our role-based analysis provides a way to connect low-level information (e.g. coming from cameras) with high-level information (e.g. coming from security protocols). For example, the concept of role allows for making explicit the conceptual dependence of a signal of alarm triggered by a particular scene that has been detected by cameras with the properties that are sufficient to trigger that signal. For example, a "suspect", according to our approach, can be modeled as a role. We can impose a constraint that specifies that only entities that are agentive physical objects (APO, cf Table 1) can be classified as suspects in our scenario (according to the (FD) condition). Moreover, we can specify the description that defines "suspect" by spelling out a set of properties, like the participation to some kinds of events, e.g. "carrying a gun", "entering in an unauthorized area". Thus, if a person (an agentive physical object) is recognized (possibly by a computer vision system that locates a set of individual qualities in the relevant places) as possessing one or more of these properties, he/she is classified as a suspect and this triggers an alarm. In order to specify such a security protocol, the system should be capable of taking into account the various layers of information involved. Consider the following example:

$$\exists x (\exists i \mathsf{V}(i, x, v_{\text{person}}, t) \wedge \exists j \exists y \mathsf{V}(j, y, v_{\text{gun}}, t) \wedge \text{next}(x, y) \wedge \neg \mathsf{CF}(x, \text{officer}, t)$$
$$\to \text{suspect}(x, t))$$

The formula above means that if a camera detects a person and another detects a gun that is next to the person (i.e. $\text{next}(x, y)$), and that person has not the role of a security officer at that moment, then the person is a suspect.

Depending on the type of agent that is provided with this system, the reaction to the alarm could be of various kinds: either send a message to some other agent that has to follow the suspect, or activate another camera with a tracking system, for example. That depends on the security protocol that is implemented in the system. Thus, we can view the inference of the proposition $suspect(x, t)$ as the alarm that triggers possible course of actions that are specified by the security protocols P, by adding constraints of the following form in our system:

$$\text{suspect}(x, t) \to P.$$

By extending the ontological treatment so to include norms, plans, preconditions, postconditions, prescriptions and so on (cf. [1]), the security protocols can be represented as formulas in our system. Obviously, a person can cease to be classified as suspect if further properties are discovered (for instance, a new video sequence may show that what at first appeared as a gun is in fact an umbrella, or it may show a police sign on the back of the person who eventually turns his/her back to the camera, and after that the same person who had been previously classified as "suspect" is subsequently classified as police officer). In particular, roles allow for linking a higher level property used by human agents involved in the system to low level properties that can be checked by means of perception (either direct, performed by human agents, or indirect, obtained by a camera).

Our role based analysis of normative information in socio-technical systems can be applied to define and make explicit the statuses of the personnel as well as the sub-organizations of a complex structure like an airport viewed as an organization, for example, pilots, officers, information desks and so on. Moreover, we could extend the treatment based on roles to concepts that may be applied to events. For example, we can apply the concept of queue to a grouping of persons and view it as a boarding event that is subject to the normative constraints defined by the airport protocols. The notion of role allows in this case to distinguish, for example, queues that are part of a boarding process from groupings or formations of persons that are due to other reasons and may trigger a security check.

4   A Multiagent Setting

We have described how to represent in an abstract way the pieces of information that are required in order to provide an analysis of socio-technical systems. In this section, we apply a multiagent perspective in order to deal with information at systemic level. We view agents as observation points in the system that are endowed with the reasoning capabilities provided by the ontology definitions in DOLCE. For example, cameras endowed with axioms that connect visual information with high-level organization concepts, as well as security officers that communicate pieces of information, are all viewed as agents in our system. The problem that we are going to tackle is how to integrate the possibly divergent information coming from different agents into a collective information that is supposed to be made available at systemic level or to the relevant subsystems that are directly involved.

4.1   Modeling Socio-Technical Systems

In order to describe a concrete scenario for applying our ontological analysis, we enrich the language of DOLCE by introducing a specific language to talk about the scenario at issue. The language contains a set of constants for particular individuals $\mathcal{C}_S$. For example, in the case of an airport, individual constants may refer to "the gate 10", "the flight 799", "the landing of flight 747", "the security officer at gate 10". According to our previous analysis of visual information, we need also constants for locations of individual qualities in their respective spaces. Moreover, the language contains a set of contextual predicates $\mathcal{P}_S$ that describe the pieces of information that agents may communicate in the intended situations. In case of an airport, we need for example to include predicates such as "being an aircraft", "being a queue", "being a gate", "being a delay", "being a landing", "being a security protocol" and so on. The set of predicates $\mathcal{P}_S$ and the set of individuals $\mathcal{C}_S$ are partitioned according to the basic categories, concepts, and individual qualities, etc. This is done by assuming a number of axioms that specify for each predicate the right category. We are taking here the suggestion to view DOLCE as a shared terminology, or Tbox, and let agents have possibly divergent knowledge bases, namely Aboxes.

4.2   Modeling Agents' Information

For the sake of simplicity, agents in our systems are modeled just as sets of (closed) formulas built by means of predicates that are either in DOLCE or in the specific language that we have sketched in the previous paragraph.

This set may include information coming from vision, propositions concerning social objects, norms, plans, etc. We denote $\mathcal{L}_S$ the language of the agents in the system: it is defined as the set of atomic formulas or negations of atomic formulas defined on the alphabet given by $\mathcal{P}_S$, $\mathcal{C}_S$ and DOLCE. We denote an agent's set of propositions by $A_i \subset \mathcal{L}_S$. For example, in case A_i is a surveillance camera, it may contain a set of visual propositions $V(i, x, v, t)$ that are triggered by the detection of the relevant individual qualities[7]. The only general requirement that we put on the A_is is that each A_i is *consistent wrt the ontology*, namely they are consistent with the definitions provided in the ontological analysis. For example, A_i cannot contain a proposition such as "a security officer is a mental object", and so on[8]. Note that the amount of information that each agent shall submit at a given moment depends on the security protocol that is implemented in the system and on the situation at issue. For example, not all the visual information that is provided by all the cameras shall be continuously made available to the whole system. Moreover, we shall make the assumption that the propositions provided by the agents of our system can be synchronized by means of the temporal parameters that are attached to them. Thus, we assume that it is possible to talk about the state of the system, or of a subsystem, at a particular moment or during a particular interval of time[9]. In this section, we shall abstract from those important issues and we simply assume that at a given moment in time, we can take the sets of propositions provided by the agents of the system.

4.3   Modeling Systemic Information

We present now our modeling of *systemic information*. We want to be able to check the status of the system with respect to a number of parameters. As the sources of information are heterogeneous, namely each agent of the system provides his/her set of propositions, the problem of evaluating the state of the system as a whole can be viewed as a problem of integrating heterogeneous information. We shall model this issue by means of techniques developed in social choice theory [4], belief merging [18], and judgment aggregation [11,20,25]. The reason is that, as we shall see, those techniques provide versatile tools to model aggregation of heterogenous types of information and they allow for spelling out

---

[7] Note that we do not want the knowledge base to be closed under negative information, namely we have to endorse an *open world assumption* on each A_i. This is because the fact that a camera does not detect a man carrying a gun does not mean that we can claim that he is not carrying a gun.

[8] We are aware that the consistency assumption may be a highly demanding condition in case we model cognitive agents. We assume it here just for the sake of simplicity, in order to directly apply the model of the next section.

[9] We are thankful to an anonymous reviewer for stressing this point. We are aware that this is a demanding assumption. For example, synchronizing surveillance cameras and human agents' communications may require interfacing two different time segmentations of events. We abstract from this issue in order to present our analysis of systemic information and in order to provide an easy application of social choice theoretic techniques.

the properties of each type of aggregation procedure. The properties that we are going to discuss shall provide a qualitative evaluation of the information of a system in a given moment.[10]

In a complex system like the one we are depicting, there may be several sources of disagreement between agents. For example, a possible disagreement may be at the level of perceptual information. Imagine three cameras that are pointing at the same scene, and such that two of them recognize an object as a gun, whereas the third does not. Furthermore, agents' knowledge bases can contain conflicting high-level information on the roles involved, and it is not clear where to place the source of disagreement.

The ontological analysis allows us to classify the types of information, thus the question is how to define suitable procedures to solve the different types of disagreement, e.g. normative, prescriptive, or visual. We briefly sketch our model. Suppose the system consists of a set $\mathcal{N}$ of n agents. Denote $\mathcal{A}(\mathcal{L}_S)$ the set of all possible sets of atomic formulas in our language $\mathcal{L}_S$ that are consistent with the ontology. A profile of agents knowledge bases is given by a vector $(A_1, \ldots, A_n)$, we denote it $\mathbf{A}$. An aggregation procedure is a function $F : \mathcal{A}(\mathcal{L}_S)^n \to \mathcal{P}(\mathcal{L}_S)$ that takes a profile of agents' knowledge bases and returns a single set of propositions. The set of propositions $F(\mathbf{A})$ represents then the systemic information according to the procedure F.

Whenever we want to consider the collective information of a particular subsystem, we simply restrict the profile $\mathbf{A}$ to the relevant agents and define F accordingly.

The ontological analysis allows us to partition the set of propositions in $\mathcal{L}_S$ into their respective types. For each predicate P in our language, we can easily check by means of DOLCE whether P is a social concept, a visual concept, a basic concept and so on. This is one of our motivations for using an ontology. Since every proposition in the A_i is an atomic formula or a negation of an atomic formula, we can easily extend the classification of predicates in order to partition the agents' propositions into visual, conceptual and factual propositions.

Given a set of formulas A_i, we denote A_i^V, A_i^C, A_i^F, the visual, conceptual and factual propositions (respectively) that are contained in A_i. Accordingly, we partition profiles wrt their type of information; we denote them $\mathbf{A}^V$, $\mathbf{A}^C$, $\mathbf{A}^F$. We shall discuss aggregators that take profiles restricted to one of the types of propositions, namely, we define aggregation functions $F^V : \mathbf{A}^V \mapsto A^V$, $F^C : \mathbf{A}^C \mapsto A^C$, and $F^V : \mathbf{A}^F \mapsto A^F$.

We introduce and discuss a number of properties of aggregators that have been widely studied in judgment aggregation and social choice theory. In particular, the application of social choice theory and judgment aggregation to ontology merging has been developed in [25], where a number of aggregation procedures

---

[10] The methodology we propose is motivated by our intention of providing an analysis of the quality of systemic information depending on a number of parameters. Although the aggregation process is centralized, more plausible, and possibly feasible, distributed mechanisms that provide the same collective information can be defined. We leave this point for future work.

for aggregating Tboxes and Aboxes are defined. In what follows, we present some arguments to evaluate to what extent those properties are relevant for our modeling tasks.

Unanimity. An aggregator F is called unanimous if $A_1 \cap \cdots \cap A_n \subseteq F(\mathbf{A})$ for every profile $\mathbf{A} \in A(\mathcal{L}_S)^n$.

Anonymity. An aggregator F is called anonymous if for any profile $\mathbf{A} \in A(\mathcal{L}_S)^n$ and any permutation $\sigma : N \to N$ of the agents, we have that $F(A_1, \ldots, A_n) = F(A_{\sigma(1)}, \ldots, A_{\sigma(n)})$.

Independence. An aggregator F is called independent if for any formula $\phi \in \mathcal{L}_S$ and any two profiles $\mathbf{A}, \mathbf{A}' \in A(\mathcal{L}_S)^n$, we have that $\phi \in A_i \Leftrightarrow \phi \in A_i'$ for all agents $i \in N$ implies $\phi \in F(\mathbf{A}) \Leftrightarrow \phi \in F(\mathbf{A}')$.

Neutrality. An aggregator F is called neutral if for any two formulas $\phi, \psi \in \mathcal{L}_S$ and any profile $\mathbf{A} \in A(\mathcal{L}_S)^n$, we have that $\phi \in A_i \Leftrightarrow \psi \in A_i$ for all agents $i \in N$ implies $\phi \in F(\mathbf{A}) \Leftrightarrow \psi \in F(\mathbf{A})$.

Monotonicity. An aggregator F is called monotonic if for any agent $i \in N$, formula $\phi \in \mathcal{L}_S$, and profiles $\mathbf{A}, \mathbf{A}' \in A(\mathcal{L}_S)^n$ such that $A_j = A_j'$ for all $j \neq i$, we have that $\phi \in A_i' \setminus A_i$ and $\phi \in F(\mathbf{A})$ imply $\phi \in F(\mathbf{A}')$.

Unanimity implies that if the agents of the system agree on a proposition ϕ, then ϕ is accepted at systemic level. We claim that unanimity is a desirable property of any aggregator, regardless the specific type of propositions. As agents are the observation points of the system, and our knowledge of the system is provided by means of agents' information, a violation of unanimity would amount to discharging information for no apparent reason (i.e. no agent against).

Anonymity implies that all agents are treated equally, namely, that we have no reason to weight the information coming from an agent more than from another. This requirement is desirable when we cannot (or we do not want to) distinguish the reliability of agents. For example, we may not want to distinguish the information provided by two security officers that are communicating on the ground of the higher reliability of the first wrt the reliability of the second. In case of visual information, anonymity may not be desirable. For example, we want to weight the information coming from a trained security officer more than the information coming from a surveillance camera. Whenever appropriate, this is intended to model the fact that human agents may double check outcomes coming from artificial agents and human agents are assumed to be more reliable than artificial ones, at least in a number of tasks.

The condition of *independence* means that the acceptance of a formula at systemic level only depends on the pattern of acceptance in the individuals' sets (e.g. the number of agents who accept ϕ). That is, the reason for accepting ϕ should be the same in any profile. Independence is a more demanding axiom than the previous two; whether or not it should be imposed is debatable. A domain of application for which it is desirable is to merge normative information, see [20]. For example, suppose that the security protocol of the airport prescribes to an officer to fire if and only if conditions c_1 and c_2 hold. Suppose such conditions have to be checked by the relevant committee of agents. In that case, we do not want the outcome of the decision to depend on a particular scenario (i.e. profile), rather a form of impartiality should be respected. On the other hand, there are cases in which the number of agents supporting ϕ is not a good criterion for any profiles; we shall present an example below.

Neutrality requires that all the propositions in the system have to be treated symmetrically. We believe that this is not desirable for our purpose in general, as we want to treat visual, factual and conceptual information according to different criteria. Moreover, there are reasons to weight certain propositions more than others even in case they belong to the same class. For example, the proposition that states that an object has been seen as a gun by a surveillance camera should be considered as highly sensible and therefore it should be taken into account at systemic level. *Monotonicity* implies that agents' additional support for a proposition that is accepted at systemic level will never lead to it being rejected. This property is desirable in most of the cases, provided the relevant agents are involved.

A further requirement that is usually viewed as a desirable property is the consistency of the systemic information.

Consistency. An aggregator F is *consistent* if for every profile $\mathbf{A} \in \mathcal{A}(\mathcal{L}_S)^n$, the set $F(\mathbf{A})$ is consistent with the ontology.

It is well-known that not every aggregator that satisfies the properties that we have seen guarantees consistency. In particular, an aggregator that satisfies anonymity, independence, and neutrality may return inconsistent outcomes, cf. [20]. For example, merging information by means of the majority rule or by a quota rule may lead to inconsistent sets of propositions[11].

For the sake of example, we introduce a class of aggregators to model systemic information that is adapted from [25]. We leave an exhaustive discussion of types of aggregators for future work. We thus present a class of procedures that can be tailored for aggregating information in our scenario. Given a set of propositions $X \subseteq \mathcal{L}_S$, we define a *priority order* on formulas in X as a strict linear order on X. Several priority orders can be defined on X, for example a *support* order $>_S$ ranks the propositions according to the number of agents supporting them: $\phi >_S \psi$ iff the number of agents supporting ϕ is greater than the number of agents supporting ψ (provided a tie-breaking rule for propositions with equal support). Moreover, we can define a priority order on propositions that depends on the reliability of the agents that support them. Given the set of agents N, we define the *expert* agents as a subset $E \subset N$. Thus, the reliability priority may be defined as $\phi >_R \psi$ iff the number of experts supporting ϕ is greater than the number of experts supporting ψ. We may also introduce more stringent conditions by imposing that ϕ has higher priority than ψ if the very experts that support ϕ also support ψ.

---

[11] These results depend on the structure of the language that the agents use. It is enough to include some minimal logical connection to generate inconsistent outcomes, cf. [20]. Even if the propositions in the agents' sets are atomic, we are evaluating consistency wrt the ontology, that contains complex propositions.

Definition 1 (Priority-based procedures). *Given a priority order $>_X$, the procedure based on $>_X$ is the aggregator mapping any profile $\boldsymbol{A}$ to $F(\boldsymbol{A}) := S$ for the unique set $S \subseteq \mathcal{L}_S$ for which (i) $\phi \in S$, where ϕ is the top proposition according to $>_X$; (ii) if $S \cup \{\psi_2\}$, $\psi_1 \in S$, $\psi_1 >_X \psi_2$ and is consistent, then $\psi_2 \in S$.*

Thus, a priority-based procedure tries to provide a consistent outcome by checking the relevant information according to the priority. That is, the procedure tries to discharge conflicting information with a lower priority. For priority based procedures, neutrality or anonymity may be violated by the priority order. Independence is also violated (because ϕ may cease to be accepted if a formula it is contradicting receives additional support). Moreover, such procedures are consistent by construction. The priority order is supposed to represent the importance of the property for the system. For example, the proposition that states the recognition of an object as a gun should receive high priority in our ordering. This amounts to assuming that the propositions concerning the presence of weapons are taken as true even if few agents actually support their truth. This may be appropriate for example in a risk averse security protocol that tries to minimize the occurrence of worst case scenarios.

Priority based procedures allow for weighting the information according to the reliability of different sources. For example, we can weight the information coming from security officers, that are viewed as experts, more than information coming from surveillance cameras. Moreover, we can weight the reports of cameras that are closer to the location at issue more than the information coming from other cameras.

Thus, priority based procedures may be used to define aggregators that provide collective information on visual propositions: $F^V : \mathbf{A}^V \mapsto A^V$. Moreover, a priority order based on the reliability of agents can be used to merge factual information $F^V : \mathbf{A}^F \mapsto A^F$, provided we single out the right class of experts in our system. A number of aggregation procedure that single out the more reliable agents in the system have been developed in [10]. Note that it may be hard to compute the systemic information, given the required consistency check. The complexity depends of course on the language that we use to implement our ontology, a study of the complexity of computing problems related to judgment aggregation has been presented in [11].

It is interesting to point at an application of non-consistent aggregators, namely aggregators that return inconsistent sets of propositions. By using the analysis of aggregators provided by judgment aggregation, it is possible to pinpoint the places where the inconsistencies in the system are generated. In particular, aggregators that may return inconsistent information are useful to pinpoint causes of normative or conceptual disagreement, namely to analyze incompatibility of norms or concepts defined in the system with the collective information gathered by the agents.

We stress that the properties of aggregation procedures that we have introduced can be viewed as normative constraints on the procedure that settle possible disagreements as well as qualitative constraints on the collective information.

Agents may be willing to cooperate and accept the outcome of an aggregation procedure, namely a collective decision that may diverge with respect to their own individual stance, in case the procedure satisfies properties that they evaluate as desirable. In this sense, the properties of aggregation procedures provide arguments and justification addressed to the individuals for the collective outcome. We simply mention that it is, at least in principle, possible to include descriptions of aggregation procedures as specific norms in our ontology (cf. Table 1) and to model agents that discuss about aggregation procedures. This would make the acceptance of the coordination of diverging agents a matter of explicit discussion and acceptance within the system. This type of coordination is useful when modeling collective decisions that are taken in cases that are not covered by the standard procedures that are supposed to be known by the agents of the system.

5   Conclusion

We have depicted and discussed a number of important conceptual elements that ground the modeling of the complex scenario of a socio-technical system. We have seen that in order to provide a faithful representation of agents' and systemic knowledge, we need to characterize agents endowed with visual, cognitive and social capabilities, as well as systemic procedures that handle complex interactions and systemic information. We have argued that the ontological analysis allows for specifying the types of information involved in the system and we have used DOLCE to classify and partition the propositions that represent the different types of information. We have proposed the application of techniques from social choice theory and belief merging in order to define and analyze several concepts of systemic information, that depend on the type of information that has to be integrated. We stress that the analysis that we have introduced can serve as a theoretical framework for evaluating procedures for integrating heterogeneous information.

Future work shall focus in particular on two directions. Firstly, we will extend the ontological analysis to model agents that are endowed with a set of actions that depend on the information state. For example, agents can send an alarm signal in case they can infer that a person is a suspect, they can communicate pieces of information to other agents, they can ask questions to other agents, they can ask other agents to perform tasks, they can prescribe actions to be taken (e.g. "close the gate 12"), etc. For instance, an observation point i can see that a person is getting close to a security area and it sends this information to agent j who can check if such information holds also on the basis of his/her visual input. Moreover, i can ask other agents to track the path of the person who has been recognized as a suspect. This extension shall provide an ontology based communication protocol for socio-technical systems.

Secondly, we plan to extend our treatment of systemic information by discussing more general classes of functions that aggregate agents' information and by viewing the composition of a number of aggregation procedures as describing the hierarchical structure of a rich system. Moreover, it is important to introduce mechanisms that capture the procedural aspects of agents' interaction, e.g. negotiation, dialogues, deliberation.

References

1. Boella, G., Lesmo, L., Damiano, R.: On the ontological status of plans and norms. Artif. Intell. Law **12**(4), 317–357 (2004)
2. Borgo, S., Masolo, C.: Foundational choices in dolce. In: Staab, S., Studer, R. (eds.) Handbook on Ontologies, 2nd edn. Springer, Heidelberg (2009)
3. Bottazzi, E., Ferrario, R.: Preliminaries to a DOLCE ontology of organizations. Int. J. Bus. Process Integr. Manage. (Special Issue on Vocabularies, Ontologies and Business Rules for Enterprise Modeling) **4**(4), 225–238 (2009)
4. Brandt, F., Conitzer, V., Endriss, U.: Computational social choice. In: Weiss, G. (ed.) Multiagent Systems. MIT Press (Forthcoming)
5. Coradeschi, S., Saffiotti, A.: An introduction to the anchoring problem. Robot. Auton. Syst. **43**(2), 85–96 (2003)
6. Dalpiaz, F., Giorgini, P., Mylopoulos, J.: Adaptive socio-technical systems: a requirements-based approach. Requir. Eng. **18**(1), 1–24 (2013)
7. Duda, R.O., Hart, P.E., Stork, D.G.: Pattern Classification, 2nd edn. Wiley, New York (2001)
8. Duin, R.P.W., Pekalska, E.: The dissimilarity space: bridging structural and statistical pattern recognition. Pattern Recogn. Lett. **33**(7), 826–832 (2012)
9. Emery, F.E., Trist, E.: Socio-technical systems. In: West Churchman, C., Verhulst, M. (eds.) Management Sciences: Models and Techniques, pp. 83–97. Pergamon, New York (1960)
10. Endriss, U., Fernández, R.: Collective annotation of linguistic resources: basic principles and a formal model. In: Proceedings of the 51st Annual Meeting of the Association for Computational Linguistics (ACL-2013), August 2013
11. Endriss, U., Grandi, U., Porello, D.: Complexity of judgment aggregation. J. Artif. Intell. Res. **45**, 481–514 (2012)
12. Farenzena, M., Bazzani, L., Murino, V., Cristani, M.: Towards a subject-centered analysis for automated video surveillance. In: International Conference on Image Analysis and Processing, pp. 481–489 (2009)
13. Ferrario, R., Oltramari, A.: Towards a computational ontology of mind. In: Varzi, A. C., Vieu, L. (eds.), Proceedings of the International Conference on Formal Ontology in Information Systems, FOIS 2004, IOS Press, pp. 287–297 (2004)
14. Ferrario, R., Prévot, L.: Special issue: formal ontologies for communicating agents. Appl. Ontol. **2**, 3–4 (2007)
15. Gärdenfors, P.: Conceptual Spaces - The Geometry of Thought. MIT Press, Cambridge (2000)
16. Hadzic, M., Wongthongtham, P., Dillon, T.S., Chang, E.: Ontology-Based Multi-Agent Systems. Studies in Computational Intelligence. Springer, Heidelberg (2009)
17. Harnad, S.: The symbol grounding problem. Physica D **42**(1), 335–346 (1990)
18. Konieczny, S., Pino Pérez, R.: Merging information under constraints: a logical framework. J. Log. Comput. **12**(5), 773–808 (2002)
19. Lauritzen, S.L.: Graphical Models. Oxford University Press, Oxford (1996)
20. List, C., Puppe, C.: Judgment aggregation: a survey. In: Anand, P., Puppe, C., Pattanaik, P. (eds.) Handbook of Rational and Social Choice. Oxford University Press, Oxford (2009)

21. Masolo, C., Borgo, S., Gangemi, A., Guarino, N., Oltramari, A.: Wonderweb deliverable d18. Technical report, CNR (2003)
22. Masolo, C., Vieu, L., Bottazzi, E., Catenacci, C., Ferrario, R., Gangemi, A., Guarino, N.: Social roles and their descriptions. In: Proceedings of the 6th International Conference on the Principles of Knowledge Representation and Reasoning (KR-2004), pp. 267–277 (2004)
23. Minh, H.Q., Cristani, M., Perina, A., Murino, V.: A regularized spectral algorithm for hidden Markov models with applications in computer vision. In: IEEE International Conference on Computer Vision and Pattern Recognition, pp. 2384–2391 (2012)
24. Perina, A., Cristani, M., Castellani, U., Murino, V., Jojic, N.: Free energy score spaces: using generative information in discriminative classifiers. IEEE Trans. Pattern Anal. Mach. Intell. **34**(7), 1249–1262 (2012)
25. Porello, D., Endriss, U.: Ontology merging as social choice. In: Leite, J., Torroni, P., Ågotnes, T., Boella, G., van der Torre, L. (eds.) CLIMA XII 2011. LNCS (LNAI), vol. 6814, pp. 157–170. Springer, Heidelberg (2011)
26. Rabiner, L.: A tutorial on hidden Markov models and selected applications in speech recognition. Proc. IEEE **77**(2), 257–286 (1989)
27. Shoham, Y., Leyton-Brown, K.: Multiagent Systems: Algorithmic, Game-Theoretic, and Logical Foundations. Cambridge University Press, Cambridge (2009)
28. Woolridge, M.: Introduction to Multiagent Systems. Wiley, New York (2008)

Intelligent Battery Strategies for Local Energy Distribution

Muhammad Yasir[(✉)], Martin K. Purvis, Maryam Purvis,
and Bastin Tony Roy Savarimuthu

Department of Information Science, University of Otago, Dunedin, New Zealand
{muhammad.yasir,martin.purvis,maryam.purvis,tony.savarimuthu}@otago.ac.nz

Abstract. Electricity is an essential element of modern life, and presently most electric power is generated using fossil fuels. Two abundant renewable energy sources, solar and wind, are increasingly cost-competitive and also offer the potential of decentralized, and hence more robust, sourcing. However, the intermittent nature of solar and wind power can present difficulties in connection with integrating them into the main electric power grid. One measure that can address this issue of local, temporal energy deficits is to organize local micro-grid societies in which excess power is traded to those members that need it by market exchange. Different communities may employ differing strategies and policies with respect to their attitudes concerning environmental sustainability and financial outcomes. In this connection it can be valuable to have modeling facilities available that can assist communities to predict what may happen under various circumstances in a society employing mixed trading and storage strategies. In this paper we present an agent-based modeling approach that can be used to examine various strategies that can be used in connection with battery storage and market-based energy trading strategies for a set of communities locally connected into an electric micro-grid. We demonstrate that by means of agent-based what-if simulations, battery strategies can be selected that provide financial advantages to local communities and also lead to reduced greenhouse gas emissions (from a policy modeling perspective).

Keywords: Micro-grid · Renewable energy · Multi-agent system · Strategies

1 Introduction

With world population predicted to reach 9 billion by 2050 [3] and increasing environmental strains caused by pervasive globalization [17], there is an increasing recognition that the world reliance on stores of non-renewable and polluting fossil fuels [2,13] will need to be reduced. Another non-renewable energy source, nuclear power, also has an uncertain future, given serious concerns about nuclear waste disposal and the possibility of wide-scale health disasters in the event of a

T. Balke et al. (Eds.): COIN 2013, LNAI 8386, pp. 63–80, 2014.
DOI: 10.1007/978-3-319-07314-9_4, © Springer International Publishing Switzerland 2014

human- or naturally-caused failures [14]. For these reasons many scientists and engineers believe that renewable energy sources are the best alternative option for future energy needs.

Electricity production from renewable energy sources, such as solar and wind, are attractive because of the abundant availability of these sources and their benign effect on the environment. The distributed, modular, and potentially decentralized nature of these renewable energy sources can make electricity diversification and distribution more available in remote areas without extending transmission lines and facilitate better energy security. Some studies have shown that it is possible to fulfill future global energy demand entirely from renewable sources (solar, wind, and water) [5,8,9]. However, the intermittent nature of solar and wind energy stands in the way of fully adopting renewable energy for 100 % electricity generation.

Various techniques to overcome the sporadic nature of renewable sources have been proposed. For example the interconnection of geographically dispersed wind farms can reduce the effect of intermittency and provide stable power output. Similarly, large renewable energy producers can use weather forecasting techniques and larger batteries at the generation site to provide more stable power to the utility grid. Thus the intermittency issue can be addressed for a local community by buying power from other communities that have excess power stored that they are willing to trade. A standard decentralized mechanism to facilitate this trading is to employ a market mechanism. This then in turn presents policy issues for local communities: what kind of power-trading strategy is appropriate for them to meet their potentially conflicting long-term goals with respect to financial outcomes and the limitation of carbon emissions? We suggest that agent-based modeling can assist in the formulation of adjustment of such policies, and in this paper we present an agent-based model of an energy grid configuration whereby micro-grids (communities connected to local renewable energy sources, such as wind farms) are interconnected into larger micro-grid networks and can thereby share power among them.

Our proposed energy-sharing micro-grid model employs multi-agent interaction in order to trade energy among the local communities and stores energy for this purpose when excess energy is available. Each local community is autonomous and can adopt its own trading and storage strategy. Our empirical evaluation of these strategies shows that the intelligent storing can not only provide improved reliability but also can offer financial benefits. In Sect. 2 we review some related work in this area. In Sect. 3 we discuss our agent-based architecture for local coordination among locally connected micro-grids. Section 4 covers three battery storage strategies. Section 5 shows our empirical comparison of different battery storing strategies, and Sect. 6 discusses some future prospects and also provides a conclusion.

2   Related Work

In recent years there has been an increasing interest in using agent-based coordination to manage local energy usage:

- Alam et al. [1] used a game-theory approach to form a coalition among trading partners to exchange power. Their paper demonstrates that the coalition can result in a reduction of battery usage and energy losses.
- Vytelingum et al. [18] proposed an agent-based micro-storage management technique which supports the coordination of individually-owned profit seeking storage devices.
- Ishowo-Oloko et al. [7] presented a model of a dynamic storage-pricing mechanism using information from renewable energy providers to generate real-time electricity prices that are communicated to the customers.
- Lagorse et al. [11] defined an agent-based energy management system for distributed power sources, using a bottom-up approach for system reliability.
- Similarly, Jun et al. [10] also defined a multi-agent based solution to manage energy for a hybrid renewable energy generation system, and argue that their approach assists system maintenance and reduces excessive load growth.
- Cossentino et al. proposed a multi-agent system for the management of micro-grids [4]. Their system provides micro-grid-based electronic market to producers and consumers. In case of mismatches between supply and demand, their system disconnects either loads or feeders depending upon the priority.

With respect to the above-mentioned proposed systems, the model of Alam et al. [1], considers energy exchanges between members of a coalition (i.e. a community of individual households), but does not consider the profitability of the individual households nor the amount of carbon emissions mitigated through coalition formation. In the second model [18], the authors defined an agent-based framework that attempts to converge the storage profiles towards a Nash equilibrium, resulting in low peak demand, and reducing the requirement of a costly and carbon-intensive generation plant. However, they do not consider the role of the prosumer (producer and consumer), and the trading of power among individuals in their system. In other three models [7,10,11], there has not been much attention given to the consideration of robust energy distribution across locally-connected communities. Cossentino et al. [4], do use a trading mechanism among the internal agents of the micro-grid to balance supply and demand inside the micro-grid's boundaries, but no attention has been given to trading across the micro-grids.

In contrast, our research here incorporates and focuses on battery storage strategies for an interconnected set of communities that not only improve energy reliability and distribution, but also take into account financial outcomes and social welfare of the societies. We consider a local community as one micro-grid that has local generators and dedicated storage devices. Typically when a micro-grid has a surplus of power, it puts all of its surplus into its battery up to its capacity. Due to the limited number of battery charging cycles (1500–4500), frequent charging reduces the lifespan of the battery. As a result batteries, which are one of the most expensive components of the renewable energy generation system, need to be replaced more often. Instead of always putting all its energy surplus into the battery, a micro-grid controller could, on the basis of weather forecasts and the current State Of Charge (SOC) of its battery, decide to sell some of its energy surplus in the local market. This way interconnected micro-grids could not only improve their reliability during energy generation deficits, but also could enhance battery life and then financial outcome.

3   Agent-Based Architecture for Local Distribution

The goal of our agent-based architecture is to provide a mechanism to enhance locally generated power usage and also provide reliability in cases of main-grid failures. This is schematically shown in Fig. 1. The combination of communities (shown by ellipses) is called a society. Each community has four fundamental components, each of which is managed by an associated agent.

1. **Generator Agent.** It manages the community's renewable energy generators within the local area, and it reports on available energy to the coordinator agent.
2. **Battery Agent.** It is responsible for regulating the battery chargers and reporting on battery energy availability to the coordinator agent.
3. **Consumer Agent.** It represents the aggregate energy consumption load of the community.
4. **Coordinator Agent.** It represents the community to the external environment and interacts with other micro-grid coordinator agents (in a power trading market) and with the main power utility. It reads the wind forecast (available for up to 24 h) and also predicts its local community demand for the next 24 h. If there is excess power available, it decides whether to store the excess power or sell it to other communities or to the main utility grid.

As shown in Fig. 1, there is a local marketplace where communities can engage in energy trade. The market mechanism here employs a double-auction algorithm to facilitate market clearing (determining the price at which a unit of energy is sold by matching bids and offers). In this procedure, the buyer making the highest bid will be matched with the seller making the lowest offer. The clearing price (unit price per Kwh) is set to be the mean of two prices (bid and offer). If there are remaining buyers and sellers, this matching process is iterated. A local community coordinator agent typically buys from the market if it has a local power deficit, or depending on prevailing market conditions, it can choose to buy power from the main utility grid. The details of different trading strategies are presented in Sect. 3.1.

Individual communities may employ differing trading strategies when they trade electricity with other communities. Some communities may be environmentally conscious and more interested in minimizing environmentally harmful emissions, while others may be more concerned about finances. Such communities will prefer to trade with other local communities, because their energy comes from renewable sources (i.e. it is **green power**).

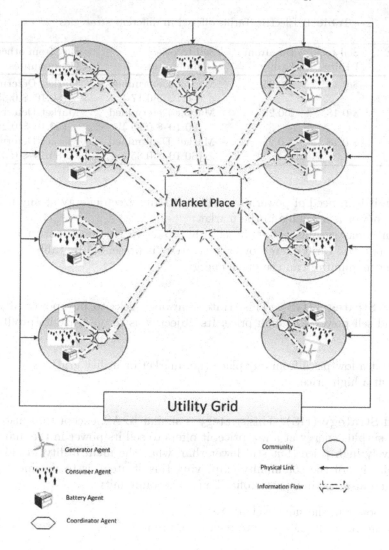

Fig. 1. Agent-based architecture for local distribution

3.1 Trading Strategies

There are three energy trading strategies that local communities can employ. In addition, we will discuss in Sect. 4 three related battery storage strategies that local communities can employ in that regard.

Altruistic Strategy (AS). The goal of a community using this strategy is to minimize carbon emissions by maximizing its use of renewable energy and getting other communities to use renewable energy, too. As a consequence,

Table 1. Electric Tariffs offered in different strategies

Strategy	Sell to Utility	Buy from Utility	Sell to other Communities	Buy from other Communities
AS	$ 0.18	$ 0.25	Market Determined ($0.10–$ 0.17)	Market Determined ($0.10–$ 0.35)
GS	$ 0.18	$ 0.25	Market Determined ($0.10–$ 0.35)	Market Determined ($0.10–$ 0.25)
HS	$ 0.18	$ 0.25	Market Determined ($0.10–$ 0.35)	Market Determined ($0.10–$ 0.35)

- When it is in need of power, it is willing to buy green energy at any price, if green power is available in the market.
- When it has surplus power, it sells the power in the local market at a low price (electric tariff offered by each strategy is presented in Table 1), so that more communities can use green energy.

Greedy Strategy (GS). This strategy always seeks to buy power at a low price and sell power at a high price. Its objective is to optimize its profits. GS always:

- Buys at a low price from any place (i.e. market or utility grid).
- Sells at a high price.

Hybrid Strategy (HS). This strategy is similar to AS, except that instead of offering surplus energy at a low price, it offers to sell its power in the market at a relatively high price (but still lower than what the main utility would pay). The objective of the community employing this strategy is to use more green power and also maximize its profit. Thus this community

- Buys power in the same way as AS.
- Sells surplus at a high price to maximize profit.

Previous studies e.g. [19] have compared trading community strategies, but they have not included intelligent strategies for battery storage. Key aspects to consider when making decisions in this regard include information about future wind patterns, the state of the battery charge (SOC), and potential financial gains and losses. By making intelligent decisions about storing surplus power, a community can not only save battery life but also increases its financial gain and improve the reliability of the local system (i.e. increase the longevity of power availability in case of a main-grid cut-off). In this paper, we propose three battery strategies for storing surplus power. We also show experimental results comparing how these strategies can be used in conjunction with market-based trading strategies and the overall effect on carbon emissions and net profits/loss.

4   Battery Storing Strategies

This section describes three battery storing strategies by means of which communities can take into account (a) future wind availability (i.e. forecast) and (b) future demand.

4.1   Battery Altruistic (BA) Strategy

The objective of this strategy is to promote green power usage within the community and also promote green power usage among other communities by offering surplus power into the market for a low price. The operation of this strategy is schematically presented in Algorithm 1. This battery strategy is in-line with the overall objectives of the Altruistic strategy (AS) discussed in Sect. 3.1 When the surplus occurs, the coordinator agent sends information to the battery agent about available excess power. The battery agent checks the state of charge (SOC) of the battery. If it is less than the predefined level (i.e. α x Batterycapacity, where value $0 < \alpha < 1$), then all the surplus goes into the battery until the SOC exceeds the predefined level. If the SOC is already above the predefined level, then the battery agent asks the coordinator agent about future generation and demand. If the same trend (i.e. future generation is greater than the future demand) exists for the future, then the current surplus will be offered to the market at a low price (so that more buyers can use green power); otherwise, it will store the surplus in the battery for future use. If no buyer is present in the market then, the offered amount will be stored in the battery.

When an energy deficit occurs, the coordinator agent sends unmatched demand information to the battery agent. If the battery storage is greater than unmatched demand, then unmatched demand is fulfilled from battery, otherwise remaining storage in the battery is used, and the remaining amount (i.e. unmet demand) is met from the market or from the utility grid.

4.2   Battery Greedy (BG) Strategy

For the BG strategy, the focus is on obtaining maximum financial advantage by selling surplus power for a high price in the market or to the utility grid. The operation of this strategy is defined in Algorithm 2. This battery strategy is in-line with the overall objectives of the Greedy Strategy discussed in Sect. 3.1.

An agent using the greedy strategy not only sells current surplus power, but also the extra power stored in the battery (i.e. the power stored above the predefined level, α x Battery capacity) for a high price either in the market or to the utility grid. During a shortage of power, the unmatched demand is met from the battery if the wind outlook is positive (i.e. future generation will be in excess of future demand) and the power stored in the battery is greater or equal to the unmatched demand. Otherwise, it goes to the market or to the utility. From the storage point of view, BA and BG are the same. They differ from each other in two aspects:

Algorithm 1. Battery Altruistic Strategy

---

1 **if** *Demand < Generation* **then**
2 | *Surplus ← Generation - Demand*;
3 | **if** *SOC < α × BatteryCapacity* **then**
4 | | **if** *Surplus + SOC < BatteryCapacity* **then**
5 | | | *SOC ← BatteryStorage + Surplus*
6 | | **else**
7 | | | *BatteryStorage ← full*;
8 | | | *leftoversurplus ← surplus - (batterycapacity - SOC)* ;
9 | | | Sell *leftoversurplus* to the Market or to the utility grid;
10 | **else**
11 | | **if** *FutureDemand < FutureGeneration* **then**
12 | | | **if** *buyer available in Market* **then**
13 | | | | Sell surplus in the market
14 | | | **else**
15 | | | | **if** *Surplus + SOC < BatteryCapacity* **then**
16 | | | | | *SOC ← BatteryStorage + Surplus*;
17 | | | | **else**
18 | | | | | *BatteryStorage ← full*;
19 | | | | | *leftoversurplus← surplus - (batterycapacity - SOC)* ;
20 | | | | | Sell *leftoversurplus* to the utility grid;
21 | | **else**
22 | | | **if** *Surplus + SOC < BatteryCapacity* **then**
23 | | | | *SOC ← BatteryStorage + Surplus*;
24 | | | **else**
25 | | | | *BatteryStorage ← full*;
26 | | | | *leftoversurplus ← surplus - (batterycapacity - SOC)* ;
27 | | | | Sell *leftoversurplus* to the utility grid;
28 **else**
29 | *UnmatchedDemand ← Demand - Generation*;
30 | **if** *BatteryStorage < UnmatchedDemand* **then**
31 | | *BatteryStorage ← 0* ;
32 | | *UnmetDemand ←* Buy from Market and\or Utility ;
| | // *Unmetdemand = Unmatcheddemand - BatteryStorage*
33 | **else**
34 | | *UnmatchedDemand* is Obtained From Battery

- BA only sells if there is a buyer in the market (line 12 of Algorithm 1), however BG sells its surplus to the utility grid if there is no buyer in the market.
- In addition to the current surplus, BG also sells the extra power stored in the battery (i.e. power stored more than the predefined level).

Algorithm 2. Battery Greedy Strategy

---

1 **if** *Demand < Generation* **then**
2 | *Surplus* ← *Generation - Demand*;
3 | **if** *SOC < α × BatteryCapacity* **then**
4 | | **if** *Surplus + SOC < BatteryCapacity* **then**
5 | | | *SOC* ← *BatteryStorage + Surplus*;
6 | | **else**
7 | | | *BatteryStorage* ← *full*;
8 | | | *leftoversurplus* ← *surplus - (batterycapacity - SOC)* ;
9 | | | Sell *leftoversurplus* to the Market/ utility grid;
10 | **else**
11 | | **if** *FutureDemand < FutureGeneration* **then**
12 | | | *Surplus* ← *Surplus + BatteryStorage (up to α× Battery Capacity)*;
13 | | | Sell *Surplus* to the Market/utility grid
14 | | **else**
15 | | | **if** *Surplus + SOC < BatteryCapacity* **then**
16 | | | | *SOC* ← *BatteryStorage + Surplus*;
17 | | | **else**
18 | | | | *BatteryStorage* ← *full*;
19 | | | | *leftoversurplus* ← *surplus - (batterycapacity - SOC)* ;
20 | | | | Sell *leftoversurplus* to the Market/ utility grid;

21 **else**
22 | Unmatched Demand ← Demand - Generation;
23 | **if** *FutureDemand < FutureGeneration* **then**
24 | | **if** *BatteryStorage < UnmatchedDemand* **then**
25 | | | *UnmetDemand* ← *Buy from Market and\or Utility* ;
   | | | // Unmet demand = Unmatched demand - Battery Storage
26 | | **else**
27 | | | *UnmatchedDemand is Obtained From Battery*
28 | **else**
29 | | *UnmatchedDemand* ← *Buy from Market and\or Utility*

4.3 Battery Conservative (BC) Strategy

The goal of the BC strategy is to store more power in the battery for its own usage in the future. Its operation is presented in Algorithm 3 and this battery is in-line with the overall objective of the Hybrid Strategy (HS) discussed in Sect. 3.1.

In this strategy, there are two parameter levels (α and β, where $\alpha < \beta$, and their values are between 0 and 1). All surplus energy initially goes into the battery until the SOC reaches more than the α-level of storage (lines 3 and 4).

After that and depending upon the forecast information, the decision whether to store or sell takes place (lines 6–18). If the anticipated future demand is less than future generation, then half of the surplus power will be stored in the battery (up until the SOC exceeds the β-level of storage, i.e. β x Batterycapacity) and the other half will be sold into the market or the utility grid for a high price. If the battery storage exceeds β x Battery capacity, then all the surplus will be sold to the market or the utility grid. However, if the future generation is anticipated to be less than the future demand, then all surplus will be put into the battery (lines 15–18). During power deficits (i.e. current generation doesn't match the demand), battery storage will be used to satisfy unmatched demand. However, if the battery storage also does not meet the unmatched demand, then the remaining unmatched demand (i.e. unmet demand) will be satisfied from the market or from the utility grid (line 22). It should be noted that BC and BA strategies have the same discharging mechanism (lines 28–34 of Algorithm 1 and lines 19–24 of Algorithm 2).

Algorithm 3. Battery Conservative Strategy

---

1 **if** $Demand < Generation$ **then**
2      $Surplus \leftarrow Generation$ - $Demand$;
3   **if** $SOC < \alpha \times BatteryCapacity$ **then**
4          $SOC \leftarrow BatteryStorage + Surplus$;
5   **else**
6   **if** $FutureDemand < FutureGeneration$ **then**
7   **if** $SOC \geq \alpha \times BatteryCapacity$ $and \leq \beta \times BatteryCapacity$ **then**
8   Sell and store the surplus by proportion of 50%
9   **else**
10   **if** $SOC > \beta \times BatteryCapacity$ **then**
11   Sell $Surplus$ into Market and\or Utility Grid

12   **else**
13   **if** $Surplus + SOC < BatteryCapacity$ **then**
14                 $SOC \leftarrow BatteryStorage + Surplus$;
15   **else**
16                 $BatteryStorage \leftarrow full$;
17                 $leftoversurplus \leftarrow surplus$ - $(batterycapacity$ - $SOC)$;
18   Sell $leftoversurplus$ to the Market/ utility grid;

19 **else**
20     $UnmatchedDemand \leftarrow Demand$ - $Generation$;
21   **if** $BatteryStorage < UnmatchedDemand$ **then**
22         $UnmetDemand \leftarrow Market$ $and\or$ $Utility$ $Grid$
        // Unmetdemand = Unmatched demand - Battery Storage
23   **else**
24         $UnmatchedDemand$ is Obtained From Battery

---

5   Experiments

5.1   Experimental Setup

In order to compare the above mentioned strategies, we set up nine communities (C1 to C9). Each community has an average hourly consumption of 1150 kWh (with a variance among them of 100 kWh) and has a wind turbine of 2000 kW generation capacity and overall battery storage capability of 4000 kWh. However, these values for an individual community will vary. Because the communities are dispersed geographically, and they have different wind speeds. Due to different wind pattern, the power produced by each community is also different. Power generated by a wind turbine is calculated by using the following formula [12]:

$$P = 1/2 \; \rho \; A \; V^3 \; C_p$$

where
   P is power in watts (W),
   ρ is the air density in kilograms per cubic meter (kg/m^3),
   A is the swept rotor area in square meters (m^2),
   V is the wind speed in meters per second (m/s), and
   C_p is the power co-efficient.

We obtained the synthetic wind speed (V) data of New Zealand from Electricity Authority New Zealand [6].

   Our experiments were conducted using the following assumptions. All communities are situated at sea level, so the value of ρ is 1.23 kg/m^3. The wind turbine blade length is 45 meter (m). The cut-in and cut-out wind speeds of the turbine are 3 and 25 meters per second (m/s), respectively. Theoretically the maximum value of C_p is 59 %, which is known as the Betz limit [12,16]. However, practically the value of C_p is in between 25 %–45 %, depending upon the height and size of the turbine. The value we used for C_p was 0.4 (i.e. 40 %). The round-trip battery efficiency (i.e. the charging and discharging efficiency) is 85 %. The depth of battery discharge (i.e. the maximum power that can be drained out from the battery) is 90 %. The self-discharge of the battery is 1 % per month. The value of α for BA and BG is 0.25, and for BC it is 0.5. The value of β for BC is 0.75. We also assume the available predicted weather information and demand to be 90 % accurate [15]. We then use randomization of existing data in order to simulate real predictions. We also assume that the utility grid is always ready to buy power and sell power to the micro-grids at a rate of 18 cents per kWh and 25 cents per kWh, respectively. To trade into the market, a community uses the market-based trading mechanisms presented in Sect. 3.1.

   We computed the values of two variables of interest during the simulation: *carbon emission* (the amount of carbon dioxide emitted during electricity production, transmission and distribution) and *net profit/loss* (i.e. energy_sales_revenue – energy_purchases_expenses – generation_costs) during the simulation by varying battery strategies employed by a community. To calculate CO_2, we used an electricity emission factor of 0.137 (kg CO_2-equivalent per kWh) for New Zealand [16]. We used two metrics to calculate the net profit/loss.

1. Net profit/loss at the *society level* is the aggregation of net profit/loss of all nine communities present in the society. If the communities only trade among each other through the market, then the total net profit/loss at the society level is zero. Selling power to the utility grid brings in a profit (i.e. financial gain at society level), and buying energy from the utility produces a loss.
2. Net profit loss at the *community level.* If a local community is self-sufficient in terms of power, then that means the community can produce more power than its local demand and can sell it externally. In that case the community will gain a net profit. However, if the community does not meet its local demand from its own generation, then the net profit/loss can be negative (since it has to pay to buy electricity from another provider).

5.2   Results

We ran all experiments for 25,000 simulated hours. During the experiments, communities having BA strategies used the Altruistic Strategy (AS) for trading. Communities with BC strategy employed the Hybrid Strategy (HS) and communities with the BG strategy employed the Greedy Strategy (GS) for trading into the market. Note that we are only comparing the impact of battery strategies on net profit/loss by using the above mentioned metrics.

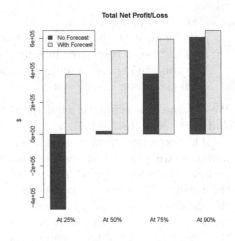

Fig. 2. Net Profit/Loss in forecast vs no forecast system

Performance of Communities Without Forecast. For comparison purposes, we generated baseline results where communities do not have a forecasting ability (i.e. are unable to foresee future wind patterns and predict future demand). For this purpose, we conducted a simple experiment where an agent sells power to the market or to the utility grid if the power in its battery is more than a certain level (e.g. 25 %, 50 %, 75 %, 90 %) of the total capacity of the battery. Note this experiment uses the BG storing strategies introduced in Sect. 4. The results are shown in Fig. 2.

As expected, the results show that the system with forecast information has financial advantages compared to the system which does not use forecast information. This is because instead of always selling surplus power after reaching a certain storage level, the forecast-equipped system can foresee future demand and generation and then choose whether to sell power or save it in the battery for future use. Results show that forecast information helped in the reduction of CO_2 up to 7 %.

Result of Heterogeneous Battery Storing Strategies. In this experiment, the 9 communities have different individual battery storing strategies. Due to space limitations, we present only 10 of the possible combinations, which are listed in Table 2:

Table 2. Ten different combinations of strategies

Combination No	Description	C 1	C 2	C 3	C 4	C 5	C 6	C 7	C 8	C 9
CMB1	7BCs, 1BA, 1BG	BC	BC	BC	BC	BC	BC	BC	BA	BG
CMB2	7BAs, 1BC, 1BG	BA	BA	BA	BA	BA	BA	BA	BC	BG
CMB3	7BGs, 1BC, 1BA	BG	BG	BG	BG	BG	BG	BG	BC	BA
CMB4	3BCs, 3BAs, 3BGs	BC	BC	BC	BA	BA	BA	BG	BG	BG
CMB5	6BCs, 3BAs	BC	BC	BC	BC	BC	BC	BA	BA	BA
CMB6	6BCs, 3BGs	BC	BC	BC	BC	BC	BC	BG	BG	BG
CMB7	6BAs, 3BCs	BA	BA	BA	BA	BA	BA	BC	BC	BC
CMB8	6BAs, 3BGs	BA	BA	BA	BA	BA	BA	BG	BG	BG
CMB9	6BGs, 3BCs	BG	BG	BG	BG	BG	BG	BC	BC	BC
CMB10	6BGs, 3BAs	BG	BG	BG	BG	BG	BG	BA	BA	BA

Figure 3 shows the total financial outcomes at the society level for the above mentioned combinations. The general observation is that the society having more green-power based strategies (with respect to both battery storing and trading) communities yield better financial advantages. In Fig. 3, the community combination, CMB7, has the highest financial gain, because the majority of the communities in this combination promote green power usage by selling power at low price among themselves. CMB5 has the second highest financial gain. Although the number of communities who want to use green power in CMB5 is the same as CMB7 (that is, they have same buying strategies), the difference comes from the selling and storing point of view, i.e. in CMB5 only 3 communities want to promote green power usage by offering at a low price (3BAs), 6 other communities (6 BCs) sell power for maximum profit, either in the local market or to the utility grid. Since 6 communities in CMB5 use the BC strategy, the surplus amount available in the market is less because BC offers surplus amount to the market only when its battery storage exceeds the level of β.

CMB3 has the worst financial outcome on the society level. Most of the communities (seven) in this combination use BG and GS for storing and trading respectively. One problem they have is that BG does not use the battery storage efficiently. Instead of using its battery storage to meet its unmatched demand, it goes to the market or to the utility if the existing trend (i.e. generation is less than demand) is expected to last for the next 24 h. In that case, instead of using stored battery power, it directly goes to the market or to the utility grid to meet unmatched demand, which is more expensive. Secondly, because of the greedy trading strategies, sellers and buyers are not bound to buy from or to sell to the market, and they may turn to the more expensive for the society utility. Note that the community configurations that ranked in the top four (CMB 1, 2, 5, 7) had significant proportions of communities using green battery strategies (i.e. BA or BC).

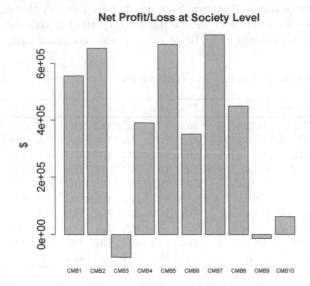

Fig. 3. Net profit/loss in heterogeneous battery strategies

Figure 4 graphically shows the total net profit/loss for each of the nine communities, as well as the average net profit/loss of each combination, when different combinations of strategies are used (i.e. for each bar in Fig. 3, there are 9 bars in Fig. 4). The individual community bars refer to the left-hand vertical scale, which shows the total net profit loss at each community level. The horizontal dashed lines refer to the right-hand vertical axis, which shows the average net profit loss of each combination of 9 communities. Note that the combinations having more BG strategies have lower average net profit/loss (CMB 3, 9 and 10) compared to the combinations having more BA or BC strategies. Also, any combination with at least one greedy community does worse than combinations containing only a mixture of BA and BC strategies. However, at the individual level, a community having BG strategy from CMB6 has the highest financial gain (the first bar in CMB6). This is because, that particular community has overall surplus power generation and the majority of the communities in this combination have BC strategy. Hence, most of the time the community can sell its surplus power in the market at a good rate (i.e. this community takes advantage of BC buyers who buy at a high price). It is also observed that communities that have low generation, have low financial loss if the other communities in their combination have green behaviour (i.e. green trading and storage). For example, the last community from the CMB2 has the least financial loss compared to the other combinations. This is because most of the communities in this combination use the BA strategy. Hence most of the time it can acquire needed power at a low price. Note also that for CMB3, CMB4, CMB6, and CMB7, the first community uses the same strategy (BG), but it has varying financial outcomes

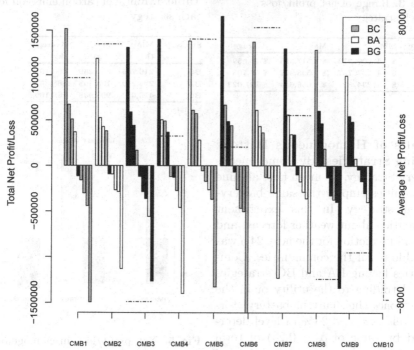

Fig. 4. Net profit/loss at community level

due to its varying market contexts with different combinations of communications employing a different mix of greedy and altruistic strategies. This shows that the net profit/loss at the community level not only depends upon which strategy a community has but also depends upon the strategies of the neighbouring communities.

Table 3 shows the total range of net profits and losses (maximum and minimum financial outcomes) for the various battery storage strategies over all of these experiments. Similarly, Table 4 shows the range of carbon emissions for each strategy. For example, if a community chooses the BG strategy, there are seven different configurations that are possible, and the maximum and minimum net profits/losses and carbon emission over the various collective combinations were $-1,334,827, $ 1,656,634, 909,938 kg, and 416,682 kg respectively. Also, on average, communities having BG netted a profit of $121,023, and average carbon emission of 668,109 kg over 25,000 h. Information like this can be used by the power management committees of a community to calculate consequences and help them decide which strategy they wish to adopt.

Table 3. Range of net profit/loss for each strategy

Strategy	Min	Max	Average
BC	$ −1,609,313	$ 1,517,325	$ 40,059
BA	$ −1,227,797	$ 1,398,997	$ 56,708
BG	$ −1,334,827	$ 1,656,634	$ 121,023

Table 4. Range of carbon emission for each strategy

Strategy	Min (kg)	Max (kg)	Average (kg)
BC	216,736	810,259	490,101
BA	224,249	798,608	488,867
BG	416,682	909,938	668,109

Results of Homogeneous Battery Storing Strategies. By Homogeneous Battery Strategy, we mean that all nine communities employ the same battery-storing strategy. In this experiment information about weather forecast and demand prediction for the next 24 h was available to all the communities. Communities having BA and BG strategies started trading to the utility or in the market once their current battery storage levels exceeded 25 % (a level determined by value of $\alpha = 0.25$) of total capacity. However, communities having a BC strategy started trading after the battery storage level exceeded 50 % (value of $\alpha = 0.5$) and had a value of $\beta = 0.75$ for regulating when they would sell to the market. Figure 5 shows the results of the simulation.

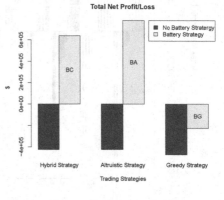

Fig. 5. Net profit/loss in homogeneous battery strategies

Figure 5 compares homogeneous societies (same strategy employed across all nine communities) with and without battery storage. The BA homogeneous society has the best overall outcome, because the communities concentrate their power trading in the local energy market. This avoids the higher costs associated with trading with the utility. The greedy all-BG society does poorest in the homogeneous circumstances, because (a) its associated greedy trading strategy (AS) leads to more frequent interactions with the more expensive utilities and (b) it less frequently uses its battery storage to meet its unmet energy demand, thereby incurring higher costs from the market. It is also observed that by the use of BA approach with it associated AS trading, carbon emission is reduced to 13 % as compared to the system using no battery strategy. Similarly, use of BC approach with HS and BA with GS trading strategy result in the reduction of CO_2 by 7.5 % and 5.2 % respectively.

6   Conclusion

Interconnected micro-grid communities, with renewable energy sources and energy storage devices have already been shown to be effective with respect to financial advantage, local autonomy, and more energy distribution. When communities engage in local power trading, their trading and storage strategies can affect their own finances and their own level of carbon emissions, as well as those of their neighbouring communities with which they interact. We have extended the kind of investigation here by presenting a set of three battery storing strategies and have shown some of the complex interactions that can take place in a micro-grid trading environment. For this reason, we believe that multi-agent modeling can be valuable in predicting and managing these operations. In this connection, we have conducted experimental simulations for a number of strategies using an agent-based architecture and employing synthetic wind data and current energy pricing data.

Since agent-based system coordination and collaboration is inherently scalable, a deployed decentralized energy-trading approach that is managed by autonomous agents can be expanded to cover much larger collectives. This offers even more grounds to employ agent-based modeling and simulation to assist in managing such communities and making predictions under various weather and system conditions (i.e. policy modeling for communities).

In the future we will be extending our agent-based analyses by conducting more elaborate examinations of more complex situations. This future research will explore:

- Greater variation in types of renewable energy. This will include solar heating and solar voltaic systems.
- More consideration of line and transfer costs between communities and with the utility grid.
- Multiple levels of complexity. Thus within communities we will explore the idea of individual prosumers having their own local storage facilities and trading among themselves at lower rates, as well as across communities. This will involve varying levels of trust among the agent energy traders.
- More dynamic and adaptable trading and storage strategies. Under these conditions, agent traders will be better able to learn from past experiences what trading strategy to adopt, and they will examine the effects of on-the-fly strategy shifts under these conditions.

References

1. Alam, M., Ramchurn, S., Rogers, A.: Cooperative energy exchange for the efficient use of energy and resources in remote communities. In: 12th Autonomous Agents and Multiagent Systems (AAMAS) Conference, pp. 731–738. Saint Paul Minnesota, USA (2013)
2. BP: BP Statistical Review of World Energy. Technical report, London, England (2013)
3. Chu, S., Majumdar, A.: Opportunities and challenges for a sustainable energy future. Nature 488(7411), 294–303 (2012)
4. Cossentino, M., Lodato, C., Pucci, M., Vitale, G.: A multi-agent architecture for simulating and managing microgrids. In: Federated Conference on Computer Science and Information Systems (FedCSIS), pp. 619–622. Szczecin, Poland (2011)

5. Delucchi, M.A., Jacobson, M.Z.: Providing all global energy with wind, water, and solar power, Part II: reliability, system and transmission costs, and policies. Energy Policy **39**(3), 1170–1190 (2011)
6. Electricity Authority: Synthetic wind data. http://www.ea.govt.nz/industry/monitoring/forecasting/analysis-of-wind-integration/synthetic-wind-data/ (2013). Accessed 01 July 2013
7. Ishowo-oloko, F., Vytelingum, P., Jennings, N., Rahwan, I.: A storage pricing mechanism for learning agents in masdar city smart grid. In: 11th International Conference on Autonomous Agents and Multiagent Systems, pp. 1167–1168. Valencia, Spain (2012)
8. Jacobson, M.: Review of solutions to global warming, air pollution, and energy security. Energy Environ. sci. **2**, 148–173 (2009)
9. Jacobson, M.Z., Delucchi, M.A.: Providing all global energy with wind, water, and solar power, Part I: technologies, energy resources, quantities and areas of infrastructure, and materials. Energy Policy **39**(3), 1154–1169 (2011)
10. Jun, Z., Junfeng, L., Jie, W., Ngan, H.: A multi-agent solution to energy management in hybrid renewable energy generation system. Renewable Energy **36**(5), 1352–1363 (2011)
11. Lagorse, J., Paire, D., Miraoui, A.: A multi-agent system for energy management of distributed power sources. Renewable Energy **35**(1), 174–182 (2010)
12. Miller, A., Muljadi, E., Zinger, D.S.: A variable speed wind turbine power control. Energy Convers. **12**(2), 181–186 (1997)
13. Moriarty, P., Honnery, D.: Rise Fall Carbon Civilisation. Resolving global environmental and resource problems. springer, London, England (2011)
14. Moriarty, P., Honnery, D.: What is the global potential for renewable energy? Renew. Sustain. Energy Rev. **16**(1), 244–252 (2012)
15. National Renewable Energy: Solar and wind forecasting. http://www.nrel.gov/electricity/transmission/resource_forecasting.html (2013). Accessed 01 July 2013
16. M. f. t. E. New Zealand: Guidance for voluntary corporate greenhouse gas reporting data and methods for the 2010 calendar year. Technical report, Ministry for the Enviornment, Welington New Zealand (2010)
17. Ramachandran, P., Singh, M., Kapoor, A.: Population GROWTH - Trends, Projections. Challenges and Opportunities. Technical report, Planning Comission. Delhi, India (2000)
18. Vytelingum, P., Voice, T.D., Ramchurn, S.D., Rogers, A. Jennings, N.R.: Agent-based micro-storage management for the smart grid. In: 9th International Conference on Autonomous Agents and Multiagent Systems: number Aamas, pp. 10–14. Toronto, Canada (2010)
19. Yasir, M., Purvis, M., Purvis, M., Tony, B. Savarimuthu, R.: Agent-based coordination of local energy resource distribution. In: workshop on Multiagent-based Societal Systems (MASS 2013). AAMAS 2013, pp. 1–7. Saint Paul Minnesota, USA (2013)

Organisations

Coordination Using Social Policies in Dynamic Agent Organizations

Kathleen Keogh[1,2](✉) and Liz Sonenberg[2]

[1] School of Science, Information Technology and Engineering,
Federation University Australia, P.O. Box 663, Ballarat, VIC 3353, Australia
k.keogh@federation.edu.au
[2] Department of Computing and Information Systems,
The University of Melbourne, Parkville, Australia

Abstract. We seek to engineer adaptive coordination between agents working in and across dynamic organizations in a complex, distributed setting. Guided by predefined social policies, agents can create social commitments at run time to achieve coordination of knowledge and behaviour. We demonstrate coordination requirements by providing example policies, drawing on the need for knowledge cultivation in an emergency management scenario.

Keywords: Multiagent systems · Coordination · Adaptation · Organizations · Social commitments · Social policies

1 Introduction

Organizations, sometimes described as coordination structures for cooperation among individual agents [1], have been used as a construct for the governance of multi-agent systems, particularly when there is a need to impose institutional constraints upon a group of agents. Agent organizations can include definitions of roles, relations between roles and agents and associated obligations, as well as defining and perhaps imposing or enforcing norms or behavioural responsibilities. A number of organizational models for agents have been proposed in the literature, for example [2–10].

In previous work we have proposed a model for adaptive agent organizations OJAzzIC [11] inspired by studying the behaviour of human teams in emergency management settings. In the emergency management domain, with multiple formal organizations being coordinated (e.g. fire, ambulance, etc.), smaller teams emerge not based on predetermined organizational structures, but comprising agents identifying a context where improvised and coordinated action can help achieve overall goals [12,13]. In this paper we refine aspects of the OJaZZIC model – specifically we explore the use of social policies and social commitments in the specification of agent behaviours.

We are seeking to establish an organizational framework that defines the coordination of knowledge and plans between and across organizations so that system

T. Balke et al. (Eds.): COIN 2013, LNAI 8386, pp. 83–102, 2014.
DOI: 10.1007/978-3-319-07314-9_5, © Springer International Publishing Switzerland 2014

objectives can be achieved and that individual agent's behaviour and operational decisions do not interfere with success. If agents have the capabilities to coordinate knowledge and plans dynamically, then such agents could be in future employed as assistants for humans working in complex and dynamic situations. This is an ambitious long term motivation for our work, and a more realistic goal is toward agents as characters in virtual organizations within simulation-driven training systems.

In emergency management, situations arise when people by necessity adapt and improvise beyond predetermined scripts and plans. Adhoc collaborations emerge that are not preplanned and such organizations have been called adhocracies [12]. Coalitions of actors are formed in adhocracies to coordinate resource use, knowledge sharing or emergent planning. Adhocracies are organizations that may persist over time and members may improvise away from existing roles in order to achieve a task. As the organization needs to coordinate, there is potential benefit in establishing a dynamic organizational structure and mechanisms to guide the adaptive and improvised management of the organization. In this environment, plan revision, appropriate knowledge transfer and mutual adjustment to fit in with others and manage interdependencies are crucial to success. Improvisation is needed to adapt pre-existing plans, revise role descriptions and make do with existing resources in order to achieve a solution in a time critical situation. This improvisation to cope with non-routine events has been described similar to the improvisation required of a jazz musician [14]. The organizations that make up a overall response system may include emergent organizations as well as organizations with pre-planned (although still adaptable) structures and policies. Collaboration and flexibility between the distributed organizations and adhocracies that form is central to effectiveness of the system [12].

Adaptive agent organizations need an ability to adapt to a changing external environment as well as cope with the arrival or departure of individual agents. The organization may contain multiple overlapping organizations and agents may belong to multiple organizations. Agents' focus of attention can change over time. Agents may need to work with new coalitions of agents to achieve a particular task, share a resource or to coordinate to split a role that was previously allocated to an agent who is no longer available. The agents' organizational context may also change so that an agent's priority may shift between multiple organizations. At design time, it is necessary to specify coordination requirements such that agents at run time can be guided toward appropriate interaction and communication to ensure knowledge is shared as needed (we refer to this as *knowledge cultivation* [15]).

Coordination and adaptive behaviour relies upon agents having a shared understanding of situational knowledge, goals and plans as well as organizational structure [15]. Sharing a mental model of the situation has been deemed important for agent coordination in a team oriented architecture [16]. The sharing of knowledge regarding plans can be achieved by agents using a strict shared mental space or agreed public commitments to particular intentions such as in SharedPlans [17]. However sharing a mental model may not of itself be enough.

It is suggested that human team cognition is all about the interactions, not just shared mental models, but how the team interacts to create and share information [18]. As elaborated below, we propose that organisations formed at run time adopt a set of social policies on formation that are accepted by all member agents and that guide the creation and modification of social commitments regarding interactions. Social policies have been used to specify that agents adopt particular interaction and coordination commitments in a particular context at run time [19–21]. Social commitments make the interaction obligations explicit. Observability and interpredictability are important aspects of teamwork involving agents and humans [22,23]. Hence it is beneficial to agents' adaptability if agents have a general understanding of the high level plans of others in the organizational space [24]. Our model uses organizational structures to identify related agents [11]. Agents can form expectations of the behaviour of other agents based on the social commitments that have been made through membership of the organization.

The policies adopted by an organization define a layer of control and coordination of knowledge at an organization level. The system at a macro level comprises multiple organizations. These organizations can be stable long term organizations defined at design time with clear roles and behaviours, or can be adhocracies. Each organization provides a level of coordination and control for a particular collective of agents within a particular context. As organizations are agentified, an agent at one level of abstraction may represent a sub-organization at a lower more detailed level.

Our OJAzzIC model includes a dynamic role model, a hierarchical goal tree, a dynamic organizational plan and contracts (social and information contracts) [11]. In this model, roles are defined at design time but can be adapted later. Relationships between roles are explicitly defined as are relationships between individual agents. When an agent (or organizational agent) is available to adopt a role, then the agent can be allocated to this role. If there is not one existing agent available with the appropriate capabilities to fully enact a role, then a goal can be decomposed and individual agents can collaborate to achieve goal objectives. In the current paper, we elaborate on the description of contracts in OJAzzIC. The social contract defines roles and member agents as well as commitments to role fulfillment in the organizational plan. The information contract defines policies for agents regarding knowledge transfer within and across organizations. Policies ensure agents commit to sharing relevant knowledge within organizations, and provide a framework to enable coordinated, improvised activity.

The structure of the remainder of this paper is as follows. In Sect. 2 we briefly justify our decision to use social commitments and policies, describe some related work, and provide example policies. We have chosen policies that make explicit the commitments between agents within an organization regarding coordination of knowledge and plans. In Sect. 3 we use a scenario from emergency management to illustrate how policies can ensure the creation of social and information contracts that achieve knowledge cultivation and coordination obligations.

In Sect. 4 we briefly discuss related work and conclude (Sect. 5) with some future possible directions for this work.

2   Social Policies and Commitments

Social commitments have been used to express an agent's commitment to another agent to perform something [20]. Social commitments are relational - based on two or more agents interacting so make behaviour explicit and predictable. This is important especially when working in a domain in which agents and humans may potentially need to interact. As we are interested in adaptability and we are not looking to pre-script interactions with strict protocols at design time, social commitments provide an observable and adaptable specification of expected agent interaction. Attention has been given by others to defining and specifying norms, obligations and sanctions between agents in the context of a society, institution or organization. Schemes have been developed to model institutions using dynamic norms [25]. We are not focusing on this level of specification nor looking to contribute to this related work. Rather we are attempting to use policies to explicitly specify and articulate the coordination needs within an emergent organization network.

Policies have been used at an institutional level, external to agent design or mental states to enforce behaviour regardless of agent acceptance, consent or cooperation e.g. KAoS policies [19]. We seek to define behaviour for agents in the context of an organization. We want to have policies that are encoded and adopted by the agents with some awareness of their organizational context, rather than enforced externally. We use policies to guide agent creation of commitments and in so doing, we are adopting the position that a policy is a higher order meta-commitment [20]. We use policies to create and modify commitments. In fact, some might argue that we could better use norms to describe our obligations rather than social policies and reserve the use of policies at the individual agent decision making level to choose commitments [20,26]. Policies have been used to describe communication protocols between agents as conversation policies [27]. Policies have also been used to describe obligations, sanctions or punishments to enforce commitments [28]. In the current context, we are not interested in defining sanctions or punishments for when agents do not adopt policies. Inspired by others, we use policies as guidelines within an organizational context to govern the creation of social commitments to ensure that we achieve appropriate coordination of knowledge and behaviour [21,29,30].

We coordinate knowledge amongst agents in an organization by a knowledge coordination policy, for example that individual agents take responsibility to form commitments to synchronize with an organization as an explicit first class entity. We use social commitments rather than sharing mental attitudes so that we do not need to maintain mutual internal mental attitudes [20]. The interaction between agents regarding commitments to goals and plans provides an externalisation of mental attitudes that is explicit and adaptable.

Carabelea and Boissier [29] proposed how social commitments could be used to represent contracts between agents defining expected behaviour of agents in an organization. We use an adaptation of their notation for social policies and commitments to explicitly define social obligations for agents in an OJAzzIC organization. This commitment notation is consistent with Singh's [30], however where Singh has a social policy as a higher order, meta social commitment, Carabelea introduces a separate notational syntax for social policies and includes the status and pre-conditions explicitly. This meta level of describing policies to guide the creation and modification of commitments is the meso-level of control within each organization. Singh proposes a clear lifecycle for commitments and goals showing how the status of a condition might change. For our purposes, in the current paper, we chose not to include a commitment id in the commitment expression. For clarity, similar to Carabelea, we use distinctive names for commitments and policies. We use SC to indicate a social commitment and SPolicy to indicate a social policy. The SPolicy is similar to the create() predicate defined by Chesani et al. [31] in that it defines the conditions when a particular commitment should be created. The social commitment is similar to the concept of conditional commitments proposed by others in which a debtor commits to the creditor to perform a particular object when a condition holds [31], however, identifying the organizational context explicitly as follows:

Social Commitment

$$SC(debtor, creditor, Org, object, status(omitted), [condition])$$

expresses that a social commitment is created between debtor agent to creditor agent in the context of the organization Org, regarding object, with the given current status and held to be valid when the given condition holds (the latter term is optional). Valid commitment status' are [30]: null, active, pending, conditional, detached, violated, satisfied, terminated, expired. In all our examples, the status of the SC is active, so we omit this for brevity in our equations.

We use social policies to externalise obligations agreed between agents in an organization. When creating commitments, organizational agents are guided by the policies that can be created at design time for particular contexts. A social policy is adopted by a given agent x within an organization, *Org* and satisfying the given constraints, *const*. The policy specifies the trigger conditions *precond*, when the specified commitment, SC is obliged to be created. We do not describe the life-cycle of policies, in the examples provided, the status is active by default and is omitted. Similar to commitments, it may be possible for policies' status to be active or not. The social policy applies under the condition *spcondition*, if provided and is expressed as follows:

$$SPolicy(x, org, const : precond =>$$
$$create(x, SC(...)), status(omittedbelow), [spcondition])$$

We adopt predicates and definitions to express detail in our social policies, some of these particular to beliefs are shown in Table 1.

Table 1. Selected predicates and definitions

$beliefset(x, [B : bel(name, val, status, type)])$	Agent x has a set of beliefs, B comprising for each belief attributes: name, value, status and type. Belief types include: domain, situation, orgstructure. status is either current or expired
$add(x, bel(b, v, current, t)$	Add a belief b with value v, type t to agent x's current belief set
$expire(x, bel(b, oldv, current, t))$ $\wedge bel(b, oldv, current, t) => bel(b, oldv, expired, t)$	Change the status of a belief, b, with current value: oldv to expired
$SC(x, z, OA, update(x, b, v), active)$	Agent x has an active commitment in organization OA to update belief b with a new value v

Due to space limitations, we do not include all definitions. When agent x has a relationship status e.g. *fullTrust, noTrust, limitedTrust* with agent y, we express this as relation(x,y, status). agentrole(x, r, org, status) expresses that agent x is enacting role r in organization org with status of: valid (capable of playing this role) or active (currently in role). rolecapabilityset(r1, C, OA) means that Role r1 in org OA has a set of capabilities, C, associated with it. Agents adopting this role must possess these capabilities. We refer to the org as OA as a reminder that the organization is a first class, agentified entity that may itself behave as an agent adopting a role in another organization.

Policies have been categorized elsewhere as either authorization or obligation (including coordination) policies [19]. In an OJAzzIC organization, there are four main areas that social policies can address. These are agreed in the information contract. Social policies govern: Authority, Obligations regarding knowledge cultivation (Belief updates), Coordination (of individual and collective plans) and Creation of Organizations. These types of policies are needed between agents to ensure that appropriate knowledge transfer occurs within the organizations. Plan coordination considers task selection and allocation of agents to tasks, agents form commitments to the organizational plan, commitments to awareness of others and commitments regarding authority to request/assign tasks to agents. Knowledge cultivation is ensured by commitments regarding updating beliefs and membership of organization. To establish an organizational social structure, agents create commitments to role definitions and responsibilities. Policies also provide governance for the conditions and process for the creation of new adhocracies.

We now provide eleven social policy examples. We choose these examples to demonstrate how social policies can be used to express the guidelines for an organization to create appropriate commitments to ensure coordination and sharing of knowledge. Social policies could be established based on domain requirements at design time or even dynamically chosen based on environmental conditions at run time based on default or selective policies. Social policies 1 and 2 define policies for authority; social policies 3 and 4 define policies for knowledge cultivation; social policies 5 through to 9 define coordination of goal selection, awareness and plan coordination; and social policies 10 and 11 define triggers for when new adhocracies should be created. When an adhocracy is created, the organizational members create social and information contracts to define roles, responsibilities and policies that define behaviour within the organization.

SPolicy1-Role-Authority-Request. If an agent x acting a role R1 in org OA is requested by another agent y in a role R2 that is higher in hierarchy than R1, then agent x is obliged to commit to any request from y so long as x is capable of fulfilling the request and is available.

$$SPolicy(x, OA, \forall y : agentrole(y, R2, OA, active) \, \forall obj \in capable(x, obj) :$$
$$request(y, x, sc(x, y, OA, obj)) =>$$
$$create(x, sc(x, y, OA, obj)), agentrole(x, R1, OA, active)$$
$$\wedge \, rolerelation(R1, R2, subordinate, OA))$$

where Agent x is capable of enacting obj if obj is in the capability set of the agent or in the capability set of role r that agent x is acting in:

$$capable(x, obj) <= agentcapabilityset(x, obj) \vee (\exists r \, \exists C : obj \in C \wedge$$
$$rolecapabilityset(r, C, OA) \wedge agentrole(x, r, OA, valid))))$$

SPolicy2-Role-Authority-RoleRequest. If an agent x is capable of acting in role R1 in org OA and is requested by another agent in OA to fulfill this role, then agent x is obliged to commit to adopting this role if possible[1].

$$SPolicy(x, OA, \forall y : member(y, OA) :$$
$$request(y, x, sc(x, y, OA, agentrole(x, R1, OA, active))) \wedge available(x)$$
$$=> create(x, SC(x, y, OA, agentrole(x, R1, OA, active))),$$
$$agentrole(x, R1, OA, valid) \wedge available(x))$$

SPolicy3-Update-OrgBeliefs. If agent x, a member of org OA or in a currently valid role in org OA, creates an active commitment (in any organizational context) to update its own belief set with a new or updated belief that is relevant to the organization (for simplicity, we reduce the relevance to be: the belief is in the current organizational belief set), or agent x is requested to update its own belief set with a new or updated belief that is related to the organization, then agent x creates a commitment to request an update by the organizational agent

---

[1] This policy may be somewhat contentious as it obliges an agent to accept a request to perform a role, however, this could be representative of command and control organizations within some domains. It is possible to declare weaker policies regarding such obligations.

to update the organization beliefs to be consistent with the update.

$$SPolicy(x, OA, \forall bel \in B1 \cap B2 : beliefset(OA, B1) \land beliefset(x, B2) :$$
$$create(x, SC(x, a, g, update(x, bel, newval)))$$
$$=> create(x, SC(x, OA, OA, request(x, OA, update(OA, bel, newval))),$$
$$member(x, OA) \lor agentrole(x, r, OA, valid))$$

In the case that agent, A is an organizational agent, then the belief set of A is the organizational belief set.

SPolicy4-Update-AgentBeliefs. If agent x is in organization OA and OA has a commitment to update a belief, then agent x is obliged to also commit to update individual beliefs to be consistent with OA organizational beliefs.

$$SPolicy(x, OA, \forall bel \in B \, beliefset(OA, B) : SC(OA, z, OA, update(OA, bel, newval))$$
$$=> create(x, SC(x, OA, OA, update(x, bel, newval)), bel \in B : beliefset(OA, B)$$
$$\land member(x, OA) \land (member(z, OA))))$$

SPolicy5-RoleResponsibility. If agent is in a role, r then agent will commit to goals in the responsibility set for that role if requested by any other agent in the org

$$SPolicy(x, OA, \forall y \in member(y, OA) \land agentrole(x, r, OA, active)$$
$$\land rolecapabilityset(r, C, OA) \, \forall goal(obj, x, pg, s, f), pg(obj), goalrequires(obj, C) :$$
$$request(y, x, SC(x, y, OA, active(obj)))$$
$$=> create(x, SC(x, y, OA, active(obj)), agentrole(x, r, OA, valid)))$$

where a goal, g for agent, x with pg is precondition of goal, s is success condition and f is fail condition is formulated as:goal(g,x,pg,s,f) [30].

Goals are represented in a hierarchical network or tree like decomposition [11,30]. We decompose goals into tasks so that where an agent is not available to adopt a role and completely achieve a goal, individual agents can coordinate activity on individual tasks within the goal to achieve the same result. A function roleachieves(g, r, pg) : goal(g) returns a value representing the value of an allocation of role r to achieve goal g. A similar function agentachieves(t, x, pg) returns a number representing the value of an allocation of agent x to achieve task t, given the precondition pg. The functions and predicates in Table 2 relate to ordering of goals.

SPolicy6-CoordinationAwareness. When an agent is deliberating, agent will consider high level guidelines of others in the space. Agents should not commit to goals that the agent believes will interfere with other agents' goals.

$$SPolicy(x, OA, member(x, OA) \land member(y, OA) : create(x, SC(x, y, OA, obj))$$
$$=> suspend(x, SC(x, y, OA, obj, active)), \exists obj2, SC(x, y, OA, obj2)$$
$$\land (interferes(obj1, obj2)))$$

Table 2. Goal predicates and functions

goal(g,x,pg,s,f)	Goal g for agent, x with pg is precondition of goal, s is success condition and f is fail condition
roleachieves(g,r, pg) : goal(g)	Function returns a number representing the value of an allocation of role r to achieve goal g
achieves(t, a)	Action a achieves task t
preceeds(obj1, obj2)	Task or goal synchronization: obj1 must be performed before obj2
concurrent(obj1,obj2)	Task or goal concurrency: obj1 must be performed concurrently with obj2
interferes(obj1,obj2)	Interference: obj1 cannot be performed concurrently with obj2

SPolicy7-CoordinationCooperation. Agents are obliged to commit to 'help' by committing to concurrent tasks if requested by any agent, if they are capable of doing so.

$$SPolicy(x, OA, \forall obj \in capable(x, obj) \wedge available(x) :$$

$$request(y, x, SC(x, y, OA, active(obj))) => create(x, SC(x, y, OA, active(obj))),$$

$$\exists obj2 \, active(obj2) \wedge concurrent(obj2, obj1) \wedge available(x))$$

SPolicy8-CoordinatePlan. If agents are working together on a common goal, they will create a commitment to ensure coordination of the shared organizational plan toward reaching that goal

$$SPolicy(x, OA, member(x, OA) \wedge member(y, OA) \wedge goal(g1) :$$

$$SC(x, OA, OA, g1) \wedge SC(y, OA, OA, g1)$$

$$=> create(x, SC(x, OA, OA, SP)), active(g1) \wedge SC(x, OA, OA, g1))$$

where SP represents the Organizational Plan. We consider the Organizational Plan to be very similar to a SharedPlan [17] using policies in the organizational contract to ensure that agents keep each other informed of changes to the plan. We do not provide further details regarding SharedPlans [17] in this paper, however we are influenced by SharedPlans. We consider the organizational plan as a mental attitude at the organizational level and similar to SharedPlans, agents create commitments to ensure they maintain coordination of the plan as it develops. The organizational plan outlines the set of actions and goals to be enacted and at least a partial allocation of agents to each.

SPolicy9-CoordinateAgents. If an agent is busy in another organization with goal g1, that agent informs the other organizations that it is member of, that it is unavailable.

$$SPolicy(x, OA, \forall org : member(x, org) \land \exists SC(x, OA, OA, g1) \land goal(g1) \land org \neq OA$$
$$=> inform(x, org, unavailable, SC(x, OA, OA, g1)), active(g1) \land SC(x, OA, OA, g1))$$

SPolicy10-CreateOrg-Trigger-Goal. If multiple agents from different organizations have a common goal, trigger creation of an adhocracy.

$$SPolicy(x, SysOrg, \exists goal(g1, x, pg, s, f) \land \exists goal(g1, y, pg, s, f) \land \not\exists org1 : member(x, org1)$$
$$\land member(y, org1) => createorg(x, y, neworg, g1), active(g1))$$

We omit details of the createorg function here. This function will instantiate a new adhocracy, neworg with member agents: x,y and the goal g1.

SPolicy11-CreateOrg-Trigger-Res. If multiple agents from different organizations have contention of a shared resource, then they need to trigger creation of an adhocracy to manage this contention

$$SPolicy(x, SysOrg, \exists resource(re) : contention(x, y, re) \land$$
$$\not\exists org1 : member(x, org1) \land member(y, org1)$$
$$=> createorg(x, y, neworg, g1) \, goal(g1, x, contention(x, y, re), manage(re, neworg),$$
$$contention(x, y, re)))$$

The policies provided in this section are representative of policies that could be used by to govern the appropriate information sharing and coordination within a complex distributed organization. These policies guide the authority to allocate agents to goals as well as coordination of plans and the creation of adhocracies. The organizations enable a selection of context to facilitate appropriate communication. We do not yet specify how to prioritise policies for agents, although this will be necessary when agents belong to multiple organizations. We have not provided details on the mechanisms for identifying relevance of knowledge other than to simplify this to the set of beliefs current in the organization. More work is needed to expand upon beliefs and the way that they are represented.

Maintaining mutual organizational and individual beliefs is not a trivial problem. In the simplest case, a leader is appointed with full authority to act on update requests. The leader has power to change organizational beliefs and require all member agents to accept these beliefs and adopt them as individual beliefs. The power of organizational beliefs over an agent in a strict organization is such that an agent may not ignore organizational beliefs. SPolicy4 provides a policy for this situation. We rely on social commitments between agents to ensure consistent beliefs rather than attempt to define mutual beliefs.

3 Demonstrating Knowledge Cultivation Through Policies

We use a scenario from the emergency management domain to demonstrate our use of OJAzzIC to ensure coordination and knowledge sharing within and between organizations. We create multiple organizations, each working somewhat autonomously on individual tasks but acting in a context of awareness of others in the distributed network. The scenario is set during the incident management phase immediately following an event such as an explosion in a built up area. The system organization has the goal to resolve the disaster - rescue the injured, give first aid, transport to hospital. The main agencies are allocated sub goals in the high level plan, based on their service for example the goals of the ambulance agency are to provide immediate medical care and casualty transport to hospital; the goals of the fire agency are to manage hazards, protect the site, extinguish fires.

The default, high level plan adopted would be to follow the goal decomposition as follows: goal G1: 'Provide Medical Care' would be allocated to the ambulance agency; goal G2: 'Manage the disaster site' would be allocated to the fire agency. Following the initiation of the scenario, the initial response would involve each agency dispatching a number of available agents and emergency response vehicles from the station center to the disaster zone.

The system organization, SysOrg is the super organization and contains two 'agents', AmbOrg and FireOrg, each of which is itself an organization. Conceptually, this means that all agents in AmbOrg and FireOrg are also in SysOrg. In practice, the communication flow is such that there is one nominated leader or spokesperson agent in each of the suborganizations who will attend to communication at the super-organization level and then be responsible for passing on relevant knowledge into each sub-organization. At the super organization (macro) level - SysOrg, the high level plan is known and each agent(sub-organization) is aware of its allocated goal in the goal tree. This means that an agent in FireOrg will be aware of the more detailed plan agreed at the FireOrg organizational level but also aware that there is a high level plan at a higher level in SysOrg.

Initially, there is no intersection or direct formal communication between individual members of AmbOrg and FireOrg other than within the sysorg plan allocation of high level goals to AmbOrg and FireOrg. As the scenario progresses, situations will arise requiring individual members to agree to coordinate to achieve goals and/or share resources. When that occurs, the individual members create new short term organizational adhocracies. Each adhocracy has an identifiable common interest - e.g. shared resource, shared knowledge goal, shared coordination goal. Explicitly representing each organization as a first class entity provides a mechanism for agents to identify which other agents are involved and thus facilitates appropriate knowledge sharing communication. These will be demonstrated later in the scenario.

In the next section, we do a paper walk through of part of the unfolding scenario to illustrate the management of coordination and how policies ensure appropriate knowledge sharing and cultivation of relationships between organizations. Table 3 shows the 9 agents, their capabilities and potential roles as well as their membership of organizations at the start of the scenario.

Table 3. Agents, potential roles, capabilities and organizations at start of scenario

Agent	Potential roles	Capabilities	Organizations
simpleagent1		carry, firstaid(1)	systemorg
fireagent1	fireFighter, driver	rescue, extinguish(2),	fireorg, systemorg
fireagent2	commandingOfficer, fireFighter, driver	commander, rescue, firstaid(1), carry, drive, extinguish(3)	fireorg, systemorg
fireagent3	firefighter	extinguish(2), rescue	fireorg, systemorg
ambagent1	firstaidOfficer, driver	firstaid(3), carry, drive	amborg, systemorg
ambagent2	firstaidOfficer, commandingOfficer, driver	firstaid(3), carry, drive, commander	amborg, systemorg
ambagent3	firstaidOfficer	firstaid(2), carry	amborg, systemorg
ambagent4	ambulanceOfficer	firstaid(2), carry	amborg, systemorg
ambagent5	firstaidOfficer, driver	firstaid(3), drive, carry	amborg, systemorg

3.1 Using Policies and Commitments

In our scenario roles are defined within the organization using relationship definitions to reflect the structural hierarchy and set permissions to which agents may request other agents to accept allocated tasks. For example *rolerelation (commandingofficer, firefighter, authority, FireOrg)*. When an organization is created, agents will instantiate a social contract and an information contract. The information contract defines the relevant current agreed organizational beliefs and obligations to share these within the organization. The social contract includes a list of member agents, roles, relationships and the organizational plan.

In order to demonstrate by example, we choose a snapshot in time during the scenario to focus upon. We will highlight some of the social policies introduced in Sect. 2 and how they ensure appropriate information flow. At some time after the scenario has begun new organizations have been created. On site, a group of fire fighter agents are working to extinguish a fire in a collapsed building. Another group of fire fighters and ambulance officers are working together to find injured people in the same collapsed building (RescueOrg) and move them to safety outside the building. This requires coordination between the fire officers who work toward securing a safe path into the collapsed building for the ambulance officers. It is also important that the fire agents who are extinguishing the fire in FireOrg do not interfere with the fire agents who are attempting to secure part of the building for safe access to the injured. Social Policy 6 will ensure that fire agents in the FireOrg do not interfere with each other. Another group of fire fighters and ambulance officers are working together to coordinate moving injured away from the collapsed buildings and to hospital (moveInjuredOrg). Due to the blocked roads, the latter group is coordinating the use of a fire truck that can navigate around the collapsed roads and across a park to move the injured to a rendezvous point to meet an ambulance vehicle on an unaffected road. Organization, MoveInjuredorg has an partial plan selected that involves using stretchers to move the injured onto the firetruck, driving the truck to meet an ambulance and then the ambulance transporting the injured to hospital. As these new organizations involve agents from within different agency organizations, new adhocracy organizations Rescueorg and MoveInjuredorg have been created.

The new adhocracies will enable the flow of information across the wider network. For example, The Rescueorg is aware of 8 injured people. This information is relevant to the AmbOrg. AmbOrg at this stage has no. injured: unknown. As ambagent1 is a member of both organizations, this agent will be informed of the knowledge shared in Rescueorg and then will propogate this information to AmbOrg (SPolicy3). Policies are adopted to obligate this knowledge sharing in the contracts created for each organization. Similarly, if MoveInjuredorg organization decides to change their Organizational SharedPlan regarding the transport of injured to the ambulance, any relevant information needs to be passed on to the AmbOrg. As agent ambagent1 is a member of both organizations agent amgagent1 will be obliged by SocialPolicy3 to pass this information to update beliefs and plans in AmbOrg as appropriate. Figure 1 shows some agent interactions at selected times during the scenario chosen to highlight how the social policies ensure appropriate information flow and coordination. We do not highlight the potential for dynamic role changes in this scenario, however, we believe that using the OJAzzIC organizational structure role definitions and allocations to agents can be changed dynamically in the organizational plan as needed in response to agents leaving the scene or becoming unavailable. We do not provide sample policies to guide this behaviour in the current paper.

The contracts define obligations accepted by agents as commitments to be adopted. In Sect. 2 we provided some default policies for knowledge sharing in the information contract. The OJAzzIC model does not specify how strict these obligations need to be. It is up to the designer of the system, based on requirements to define such obligations, however for simplicity in our example, we assume that the contract is agreed by adopting policies that enforce agents within each organization to maintain individual beliefs consistent with organizational beliefs.

4   Related Work

Various models have been proposed for adaptive organizational agent systems. We have looked particularly at the following models: OMACS [32], KB-ORG [10], and OperA [3]. We have also looked at shared mental models e.g. SharedPlans [16,17]. Each addresses part of our requirements. We have also considered adaptivity in relationships achieved by associating Agents to Roles and Goals as discussed, for example, in previous work by Ferber et al. [4] and Odell et al. [33]. We have chosen to make a distinction between goals and objectives for an organization and the roles that might achieve those objectives. Our adaptive design allows for a situation when there may not be agents available who can enact a role completely, but individual agents can collaborate dynamically to each achieve tasks equivalent to one 'role'.

This approach has also been adopted in AGR [4] and in the MOISE system [34] where a distinction is made between a separate structural specification

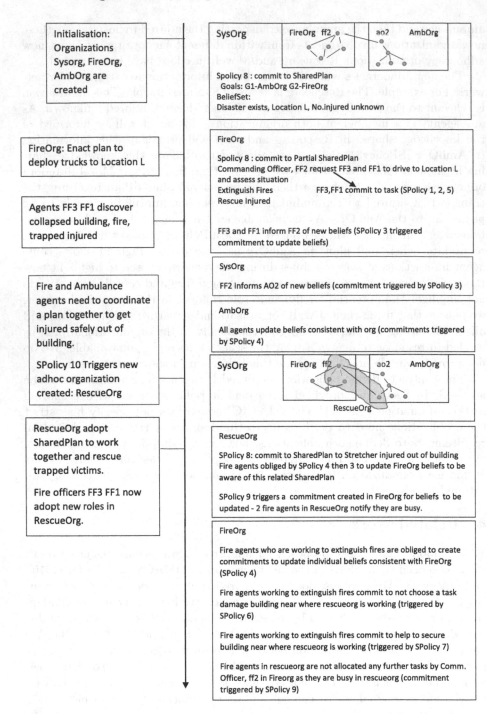

Fig. 1. Social policies coordinating knowledge flow and cooperation across the organization

and a functional specification. In MOISEInst [6], goals are decomposed into missions, then allocated to a set of responsible agents. The goal tree specifies potential tasks that can be associated with individual plan recipes that achieve each leaf goal [5, 10].

The context of our interest in dynamic and improvised organizations is similar to broader work toward adaptable, open, heterogeneous agent systems. Planned emergence describes situations where agents dynamically combine to form a complex system [35]. In these systems, collective awareness between agents can be established by using layers of control. Agents operate individually at a micro level, however in order to ensure macro level success of the collective system, meso-level mediation and control can ensure that micro-level, operational decision making does not interfere with or cause undesirable macro outcomes [35]. The meso-level is akin to a middleware layer that provides an interface between macro and micro levels of decision making and control. Our focus on creating organizations of agents is at the meso-level. Each organizational context defines constraints on member agents in terms of roles and responsibilities as well as contracts defining obligations toward knowledge cultivation. Agents in our system are aware of the organization and are assumed to adopt the organizational objectives. Such a system could be described as a combination of a restricted-agent system and a restricted-middleware system [36]. The middleware organizational layer helps the agents to coordinate and may be responsible for delegating tasks, but agents are aware of the organization, have organizational beliefs and ability to choose and delegate tasks. It has been argued that self-organizing, self-governing, open, distributed systems can be considered as institutions that require an explicit contractualisation or encoding of policies to be adopted to ensure endurance of the system [37]. We aim for a self-organizing system that is somewhat dynamic and similar to Pitt, we adopt the premise that making the meso-level collective rules explicit is helpful to a sustainable system. Singh also argues that making the interactions and relationships between agents explicit is helpful toward codifying these relationships, rather than relying on agents forming mutual beliefs or joint intentions with one another [20].

We are not unique in articulating agent interactions as requirements and modelling these separately in the design process for an agent system e.g. [13]. We are not alone in using social-based approaches to explicitly define relationships, interactions and obligations. There are advantages in using a declarative, social approach to modelling agent interaction when agents are working without necessarily sharing common internal mental attitudes such as goals, desires or intentions [20].

High level guidelines have been used to describe constraints on how organizational objectives should be decomposed in a hierarchy. Separately, operational objectives represented as leaf goals in their goal decomposition can be operationally coordinated as required by the individuals involved in each team [10, 24]. This abstraction to 'leave the details' to the smaller groups is similar to ours, although we make the distinction that these smaller groups may be considered as temporary adhoc organizations with the infrastructure associated with an organization, rather than teams that may not necessarily have a formal structure[2]. We are interested in a distributed network, where agents are working with some autonomy within individual organizations, but need to have a general awareness of others to avoid interference and ensure success of a high level shared goal. Representing a network of agents in organizations enables levels of abstraction or hiding of detail so that agents can have multiple individually defined contexts (associated with each organization). Each organization can have a detailed awareness of its own goals, plans, membership and a more general awareness of others at a higher, less detailed level of abstraction [38]. The value in creating short to medium term organizations, is that for the duration of the organization, obligations and shared organizational mental attitudes can be used to help ensure that our complex, dynamic, coordination requirements are addressed.

There are various extensions and adaptations of the basic notion of social commitment including probabilistic commitments, time constraints and sanctions as part of the definition. These do not contribute to the focus of our use of commitments currently, so we do not use these. Our focus is on describing obligations for coordination that would be adopted during the active life-cycle of an organization and particular to each organization.

In related work, norms have been used to create obligations which are very similar to social commitments in a language, NOPL [39]. In NOPL, norms express conditions that result in obligations or a fail status. Norms can also be used to define regimented rules that must hold and cannot be ignored. One main difference in our approach is that we allow for obligations to be defined particular to each organizational context that an agent may belong to. In NOPL, the obligations are defined related to roles in groups, whereas in our case, our policies would relate to the group. Also, our obligations are not necessarily relating to a change in the state of the world, but may relate to communication and interaction obligations. In NOPL, the obligations are defined as a result of a norm declaration. The obligations are related to goals that can be fulfilled when a declared state is achieved. In our case, the type of obligations we are considering will remain active unless the condition for creation no longer holds and they become inactive. However, our social policies are very similar to the norms in NOPL and the obligations created from norms in NOPL are similar to our social commitments if very specific obligations are created, particular to goals for communicative acts.

Others have described the social context of an organization or coordinating group of agents with various names including an Organizational Adhocracy [12]. Collective Obligations have been used to collectively represent a group of agents who share responsibility for a particular obligation. Using policies, the obligations are then mapped to individual obligations on agents [21]. Whatever the term used, it is necessary to place a boundary around the organizational social context within which social policies and commitments are defined.

---

[2] A team could of course also have infrastructure such as roles and responsibilities, obligations and norms however an organization must have these.

The organizations that make up an overall system may include emergent adhocracies as well as formal organizations with pre-planned (although still adaptable) structures, roles and policies. Collaboration and flexibility within the distributed organization including adhocracies that form is central to effectiveness of the system [12].

Others have previously used social contracts with landmarks to define agent interactions, e.g. [40]. In OperA [3], which involves three distinct models: organizational, social and interaction, a top-down approach is used for the design of organizations: the organization is specified first, then agents are allocated to it. We take a combined approach, with some top down specification of organizations as well as a bottom up approach to the runtime creation of adhocracies. Another difference between the approach taken in OperA [36,40] and our approach is our decision to decompose functionality as a goal and task hierarchy rather than as a set of role descriptions. We chose to do this as it seems to better address the dynamic coordination of individual as well as organizational plans. OperA+, which extends the social structure in OperA, provides a modelling framework with constructs to represent multi-organizational interactions in two dimensions [38]. The *specification* dimension presents the regulating structures in terms of connected roles and organizations while the *enactment* dimension presents the acting components in terms of agents enacting the roles. In OperA+, composite roles and composite agents yield a multi-level modelling environment. The higher-level specification captures the commonalities of organizational collaborations while the lower-level specifications present the individualities by layers of customization according to more specific requirements.

5 Conclusion and Future Work

We have provided a description of interactions within and across agent organizations. We have used the construct of social policies to elaborate our previous OJAzzIC framework and define knowledge cultivation obligations for agents. Agents adhering to such policies will create commitments within the context of the organization in order to coordinate plans and knowledge.

Our contribution is in the way we propose to use the social policies as high level guidelines that result in agent commitments for coordination. We suppose agents may belong to multiple organizations at any time and so the overlapping of these organizations allows for agents to identify when beliefs are related to each organization and to share knowledge and plans appropriately.

OJAzzIC organizations would be suited to working in dynamic, complex domains that require flexible adaptive interactive behaviour. These could include emergency management decision support systems, naval management coordination and situations in military command and control when local decision making occurs independently from the formal vertical command hierarchy. Where short term coordinated tasks are to be performed by a group of agents and are well specified and not likely to change during execution of a plan, an organizational structure is not necessary. In these cases, agents might form a different less structured collective such as a group with a SharedPlan [17].

In this paper we have provided some example policies, but further work is needed to specify the details of the information and social contracts for OJAzzIC organizations and to consider adequacy and perhaps completeness of policy sets. In addition, there is potential to explore a more formal approach to the creation of social commitments if we define social commitments using the event calculus framework as proposed by Chesani et al. [31]. More detailed coverage of interference and relevance is also desirable. In this paper, we have simplified these by presuming we have predicates to define when actions might interfere; and to identify relevant information between agents beyond a simplification to beliefs. Further work could include a framework for the design process and methodology for implementation of an OJAzzIC network.

Acknowledgements. The authors thank Dr. Gil Tidhar for his conversations and suggestions regarding OJAzzIC. Also, thanks to the anonymous reviewers for their constructive suggestions and to the participants in the COIN workshop at PRIMA 2013 for their feedback.

References

1. Castelfranchi, C.: Grounding organizations in the minds of the agents. In: Dignum, V. (ed.) Handbook of Research on Multi-Agent Systems: Semantics and Dynamics of Organizational Models, pp. 242–262. IGI Global, Hershey (2009)
2. DeLoach, S., Miller, M.: A goal model for adaptive complex systems. Int. J. Comput. Intell. Theor. Pract. **5**(2), 83–92 (2010)
3. Dignum, V.: The role of organization in agent systems. In: Dignum, V. (ed.) Handbook of Research on Multi-Agent Systems: Semantics and Dynamics of Organizational Models, pp. 1–6. IGI Global, Hershey (2009)
4. Ferber, J., Gutknecht, O., Michel, F.: From agents to organizations: an organizational view of multi-agent systems. In: Giorgini, P., Müller, J.P., Odell, J.J. (eds.) AOSE 2003. LNCS, vol. 2935, pp. 214–230. Springer, Heidelberg (2004)
5. Horling, B., Lesser, V.: A survey of multi-agent organizational paradigms. Knowl. Eng. Rev. **19**(4), 281–316 (2005)
6. Hübner, J., Kitio, R., Ricci, A.: Instrumenting multi-agent organisations with organisational artifacts and agents 'giving the organisational power back to the agents'. Auton. Agent. Multi-Agent Syst. **20**, 369–400 (2010)
7. Odell, J.J., Van Dyke Parunak, H., Fleischer, M.: The role of roles in designing effective agent organizations. In: Garcia, A.F., de Lucena, C., Zambonelli, F., Omicini, A., Castro, J. (eds.) SELMAS 2002. LNCS, vol. 2603, pp. 27–38. Springer, Heidelberg (2003)
8. Matson, E., DeLoach, S.A.: Autonomous organization-based adaptive information systems. In: IEEE International Conference on Knowledge Intensive Multiagent Systems (KIMAS '05), Waltham, MA, April 2005 (2005)
9. McCallum, M., Norman, T., Vasconcelos, W.: A formal model of organizations for engineering multi-agent systems. In: Proceedings of ECAI 2004 Workshop on Coordination in Emergent Agents Societies (2004)
10. Sims, M., Corkill, D., Lesser, V.: Automated organization design for multi-agent systems. Auton. Agent. Multi-Agent Syst. **16**, 151–185 (2008)

11. Keogh, K., Sonenberg, L.: Adaptive coordination in distributed and dynamic agent organizations. In: Cranefield, S., van Riemsdijk, M.B., Vázquez-Salceda, J., Noriega, P. (eds.) COIN 2011. LNCS (LNAI), vol. 7254, pp. 38–57. Springer, Heidelberg (2012)

12. Mendonca, D., Jefferson, T., Harrald, J.: Emergent interoperability: collaborative adhocracies and mix and match technologies in emergency management. Commun. ACM **50**(3), 45–49 (2007)

13. Zhao, K., Yen, J., Ngamassi, L.M., Maitland, C., Tapia, A.: From communication to collaboration: simulating the emergence of inter-organizational collaboration network, pp. 413–418 (2010)

14. Mendonca, D., Wallace, W.A.: A cognitive model of improvisation in emergency management. IEEE Trans. Syst. Man Cybern. Part A **37**(4), 547–561 (2007)

15. Keogh, K., Sonenberg, L., Smith, W.: Coordination in adaptive organisations: extending shared plans with knowledge cultivation. In: Vouros, G., Artikis, A., Stathis, K., Pitt, J. (eds.) OAMAS 2008. LNCS (LNAI), vol. 5368, pp. 90–107. Springer, Heidelberg (2009)

16. Yen, J., Fan, X., Sun, S., Hanratty, T., Dumer, J.: Agents with shared mental models for enhancing team decision-makings. J. Decis. Support Syst. (Special issue on Intelligence and Security Informatics) **41**(3), 634–653 (2006)

17. Grosz, B., Hunsberger, L.: The dynamics of intention in collaborative activity. Cogn. Syst. Res. **7**(2–3), 259–272 (2006)

18. Cooke, N., Gorman, J., Myers, C.W., Duran, J.: Interactive team cognition. Cogn. Sci. **37**, 255–285 (2013)

19. Bradshaw, J., Uszok, A., Breedy, M., Bunch, L., Eskridge, T., Feltovich, P., Johnson, M., Lott, J., Vignati, M.: The KAoS policy services framework. In: Eighth Cyber Security and Information Intelligence Research Workshop (CSIIRW 2013), January 2013 (2013)

20. Singh, M.: Commitments in multiagent systems: some history, some confusions, some controversies, some prospects. In: Paglieri, F., Tummolini, L., Miceli, M., Falcone, R. (eds.) The Goals of Cognition: Essays in Honor of Cristiano Castelfranchi, pp. 1–29. College Publications, London (2012)

21. van Diggelen, J., Bradshaw, J.M., Johnson, M., Uszok, A., Feltovich, P.J.: Implementing collective obligations in human-agent teams using KAoS policies. In: Padget, J., Artikis, A., Vasconcelos, W., Stathis, K., da Silva, V.T., Matson, E., Polleres, A. (eds.) COIN@AAMAS 2009. LNCS, vol. 6069, pp. 36–52. Springer, Heidelberg (2010)

22. Bunch, L., Carvalho, M., Bradshaw, J., Eskridge, T., Feltovich, P., Lott, J., Uszok, A.: Policy-based governance within luna: why we developed yet another agent framework. In: Software Agent Teamwork for the Semantic Web 2012 Workshop in Conjunction with WI-IAT 2012, December 2012 (2012)

23. Jennings, N.: Commitments and conventions: the foundation of coordination in multi-agent systems. Knowl. Eng. Rev. **8**(3), 223–250 (1993)

24. Corkill, D., Durfee, E., Lesser, V., Zafar, H., Zhang, C.: Organizationally adept agents. In: 12th International Workshop on Coordination, Organization, Institutions and Norms in Agent Systems (COIN@AAMAS 2011), Taipei, Taiwan, May 2011, pp. 15–30 (2011)

25. Frantz, C., Purvis, M.K., Nowostawski, M., Savarimuthu, B.T.R.: Modelling institutions using dynamic deontics. In: Balke, T., Dignum, F., van Riemsdijk, M.B., Chopra, A.K. (eds.) COIN 2013. LNCS (LNAI), vol. 8386, pp. 211–233. Springer, Heidelberg (2014)

26. Singh, M.P.: Norms as a basis for governing sociotechnical systems. ACM Trans. Intell. Syst. Technol. **5**(1), 21:1–21:23 (2013)
27. Kremer, R., Flores, R.A.: Flexible conversations using social commitments and a performatives hierarchy. In: Dignum, F.P.M., van Eijk, R.M., Flores, R. (eds.) AC 2005. LNCS (LNAI), vol. 3859, pp. 93–108. Springer, Heidelberg (2006)
28. Martínez, E., Kwiatkowski, I., Pasquier, P.: Towards a model of social coherence in multi-agent organizations. In: De Vos, M., Fornara, N., Pitt, J.V., Vouros, G. (eds.) COIN 2010. LNCS (LNAI), vol. 6541, pp. 114–131. Springer, Heidelberg (2011)
29. Carabelea, C., Boissier, O.: Coordinating agents in organizations using social commitments. Electron. Notes Theoret. Comput. Sci. **150**, 73–91 (2006)
30. Telang, P.R., Meneguzzi, F., Singh, M.P.: Hierarchical planning about goals and commitments. In: Proceedings of the 12th International Conference on Autonomous Agents and Multiagent Systems (AAMAS 2013), May 2013, pp. 877–884 (2013)
31. Chesani, F., Mello, P., Montali, M., Torroni, P.: Representing and monitoring social commitments using the event calculus. Auton. Agent. Multi-Agent Syst. **27**, 85–130 (2013)
32. DeLoach, S.A.: OMACS: a framework for adaptive, complex systems. In: Dignum, V. (ed.) Multi-Agent Systems: Semantics and Dynamics of Organizational Models. IGI Global, Hershey (2009). ISBN: 1-60566-256-9
33. Odell, J.J., Nodine, M., Levy, R.: A metamodel for agents, roles, and groups. In: Odell, J.J., Giorgini, P., Müller, J.P. (eds.) AOSE 2004. LNCS, vol. 3382, pp. 78–92. Springer, Heidelberg (2005)
34. Gâteau, B., Khadraoui, D., Dubois, E., Boissier, O.: MOISEInst: an organizational model for specifying rights and duties of autonomous agents. In: Proceedings of Third European Workshop on Multi-Agent Systems (EUMAS 2005), pp. 484–485. Elsevier Science B.V (2005)
35. Pitt, J., Bourazeri, A., Nowak, A., Roszczynska-Kurasinska, M., Rychwalska, A., Rodriguez Santiago, I., Lopez Sanchez, M., Florea, M., Sanduleac, M.: Transforming big data into collective awareness. Computer **46**(6), 40–45 (2013)
36. Jensen, A., Alderwereld, H., Dignum, V.: Dimensions of organizational coordination. In: Hindriks, K., de Weerdt, M., van Riemsdijk, B., Warnier, M. (eds.) Proceedings of the 25th Benelux Conference on Artificial Intelligence, pp. 80–87 (2013)
37. Pitt, J., Schaumeier, J., Artikis, A.: Axiomatization of socio-economic principles for self-organizing institutions: concepts, experiments and challenges. ACM Trans. Auton. Adapt. Syst. **7**(4), 39:1–39 (2012)
38. Jiang, J., Dignum, V., Tan, Y.-H.: An agent-based inter-organizational collaboration framework: OperA+. In: Cranefield, S., van Riemsdijk, M.B., Vázquez-Salceda, J., Noriega, P. (eds.) COIN 2011. LNCS, vol. 7254, pp. 58–74. Springer, Heidelberg (2012)
39. Hübner, J.F., Boissier, O., Bordini, R.H.: A normative organisation programming language for organisation management infrastructures. In: Padget, J., Artikis, A., Vasconcelos, W., Stathis, K., da Silva, V.T., Matson, E., Polleres, A. (eds.) COIN@AAMAS 2009. LNCS (LNAI), vol. 6069, pp. 114–129. Springer, Heidelberg (2010)
40. Weigand, H., Dignum, V., Meyer, J.-J.C., Dignum, F.P.M.: Specification by refinement and agreement: designing agent interaction using landmarks and contracts. In: Petta, P., Tolksdorf, R., Zambonelli, F. (eds.) ESAW 2002. LNCS (LNAI), vol. 2577, pp. 257–269. Springer, Heidelberg (2003)

Monitoring the Impact of Norms upon Organisational Performance: A Simulation Approach

Chris Haynes[✉], Simon Miles, and Michael Luck

Department of Informatics, King's College London, London, UK
christopher.haynes@kcl.ac.uk

Abstract. Normative organisations use norms to guide and constrain agent behaviour in order to facilitate cooperation. Norms and their associated enforcement strategies are chosen to further organisational goals, but the effect that a norm has upon organisational performance may change over time in a dynamic environment and behaviour that is desirable in one environment may come to be harmful in another. In this paper we seek to answer the question — how can an organisation detect when a norm is no longer supporting its goals? Specifically, how can it monitor the impact of a norm upon its performance? This paper has three contributions: first, we detail a model which relates an organisation's norms to its performance, second, we propose a mechanism for monitoring the impact of a norm upon that performance using a simulation approach, and finally we describe an implementation of our mechanism.

Keywords: Norms · Normative organizations · Organisational performance · Monitoring · Simulation

1 Introduction

In organisations, agents work together to achieve goals that are difficult or impossible to achieve by a single agent alone. Cooperating agents within an organisation can solve problems with distributed resources, data or expertise, as well as long term problems in timescales beyond the life of an individual [5]. However, this cooperation can be complex to orchestrate, especially as the number of agents increases. In particular, agents may interfere with one another while performing actions, or come into conflict over shared resources.

Norms have been proposed as a solution to these coordination problems [9], and constrain agent behaviour by prohibiting, or obligating, certain actions or states of affairs. Autonomous agents may violate norms in exceptional circumstances, when the benefits outweigh the costs of punishment, so a normative organisation may be more flexible and robust in the face of unexpected problems, such as environmental changes. Conflicts may thus be reduced and goal achievement facilitated without rigid rules. This follows the example of the use of norms

T. Balke et al. (Eds.): COIN 2013, LNAI 8386, pp. 103–119, 2014.
DOI: 10.1007/978-3-319-07314-9_6, © Springer International Publishing Switzerland 2014

within human organisations as a means of management control over employee behaviour in order to improve organisational performance [22]. However, the design of norms is complex and challenging [21] with behavioural controls leading to unintended consequences (as Merchant notes in human organisations [16]). Offline design of norms allows an organisation to select its initial norms [21], but if the environment is dynamic or largely unknown at design time, norms may come to have different practical effects from their designed purpose, so that the *impact* of the norms may change. This effect has been noted and studied in human organisations [23].

The problem of norms becoming counter-productive is considered by Boella et al. [2], who take the view that each norm is designed with an intended goal in mind, much like a plan, and that in each situation the norm must be interpreted to determine if it furthers that goal. They propose a logical framework to allow such interpretation, either by an agent choosing whether to comply with a norm, or by an enforcement mechanism deciding whether to sanction a violation. This interpretation makes use of constitutive norms that specify counts-as rules for variables that make up the regulative norms. While the approach is a valuable way to ensure that the effect of norms remains true to their intended purpose, it relies on agents (or the enforcement mechanism) having the capability and knowledge to perform such reasoning. Moreover, it does not concern itself with the situation where changing circumstances render the intended purpose of the norm itself harmful to the organisational performance. It is this latter problem that we seek to address in this paper — how can an organisation detect when a norm is no longer supporting its wider goals? More specifically, how can it monitor the changing impact of a norm over time in a dynamic environment?

This paper thus has three contributions. First, we propose a model of *norm impact* that links organisational norms to organisational performance. Second, we detail a mechanism to monitor norm impact within an organisation. Finally, we implement our mechanism and show how it reveals a change in impact in a dynamic environment.

As a motivating example, we use a mobile distributed sensor network (MDSN): specifically, a group of unmanned aerial vehicles (UAVs) undertaking a search and rescue task in which they seek to locate victims and report their locations to a control centre [11], described in Sect. 2. The model of organisational performance and norm impact is then detailed in Sect. 3, and the monitoring mechanism is described in Sect. 4, where we consider how to determine what is required in order to monitor norm impact within an organisation, and propose a method to do so. In Sect. 5 we describe an implementation of the norm impact monitoring system and present results. We finish with a review of related work in Sect. 6, and conclusions in Sect. 7.

2   The Scenario: UAV Search and Rescue

In order to motivate and illustrate our work, we adopt a search and rescue scenario involving an organisation using a team of UAVs to search for hidden victims. The organisation consists of a static *controller* and five mobile agents (representing the UAVs) who play the roles of *team leader* and *sensors*. The environment is represented by a grid of 50×50 cells in which some are open ground while others contain either bushes or trees. The *sensors* traverse the environment searching for victims, but their range of detection is limited to the cell they occupy and to adjacent cells.

If a victim is found, a *sensor* sends its location to the *team leader* and the information is relayed to the *controller* which keeps count of located victims. Another victim then appears at a random location, so that at any time there are always 6 hidden victims. Organisational performance is measured by the cumulative number of victims located.

A single norm (*avoidTrees*) prohibits a UAV from flying below 50 m in a cell containing trees. As well as punishment for norm violation, flying low over trees gives a small risk of crashing, resulting in an agent being disabled for 80 time steps. If agents comply with the norm, they will not crash. The probability of a *sensor* detecting a victim depends on the contents of the cell (open, bush or tree) and the altitude of the sensor (flying low increases the probability). This is high in open ground, lower in bushes and even lower in trees. Over trees there is thus a tension between flying low to increase the chance of detecting a victim and flying high to reduce the chance of crashing.

The probability of crashing depends on conditions that can change over time, so it is possible that the usefulness of the norm to the organisation may also change. For example, on a calm, clear day, a UAV is able to fly at a low altitude over trees with barely any chance of crashing, and in such an environment the norm may harm performance by obliging it to fly high unnecessarily. In contrast, on a windy day, flying low makes a crash very likely, and the norm may greatly benefit performance. Note that in both cases, the goal of the norm (to stop UAVs crashing) has not changed, merely its impact. It is this change in norm impact that we seek to detect.

3   A Model of Organisational Performance

The term *organisation* encompasses many different types of multi-agent groupings, from hierarchies for specific tasks to loose congregations with common interests [13]. There are several well-established organisational models in the literature (e.g. MOISE [12]) but, in order to maintain generality as far as possible, we do not use an existing one here. However, since we are concerned with the impact of norms upon organisational performance, we do have some requirements. In particular, we are concerned with organisations with three characteristics: they have explicit, measurable goals; they comprise agents playing roles, each with defined responsibilities and tasks, so as to achieve those goals; and they use norms as a flexible means to guide and constrain behaviour.

With these characteristics in mind we represent an organisation as a tuple: $O = \langle G, R, N, A, Mem, rwd \rangle$, where G is the set of goals, R is the set of roles, N is the set of organisational norms, A is the set of agents within the organisation,

Mem is the organisational memory and *rwd* is the reward function that the organisation uses to measure its success at achieving its goals. We define these elements in the following sections.

3.1 Organisational Goals and Roles

Organisations can be seen as goal-directed systems designed to solve problems that are too large (either spatially or temporally) or too complex to be solved by individual agents [5]. In this work, we specifically concern ourselves with organisations that have a set of explicit goals, G, such that success at meeting those goals can be measured by a reward function, rwd. A goal in this context is a state of affairs that the organisation wishes to achieve or maintain. This requirement is driven by our need to measure the performance of the organisation, which we consider in Sect. 3.5.

A *role* can be seen as a building block of an organisation, representing some service or function that must be performed by it, and related to other roles by interaction and authority relationships [8]. Designing organisations using roles allows the designer to abstract away from specific agents and instead impose goals and norms onto roles rather than individuals. During the operation of the organisation, these roles are filled by agents who seek to achieve the goals under the constraints of applicable norms.

3.2 Organisational Norms

We take norms to be obligations, prohibitions and permissions that constrain and guide behaviour [1,15]. We consider prohibitions as negative obligations: one is obliged to see to it that the prohibited action or state does not occur. In our model, a norm is represented[1] as: $n = \langle target, type, content, context, punishment \rangle$ where *target* is the role to which the norm applies, $type \in \{obl, per\}$ is the deontic type of the norm (either obligation or permission), *content* is the action or state referred to by the norm, *context* is a statement of under which circumstances the norm applies, and $punishment \in \mathbb{R}^+$ is the penalty for violating the norm. Permissions cannot be violated, so have no associated punishment. Note that this representation does not consider norms where the punishment is the imposition of a contrary-to-duty norm. Both *content* and *context* are boolean expressions that can be understood by agents playing the roles, and can thus use environmental variables, internal agent variables, or actions. For example, a norm, *avoidTrees*, which prohibits an agent playing a *sensor* role from flying below fifty metres in altitude over trees is represented in the following way: $avoidTrees = \langle sensor, obl, altitude > 50, isOverTrees, 35 \rangle$.

Norms apply to any agent playing the targeted role and, if agents play multiple roles, the norms from all the roles apply. The organisational norm set,

---

[1] Our representation is a simpler version of Andrighetto et al.'s [1]; we do not include norm defender or source since norms are imposed by the organisation and self-enforced by agents themselves.

$N = \{n_1, n_2, ..., n_i\}$, contains the norms used by the organisation. $N_{r_i} \subset N$, is the set of norms that apply to role r_i (and hence any agents playing that role). In our UAV scenario, there is a single norm, *avoidTrees*, applying to the *sensor* role, so $N = N_{sensor} = \{avoidTrees\}$.

3.3   Agents

Agents play the roles within an organisation and it is the aggregate actions of these agents that make up the organisation activity. An agent playing a role in the organisation commits to try to achieve certain goals at certain times. These goals may be sub-goals of larger missions performed by multiple agents. We assume that agents are benevolent towards their organisation, and that they will attempt to achieve their goals. However, since agents are autonomous, they have leeway in *how* they achieve the goals. They may also have multiple goals at any one time and so must decide the order in which to pursue those goals. In this section, we consider how agents within normative organisations choose which actions to take. We specifically examine BDI agents using offline planning.

BDI agents [4], such as those using AgentSpeak(L) [19], perform offline planning using libraries of pre-compiled plans to achieve goals and react to events. To enable flexible plan selection in the presence of norms, we follow the approach of Oren et al. [18], where each agent has some utility function that it seeks to maximise and in this respect, achieving goals increases its utility, while violating norms decreases its utility. There is no requirement for an agent's utility function to directly relate to the organisation's reward function (described in Sect. 3.1), in particular the agent may lack the wider knowledge required to determine whether its actions are ultimately beneficial to the organisational goals. Now, since agents are benevolent towards the organisation, they automatically reduce their utility for norm violations, so in effect punish themselves rather than rely on external enforcement — they do not wish to evade the consequences of their violations.

Given this, we can model an agent, a as $a = \langle G_a, \Pi_a, B_a, R_a, C_a, Plan\ Selection_a \rangle$ where G_a is the set of current goals, Π_a is the set of available plans, B_a is the set of agent's beliefs (including its representation of the environment), R_a is the set of roles currently played by the agent. C_a is a set of capabilities $\{c_1, c_2, ..., c_n\}$, $c_i = \langle \alpha, comp \rangle$, where α is some action that the agent can perform and $comp \in [0, 1]$ represents the agent's level of competence at performing the action. The set of plans, $\Pi_a = \{\pi_1, ..., \pi_n\}$ represent the contents of the agent's *plan library*. *PlanSelection_a* is the set of two functions, *selectPossiblePlans_a* and *selectBestPlan_a* that the agent uses to select a plan from the plan library when deciding upon a course of action.

An agent chooses its plan based upon its current goals, beliefs, capabilities and norms. Since violating a norm reduces utility, agents prefer to comply with applicable norms, but if a goal is very important and yields a high utility, then it may make sense for an agent to violate a norm in order to achieve it.

In order to choose a plan, first the agent generates a set of possible plans, Π_{pos}, using *selectPossiblePlans_a*$(G_a, \Pi_a, B_a, C_a) \rightarrow \Pi_{ap}$. Then it selects the plan yielding the highest utility, π_{N_a}, using $selectBestPlan_a(\Pi_{pos}, B_a, C_a, N_a)$ $\rightarrow \pi_{N_a}$, where N_a is the set of norms applicable to the agent. Using this method of plan selection, if all else is equal, the selected plan, and hence the agent's behaviour, is dependent upon the norms.

3.4 The Environment and Agent Activity

An organisation acts within and upon an environment in order to achieve its goals, and this activity may change the environment. We must therefore represent this environment, and also the activity itself. We model the environment as a set of variables, with each variable referring to a property of the world. At a specific time t_i, the environment is E_{t_i}, where $e \in E_{t_i}$ is an environmental property.

The *activity* of an organisation is the aggregate actions of all the member agents. AC_{org,N,t_i} is the organisational activity at time t_i and is defined as

$$AC_{org,N,t_i} = \bigcup_{j=0}^{|A|} AC_{a_j,N,t_i}$$

where A is the set of all agents in the organisation, and AC_{a_j,N,t_i} is the set of actions taken by agent a_j, at time t_i, with organisational norm set N.

To represent the changes that an organisation's behaviour makes upon the environment we specify an environment transformation function, $\mathcal{ETF}(E_{N,t_i}, AC_{org,N,t_i}) \rightarrow E_{N,t_{i+1}}$, where AC_{org,N,t_i} is the *organisational activity* at time t_i using organisational norm set N, and $E_{N,t_{i+1}}$ is the environmental state arrived at after one 'tick' of activity by the organisation. Note that the environment may change without the involvement of agents.

Over a time period longer than a single 'tick' (from t_0 to t_n), if the norm set N does not change, we can define an extended transformation function:

$$\mathcal{ETF}_{t_0 \rightarrow t_n}\left(E_{N,t_0}, \bigcup_{i=0}^{n} AC_{org,N,t_i}\right) \rightarrow E_{N,t_n}$$

where E_{N,t_0} is the environmental state at t_0, and E_{N,t_n} is the state at t_n.

3.5 Organisational Performance and Norm Impact

We are interested in how the norms of an organisation help it to perform its tasks given a specific environment and set of agents playing its roles. We informally define organisational performance over a time period as the increase in organisational utility over that period; this may be positive (if utility increases), negative (if it decreases) or zero. In this section, we consider how an organisation may calculate this performance, and propose a definition for norm impact.

An organisation's reward function may not depend purely on the current environmental state, but may also depend on past states and organisational behaviour. To accommodate this we use the concept of *organisational memory*, a repository of information that an organisation updates over time (though simple organisations may not require such a memory). We denote organisational memory at time t_i as Mem_{N,t_i}, where N is the organisational norm set (which has not changed from t_0 to t_i), and $m \in Mem_{N,t_i}$ is some variable derived from environmental, organisational or agent properties over time.

The reward function is defined as $rwd(E_{N,t_i}, Mem_{N,t_i}) \rightarrow utility_{N,t_i}$, where $utility_{N,t_i} \in \mathbb{R}$ is the organisational utility, and E_{N,t_i} is the state of the environment at time t_i resulting from the activity of the organisation using norm set N (see Sect. 3.4). $utility_{N,t_i}$ indicates how well the organisation is performing at time t_i using norm set N. In our UAV scenario, the number of victims found measures the performance of the organisation over the mission: a higher number indicates better performance.

We define organisational performance over a time period t_s to t_f as the difference between the utility values at those times (so long as N does not change over the period):

$$perf_{N,t_s \rightarrow t_f} = utility_{N,t_f} - utility_{N,t_s}$$

Thus performance is the measure of change in the organisation's utility from t_s to t_f.

We define *norm impact* as the effect of a specific norm upon organisational performance. Formally, the impact of norm n between time t_s and t_f is

$$impact_{n,t_s \rightarrow t_f} = perf_{N,t_s \rightarrow t_f} - perf_{N',t_s \rightarrow t_f}$$

where $N' = N\backslash\{n\}$, and $perf_{N',t_s \rightarrow t_f}$ is the performance that would have occurred if the organisation had been using norm set N' over the time period. The impact of a set of norms can also be derived in a similar way.

The challenge is to derive the performance for both norm sets, N and N', over the same time period, since only one norm set would actually be applied within the organisation at any one time. If N is the applicable norm set, the performance under N' must be estimated. In the remainder of this paper, we describe our proposal to estimate this performance using a simulation approach.

4   Monitoring Norm Impact

In this section we propose a method to monitor the impact of a norm, n, upon the performance of an agent organisation. We do not measure norm impact directly, but, instead, use a simulation approach where the activity of the organisation is modelled twice: first, using the existing set of organisational norms, N, and then under the norm set, N', where $N' = N/n$. Each simulation starts from the same state derived from the state of the organisation and environment at a specific time, but with different norms. First, we specify the process and provide a monitoring algorithm, then we examine the process in more detail.

4.1   The Monitoring Process

The monitoring entity may be an agent (for example, one playing a monitoring or leadership role), or it may be some program either internal or external to the organisation. We make no assumptions about its nature, but refer to it as the *monitor*. The monitoring process has two stages. First, the *monitor* captures information about the organisation, agents and the environment at a single point in time — the *snapshot*, which is the state of the system at that moment in time (in Sect. 4.2 we examine what needs to be in this snapshot). The *monitor* uses the snapshot to build a model of the environment and the agents. In the second stage, the *monitor* uses these models to simulate agent activity over the time period required, both with and without the norm of interest. Multiple runs of each simulation may be needed to get an average performance if the environment is non-deterministic.

Algorithm 1. The monitoring process, for a single monitoring period

---

Require: A multi-agent organisation to be monitored, MAS
Require: Its norm set N
Require: Its set of agents A
Require: Its organisational specification, Org
Require: The norm to be investigated n.
Require: A monitoring time period, $mt = \langle t_s, t_f, length \rangle$
1: Generate norm set $N' \leftarrow N/ \{n\}$
2: **while** MAS is active **do**
3:   **if** time $= t_s$ (the start of a monitoring period) **then**
4:     Gather snapshot of environment properties, E_{N,t_s}
5:     Gather snapshot of agent states, AS_{N,t_s}
6:     Gather snapshot of organisational memory, Mem_{N,t_s}
7:     Create simulation, $sim_N \leftarrow createSim(A, E_{N,t_s}, Mem_{N,t_s}, Org, N, AS_{N,ts})$
8:     Create simulation, $sim_{N'} \leftarrow createSim(A, E_{N,t_s}, Mem_{N,t_s}, Org, N', AS_{N,ts})$
9:     Run simulation, $E_{N,t_f}, Mem_{N,t_f} \leftarrow runSim(sim_N, length)$
10:    Run simulation, $E_{N',t_f}, Mem_{N',t_f} \leftarrow runSim(sim_{N'}, length)$
11:    Estimate performance, $p_N \leftarrow rwd(E_{N,t_f}, Mem_{N,t_f}) - rwd(E_{N,t_s}, Mem_{N,t_s})$
12:    Estimate performance, $p_{N'} \leftarrow rwd(E_{N',t_f}, Mem_{N',t_f}) - rwd(E_{N,t_s}, Mem_{N,t_s})$
13:    Calculate norm impact, $impact_{n,t_s \rightarrow t_f} \leftarrow p_N - p_{N'}$
14:   **end if**
15: **end while**

Algorithm 1 shows the monitoring process algorithm for a single time period, from time t_s to t_f, of *length* 'ticks'. Norm set N' is generated by removing the investigated norm, n, from the organisational norm set, N (line 1). At t_s the *monitor* gathers the snapshots (lines 4–6). Using this information it creates two simulations, sim_N and $sim_{N'}$, differing only in the norm sets used (lines 7 and 8). The organisational performance under each set of norms, p_N and $p_{N'}$, is estimated by running the simulation for the required number of 'ticks' to obtain the environment state and organisational memory at time t_f, and then calculating the performance based on the organisational reward function (lines 9–12). Finally, norm impact, $impact_n$, is calculated by a simple subtraction (line 13).

We choose to create sim_N and generate p_N rather than compare $p_{N'}$ directly to the performance seen in reality for two reasons. First, in a non-deterministic environment, a single run of the system may produce a performance that is exceptionally good or bad due to random chance, and this may obscure the impact of the norms. Using an average performance derived from multiple runs reduces this effect. Second, by comparing the performance in the real system to p_N the organisation may be able to detect problems with the simulation models. For example, if p_N is very different from the real performance (beyond that which could be derived from random chance), it is possible that the models used to create the simulations are not fit for purpose.

The remainder of this section examines the steps of the process in more detail. In Sect. 4.2 we consider the snapshot information and discuss what must be included, then we discuss the creation and running of the simulations in Sect. 4.3.

4.2   The Snapshot Information

The snapshots form the initial state of the simulations, as they capture the moment in time from which the simulated activity begins. The *monitor* gathers this information from the multi-agent system (MAS) either directly, or via the organisational agents themselves. There are three sources of snapshot: the environment, the organisational memory and the agents. In our model, the environment snapshot at time t_s is E_{N,t_s}, the set of environment variables at time t_s. Similarly, the organisational snapshot is Mem_{N,t_s}, the organisational memory at time t_s. The snapshot of an agent is the state of that agent at a moment in time, so if the MAS and the simulation use the same software framework, it may be possible simply to copy the entire internal state of the agent from the MAS and then use it in the simulation. However, we cannot make this assumption about the nature of the MAS and the simulation without overly constraining the generality of our work. Therefore, in this section, we consider which parts of an agent's internal state must be included in a snapshot in order to simulate its behaviour.

The *monitor* must simulate the behaviour of the organisational agents during the monitoring period. First, agents select a goal based on their role, their available plans, and the environment. Second, they select a plan from the set of those applicable, based upon the norm set and the environment. Third, they perform the actions from the plan until the task is complete or abandoned. In our model, we represent the agent's plan selection mechanism as two functions: *selectPossiblePlans* and *selectBestPlan* (see Sect. 3.3); these are the functions that the *monitor* must simulate. In order to do so under norm set N_a', the *monitor* needs eight pieces of information as shown in Table 1.

Table 1. Information required to simulate agent a's goal and plan selection

Item	Description	Source
$selectPossiblePlans_a$	Function to select possible plans	Agent
$selectBestPlan_a$	Function to select best plan	Agent
R_a	Set of roles played by the agent	Agent
G_a	Set of a's goals	Organisation
N'_a	Set of norms applicable to a	Organisation
Π_a	Set of plans in a's Plan library	Agent
B_a	Set of a's beliefs	Agent
C_a	Set of a's capabilities	Agent

Agents within an organisation have goals imposed upon them as a result of their acceptance of a role; these organisational goals take precedence over any individual agent goals. Role-based goals are available to the *monitor* via the organisation's specification, so the *monitor* can obtain G_a. It also has access to the organisational norm set and can thus derive N'_a, which are the norms applying to a without the norm of interest, n.

The *monitor* must rely upon the agents to provide the other information. However, in this paper we assume that most of these elements do not change over the lifetime of the MAS[2]. Specifically, we assume that the two selection functions ($selectPossiblePlans_a$ and $selectBestPlan_a$), the plan library, Π_a, the roles played by the agent, R_a, and its capabilities, C_a, do not change. The *monitor* therefore receives this information once when the MAS starts and uses the same information throughout its lifetime. This leaves the beliefs, B_a as information that must be provided in the agent snapshot.

If an agent is following one or more plans at time t_s, they must be recorded in the snapshot, because these plans may still be valid and sound under the new norm set. We should not require the agent to discard an existing plan purely because the norm set has changed. In the case of a long term plan this could severely harm organisational performance, though the effect could be minor and acceptable if the plans are short compared to the length of the time period of the simulation.

An agent may gather percepts from the environment (or other agents) but not process them immediately. For example, if an agent able to process a single message per time step receives multiple messages, then it must store messages until able to process them. When taking a snapshot of such an agent, we must include those messages in our snapshot. Likewise, if an agent stores events for future processing, this event queue must be included, even though these events occurred before t_s. Percepts and messages processed by the agent prior to t_s need not be recorded in the snapshot because these will have been incorporated into the agent's beliefs and intentions if necessary.

---

[2] If the agent playing a role changes, then these assumptions may be incorrect — we leave this for future work.

4.3   Creating the Simulations

The direct effect of agent actions is one cause of environmental change, but there are other causes that must be considered. The actions of agents have a direct effect on the environment (or agents), but may also cause side-effects on either the environment or the agents. There may also be an element of environmental dynamism that is unrelated to the organisation's agents. The *monitor* must thus simulate three aspects: the behaviour of the agents and their direct effect on the environment; the indirect side-effects of those actions; and other elements of dynamism unrelated to agent actions.

In order to model indirect changes, the *monitor* requires a model of the environment to determine likely side-effects of agent actions upon the environment and also to simulate changes arising from environmental dynamism. This may include modelling physical effects (if the MAS exists within a physical environment). For example, in our UAV scenario the simulation must model the probability of a low-flying UAV crashing into a tree. Also, it must have a model of other agents sharing the environment with the organisation, so that their actions can be simulated.

Algorithm 2. Starting an agent from a snapshot.

Require: Agent beliefs from snapshot B_{snap}
Require: Current plan from snapshot π_{snap}
Require: Agent goals G_a, and agent capabilities C_a
Require: Norm set used in simulation N_{sim}.
Require: Set of roles played by agent R_a
Require: Agent plan library Π_a
1: $B_a \leftarrow B_{snap}$
2: $N_a \leftarrow setNorms(R_a, N_{sim})$
3: $\pi_a \leftarrow \pi_{snap}$
4: **if** not $sound(\pi_a, I, B_a)$ **then**
5:    $\Pi_{pos} \leftarrow selectPossiblePlans(G_a, \Pi_a, B_a, C_a)$
6:    $\pi_{N_a} \leftarrow selectBestPlan(\Pi_{pos}, B_a, C_a, N_a)$
7: **end if**
8: **while** true **do**
9:    Continue Agent Activity
10: **end while**

Starting a simulation from a snapshot requires the agents to begin *in media res*, that is, as if they were in the middle of whatever situation they were in when the snapshot was taken. Algorithm 2 shows the required steps for an agent starting from a snapshot — beliefs and the current plan are derived from the snapshot, and the set of applicable norms are generated from the new organisational norm set, N_{sim} and the set of roles played by the agent, R_a. The agent must determine whether the current plan is sound (possible and desirable), and if not then it reconsiders its course of action.

4.4   Calculating Performance and Norm Impact

Once the simulations (sim_N and $sim_{N'}$) have been created, the next step is to run them and calculate the organisational performance. As in Algorithm 1, each simulation is run over the time period of interest (t_s to t_f) and the simulated environmental state and organisational memory at the end of the run are used in the reward function to calculate organisational utility at time t_f under both norms sets, N and N'. If the environment is non-deterministic, then multiple runs may be performed and an average utility calculated for each norm set. Performance is then calculated by subtracting the starting utility (which is calculated from the snapshot information). Finally, the norm impact is calculated by subtracting the performance under N' from the performance under N.

5   An Implementation of the Monitoring System

To evaluate our monitoring mechanism, we implemented a monitoring system for our UAV scenario (described in Sect. 2). In this section we describe our implementation in a broad fashion, but for reasons of brevity and clarity have omitted much of the detail.

A MAS representing our UAV scenario was built using the Jason AgentSpeak framework [3]. It consists of a single *controller* and five *sensor* agents, one of the latter also plays the *team leader* role. The *sensors* have a library of plans allowing them to search the environment as a team, coordinated by the *controller* and *team leader*. The victims are also agents. As described above, the probability of detecting a victim located in a cell varies with terrain type and altitude, shown in Table 2a.

Table 2. Scenario Parameters

(a) Detection probabilities

Cell	Probability	
Terrain	(fly low)	(fly high)
open	1.0	0.7
bush	0.8	0.4
tree	0.5	0.1

(b) Plan properties

Plan	Properties		Weight
	success	reward	
searchHigh	0.1	40	4.0
searchLow	0.5	5	2.5

We do not implement a full normative plan selection mechanism as described by Oren et al. [18], but instead the *sensors* have two plans for searching a tree-filled cell, one compliant (*searchHigh*) and one that violated the norm (*searchLow*). The plans are annotated with two properties, *success* and *reward*, to reflect the probability of successfully searching a cell, the reward for doing so, and the reward reduction for violating a norm. The reward is set to a value of 40 and the punishment for violating the norm is set to 35. The *success* property is determined by the values in Table 2a.

The plan selection function, *selectBestPlan* uses weights derived by multi-plying the plan properties, *success* and *reward* to give an expected reward for following each plan (see Table 2b). The agents then choose the plan with the highest weight. Given these weightings, agents choose to comply with the norm since the expected utility gain is higher from the compliant plan. The organi-sational performance over a time period is measured by the number of victims located during that period. For example, if at time t_1, 6 victims have been found, and at time t_2, 11 victims have been found, the organisational performance is 5. This count of located victims is performed by the *controller*, so we do not use an explicit organisational memory.

In order to implement Algorithm 1, we first need to create snapshots of the environment and agents. The environment snapshot is a file generated by Jason that records the environmental state at the start of the monitoring period. To generate the agent snapshots, we use a new Jason internal action[3], *dumpState*, to record an agent's beliefs and message queue in a file. This internal action is performed as part of a plan triggered at the start of each monitoring period.

The simulations were also built using Jason, with the environment and the agents reading in the snapshot information at the start of the simulation. A new internal action, *bootstrap*, allows an agent to copy the beliefs and message queue from the snapshot, and a plan is triggered on start-up to restart agent activity based on beliefs (specifically, the point reached in traversal of the area, and whether currently disabled due to a crash). One simulation uses the *avoidTrees* norm, the other does not — implemented by changing the *reward* property for the *searchLow* to 40 (to represent the absence of a penalty). Each simulation is run 100 times, and the organisational performance calculated from the number of victims found over the period.

5.1   Experiments and Results

The MAS ran for 3000 time steps and norm impact was monitored over periods of 500 time steps, beginning respectively at time 500, 1500 and 2500. We performed experiments to represent three environments differing in the probability of a UAV crashing if flying too low over a tree: a high crash, low crash, and varying environment. The consequences of a crash were the same in all environments; Table 3 details the values of these properties. The varying environment began as a high crash one until time 1251, then became a mid crash environment until time 2251 when it became a low crash one.

Snapshots of the system were taken at time 500, 1500 and 2500, and used as the basis of simulated activity both with and without the norm, *avoidTrees*. Norm impact over the monitoring period was then calculated, with results dis-played in Fig. 1. The norm had a positive impact in the high crash environment and a negative impact in the low crash environment. In the varying environment,

---

[3] Jason internal actions are Java functions that allow agents to perform actions not related to their environment, such as writing to a log file.

Table 3. Environmental properties

Environment	Crash probability	Delay time
Low crash	0.005	80
Mid crash	0.05	80
High crash	0.1	80

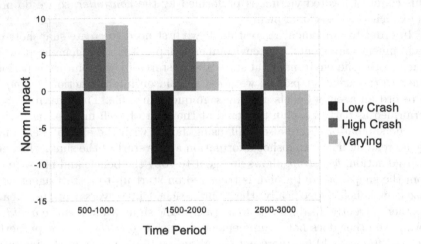

Fig. 1. Impact of norm *avoidTrees* in different environments over three time periods

norm impact begins positive, but changed to become negative as the probability of crashing reduces. These results show that it is possible to quantitatively measure norm impact and to measure the change of this impact as the environment changes. An organisation using such a monitoring mechanism is thus able to detect when a norm is becoming less useful, or indeed harmful, to its overall goals.

6   Related Work and Conclusions

The two main approaches to the design of norms are offline design [21] (where norms are designed prior to execution), or an emergent approach where satisfactory norms are converged upon by agents through a learning process [20]. Both have problems for situations in which an organisation wishes to use norms to regulate behaviour in a dynamic environment. With an offline approach, norms are designed for a specific range of environments, and if the environment changes sufficiently then norms may become unsuitable. An emergent approach can cope with a changing environment, but by its very nature the organisation has little control over the norms that arise, and the learning process can be lengthy.

Our approach allows the impact of norms designed offline to be monitored, so that poorly performing norms can be identified and replaced.

Centeno and Billhardt propose an adaptive normative system that tailors incentives to individual agents [6]. Their work provides a way to modify norms that are no longer useful because they are violated by agents since the incentives can be modified to ensure that agents will comply. However, they do not consider situations where compliance with a norm is itself detrimental to the organisation. Boella et al. do consider this situation [2] by using the concept of norm goals, where each norm has an associated intended goal, and provide a logical framework with which an agent can reason about the desirability of compliance. However, this does not detect if the goal of the norm becomes detrimental, and raises the need for possibly sophisticated agent reasoning.

Regarding organisational performance, Centeno et al. provide a formal model of a normative organisation that includes the notion of a useful regulative system (or normative system) as one that improves organisational utility [7]. However, they do not quantify the effect of particular norms on organisational performance, instead considering the normative system as a whole, whereas our work specifically looks at individual norms. Dignum and Dignum investigate the fitness of an organisation's structure to its task [10] and propose a simulation approach to determine the effectiveness of that structure. We likewise use a simulation approach, although we focus upon the normative aspect of an organisation rather than its structure.

Norm monitoring within the literature has focused upon compliance issues (for example, [17]), rather than determining whether a norm is effective. With respect to changing norms to improve organisational performance, Koeppen et al. propose and implement a method to select efficient norms using case-based reasoning [14]. Their approach builds up a library of cases to select the best norm to improve simulated traffic flow in a multi-agent system, based on organisational goals.

7   Discussion and Further Work

We have presented a model that links the norms of an organisation to its task performance. The model considers the plan selection mechanism of the agents and how this selection is influenced by applicable norms. This in turn affects the actions taken by the agents in pursuit of their goals, and hence the changes in the environment that lead to the organisational goals being achieved, or not. We proposed a mechanism to enable an organisation to monitor the impact of norms upon performance over time, and implemented it using a scenario based upon a team of UAVs undertaking a search and rescue mission. Our experimental results showed that it is possible to quantitatively measure this impact, and to measure the change of impact as the environment changes.

Our scenario is simplistic, with a single norm and only limited reasoning by the agent about whether to comply or not. A more sophisticated implementation could include agents using local knowledge to determine whether it is valuable to violate a norm and hence investigate the tension between organisational norms intended to encourage long-term success and agent decisions geared toward short-term success.

In addition, in an organisation with multiple norms it may not be feasible to monitor the impact of every norm and possible subset of norms using our approach[4], so we need a method to decide which norms to monitor. Possible approaches include: assessing how sensitive a norm's impact is to environmental change, and then monitoring those most sensitive; grouping norms according to the roles and tasks to which they apply, and monitoring those applying to the most critical tasks.

Finally, it is important to note that the quality of the impact estimation is tied to the accuracy of the simulation. In a real world UAV scenario, it may be challenging to adequately model factors such as system failures and probability of victim detection.

References

1. Andrighetto, G., Campenni, M., Conte, R., Paolucci, M.: On the immergence of norms: a normative agent architecture. In: Proceedings of the AAAI Symposium, Social and Organizational Aspects of Intelligence (2007)
2. Boella, G., Governatori, G., Rotolo, A., van der Torre, L.: *Lex Minus Dixit Quam Voluit, Lex Magis Dixit Quam Voluit*: A formal study on legal compliance and interpretation. In: Casanovas, P., Pagallo, U., Sartor, G., Ajani, G. (eds.) AICOL Workshops 2009. LNCS, vol. 6237, pp. 162–183. Springer, Heidelberg (2010)
3. Bordini, R.H., Hübner, J.F.: BDI agent programming in AgentSpeak using *Jason*. In: Toni, F., Torroni, P. (eds.) CLIMA 2005. LNCS (LNAI), vol. 3900, pp. 143–164. Springer, Heidelberg (2006)
4. Bratman, M.E., Israel, D.J., Pollack, M.E.: Plans and resource-bounded practical reasoning. Comput. Intell. 4(4), 349–355 (1988)
5. Carley, K.M., Gasser, L.: Computational organization theory. In: Weiss, G. (ed.) Multiagent Systems: A Modern Approach to Distributed Artificial Intelligence. MIT Press, Cambridge (1999)
6. Centeno, R., Billhardt, H.: Using incentive mechanisms for an adaptive regulation of open multi-agent systems. In: Proceedings of the 22nd International Joint Conference on Artificial Intelligence, pp. 139–145 (2011)
7. Centeno, R., Billhardt, H., Hermoso, R., Ossowski, S.: Organising MAS: a formal model based on organisational mechanisms. In: Proceedings of the 2009 ACM Symposium on Applied Computing, pp. 740–746. ACM (2009)
8. Dastani, M., Dignum, V., Dignum, F.: Role-assignment in open agent societies. In: Proceedings of the 2nd International Joint Conference on Autonomous Agents and Multiagent Systems, pp. 489–496. ACM (2003)
9. Dignum, F., Morley, D., Sonenberg, E.A., Cavedon, L.: Towards socially sophisticated BDI agents. In: Proceedings of the 4th International Conference on Multi-Agent Systems, pp. 111–118 (2000)

---

[4] In a MAS with n norms, there are potentially 2^n combinations that could be monitored.

10. Dignum, V., Dignum, F.: Understanding organizational congruence: formal model and simulation framework. In: Proceedings of the 2007 Spring Simulation Multi-conference, vol. 2, pp. 178–184 (2007)
11. Doherty, P., Rudol, P.: A UAV search and rescue scenario with human body detection and geolocalization. In: Orgun, M.A., Thornton, J. (eds.) AI 2007. LNCS (LNAI), vol. 4830, pp. 1–13. Springer, Heidelberg (2007)
12. Hannoun, M., Boissier, O., Sichman, J.S., Sayettat, C.: MOISE: an organizational model for multi-agent systems. In: Monard, M.C., Sichman, J.S. (eds.) IBERAMIA-SBIA 2000. LNCS (LNAI), vol. 1952, pp. 156–165. Springer, Heidelberg (2000)
13. Horling, B., Lesser, V.: A survey of multi-agent organizational paradigms. Knowl. Eng. Rev. **19**(4), 281–316 (2004)
14. Koeppen, J., Lopez-Sanchez, M., Morales, J., Esteva, M.: Learning from experience to generate new regulations. In: De Vos, M., Fornara, N., Pitt, J.V., Vouros, G. (eds.) COIN 2010. LNCS, vol. 6541, pp. 337–356. Springer, Heidelberg (2011)
15. Lopez y Lopez, F., Luck, M.: Modelling norms for autonomous agents. In: Proceedings of the 4th Mexican International Conference on Computer Science, pp. 238–245, September 2003
16. Merchant, K.A.: The control function of management. Sloan Manag. Rev. **23**(4), 43–55 (1982)
17. Modgil, S., Faci, N., Meneguzzi, F., Oren, N., Miles, S., Luck, M.: A framework for monitoring agent-based normative systems. In: Proceedings of the 8th International Conference on Autonomous Agents and Multiagent Systems, pp. 153–160 (2009)
18. Oren, N., Vasconcelos, W., Meneguzzi, F., Luck, M.: Acting on norm constrained plans. In: Leite, J., Torroni, P., Ågotnes, T., Boella, G., van der Torre, L. (eds.) CLIMA XII 2011. LNCS, vol. 6814, pp. 347–363. Springer, Heidelberg (2011)
19. Rao, A.S.: AgentSpeak(L): BDI agents speak out in a logical computable language. In: Van de Velde, W., Perram, J.W. (eds.) Agents Breaking Away. LNCS, vol. 1038, pp. 42–55. Springer, Heidelberg (1996)
20. Sen, S., Airiau, S.: Emergence of norms through social learning. In: Proceedings of the 20th International Joint Conference on Artifical Intelligence, pp. 1507–1512 (2007)
21. Shoham, Y., Tennenholtz, M.: On social laws for artificial agent societies: off-line design. Artif. Intell. **73**(1–2), 231–252 (1995)
22. Simons, R.: Control in an age of empowerment. Harvard Bus. Rev. **73**(2), 80–88 (1995)
23. Streeck, W., Thelen, K.: Introduction: institutional change in advanced political economies. In: Streeck, W., Thelen, K. (eds.) Beyond Continuity: Institutional Change in Advanced Political Economies, pp. 1–39. Oxford University Press, Oxford (2005)

Norms in Distributed Organizations

Bas Testerink$^{(\boxtimes)}$, Mehdi Dastani, and John-Jules Meyer

Utrecht University, Utrecht, The Netherlands
{b.j.g.testerink,m.m.dastani,j.j.c.meyer}@uu.nl

Abstract. Due to external requirements we cannot always construct a centralized organization, but have to construct one that is distributed. A distributed organization is a network of organizations which can locally observe and control the environment. In this paper we analyze how norms can be enforced through the joint effort of the individual local organizations. Norm violations are detected by monitoring. Sanctioning compensates the violations of norms. The main problem is to map the required data for monitoring, and the required control capabilities for sanctioning, to the local observe/control capabilities of organizations. Our investigation focuses on exploring the solution space of this problem, the properties of proper solutions and practical considerations when developing a solution.

Keywords: Normative organizations · Exogenous organizations · Distributed organizations

1 Introduction

In open multi-agent systems, organizations are used to promote global system behavior. This paper concerns normative organizations where norms are used to control and coordinate agents. Over the years there have been investigations in many aspects of organizations. This has led to different frameworks (e.g. [4,6,10]) and programming languages for organizations (e.g. [2,7]). Some of the works expand organizations with roles, hierarchical structures and empowerment definitions. We consider only organizations that are exogenous to agents and the environment, and have explicit norms.

Such organizations are useful because it separates the regulation concerns from the rest of the multi-agent system (i.e. agents, middleware, etc.). This in turn allows for independent maintenance and debugging of the organization. Also the use of violable norms is often preferred over hard constraints. This is because norms preserve to a greater extent the autonomy of agents. Agents still have a choice whether or not to violate norms if they are aware of them. But also if an agent is not aware of norms then still the organization can repair or compensate violations of norms if they occur. For instance a tourist can be incarcerated for violating a law during vacation, regardless whether he or she was aware of the law.

There is an abundant collection of norm formalisms that allow us to specify a norm set. One of the most basic methods is to specify the desired behavior and

T. Balke et al. (Eds.): COIN 2013, LNAI 8386, pp. 120–135, 2014.
DOI: 10.1007/978-3-319-07314-9_7, © Springer International Publishing Switzerland 2014

the consequences if that specification is violated. One can implement all norms with this principle as was done in [2,7]. We shall also adopt this view. Monitoring is required to detect violation, which we shall capture with rules that indicate which agent behaviors should be considered as violations. Sanctioning is needed to respond to violations, i.e. to enforce norms. For enforcement we shall use rules that tie a norm violation to a consequence. We separate the rules because they can be maintained independently, which happens a lot in practice. For instance the velocity that counts-as speeding is often quite static whereas the sanction is not (usually the fines gradually get higher). Monitoring and sanctioning require two core capabilities of an organization given an environment: what can be observed and what can be controlled in that environment.

In this paper we address distributed organizations. These distributed organizations are comprised of a network of organizations each of which has their own sense and control capabilities. There are different kinds of distribution in a distributed organization. We can distribute the monitoring of a norm, the application of a sanction to repair/compensate a violation, the task of determining violations based on monitored data and the task of determining the sanction based on a norm violation.

As an example of a distributed organization we look at an application called smart roads. In the smart roads system each highway is enriched with an organization to increase the safety and throughput. For instance speed limits can be adapted to fit the current circumstances on the road. Sensors and cameras are attached to the infrastructure so the highways can be monitored. The government's regulations for traffic are adopted as norms in the organizations. The organizations are given the power to give drivers a fine whenever for instance a speed limit is violated. The highway organizations are geographically distributed. But there is also functional distribution. Namely, aside from the highway organizations there are other support organizations to for instance manage the fines of agents.

Having a network of organizations, rather than a single organization for all roads, increases the robustness of the system and is scalable if new highways are added to the system. Because there are many agents in the smart roads application, the data that is generated by monitoring the highways can form a bottleneck if it is processed by a single organization.

The regulations for traffic are defined *independently* of the actual individual highways and their infrastructures. Similarly the norms that follow from the traffic regulations are not designed for the individual organizations. Situations can arise where only through joint effort of the organizations the norms can be enforced. As an running example we shall use a scenario from the smart roads application where joint effort is required.

In Fig. 1 a scenario is schematically depicted. There are four organizations: one manages a permit database, one manages a fine register, and two manage separate highways. The highway organizations are connected to each other and to the two other organizations. For the highway organizations monitoring entails the observation of cars while influence entails, for instance, the possibility to

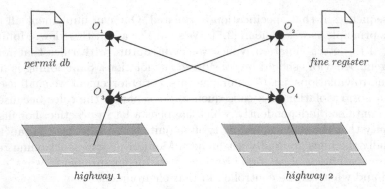

Fig. 1. Example scenario from the smart roads application. Arrows indicate the capability for communicating about violations of norms, observations and control. Lines indicate which organization monitors/controls what part of the environment. The green lane is a priority lane (Color figure online).

change the speed limit. Having a limited area per organization where it can monitor and influence the highway leads to different situations in which it becomes problematic to monitor norms or impose sanctions. In our example scenario we will have a norm that can only be monitored if the four organizations share their local observations.

Imagine that traffic flows from highway 1 to highway 2. The upper lanes of the highways are priority lanes to increase the throughput of vehicles with a permit such as taxis and car repair services. The priority lanes only come into effect at peak hours. Peak hours are detected if the traffic density on highways are above a certain threshold. The norm is: "*if the traffic density is high, then cars are only allowed to drive on the priority lane when they have a permit*". Violations of this norm will be sanctioned by a fine. There is no organization that can check if a car has a permit and whether the highways' densities are high. In this situation the organizations have to share this information in order to determine whether a violation is occurring. The fine register organization creates a fine in case of violation. We will investigate the problem of how norms can be enforced in general within a distributed organization.

In particular we are interested in the question whether, given a network of organizations, a set of norms *can* be enforced (e.g. are the required monitoring capabilities for detecting norm violations present?). And if we can enforce norms, what are our possibilities in terms of distributing the norm monitoring and violation sanctioning tasks? To answer these questions we will formally define norms, distributed organizations and enforcement (Sect. 4). Then we shall describe how the norm monitoring and violation sanctioning tasks can be distributed in the network (Sect. 5). But first we stress the importance of investigating distributed organizations (Sect. 2) and the related work on this topic (Sect. 3).

2 Why We Should Investigate Distributed Organizations

The COIN workshop provides for several years now a platform to debate different aspects of organizations. One of the main themes is the construction of formal models to investigate organizations. Often models of organizations and/or institutions with explicit norms are made to research regulatory concepts of open multi-agent systems. Usually these models do not take networks of organizations into account. For instance in this volume the works [3,5,8] concern multi-agent systems where there is assumed to be a single organization/institution. Like us, they do use organizations with explicit sets of norms. We will define a model for distributed organizations and investigate the enforcement of norms. This fits the topic of large scale multi-agent systems in this volume as well. Because in large scale systems one has to inevitably deal with the scalability of deployed organizations. Applying decentral enforcement can help with that.

We are interested in distributed organizations because centralized software systems come with plenty of disadvantages such as single point of failures, scalability issues and maintenance of always-on applications. Typically multi-agent systems are distributed by nature, with agents being distributed among platforms and entities. Imposing a centralized organization on a multi-agent system would diminish the systems advantages that are obtained from distribution.

But it is not that distribution is just a design choice. Sometimes external factors require the use of a distributed organization. When we introduce agents in corporate business then the organization of the agents will likely be a reflection of the human organization. And human organizations are typically a network of departments, task-forces, commissions, etc., i.e. distributed organizations.

Given that distributed organizations exist, one can wonder whether the organizational theories/techniques/methodologies that we have are appropriate. We believe this question to be answered in the negative for the general case. To our best knowledge all current work on distributed organizations is focused on techniques with which one can make organizations that have some form of distribution (more in Sect. 3). What is not investigated is how we could distribute some given norms in a given distributed organization.

Informally, the challenges lie in the fact that organizations only have local observation and control capabilities, though norms span over the entire distributed organization. We divide the functionality of a (distributed) organization into observing - detecting violations of norms - and sanctioning - to give norms meaning. Without sanctioning there would be no point in having norms[1]. A distributed organization has a global specification of norms. The practical issue is to transfer the global specification to norms per organization, such that overall the distributed organization enforces the norms. There has not yet been an investigation to describe this problem.

---

[1] At least when the organization is exogenous to agents. If norms are integrated in agents then this does not hold, but then we would require no exogenous organization for control and coordination.

Our effort is not targeted to defining a function that given norms and a distributed organization distributes the norms. Rather we want to describe the solution space of these functions. The reason is that it differs greatly per application what kind of solutions are desired. For instance, in the distributed highway organization example we have a lot of data to process because the system is huge. It can be unfeasible to let all organizations send their observation data to a central point for processing. Rather it would be preferable to distribute a set of norms among local organizations so they can enforce them locally, if possible. But if one of our external constraints is that only the police organization might impose fines on agents, then for the violations that result in fines the highway organizations should send the information to the police organization.

3   Distributed Organizations in Related Work

Distributed organizations have been addressed in several works. In [7] norms are programmed per scenario, where a scenario is a coherent series of (possibly parallel) activities. Their data consists only of executed speech acts and institutional facts (prohibitions, obligations and permissions). The scene rules describe how actions from one activity can affect institutional facts concerning other activities. Scenes are independent, meaning that all relevant speech acts and institutional facts are stored in its state. In [12] the main consideration is the distribution of norms in a spatial environment. Objects and places in the environment may convey norms to agents so that they can decide to follow them. Their work does not include the monitoring system or sanctioning (other than the statement that special supervision agents might check compliance). In [11] the control mechanism is based on group interactions. Each group is governed by a law which does not span multiple groups. In [14] organizations can be programmed and run separately, but are able to communicate about environment states and brute/institutional changes which occur locally. In [1] multi-institutes, which are similar to our distributed organizations, are defined, plus an action language (InstAl) to specify them.

In the related work we see existing techniques/languages for which some form of distributive properties are described, or distributed organizations are specified by fully specifying the local organizations. None of the works however analyze the issue of distributing global norms among local organizations in order to enforce them.

What is missing from current research is an analysis of if and how we can translate a given norm set to a network of organizations, where the norm set is assumed to be developed independently of the network. Especially the issue of norms that cannot be to locally enforced (i.e. both monitoring and sanctioning of a norm cannot be done in one organization) has not been addressed properly. In this paper we move away from implementations and analyze norms in distributed organizations from a more abstract point of view. The results of our research will help to develop more general norm technologies. Also a deeper understanding of design choices when constructing a norm set will be obtained. This aids the process of designing a norm set for a distributed organization.

4 Norms, Distributed Organizations and Enforcement

In this section we shall define norms, (distributed) organizations and enforcement. The definitions rely on environment state descriptions and observation/control capabilities. We use propositional logic to describe the state of a multi-agent system environment and organization.

4.1 Defining Norms

In an open multi-agent system, active monitoring is required to detect the violation of norms, and sanctioning realizes the consequences of violations. There are many ways to represent norms using preconditions, deadlines, deontic concepts etc. For our purposes we take the most basic representation which are counts-as rules. For describing the compensations of violations we use sanction rules. The reading of a counts-as rule $\varphi \Rightarrow v$ is that the system states that satisfy φ are violated states. Or to put it differently, states that satisfy φ are forbidden states. The violation of this prohibition is identified by v. The reading of a sanction rule $v \Rightarrow \psi$ is that violated states have to be updated with ψ to compensate for violation v. Violation atoms are considered to be institutional facts. Each norm has a unique violation atom. Counts-as/sanction rule context is omitted for simplicity. Thoughts on incorporating context in counts-as rules can be found in Sect. 8. A matching norm and sanction pair is a norm of which the violation is sanctioned by the sanction (Definition 1).

Definition 1 (Matching norms and sanctions). *A norm is represented by a counts-as rule of the form $\varphi \Rightarrow v$, where φ is a conjunction of literals and v is a violation atom. A sanction is represented by a sanction rule of the form $v \Rightarrow \psi$, where v is a violation atom and ψ is a conjunction of literals that has to be made true in case violation v has occurred. A norm n matches a sanction s iff $n = \varphi \Rightarrow v$ and $s = v \Rightarrow \psi$, i.e. sanction s responds to violations of norm n.*

For instance a speed higher than 130 km/h, $speed_{>130}$, may count as a speeding violation $speed_{>130} \Rightarrow speeding$, which can be sanctioned with a fine $speeding \Rightarrow fine$.

We limit the use of institutional facts to violations. Complex regulative systems often use constitutive norms to define institutional facts [13]. However, as violations are the only institutional facts, and they are already defined by counts-as rules, we do not include the use of constitutive norms.[2]

4.2 Defining (Distributed) Organizations

A distributed organization is a set of organizations that can communicate (Definition 2). For convenience and reasons explained in Sect. 4.3 we use two separate communication relations. One communication relation, which we call the regular

---

[2] More on this in Sect. 8.

communication, is for the communication about observations and to be imposed sanctions. The other relation is called the institutional communication and is reserved for the communication of violation atoms.

Definition 2 (Distributed organization). *A distributed organization is a tuple $DO = \langle \mathbb{O}, R_r, R_i \rangle$, where $\mathbb{O}$ is a set of organizations, and $R_r, R_i \subseteq \mathbb{O} \times \mathbb{O}$ are the regular and institutional communication relations among organizations.*

Consider for example the interaction between the police, courthouse and jail. The police monitors norm violations and sends those to the court. That communication concerns a norm violation and is thus institutional. The court then determines the compensation/sanction. In case of incarceration the court informs the jail for how long and under which circumstances an agent is detained. We call the communication between the court and the jail regular, as it is communication that does not concern institutional facts.

Organizations in the network are described by their observation capabilities and their control capabilities (Definition 3). The specification of what exactly the observe and control capabilities are will be part of future work. We do not intend to specify an observation/control logic here, as it is besides the point. The entailment operator $\vDash_{c/o}$ can be seen as a reasoning engine that gives us the answer whether some environment state is observable or controllable. A simple example of a capability description is a set of literals that represent the observables and controllables of an organization.

Definition 3 (Organization specification). *An organization is specified by a tuple $O = \langle \Gamma_{obs}, \Gamma_{con} \rangle \in \mathbb{O}$. Γ_{obs} is a specification of the observation capability of O. Γ_{con} is the specification of the control capability of O. Let φ and ψ be formulas denoting the state of the environment, $O \vDash_o \varphi$ indicates that φ can be locally observed by organization O. $O \vDash_c \psi$ indicates that ψ can be locally controlled by organization O.*

4.3 Enforcement

For norm enforcement it is needed to have the correct observation and control capabilities available. The presence of these capabilities can be local or available through communication. If the capabilities are not local then the regular communication relation is used. In case the capabilities are present, there is also a choice which organizations do the monitoring and which organizations do the sanctioning. This leads to a distinction between centralized and decentralized enforcement. Decentralized enforcement, where monitoring and sanctioning is performed by a number of organizations, uses the institutional communication relation. By splitting communication in regular and institutional communication we can clearly describe the distribution of control and observe capabilities and the distribution of enforcement.

We will define the characteristics of each possible way that norms can be enforced in a distributed organization. We begin with defining local and global monitoring and sanctioning in an organization that is part of the distributed organization. For a norm to be applicable it means that the norm can be monitored, and for a sanction to be applicable, it means that the sanction can be imposed. We assume that the sanctioning of violations is described in terms of what organizations can do. For instance, the highway organizations can ultimately only give fines and not force agents to pay them (though not paying a fine could result in the notification of some other authority that can).

Local application in an organization can only happen if the right observation and control capabilities are locally present. If a norm or sanction is locally applicable, then no communication needs to burden the network. For a norm to be locally monitorable in an organization it must be possible to locally observe all the occurring literals in the norm. Similarly for sanctions all occurring literals in the sanction must be locally controllable.

Definition 4 (Local monitoring and sanctioning). *Let N be a set of norms, S a set of sanctions and $\langle \mathbb{O}, R_r, R_i \rangle$ a distributed organization. Then, we say that $O \in \mathbb{O}$ can locally monitor N iff $\forall (\varphi \Rightarrow v) \in N : O \vDash_o \varphi$, and $O \in \mathbb{O}$ can locally sanction violations using S iff $\forall (v \Rightarrow \psi) \in S : O \vDash_c \psi$.*

Global monitoring and sanctioning concerns subparts of the network of organizations (Definition 5). An organization O can globally monitor a norm or apply a sanction if the reachable organizations for O together have the required capabilities. Given the regular communication relation among organizations, one can treat observable/controllable atoms in a connected network as distributed knowledge/controllability. Again the norm and sanctions look alike in their application. For norms the required literals for determining violation must be locally observable, or observable in a connected organization. All occurring literals in a sanction must be locally controllable or controllable in a connected organization. In the following we use $lit(\varphi)$ for the set of literals that occur in φ.

Definition 5 (Global monitoring and sanctioning). *Let N be a set of norms, S a set of sanctions and $\langle \mathbb{O}, R_r, R_i \rangle$ a distributed organization. Then, we say $O \in \mathbb{O}$ can globally monitor N iff*
$\forall (\varphi \Rightarrow v) \in N, \forall l \in lit(\varphi), \exists (O, O') \in R_r : O' \vDash_o l.$
We also say that $O \in \mathbb{O}$ can globally sanction violations using S iff
$\forall (v \Rightarrow \psi) \in S, \forall l \in lit(\psi), \exists (O, O') \in R_r : O' \vDash_c l.$

Observation 1. If R_r is reflexive, then local applicable norms and sanctions are also globally applicable because the pair $(O, O) \in R_r$ for all $O \in \mathbb{O}$ can globally apply norms/sanctions that are locally applicable by O.

To enforce norms, first monitoring takes place to determine violations. Then sanctioning takes place to compensate for the violations that occurred. There is a choice whether this process is centralized or decentralized in organizations.

Central enforcement of norms in an organization means that both the monitoring and the sanctioning of norms/violations is done by the same organization. The monitoring and sanctioning can however be either locally or globally done

(Definition 6). Note that for a norm set N to be enforceable using S it must hold that for each norm $\varphi \Rightarrow v \in N$ there must be at least one corresponding sanction $v \Rightarrow \psi \in S$, otherwise the violation cannot be sanctioned.

Definition 6 (Centralized enforcement). *Let N be a set of norms, S a set of sanctions and $\langle \mathbb{O}, R_r, R_i \rangle$ a distributed organization. $O \in \mathbb{O}$ can centrally enforce N by S iff O can locally or globally monitor N and O can locally or globally sanction violations using S.*

Decentralized enforcement entails that monitoring and sanctioning can happen in two different organizations. Though the organizations do have to be able to communicate about the detected violations (Definition 7).

Definition 7 (Decentralized enforcement). *Let N be a set of norms, S a set of sanctions and $\langle \mathbb{O}, R_r, R_i \rangle$ a distributed organization. $O \in \mathbb{O}$ and $O' \in \mathbb{O}$, $O \neq O'$, can decentrally enforce N by S iff $(O, O') \in R_i$ and O can locally or globally monitor N and O' can locally or globally sanction violations using S.*

Observation 2. If R_i is reflexive, then centrally enforceable norms and sanctions are also decentrally enforceable, because the pair $(O, O) \in R_i$ for all $O \in \mathbb{O}$. So if O can locally or globally monitor N and locally or globally sanction using S, then the pair (O, O) can do this decentrally.

Consider two organizations $O_1 = \langle \Gamma^1_{obs}, \Gamma^1_{con} \rangle$ and $O_2 = \langle \Gamma^2_{obs}, \Gamma^2_{con} \rangle$, which are connected in R_r and R_i. O_1 can monitor whether a car is driving too fast ($\Gamma^1_{obs} \models_o speed_{>130}$) and O_2 can issue a fine ($\Gamma^2_{con} \models_c fine$). Furthermore we have a norm $speed_{>130} \Rightarrow speeding$ and a sanction $speeding \Rightarrow fine$. O_1 can locally monitor the norm and globally sanction its violation. O_2 can globally monitor the norm and locally sanction its violation. Either organization can centrally enforce the norm, as both can locally or globally monitor and sanction it. But together they can also decentrally enforce the norm, in which case only the communication of a violation is required between the monitoring organization, and the one that applies the sanction rule.

A distribution of a set of norms and sanctions is a set of pairs that contain a subset of the norms and a subset of the sanctions. To be correctly enforced, each possible detection of a violation must be present in the distribution (i.e. all occurring norms must together be the set of all norms). But it must also be the case that if a violation is monitored, that then the sanction concerning that violation will always be imposed when the violation occurs. Thus for each norm and sanction concerning the same violation there must be a pair in the distribution such that both the norm and the sanction occur in the pair (Definition 8).

Definition 8 (Distribution). *Let (N, S) be a pair consisting of a set of norms N and a set of sanctions S. A distribution of (N, S) is a set $\{D_0, \ldots, D_n\}$, where $D_i = (N_i, S_i)$, $N_i \subseteq N$ and $S_i \subseteq S$. Furthermore, for each matching norm-sanction pair (n, s), $n \in N$, $s \in S$, we require the existence of $D_i = (N_i, S_i)$ in the distribution such that $n \in N_i$ and $s \in S_i$.*

We have defined enforcement of norms and their sanctions for a specific organization or a pair of organizations, but not yet for the distributed organization as a whole. In Definition 9 we define whether norms and their sanctions are enforceable in a distributed organization. This is the case if there is a distribution such that each of the norm subset and sanction subset pairs in that distribution are enforceable by some organization or pair of organizations.

Definition 9 (Global enforcement). *Let N be a set of norms, S a set of sanctions and $\langle \mathbb{O}, R_r, R_i \rangle$ a distributed organization. $\langle \mathbb{O}, R_r, R_i \rangle$ can globally enforce N by S iff there is a distribution $\{D_0, \ldots, D_n\}$ of (N, S) such that for each D_i there either exists an organization $O \in \mathbb{O}$ that can centrally enforce D_i or there exists a pair of organizations $(O, O') \in R_i$ such that (O, O') can decentrally enforce D_i.*

4.4   Subtypes of Enforcement

We have discussed local/global availability of observe and control capabilities, and we have discussed centralized versus decentralized enforcement. In Definition 9 we required a distribution for which each element was either centralized or decentralized enforced, and each norm/violation was either locally or globally monitored/sanctioned. But we can get some interesting properties of enforcement by ruling out types of enforcement and the types of norm and sanction application. We do this by restricting the communication.

Global monitoring and sanctioning (Definition 5) is impossible if $R_r = \emptyset$, so only local monitoring and sanctioning (Definition 4) then remains. This is useful if the data for norm monitoring is very big in an application. The communication of violation atoms is likely to be very cheap.

Decentralized enforcement (Definition 7) is impossible if $R_i = \emptyset$, so only centralized enforcement (Definition 6) then remains. This kind of enforcement is useful because we do not need to create an institutional infrastructure. It also increases security as important data concerning enforcement (the violations) cannot be intercepted.

If both global monitoring and sanctioning, and decentralized enforcement are impossible, i.e. $R_r = \emptyset$ and $R_i = \emptyset$ then there is no communication needed for enforcement. This kind of enforcement is needed if we want to implement norms using a language that does not allow for inter-organizational communications (such as 2OPL [2] and NPL [9]).

Observation 3. If $\langle \mathbb{O}, R_r, \emptyset \rangle$ can globally enforce N by S then no subsets of N and S can be decentrally enforced. If $\langle \mathbb{O}, \emptyset, R_r \rangle$ can globally enforce N by S then only local monitoring and sanctioning of N and S respectively is possible. If $\langle \mathbb{O}, \emptyset, \emptyset \rangle$ can globally enforce N by S then only local monitoring and sanctioning of N and S respectively is possible and only centralized enforcement.

5   Assigning Norms and Sanctions to Organizations

In an organization each norm has to be monitored. This requires computational effort. Similarly, each sanction to be imposed costs computational effort as well.

In a distributed organization we have the possibility to distribute this computational effort in the network of organizations. We want to assign to organizations norms and sanctions that they must monitor/impose.

The assignment of a global set of norms and sanctions to local organizations should provide the information about which organization exactly monitors which norms and which sanctions. We define this by creating two sets of pairs. The first set couples organizations with norms, the second set couples organizations with sanctions. All the given norms and sanctions must be assigned to at least one organization. Furthermore, all assigned norms must be monitorable in the organizations to which they are assigned. And equally all assigned sanctions must be imposable by the organizations to which they are assigned. Lastly it is needed that each detectable violation can reach the sanction that handles that violation.

Definition 10 (Assignment). *Let (N, S) be a pair consisting of a set of norms N and a set of sanctions S and $\langle \mathbb{O}, R_r, R_i \rangle$ a distributed organization. An assignment A is a pair (A_N, A_S), where $A_N \subseteq \mathbb{O} \times N$ and $A_S \subseteq \mathbb{O} \times S$. For every $(O, n) \in A_N$ and $(O, s) \in A_S$, n can be monitored locally or globally by O and s can be locally or globally used by O to sanction. Furthermore for each matching norm-sanction pair (n, s), $n \in N$, $s \in S$, either there exists an $O \in \mathbb{O}$ s.t. $(O, n) \in A_n$ and $(O, s) \in A_S$ and O can centrally enforce n by s, or there exists $(O, O') \in R_i$ s.t. $(O, n) \in A_n$ and $(O', s) \in A_S$ and (O, O') can decentrally enforce n by s.*

Observation 4. Let N be a set of norms, S a set of sanctions and $\langle \mathbb{O}, R_r, R_i \rangle$ a distributed organization. (A_N, A_S) is an assignment if and only if $\langle \mathbb{O}, R_r, R_i \rangle$ can globally enforce N by S. An assignment can be transformed into a distribution $\{D_0, \ldots, D_n\}$ by creating for each matching norm-sanction pair (n_i, s_i), $(O, n_i) \in A_N$, $(O, s_i) \in A_S$, a distribution element $D_i = \{(\{n_i\}), (\{s_i\})\}$. Likewise the distribution $\{D_0, \ldots, D_n\}$ that is required for global enforcement can be transformed in an assignment. We know that for each matching norm pair (n, s) there exists a $D_i = (N_i, S_i)$ and $n \in N_i$ and $s \in S_i$. We also know that there exists an organization O s.t. O can centrally enforce n by s or two organizations O, O' s.t. they can decentrally enforce n by s. In the first case the assignment will contain $(O, n) \in A_N$ and $(O, s) \in A_S$. In the second case the assignment will contain $(O, n) \in A_N$ and $(O', s) \in A_S$.

6   Example Revisited

In Sect. 1 we described a distributed organization to regulate the traffic on highways. The example norm was *"if the traffic density is high, then cars are only allowed to drive on the priority lane when they have a permit"*. The sanction for riding on a priority lane when it is forbidden is a fine. We will model this scenario with the following atoms w.r.t. an arbitrary vehicle:

– d_1 and d_2 stand for *"high density"* on highway 1 or 2 respectively.

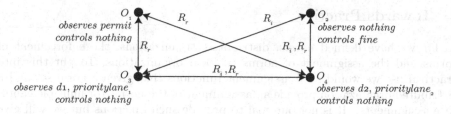

Fig. 2. More detailed depiction of the smart roads example. Arrows are labeled with whether they are regular or institutional communication lines or both.

- *prioritylane$_1$* and *prioritylane$_2$* stand for "*the vehicle is driving on the priority lane*" on highway 1 and 2 respectively.
- *permit* stands for "*the vehicle has a permit*".
- *fine* stands for the "*the vehicle is fined*".

The norm holds for both segments. We have two counts-as rules for the norm and a sanction rule:

- $c_1 = d_1 \wedge \neg permit \wedge prioritylane_1 \Rightarrow v.$
- $c_2 = d_2 \wedge \neg permit \wedge prioritylane_2 \Rightarrow v.$
- $s = v \Rightarrow fine.$

The distributed organization is formally $\langle \mathbb{O}, R_r, R_i \rangle$ where:

- $\mathbb{O} = \{O_1 : \langle \Gamma^1_{obs}, \Gamma^1_{con} \rangle, O_2 : \langle \Gamma^2_{obs}, \Gamma^2_{con} \rangle, O_3 : \langle \Gamma^3_{obs}, \Gamma^3_{con} \rangle, O_4 : \langle \Gamma^4_{obs}, \Gamma^4_{con} \rangle\}.$
- $\Gamma^1_{obs} \vDash_o permit$, $\Gamma^2_{con} \vDash_c fine$, $\Gamma^3_{obs} \vDash_o d_1$, $\Gamma^3_{obs} \vDash_o prioritylane_1$, $\Gamma^4_{obs} \vDash_o d_2$, $\Gamma^4_{obs} \vDash_o prioritylane_2$ (and similar for each negation of atoms).
- R_r and R_i are depicted in Fig. 2.

Let us consider the norm-sanction pair (c_1, s). The norm is not locally monitorable as no organization can locally observe d_1, *permit* and *prioritylane$_1$*. Therefore there can be no local monitoring. The sanction is locally imposable by organization O_2, because all literals (i.e. *fine*) are locally controllable by O_2. The norm is centrally and decentrally enforceable. For instance O_3 can centrally enforce the norm because together with O_1 it can globally monitor the norm, and together with O_2 globally sanction the norm. The pair O_2 and O_4 is able to decentrally enforce the norm (among other pairs). O_4 would then globally monitor it with O_1 and O_3, and O_2 would locally sanction violations. The pair O_1 and O_2 is not able to decentrally enforce the norm. Though O_1 can globally monitor all necessary data, it has not the possibility to send violations to O_2.

For norm assignments there are several options. However from all the possible assignments there will be some more preferable in practice. As an illustration, if we assign the norm and the sanction (c_1, s) to O_3 and (c_2, s) to O_4, then there is no need for communication of violations. But we could also assign c_1 to O_3, c_2 to O_4 and s to O_2. In that case the sanction rule can be maintained together with the organization that imposes it, which from a designer's perspective is preferable.

7 Towards Practice

So far we have defined norms, distributed organizations, the enforcement of norms and the assignment of norms to local organizations. To put this into practical use we would need assignment functions that given a norm set and a distributed organization provide an assignment of the norms (or multiple candidate assignments). It is not our goal to provide such functions but we will give some examples of how they are related to our definition of norm and sanction assignments.

The solution space of assignment functions is the set of all possible assignments as per Definition 10. Depending on the requirements of a distributed organization, the used distribution function can access a subset of the solution space. For instance let (A_N, A_S) be an assignment of norms consider the following restrictions:

1. $\forall n \in N : \exists!(O, n) \in A_N$ and $\forall s \in S : \exists!(O, s) \in A_S$
2. $\forall n \in N : \exists(O, n) \in A_N, (O', n) \in A_N : O \neq O'$ and
   $\forall s \in S : \exists(O, s) \in A_S, (O', s) \in A_S : O \neq O'$

Assignments under the first restriction have no redundancy in the assignment of norms and sanctions, which increases efficiency. Assignments under the second restriction have at least two organizations per norm and sanction. This increases robustness of the distributed organization. If one organization fails then the norms are still properly enforced. It depends on the designer of the distributed organization which kind of properties should hold for assignments. Having a clear definition of assignments helps to think about what properties are possible.

If the accessed subset of the assignment solution space is not a singleton set, then an ordering is needed to determine the best assignments. For instance if we have a low bandwidth in the communication channels among organizations then those assignments are preferred where as little as possible communication is needed. Such a preference can be captured by for instance counting the amount of norm assignments where the norm cannot be locally monitored.

In our definition of global monitoring and sanctioning (Definition 5) we have not touched upon the issue of how to exactly get information from one organization to another. We stated the conditions such that it is possible. In an implementation it would be required to use a distribution annotation such that organizations know where to get which information. Future research can expand upon these issues.

8 Discussion

Norms were our main focus in this paper. We can also incorporate other organizational aspects. For instance there are interesting aspects to the use of constitutive norms when it comes to distribution. Constitutive norms relate brute facts to institutional facts. E.g. certain vehicles will count as trucks. The brute facts that are required for applying constitutive norms can also be locally or globally acquired. For monitoring and sanctioning in an organization the applicability of norms/sanctions would depend on whether the used institutional facts in those norms/sanctions can be derived by that organization.

We represented norms with counts-as rules that do not have context. Usually counts-as rules have the form $A \Rightarrow B\ in\ C$, where C is the context in which A counts as B. Context specifies under which circumstances obligations hold. For instance an obligation to have a maximum velocity of 120 km/h might only hold at daytime. Adding context to our framework would require a description of how the context is evaluated and how the required information for this is gathered. If the information is possibly distributed then the applicability of norms and sanctions can alter.

Also empowerment as investigated in [1] forms an interesting topic in the context of distributed organizations. If only a selection of organizations is empowered to determine an institutional fact, then this poses limits to the possible assignments of norms. Also information access among organizations can differ. We can filter out assignments where certain organizations need to acquire information for an observation to which they have no access. A topic that is related to empowerment is the notion of hierarchies among organizations. For instance it might be interesting to let organizations delegate monitoring and sanctioning tasks to other organizations.

We have split communication in two different communication channels to clearly distinguish different types of distribution. The assumptions we made about communication, such as costless data transfer, do not allow for a sophisticated interaction model between organizations. Also with an eye on earlier mentioned topics such as hierarchies and communication restrictions, it is necessary to expand upon this in future work.

Lastly, we have paid little attention to agents. We followed lines of earlier research where organizations can observe and act on their own as entities, rather than being implemented endogenously inside agents. This does leave questions open such as whether norm awareness in distributed organizations is different from centralized organizations. Or if an organization depends on an agent to control an environment state, what happens if that agent leaves? We do not have readily available answers to such questions. Though the latter is related to capability dynamics, which is something we aim to look at.

9 Future Work

Our work is to be a basis for further investigations of distributed organizations. In this paper we have described their nature and some considerations when one designs a distributed organization. There are still many research opportunities.

We saw in the example scenario that the textual norm was converted to atoms which are locally available in at least one organization. This indicates that there is some conversion between an abstract description of norms, which has to be translated to enforceable concrete norms in the distributed organization. We still want to investigate this translation.

In the future we also want to move the work from the abstract level to more concrete levels such as programming frameworks for organizations. When doing so we want to also include organizational dynamics. A given infrastructure does not have to be permanent. We can imagine some distributed organization to be expandable with new organizations and communication relations among them. For instance the highway network can be expanded with new highway organizations, or become connected to other organizations. It would be interesting to investigate enforcement under the possibility of a dynamic distributed organization. Our final goal is to have a running network of organizations that in case of failing organizations or dynamic circumstances can restore itself and keep enforcing the norms.

10   Conclusions

To keep up with the decentralizing trend in software engineering it is important to investigate the use of distributed organizations. A distributed organization is described as a network of organizations. Each organization has observation capabilities to observe the environment and control capabilities to manipulate the environment. Norms have to be monitored for determining whether violation has occurred, and their violations have to be sanctioned to be enforced.

We have described the possible ways in which the enforcement overhead of norms can be distributed in a distributed organization. There are different approaches for the enforcement of norms. With centralized enforcement an organization applies both the norms and the sanctions. With decentralized enforcement a pair of organizations together enforces norms by letting one monitor the norms and the other impose the sanctions. Using these definitions we have described what proper norm assignments are. The result can be used as a basis for further investigations of distributed organizations and as a guideline for functions that produce assignments of norms for distributed organizations. In future work we plan to move the results to other organization aspects beside norms and towards a more concrete level.

Acknowledgments. We thank the reviewers for insightful comments and discussion points. This research is funded by Next Generation Infrastructures, http://www. nextgenerationinfrastructures.eu.

References

1. Cliffe, O., De Vos, M., Padget, J.: Specifying and reasoning about multiple institutions. In: Noriega, P., Vázquez-Salceda, J., Boella, G., Boissier, O., Dignum, V., Fornara, N., Matson, E. (eds.) COIN 2006. LNCS (LNAI), vol. 4386, pp. 67–85. Springer, Heidelberg (2007)
2. Dastani, M., Tinnemeier, N., Meyer, J.-J.C.: A programming language for normative multi-agent systems. In: Dignum, V. (ed.) Multi-Agent Systems: Semantics and Dynamics of Organizational Models, pp. 397–417. IGI Global, Hershey (2008)

3. de Brito, M., Hübner, J.F., Bordini, R.H.: Analysis of the use of events and states as brute facts in modelling of institutional facts. In: Balke, T., Dignum, F., van Riemsdijk, M.B., Chopra, A.K. (eds.) COIN 2013. LNCS (LNAI), vol. 8386, pp. 177–192. Springer, Heidelberg (2014)
4. Dignum, V.: A model for organizational interaction: based on agents, founded in logic. Ph.D. Thesis, Universiteit Utrecht (2004)
5. Dybalova, D., Testerink, B., Dastani, M., Logan, B.: A framework for programming norm-aware multi-agent systems. In: Balke, T., Dignum, F., van Riemsdijk, M.B., Chopra, A.K. (eds.) COIN 2013. LNCS (LNAI), vol. 8386, pp. 364–380. Springer, Heidelberg (2014)
6. Esteva, M.: Islander: an electronic institutions editor. In: AAMAS'02: Proceedings of the First International Conference on Autonomous Agents and Multiagent Systems, pp. 1045–1052. ACM Press (2002)
7. Gaertner, D., Garc'ia-camino, A., Noriega, P., Vasconcelos, W.: Distributed norm management in regulated multi-agent systems. In: AAMAS'07: Proceedings of the 6th International Conference on Autonomous Agents and Multiagent Systems, pp. 624–631 (2007)
8. Haynes, C., Miles, S., Luck, M.: Monitoring the impact of norms upon organisational performance: a simulation approach. In: Balke, T., Dignum, F., van Riemsdijk, M.B., Chopra, A.K. (eds.) COIN 2013. LNCS (LNAI), vol. 8386, pp. 103–119. Springer, Heidelberg (2014)
9. Hübner, J.F., Boissier, O., Bordini, R.H.: A normative programming language for multi-agent organisations. Ann. Math. Artif. Intell. **62**, 27–53 (2011)
10. Hübner, J.F., Sichman, J.S., Boissier, O.: Moise+: towards a structural, functional, and deontic model for MAS organization. In: AAMAS'02: Proceedings of the First International Conference on Autonomous Agents and Multiagent Systems, pp. 501–502, New York, NY, USA (2002)
11. Minsky, N.H., Ungureanu, V.: Law-governed interaction: a coordination and control mechanism for heterogeneous distributed systems. ACM Trans. Softw. Eng. Methodol. (TOSEM) **9**, 273–305 (2000)
12. Okuyama, F.Y., Bordini, R.H., da Rocha Costa, A.C.: A distributed normative infrastructure for situated multi-agent organisations. In: AAMAS'08: Proceedings of the 7th International Joint Conference on Autonomous Agents and Multiagent Systems, vol. 3, pp. 1501–1504, Richland, SC (2008)
13. Scarle, J.R.: Construction of Social Reality. Free Press, New York (1995)
14. Testerink, B., Dastani, M.: A norm language for distributed organizations. In: BNAIC'12: Proceedings of the 24th Belgium-Netherlands Artificial Intelligence Conference, pp. 234–241 (2012)

Contextualized Institutions in Virtual Organizations

Tingting Li[1][(✉)], Jie Jiang[2], Huib Aldewereld[2], Marina De Vos[1],
Virginia Dignum[2], and Julian Padget[1]

[1] University of Bath, Bath, UK
{t.li,mdv,jap}@cs.bath.ac.uk
[2] TU Delft, Delft, Netherlands
{jie.jiang,h.m.aldewereld,m.v.dignum}@tudelft.nl

Abstract. Within a virtual organization, more than one institution might be involved in the regulation of actors' behavior. Each institution specifies a set of norms covering a specific aspect of the problem domain with a governance scope defining its remit. Together, they govern the participants and reflect the objectives of the organization. With actors' behavior being simultaneously regulated by more than one institution, normative conflicts can appear. In this paper, we formalize the notion of governance scope and propose a computational approach to identify weak and strong norm conflicts in virtual organizations. This is achieved by explicitly modeling the governance scopes of institutions through context models. We illustrate our approach by means of a case study concerning food security in international trade.

1 Introduction

Virtual organizations (VOs) [11] can employ various institutions to cover different aspects of regulating the behaviour of the participating actors in order to achieve the VO's goals. The norms that make up an institution inherently serve to restrict its applicability, but the variables, in terms of which those norms are expressed, are also typically intended to be restricted to specific, meaningful ranges within the domain being modelled. That is to say, some combinations of event and metadata are meaningful and others are not. We use the term *governance scope* to describe this set of concrete observable/exogenous events and associated values (event metadata) that can affect the state of an institution and hence characterize the situations (being particular combinations of contextual information such as time, location, weather, relations, and system states) in which a given institution has competence.

When an event occurs, several institutions might respond to regulate the behaviour. Regardless of the outcome of the individual regulation processes, we call this situation a *governance overlap*. The activation of multiple institutions can cause problems, in that a single event might be interpreted differently and could result in conflicting consequences. For example, when a Dutch citizen applies for a visa to the US, several institutions might be triggered, e.g.,

T. Balke et al. (Eds.): COIN 2013, LNAI 8386, pp. 136–154, 2014.
DOI: 10.1007/978-3-319-07314-9_8, © Springer International Publishing Switzerland 2014

US embassy, Dutch government, and a conflict could exist between information requirements from the US embassy and privacy policies from the Dutch government. We contend that in VOs governed by multiple institutions, the existence of normative conflicts cannot be avoided just by defining mutually exclusive deontic expressions, since that would preclude any institutionally common event. Clearly, careful definition of institutional competence is needed and its overlap between different institutions is a necessary precondition for norm conflicts in VOs. Consequently, we regard the process of designing an institution as not only the definition of a set of norms but also the characterization of its governance scope, i.e., what kinds of situations are under control of the institution, since this is what gives the institution its 'footprint'. That is, the same set of norms with different governance scopes results in different *contextualized institutions*. Furthermore, the occurrence of external events, that fall within the governance scope of an institution, initiates state transitions for that institution. In this way, different sets of norms in the VO are activated to regulate behaviour.

This paper introduces an approach that: (i) formalizes the governance scope of an institution through context models and hence captures the relations between institutions, and (ii) provides a mechanism to analyze institutional governance scope, as a precursor to detecting norm conflicts. We operationalize our approach by adapting an existing computational model, which we then use to demonstrate how our proposal works using a case study.

The rest of the paper is organized as follows. In the next section, we present a simplified scenario concerning food security from the domain of international trade. In Sect. 3, we introduce the formal model of the *contextualized institution*. In Sect. 4, we discuss the relations between *contextualized institutions* in VOs and define two categories of *norm conflict*. Section 5 presents an operational model of contextualized institutions, which is then used to identify norm conflicts through a case study in Sect. 6. Related work is discussed in Sect. 8. Finally, we conclude and identify directions for future work in Sect. 9.

2   Scenario

The World Customs Organization (WCO) has defined a framework called the Authorized Economic Operator (AEO) program [1] in order to address the tensions created by the simultaneous growth in international trade and requirements for increased security. The European Communities' implementation of AEO permits various customs administrations to grant AEO certificates to qualified companies under which they enjoy special privileges. Taking the scenario of importing food from a country outside the EU to the Netherlands, a number of governmental authorities and companies are involved, which together form a virtual organization. Such a virtual organization is governed by different sets of regulations concerning different aspects of the food importation process. For example, the EU has a set of general regulations in which one is that the food authority is *obliged* to carry out a food quality inspection. With the introduction of the AEO programme, the Dutch government introduced new regulations for

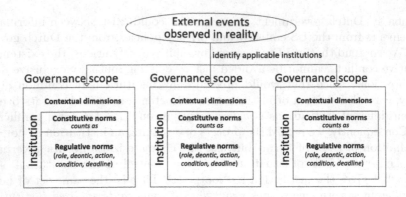

Fig. 1. Governance scopes in virtual organization.

the specific domain of AEO-certified goods in order to improve trading efficiency. For example, one regulation is that a food authority is *forbidden* to carry out a food quality inspection, if customs has already done so. Additionally, companies such as container terminals play an important role and bring their own regulations, e.g., a regulation at one container terminal is that carriers are *obliged* to transport their goods thence within two days after unloading. Given these different sets of regulations, it is essential to capture not only their individual functionalities but also their interrelations concerning the governance of real world events.

3   Formal Model

The virtual organization in Fig. 1 has three parts: (i) *external events* observed in the real world, each of which has associated contextual information (ii) *institutions* comprising sets of norms, in which *constitutive norms* translate external events into institutional events which are further mapped to institutional states, and *regulative norms* (permissions, obligations, prohibitions) react to the occurrence of institutional events and states, and (iii) *governance scopes* that delineate the control boundary of institutions through a set of contextual dimensions. With governance scopes, contextualized institutions are built, which facilitates the identification of applicable institutions for a given event. We now explain each of these components in more detail.

To capture the contextual information of events and the governance scope of institutions, we introduce the concept of *contextual dimension*.

Definition 1 (Contextual Dimension). *A contextual dimension D_i, $i \in \{1, ..., n\}$ is a situational variable whose values are from a value set V_i comprising a set of atomic values.*

Contextual dimensions concern, but are not restricted to, aspects such as individuality, activity, time, location, and relation [17]. The values of each contextual dimension are assumed to come from some structured domain. For example, we can have a contextual dimension of $D_i = Location$ with a value set $V_i = \{NL, France, Germany, ...\}$.

3.1 Events

We differentiate two kinds of events. One is external events observed in reality and the other is institutional events defined by institutions, which serve as the triggers of institutional evolution. A basic element of an event is an action and other contextual information, such as who, when and where the action is performed, can also be included to refine the occurrence of the event. Therefore, we define an event as an action associated with a set of contextual elements, which permits us to correlate events with the customized contextual dimensions of governance scopes.

Definition 2 (Event). *An event e is a tuple $\langle action, c \rangle$ where*

- *action indicates the fact or process of doing something,*
- $c \in \prod_i V_i, i \in \{1, \ldots, n\}$ *characterizes the situation where the event occurs, with respect to a flexible set of contextual dimensions.*

The contextual dimensions that are used to characterize the occurrence of an event is not fixed, i.e., c can relate to an arbitrary set of contextual dimensions. For example, given two dimensions $\{Location, Time\}$, an event could be $e = \langle eat, \langle McDonald's, 12pm \rangle \rangle$, indicating that the action of eating occurs at the time of 12pm and at the location of McDonald's.

3.2 Governance Scope

Governance scopes are used to delineate the control boundary of institutions, determining which situations are under their control. To capture the governance scope of an institution, we adopt the context model proposed by Giunchiglia and Bouquet [8]. The model is based on three elements: a set of parameters, a value for each parameter, and a state of affairs or a domain, which draws a sort of boundary between what is in and what is out.

Correspondingly, we characterize a governance scope as a set of contextual dimensions. Different contextual dimensions indicate different ways of establishing the governance scope of an institution. For example, an institution can specify its governance scope by defining a contextual dimension of *Individuality*, indicating that as long as the entities evolved in an event belongs to a set of individuals, the institution has the right to govern the behaviour. Similarly for *Location*, an institution can indicate that as long as the observed location of an event belongs to a set of locations, the behaviour is in the governance scope of the institution.

Definition 3 (Governance Scope). *A governance scope gs is a tuple $\langle Action, C \rangle$ where*

- *Action is a set of actions,*
- $C \in \prod_i 2^{V_i}, i \in \{1, \ldots, n\}$, *relating to a flexible set of contextual dimensions.*

It can be seen that gs specifies a multi-dimensional space by assigning each contextual dimension a set of values it accepts. Note that we separate the set of actions from the contextual dimensions only to match the definition of event. A governance scope might have no constraint on a particular contextual dimension. In this case, a value of universal set denoted as U is assigned to that dimension and we consider the governance scope covers the whole value set of that contextual dimension. For example, a governance scope could be $\langle Action = \{import, export\}, \langle Location = \{NL\}, Time = U \rangle \rangle$.

3.3   Institution Model

Following Searle's notion of the construction of social reality [13], we differentiate two kinds of institutional norms, i.e., constitutive norms and regulative norms. Constitutive norms specify how an institution (and hence all of the members of the society associated with it) should interpret the events happened in reality, while regulative norms are used to regulate the behaviour of agents in terms of permissions, obligations and prohibitions.

Constitutive norms in our institution model are of two kinds. One is to translate external events to institutional events, denoted by function f_{CA}. The other is to derive institutional states from institutional events subject to certain institutional states, expressed by function $\mathcal{C}$. Adapted from [3], we use the concept of fluents $\mathcal{F}$, i.e., a set of facts, to characterize institutional states. Definition 4 gives the formalization.

Definition 4 (Constitutive Norm). *A constitutive norm is defined as* $n_c = \langle \mathcal{E}_{ex}, \mathcal{E}_{inst} \rangle | \langle \mathcal{E}_{inst}, \Sigma_i, \Sigma_{i+1} \rangle$, *constructed from two functions:*

- *institutional mapping function* $f_{CA} : \mathcal{E}_{ex} \rightarrow \mathcal{E}_{inst}$ *which relates external events* $\mathcal{E}_{ex}$ *to institutional events* $\mathcal{E}_{inst}$,
- *institutional consequence function* $\mathcal{C} : \mathcal{E}_{inst} \times \Sigma_i \rightarrow \Sigma_{i+1}$ *in which* $\Sigma_i, \Sigma_{i+1} = 2^{\mathcal{F} \cup \neg \mathcal{F}}$ *respectively indicate the current and successor institutional states.*

Predicated on institutional events and states, regulative norms specify a set of dos and don'ts. Adapting the *ADICO* syntax proposed by Ostrom [12], we give the definition of a *Regulative Norm*.

Definition 5 (Regulative Norm). *A regulative norm is defined as a tuple* $n_r = \langle role, deontic, action, condition, deadline \rangle$ *such that:*

- *role indicates the type of entities to whom the norm applies;*
- *deontic indicates the deontic type of the norm, i.e., Permitted, Obliged or Forbidden;*
- *action specifies the particular institutional action to which the deontic is assigned;*

- *condition is expressed as $\langle \Sigma, E \rangle$, where Σ describes the states under which the norm holds and E is a sequence of events.*
- *deadline, expressed as an event, describes the latest time by which the norm (usually obligations) should be complied with otherwise a violation is generated.*

From the definition, we can see that a regulative norm is a conditional deontic expression with a deadline, which indicates that when the *condition* is fulfilled, agents enacting the *role* have a permission, obligation or prohibition to perform the *action* before the *deadline*. If a regulative norm does not specify a particular role, the default value is for all participants. Condition and deadline can also be empty, indicating the norm always holds under any conditions. Obligations may be assigned a deadline event, i.e. the *action* is obliged to perform before the deadline event occurs. In particular, obligations and prohibitions may have corresponding sanctions when the norms are violated. Sanctions are triggered when violations are detected. In this sense, the violation of certain norms serve as the conditions of other norms about sanctions.

Roles specified in regulative norms are enacted by real world actors. When an external event occurs, constitutive norms create a link between the actors in reality and the roles they enact in an institution. In this sense, the identity information of actors captured in the contextual information of external events are linked to institutional roles.

As stated before, institutions are not only a set of norms but also characterized by governance scopes which reflect their control boundaries. Therefore, we introduce the definition of *Contextualized Institution*.

Definition 6 (Contextualized Institution). *A contextualized Institution is defined as a tuple $\mathcal{I} = \langle \Sigma_0, \mathcal{F}, gs, CN, RN \rangle$, where*

- Σ_0 *indicates the initial state of the institution,*
- $\mathcal{F}$ *is a set of facts, characterizing institutional states,*
- *gs is the governance scope of the institution,*
- *CN is a set of constitutive norms,*
- *RN is a set of regulative norms.*

Each institution is assigned an initial state specifying where the institution starts. Associated with a governance scope, an institution identifies all the situations that are under its control. The set of constitutive norms CN, on the one hand, connects external events to the institution in the sense that external events *counts-as* institutional events constrained by the governance scope, and on the other hand, drives institutional state evolution. Given the institutional events and states, the set of regulative norms RN activates corresponding permissions, obligations and prohibitions so that the real world behavior can be regulated. Given an external event, we first use the values of its contextual dimensions to determine whether the event falls in the governance scope of an institution. If so, the event will be (partially) translated to institutional events since some of the contextual information might not be relevant for regulative norms and are only needed for the determination of governance scopes.

Given sequences of events occurring in reality, institutions relate the effects to the conditions of its regulative norms. In this way, institutions can respond to the real world behavior by initiating and terminating some of the regulative norms. Details about the dynamics of institutions will be explained in Sect. 5.

However, since regulative norms are based on institutional events, it is necessary to trace back the originating external events when determining the behavior in the real world that regulative norms refer to. Therefore, we defined *Reverse CountsAs Function* as below:

Definition 7 (Reverse CountsAs Function $\tilde{f}_{CA}$). *Given an institutional event e' and a set of constitutive norms CN, $\tilde{f}_{CA}(e') = \{e | \langle e, e' \rangle \in CN\}$.*

It can be seen that $\tilde{f}_{CA}$ maps the responses of the institution to the reality so that the real world behavior can be addressed and hence governed.

4   Institutions in Virtual Organizations

Individual institutions are designed originally for their own objectives and thus have specific governance scopes. As long as the institutions are internally consistent, they can successfully operate independently. In virtual organizations, however, when interactions are governed by multiple institutions, mutually exclusive norms might be provided from the institutions with overlapping governance scope. Therefore, we aim to detect such kind of conflicts in VOs.

4.1   Collective Institutions

Figure 2 shows how institutions evolve with a sequence of events occurred in a virtual organization. At the initial state Σ_0, each institution of the virtual organization is initialized. When an event occurs, the institutions whose governance scope covers that event will be activated.

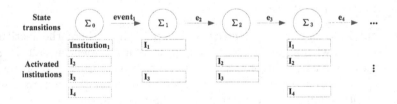

Fig. 2. Institutions.

We can see that at different time instants, there are different sets of institutions activated by the same event. That is, the contextual information of an event simultaneously maps to the governance scope of some institutions. To represent these simultaneously activated institutions, we introduce the concept of *Collective Institution Set* in Definition 8.

Definition 8 (Collective Institution Set). *In a virtual organization governed by a set of institutions* $\{\mathcal{I}_1, \ldots, \mathcal{I}_m\}$, $\mathcal{I}_j = \langle \Sigma_0^j, \mathcal{F}_j, gs_j, CN_j, RN_j \rangle$, $1 \leq j \leq m$, *given an event* e *occurred at time instant* k, *a collective institution set is defined as* $\mathcal{V}_k = \{\mathcal{I}_j | action_e \in A_{gs_j}, and\ \forall D_i, \pi_{V_i}(c_e) \in \pi_{V_i}(gs_j), 1 \leq j \leq m\}$ *where* $\pi_{V_i}(c_e)$ *and* $\pi_{V_i}(gs_j)$ *respectively indicate the value (values) that the event* e *and the governance scope* gs_j *take for the contextual dimension* D_i.

At any time instant k, the set of all institutions whose governance scope covers the contextual information of the event that occurs at time k is called a collective institution set, indicating all the activated institutions given the occurrence of an event. The governance scopes of these institutions overlap with each other and thus they all have governance competence on the same event.

4.2   Governance Overlap

In a collective institution set, the overlap relation between governance scopes is indicated by the same substantive event covered by a set of institutions. Generally, the overlap relation is determined by the values of each contextual dimension with respect to different governance scopes. To represent the overlap between the governance scopes of different institutions, we introduce the concept of *Governance Overlap*.

Definition 9 (Governance Overlap). *Given two governance scopes* $gs = \langle A, C \rangle$, $gs' = \langle A', C' \rangle$, *the governance overlap between* gs *and* gs' *is defined as* $\Omega(gs, gs') = (A \cap A') \times \prod_i \pi_{V_i}(gs) \cap \pi_{V_i}(gs')$.

If $\Omega(gs, gs') \neq \varnothing$, we say gs and gs' have a non-empty overlap. Particularly, in a collective institution set $\mathcal{V}_k = \{\mathcal{I}_1, \ldots, \mathcal{I}_n\}$, $\forall \mathcal{I}_i \in \mathcal{V}_k, \forall \mathcal{I}_j \in \mathcal{V}_k, \Omega(gs_i, gs_j) \neq \varnothing$.

4.3   Norm Conflicts

When an event simultaneously activates multiple institutions with overlapping governance scopes, these institutions should be consistent with each other. However, since the individual institutions are designed originally for their own use, there might be conflicting norms between them. The focus of this paper is on the conflicts between regulative norms that are simultaneously applied to the same agent possibly enacting different roles in different institutions, but associated with inconsistent deontic modalities. Definition 10 illustrates the concept of *Norm Conflicts* considered in this paper.

Definition 10 (Norm Conflict). *Within a collective institution set* $\mathcal{V}_k = \{\mathcal{I}_1, \ldots, \mathcal{I}_n\}$, *a norm conflict can be defined between any two institutions* $\mathcal{I}_i, \mathcal{I}_j \in \mathcal{V}_k$, $\mathcal{I}_i = \langle \Sigma_0^i, \mathcal{F}_i, gs_i, CN_i, RN_i \rangle$ *and* $\mathcal{I}_j = \langle \Sigma_0^j, \mathcal{F}_j, gs_j, CN_j, RN_j \rangle$ *iff* $\exists \langle role_i, deontic_i, action_i, condition_i, deadline_i \rangle \in RN_i$, $\exists \langle role_j, deontic_j, action_j, condition_j, deadline_j \rangle \in RN_j$, *such that*

– *both* $condition_i$ *and* $condition_j$ *are fulfilled,*

- *neither deadline$_i$ nor deadline$_j$ has expired,*
- $\tilde{f}_{CA}(e'_i) \cap \tilde{f}_{CA}(e'_j) \neq \varnothing$ *where* $e'_i = \langle action_i, v_{i1}, \ldots, v_{im} \rangle \in \mathcal{E}^i_{inst}$,
  $e'_j = \langle action_j, v_{j1}, \ldots, v_{jn} \rangle \in \mathcal{E}^j_{inst}$,
- *if deontic$_i$ = P and deontic$_j$ = F, we term this conflict as a weak conflict,*
- *if deontic$_i$ = O and deontic$_j$ = F, we term this conflict as a strong conflict,*

As expressed in the definition, given any two institutions $\mathcal{I}_i$ and $\mathcal{I}_j$ within a collective institution set, if their governance scopes overlap somehow and there are two norms initiated by two institutions simultaneously, both of which refer to the same event in reality, but associated with contradictory deontic modalities, we term this situation as a norm conflict.

Specifically, we differentiate two kinds of norm conflicts, i.e., weak conflicts and strong conflicts. A weak conflict is defined between a permission (P) and a prohibition (F), which *might* lead to violation. That is, if the action specified in both of the norms is performed, the prohibition is violated, while if not, there will not be any violation. A strong conflict is defined between an obligation (O) and a prohibition (F), which *must* lead to violation no matter the action specified in both of the norms is performed or not. That is, if the specified action is performed, the prohibition is violated, while if not, the obligation is violated. Therefore, weak conflicts might be avoided as long as the specified actions are not performed, but strong conflicts cannot.

5   Operational Model

We adapt ideas from the institutional action language *InstAL* [3], to operationalize the normative framework of Sect. 3. For each individual institution, the modeling process defines an explicit governance scope and formalizes the norms (both constitutive and regulative) for each institution. Subsequent translation into a computational model allows users to verify the resulting institutional states against a sequence of external events.

The computational model is implemented by *Answer Set Programming (ASP)* [7], which is a declarative logic programming paradigm. *AnsProlog* is chosen here to be the language because several efficient solvers exist for it. The fundamental elements of *AnsProlog* are atoms assigned with truth values. Atoms can be negated by means of *negation as failure*. A literal in *AnsProlog* is either an atom or a negated atom, and then constitute rules of the general form : $a : -b_1, ..., b_m, not\ c_1, ..., not\ c_n$ where a, b_i and $not\ c_j$ are all atoms. The rule can be read intuitively as *if all atoms b_i are known/true, and no c_j is known/true, then a must be known/true*. Of the form, a is referred as the head of the rule while b_i and $not\ c_j$ are the body. Additionally, there are two special forms of rules: *facts* which have no body part and *constraints* that have no head part. *Constraints* are normally used to filter the results by specifying the undesirable features of solutions to the problem. A normal answer set program is denoted by a conjunction of rules. The results of the programs are represented by a set of answer sets. Each answer set is a minimal and consistent set of atoms assigned with truth values satisfying all the rules in the program and thus each answer set is a solution to the problem.

We build our operational model based on two basic elements fluents $\mathcal{F}$ and events $\mathcal{E}$. Fluents characterize institutional state, as a set of facts, and their presence denote that some facts are true, and their absence indicate the facts are false. Consequently, institutional states can be denoted by any combination of the fluents and their negated forms. Events, both external and institutional, are defined as a tuple and encoded as ev(a, v1, ...vn). For example, an event $\langle transport, terminal_a, AEO\ beef \rangle$ is encoded as ev(trans, ta, abf).

Governance scope gs has been introduced to build contextualized institutions. As defined in Sect. 3.2, the gs of an institution is represented as a tuple $\langle Action, C \rangle$. C is indicated by a set of contextual dimensions, each of which defines the set of values the contextual dimension can take with regard to this governance scope. Therefore, we model the gs of an institution by a set of action(a) indicating the governed actions, and a set of scope(i, v) describing the corresponding values for a specific dimension with index i. In this way, the gs of an institution is explicitly defined by a multi-dimensional space. In order to examine whether an external event is within the gs of an institution, we assume that the event contains a full set of the contextual dimensions as defined in gs and specified in the same order. Whether a gs covers an event e is determined by comparing their attached value(s) regarding the same contextual dimension, and finally yields governed(A, V1, ..., Vn) if the event is covered by gs.

Institutional state transitions are driven by the occurrence of external events $\mathcal{E}_{ex}$ starting from a specified initial state Δ. The evolution of institutional states is based on both constitutive norms(CN) and regulative norms (RN): (i) CN interprets observed external events $\mathcal{E}_{ex}$ as institutional events $\mathcal{E}_{inst}$ subjected to the governance scope. Afterwards, the generated institutional events promote the transitions of institutional states. (ii) RN specifies norms at certain institutional states. If the conditions are satisfied, norms about permissions, prohibitions and obligation are activated. While the deadlines expire, the norms are deactivated.

In Fig. 3, we illustrate the mapping from the formal model to *AnsProlog* literals. The atoms fluent(s) and ev(a, v1, ..., vn) encode the fluents and events respectively. To operationalize CN, firstly the corresponding institutional event is generated (occ) by an external event (obs) if being covered by gs. At the same time, a literal countAs is generated to reflect the generation relation between external entities and institutional entities, including actions and other contextual entities carried with events. All the observed and occurred events are considered as happened events happened(E, T). Moreover, CN also specifies the effects of institutional events. A state formula $\mathcal{X}(\Sigma, T)$ denotes the institutional states at time T, which is expressed by a set of holdsat(s, T) and not holdsat(s, T). Regarding regulative norms RN, three literals are defined to encode Permissions (norm(perm(a, r), T)), Prohibitions (norm(forb(a, r), T)) and Obligations (norm(obl(a, r), T)), holding at time T. Certain conditions ($EX(\Sigma, T)$) have to be satisfied at time T to activate a regulative norm, which requires a sequence of happened events ($\mathcal{H}(E, T)$). The fluents holding at the initial states Σ_0 are translated into holdsat(s0, 0).

$$s \in \Sigma \Leftrightarrow \texttt{fluent(s)}.$$
$$e : \langle a, v_1, ..., v_n \rangle \in \mathcal{E}_{ex} \Leftrightarrow \texttt{ev(a, v1, ..., vn)}.$$
$$e' : \langle ia, iv_1, ..., iv_n \rangle \in \mathcal{E}_{inst} \Leftrightarrow \texttt{ev(ia, iv1, ..., ivn)}.$$
$$gs = \langle A, R1, ..., Rn \rangle \Leftrightarrow \forall a \in A, \texttt{action(a)}. \ \forall v \in Ri, \texttt{scope(i, v)}.$$
$$\texttt{governed(A, V1, ..., Vn)} : - \texttt{action(A)},$$
$$\texttt{scope(1, V1), ..., scope(n, Vn)}.$$
$$\forall \langle \langle a, v_1, ..., v_n \rangle, \langle ia, iv_1, ..., iv_n \rangle \rangle \in CN \Leftrightarrow \texttt{occ(ev(ia, iv1, ..., ivn), T)} : - \texttt{obs(ev(a, v1, ..., vn), T)},$$
$$\texttt{governed(a, v1, ..., vn)}.$$
$$\texttt{countAs(ev(a, v1, ..., vn), ev(ia, iv1, ..., ivn), Inst), inst(Inst)}.$$
$$\forall \langle \langle ia, iv_1, ..., iv_n \rangle, \Sigma_t, \Sigma_{t+1} \rangle \in CN \Leftrightarrow \texttt{holdsat(s, T + 1)} : - \texttt{occ(ev(ia, iv1, ..., ivn), T)}, \mathcal{X}(\Sigma, T).$$
$$\texttt{happened(ev(a, v1, ..., vn), T)} : - \texttt{obs(ev(a, v1, ..., vn), T)}.$$
$$\texttt{happened(ev(ia, iv1, ..., ivn), T)} : - \texttt{occ(ev(ia, iv1, ..., ivn), T)}.$$
$$\forall n_r \in RN, n_r = \langle r, perm, a, \langle \Sigma, E \rangle \rangle \Leftrightarrow \texttt{norm(perm(a, r), T)} : - EX(\Sigma, T), \mathcal{H}(E, T), \texttt{action(a), role(r)}.$$
$$\forall n_r \in RN, n_r = \langle r, forb, a, \langle \Sigma, E \rangle \rangle \Leftrightarrow \texttt{norm(forb(a, r), T)} : - EX(\Sigma, T), \mathcal{H}(E, T), \texttt{action(a), role(r)}.$$
$$\forall n_r \in RN, n_r = \langle r, obl, a, d, \langle \Sigma, E \rangle \rangle \Leftrightarrow \texttt{norm(obl(a, r), T)} : - EX(\Sigma, T), \mathcal{H}(E, T), \texttt{not happened(d, T)},$$
$$\texttt{action(a), role(r)}.$$
$$\mathcal{H}(E, T), \forall e_i \in E \Leftrightarrow \texttt{happened(ei, Ti), before(Ti, T)}.$$
$$\mathcal{X}(\Sigma, T) \Leftrightarrow \forall s \in \Sigma, \texttt{holdsat(s, T)}. \ \forall s \notin \Sigma, \texttt{not holdsat(s, T)}.$$
$$EX(\Sigma, T), \forall s \in \Sigma \Leftrightarrow \texttt{holdsat(s, T)}.$$
$$s_0 \in \Delta \Leftrightarrow \texttt{holdsat(s0, 0)}.$$

Fig. 3. Operational Model in *AnsProlog*

6   Case Study

To demonstrate our approach, we formalize a specific case from the scenario described in Sect. 2. Based on the operational model, we further illustrate how to identify collective institution sets and detect norm conflicts in the case study.

6.1   Modeling Contextualized Institution

In this case study, we mainly consider three institutions $\{\mathcal{I}_1, \mathcal{I}_2, \mathcal{I}_3\}$, whose governance scopes are based on three contextual dimensions $\{Individuality, Location, Food\}$, and a set of actions $Action$ that are specified by the regulative norms of the institutions. We use $RN_{action}(\mathcal{I}_i)$ to represent the set of actions that each institution defines in its set of regulative norms. $Individuality$ refers to agents participating in the case study $\{ag, ag1\}$. $Location$ is provided with a set of values $\{t_a, t_b, t_c, w_a\}$ in which the first three elements represent three container terminals and the fourth element represents a warehouse. $Food$ also has a corresponding value set $\{AEO$ beef, non-AEO beef$\}$. Note that in this paper we only consider parts of the value sets which are most relevant to our analysis. Table 1 gives the details of the three institutions.

As mentioned in Sect. 3.2, contextual dimensions are used to define the governance scope of an institution. We next discuss how governance scope can be formalized in our operational model. Each contextual dimension is encoded as a variable and the corresponding range of values is specified by a set of facts `scope` and `action`. Furthermore, the literal `governed` assures that the governance scope of an institution will be bounded by all these scopes. As illustrated in Table 1, the three institutions share three dimensions $Individuality$, $Location$ and $Food$, which are constrained by different sets of values. For example, $\mathcal{I}_1$ governs all European terminals and warehouses when importing food to the EU countries. Therefore the scopes are initiated as ASP literals for $\mathcal{I}_1$: `scopeEU(1, ag; ag1)`, scopeEU(2, ta; tb; tc; wa), scopeEU(3, abf; nabf). $\mathcal{I}_2$ represents Dutch government, concerning importing AEO certified food via Dutch terminals and warehouses, e.g. t_a, t_b, w_a and AEO beef, while the terminal company $\mathcal{I}_3$ regulates all the food imports through terminal t_a only. All corresponding literals are defined and shown in Table 1. Different suffixes are attached with literal names to denote which institution the literal belongs to, e.g. scopeEU is for $\mathcal{I}_1$, scopeNL for $\mathcal{I}_2$ and scopeTE for $\mathcal{I}_3$.

Table 1. Institution Model for the case study

gs	CN	RN
$\langle RN_{action}(\mathcal{I}_1), \langle\{ag,ag_1\},$ $\{t_a, t_b, t_c, w_a\},$ $\{$AEO beef, non-AEO beef$\}\rangle\rangle$ $\mathcal{I}_1$	transportfood to EU counts as food passes border	O(food authority, inspect quality, after unloading), F(carrier, pass border, before inspection is finished), F(any food,choose inspection location)
scopeEU(1, ag; ag1). scopeEU(2, ta; tb; tc; wa). scopeEU(3, abf; nabf).	occ(ev(inPass, carr, ta, abf), T) :-obs(ev(trans, ag1, ta, abf), T), governedEU(ag1, ta, abf).	norm(obl(inInspect, foodAuth), T) :-happened(ev(informLoc, ag, ta, abf), K), not happened(ev(trans, ag1, ta, abf), T), before(K, T), role(foodAuth).
$\langle RN_{action}(\mathcal{I}_2), \langle\{ag,ag_1\},$ $\{t_a, t_b, w_a\},$ $\{$AEO beef$\}\rangle\rangle$ $\mathcal{I}_2$	transportfood to EU counts as food passes border	F(food authority, inspect quality, if customs did), F(carrier, pass border, before inspection is finished), P(AEO Food, choose inspection location)
scopeNL(1, ag; ag1). scopeNL(2, ta; tb; wa). scopeNL(3, abf).	occ(ev(inPass, carr, wa, abf), T) :-obs(ev(trans, ag1, wa, abf), T), governedNL(ag1, wa, abf).	norm(forb(inInspect, foodAuth), T) :-happened(ev(inInspect, customs, wa, abf), K), before(K, T),role(foodAuth; customs). norm(perm(inChooseLoc, carr), T) :-happened(ev(informLoc, ag, wa, abf), K), role(carr), before(K, T).
$\langle RN_{action}(\mathcal{I}_3),$ $\langle\{ag,ag_1\}, \{t_a\},$ $\{$AEO beef, non-AEO beef$\}\rangle\rangle$ $\mathcal{I}_3$	transportfood to EU counts as food leaves terminal	O(carrier, leave terminal, in 2 days after unload), O(carrier, pay fine, iff ood does not leave terminal after two days from unloading)
scopeTE(1, ag; ag1). scopeTE(2, ta). scopeTE(3, abf; nabf).	occ(ev(inLeave, carr, ta, abf), T) :-obs(ev(trans, ag1, ta, abf), T), governedTE(ag1, ta, abf).	norm(obl(inLeave, carr), T) :-happened(ev(waitForInsp, ag1, ta, abf), K), not happened(ev(deadline), T), before(K, T), role(carr).

To operationalize the three institutions, we generate the computational model for each individual institution based on the rules in Fig. 3. Due to space limitation, only the most significant rules are included in Table 1. The EU commission $\mathcal{I}_1$ specifies that transporting food to EU *counts as* passing the border, and food authorities are obliged to inspect the food before it passes the border. The relevant ASP programs are shown in Table 1. An external event is observed obs(ev(trans, ta, abf), T), which then generates an institutional event occ(ev(inPass, ta, aeofood), T) for $\mathcal{I}_1$ if all the dimensions are covered by the *gs* of $\mathcal{I}_1$. After informing the inspection location happened(informLoc), the obligation norm(obl(inInspect, foodAuth), T) is activated before the deadline event trans happens. $\mathcal{I}_2$ formalizes a regulative norm that after customs inspect the food happened(inInspect(wa, abe- ef, customs)), food authorities are forbidden to inspect again norm (forb(inInspect, foodAuth), T), while the permission for passing border is granted. Besides, $\mathcal{I}_2$ permits carriers to choose inspection location when importing AEO food norm(perm(inChooseLoc, carr), T).

$\mathcal{I}_3$ only considers those external events ev(trans, ta, abf) within its governance scope, which then trigger the institutional event leaving the terminal ev(inLeave, ta, abf). The obligation of leaving the terminal norm(obl(inLeave, carr), T) before a deadline is issued for all the food waiting for inspection at terminal *ta*.

6.2   Identification of Collective Institution Sets

As defined in Sect. 4.3, conflicts are detected between institutions in a collective institution set. That is, given an external event, all institutions within the set can interpret the event (i.e. the event is covered by the *gs* of the institutions) and therefore are activated. The literal governed/3 defined for each institution is used to examine whether all contextual values carried with the event are covered by the *gs* of an institution. For example, if an event ev(inspect, ag, wa, abf) is observed at time T and covered by the *gs* of $\mathcal{I}_2$, then inst2 is added into the collective institution set at time T, collectiveInstSet(inst2, T). The corresponding ASP rules are as follows:

$$collectiveInstSet(inst2, T) : -$$
$$obs(ev(inspect, ag, wa, abf), T),$$
$$governedNL(ag, wa, abf).$$

6.3   Conflict Detection Mechanism

In this section, we present the computational mechanism for detecting norm conflicts between institutions. Because we modelled each institution by *Ans-Prolog* , the same technology can be adopted to detect norm conflicts between them. On the one hand, we can generate all the possible observed event traces to determine which traces will lead to conflicts. On the other hand, an deliberate event trace can be provided to test whether it would lead to any conflicts at any time instant. The ASP programs for detecting weak and strong conflicts are respectively shown as follows:

```
%% weak conflict
weakConflict(perm(AX, RX, InstX), forb(AY, RY, InstY), T) : -
    norm(perm(AX, RX), T), norm(forb(AY, RY), T),
    countAs(ev(A, V1, .., Vn), ev(AX, VX1, ..., VXn), InstX),
    countAs(ev(A, V1, .., Vn), ev(AY, VY1, ..., VYn), InstY),
    collectiveInstSet(InstX; InstY, T).

%% strong conflict
strongConflict(obl(AX, RX, InstX), forb(AY, RY, InstY), T) : -
    norm(obl(AX, RX), T), norm(forb(AY, RY), T),
```

countAs(ev(A, V1, .., Vn), ev(AX, VX1, ..., VXn), InstX),

countAs(ev(A, V1, .., Vn), ev(AY, VY1, ..., VYn), InstY),

collectiveInstSet(InstX; InstY, T).

Following Definition 10, within a collective institution set, it is supposed that there is a permission(obligation) regarding an action AX performed by an agent enacting role RX at time T in one institution, and there is also a prohibition regarding action RY performed by an agent enacting role RY at the same time in another institution, if the institutional events associated with action AX and AY can be traced back to the same external event (i.e. including the same action and agent), a weak(strong) conflict is detected. We define two literals for weak and strong conflicts, weakConflict and strongConflict. Of these two literals, the first two arguments refer to the action and role to which the conflicts are related, and the third arguments indicate the two conflicting institutions. The literal countAs maps external events to institutional events, including actions and other contextual dimensions carried with them. collectiveInstSet constrains that the institutions are in the same collective institution set, which can be computed by the ASP programs proposed in Sect. 6.2.

Table 2. Norm Conflicts in the case study

(ta, abf)	strongConflict(obl(inLeave,carr,inst3),forb(inPass,carr,inst1),5)
	strongConflict(obl(inLeave,carr,inst3),forb(inPass,carr,inst2),5)
	strongConflict(obl(inInspect,foodAuth,inst1),forb(inInspect,foodAuth,inst2),6)
	weakConflict(perm(inChooseLoc,carr,inst2),forb(inChooseLoc,carr,inst1),3)
(ta, nabf)	strongConflict(obl(inLeave,carr,inst3),forb(inPass,carr,inst1),4)
(wa, abf)	strongConflict(obl(inInspect,foodAuth,inst1),forb(inInspect,foodAuth,inst2),6)
(tb, nabf)	none

Figure 4 shows a part of institutional evolutions in our case study. In general, when an external event occurs(denoted as the literals above/below arrows), the first task is to identify which institutions have governance competence, and then identify which norms in these institutions are triggered. It can be seen that at different time instants, there are different sets of institutions that are initiated concerning the occurrence of the event characterized by the attached contextual information. Each circle represents institutional states at a specific time, and a column of institution I_i above/below the circle indicates the collective institutions set at the time. For example, for the states Σ_3 and Σ_3', the activation of I_3 depends on whether the location informed for inspection is within the governance scope of I_3, i.e., the terminal t_a. Therefore, I_3 is not activated at Σ_3' when the informed location is t_b. While more than one institutions are activated, different sets of regulative norms from different institutions are triggered to constrain the behavior, which might cause conflicts. For example, three norms from the three institutions are triggered simultaneously at Σ_5, between which two strong conflicts occur. In this case study, there are in total five pairs of strong conflicts(indicated by a line with a cross) and one weak conflict (indicated by a line with a bullet) by providing four different event traces. Details about these conflicts are listed in Table 2. For example, a strong conflict is detected at time 5 between an obligation of the institutional event `inLeave` and a prohibition of the institutional event `inPass` because these two institutional events can be traced back to the same external event `trans` with regard to the reverse count-as function in Definition 7.

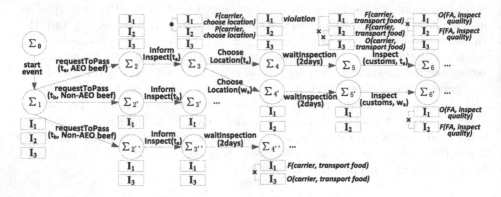

Fig. 4. Collective institution set and norm conflicts.

7   An Overview of Conflict Resolution

When the potential for norm conflict between the institutions of a collective are detected, an effective method of either preventing their actual occurrence, or a way of resolving those conflicts is needed. Unlike the approaches put forward in the literature [6,16] in which the less important norm in a conflict pair is ignored or deleted, we take a finer-grain approach by revising the less important norm to be consistent with the other. We believe that such approach can actually resolve the conflicts by tracking and fixing the origins of them, rather than simply avoiding them. This approach to conflict resolution has been successfully applied to legal conflicts between cooperating legal systems [10] and because of the similarity, at the technical level, to the circumstances described here, we believe the same solution may be applied, perhaps save some minor details. By viewing each institution in a collective set (i.e. with overlapping governance scopes) as a participating legal specification – to use the terminology of our earlier work [10] – the procedure is able to compute automatically all possible revisions of the existing norms in the light of the detected conflicts. In order to keep this paper self-contained, we provide a brief introduction to the conflict resolution approach, but for more details of the approach, please refer to [10].

The approach uses the symbolic machine learning technique *Inductive Logic Programming*, through which the system is able to learn new norms or revisions to existing norms by generalising the given positive and negative examples.

Those provided examples are the concrete reflection of the desirable and undesirable properties the resulting institutions should satisfy. Here we synthesize the negative examples by using the findings (i.e. conflict traces and conflicts) from conflict detection and feed them to the ILP learning system. We assume there is a strict total precedence order over the institutions in a (virtual) organization, e.g. EU $\succ$ NL $\succ$ TE,[1] which is then used to label the institutions in a given conflict pair, so that the one with lower precedence is referred to as the *revisable institution* and the other as the *background institution*. Keeping the background institution unchanged, the ILP learning system computes all possible revisions to the revisable institution that satisfy the properties of the examples, i.e. absence of conflict. Subsequently, it is necessary to select one of the proposed revision plans, for which criterion we use the plan with the minimum number of changes, in order to minimize the differences between the revised institution and the original. Each possible revision suggests a set of change operations, comprising:

- adding a new body condition to an existing norm, or
- removing a body condition from an existing norm, or
- forming a completely new norm.

The revision procedure, to which we refer above, is implemented in ASP, making it fully compatible with our modelling language for institutions and conflict detection. Given the operational models of the revisable institutions, we can construct the search space of all possible revisions with the help of *mode declarations* [4]. Consequently, an answer set solver (we use CLINGO), can generate a set of answer sets from: (i) the operational model of the background institution, using (ii) negative examples (i.e. conflict traces and conflicts) as constraints, and the (iii) revisable institutions. Each answer set is a candidate revision. We assign costs to each operation – the default is the unit cost for addition or deletion – and hence the total cost of a revision is then the number of operations included in the revision. The final step uses the *aggregate* technique in CLINGO to select the answer set with minimum cost. Following the application of the revision described in the answer set, the revised institution no longer causes the conflicts described in the learning examples.

8   Related Work

Interest has been steadily growing in the use of norms to regulate and coordinate agent behaviour in MAS, as a result of progress in two complementary areas: (i) institutional modeling, and (ii) norm conflict detection.

We first review some representative research on normative modelling. Singh proposes the use of commitments to capture normative concepts in MAS and defines norms as a tuple of subject, object, context, antecedent and consequent [14], which provides an intuitive way to characterize the bounds of autonomy

---

[1] EU, NL and TE refer to the three institutions in the case study: EU being European Union, NL the Netherlands and TE the terminal and warehouse.

and interdependence between agents. Boella and van der Torre presented a logic architecture for a normative system and study logic relations between counts-as conditionals, institutional constraints, obligations and permissions [2]. This architecture gives a clear vision of how input/output operations correspond to the functionality of components that constitute normative systems. However, both of these studies are at the level of norms, while in contrast our work considers a set of institutions, each of which defines a set of norms, and their interrelations in the setting of virtual organizations.

We introduce the notion of *governance scope* and demonstrate how governance scope functions in institution modeling and conflict detection. The ideas presented in [5, 16] have some similarities. Vasconcelos et al. [16] define the *influence scope* of norms to constrain the effects of individual norms. This contrasts with our approach, where governance scope is defined at the level of institutions, with the aim of illustrating how *multiple* institutions can be situated within a virtual organization and how institutions are activated when responding to observed events. Elhag et al. [5] informally proposes the concept "world knowledge" that describes the context in which norms are intended to apply, along with the definition of key terminological concepts. The governance scope and constitutive norms defined in our work can capture the same concepts, but more importantly, governance scope is modeled explicitly and is operationalized in institutional reasoning.

We now turn to existing work on norm conflicts. Vasconcelos et al. [15, 16] consider both the detection and resolution of norm conflicts. They present an algorithm that uses *first-order unification* to determine substitutions, called *undesirable* sets, for the variables of norms that would lead to norm conflicts. Once the values are identified, conflicts can be avoided, by not allowing those values. In contrast, the conflict detection mechanism presented here is not only operationalized, but significantly, deals with conflicts that emerge through the interaction of institutions, which goes beyond the static analysis of individual norms. Using ideas similar to those in [15, 16], the practical reasoning agents of [9] include resolution mechanisms that enable them to handle conflicting norms themselves via negotiation with a norm issuer. An alternative resolution approach is proposed by García-Camino et al. [6], in which a simple priority mechanism is used to rank norms and hence resolve conflict by discarding lower priority norms.

9   Conclusions

Targeting virtual organizations, this paper presents a full illustration of *what* an institution consists of and *how* it evolves to the changes of reality. By explicitly incorporating the concept of governance scope, we know that an institution is not only a set of norms that are used to regulate the real world behavior, but is also characterized by the control boundary that determines what kinds of events are in the competence of the institution. Furthermore, the operational model provides a computational expression of institution dynamics, i.e., how institutions respond to the occurrence of external events.

The contributions of this paper are three-fold. First, governance scope is explicitly captured by institutions through context models, which facilitates the identification of applicable institutions in virtual organizations. Second, the relations between institutions are studied from the perspective of governance overlap. Third, based on our institution model, two definitions of strong and weak norm conflicts are proposed to the specific requirements of virtual organizations. To validate our proposal, we present an operational model, which enables an implementation of detecting strong and weak norm conflicts by a case study.

In this paper, we propose a framework for modelling institutions and their governance scopes. The framework not only provides the components for capturing the regulative properties of institutions but also their constitutive nature. Moreover, by explicitly modelling the governance scope of institutions, the framework enables a clear representation of the regulation boundaries of multiple institutions, which is an essential aspect that has to be considered for conflicts detection. Though the framework intends to provide a general approach for the problem undertaken, there are several issues that have to be considered when applying the framework:

- We assume that the ontologies used for contextualizing different institutions are aligned. That is, the contextual information is shared among different institutions. If this is not the case, additional work concerning ontology alignment needs to be done, which is itself a separate research topic.
- Sometimes, the governance scope of an institution is implicit and has to be derived from the description of its norms. In this case, one needs an overview understanding of the institution and generalize the contextual dimensions of its regulation boundaries.
- The conflict detection mechanism is dependant on the aligned semantics among institutions, i.e. the same entity has to be represented by the same logic notation in different institutions.

In future work, we intend to extend the institution model to multiple levels through hierarchical context models, and study how institutions are related from abstract to concrete. Furthermore, we will make refinement on different kinds of regulative norms and their relations, which will enrich the definition of norm conflicts and thus the detection mechanisms.

References

1. http://ec.europa.eu/taxation_customs/customs/
2. Boella, G., van der Torre, L.: An architecture of a normative system. In: AAMAS (2006)
3. Cliffe, O., De Vos, M., Padget, J.: Specifying and reasoning about multiple institutions. In: COIN (2007)
4. Corapi, D., Russo, A., Vos, M.D., Padget, J.A., Satoh, K.: Normative design using inductive learning. TPLP **11**(4–5), 783–799 (2011)
5. Elhag, A., Breuker, J., Brouwer, P.: On the formal analysis of normative conflicts. Inf. Commun. Technol. Law **9**(3), 207–217 (2000)

6. García-Camino, A., Noriega, P., Rodríguez-Aguilar, J.-A.: An algorithm for conflict resolution in regulated compound activities. In: O'Hare, G.M.P., Ricci, A., O'Grady, M.J., Dikenelli, O. (eds.) ESAW 2006. LNCS (LNAI), vol. 4457, pp. 193–208. Springer, Heidelberg (2007)

7. Gelfond, M., Lifschitz, V.: Classical negation in logic programs and disjunctive databases. New Gener. Comput. **9**, 365–386 (1991)

8. Giunchiglia, F., Bouquet, P.: Introduction to contextual reasoning. An artificial intelligence perspective. In: Kokinov, B. (ed.) Perspectives on Cognitive Science. NBU Press, Sofia (1996)

9. Kollingbaum, M., Norman, T., Preece, A., Sleeman, D.: Norm refinement: informing the re-negotiation of contracts. In: COIN@ECAI (2006)

10. Li, T., Balke, T., De Vos, M., Padget, J., Satoh, K.: A model-based approach to the automatic revision of secondary legislation. In: Proceedings of the Fourteenth International Conference on Artificial Intelligence and Law, ICAIL'13, pp. 202–206. ACM, New York (2013)

11. O'Leary, D.E., Kuokka, D., Plant, R.: Artificial intelligence and virtual organizations. Commun. ACM **40**(1), 52–59 (1997)

12. Ostrom, E.: Understanding Institutional Diversity. Princeton University Press, Princeton (2005)

13. Searle, J.: The Construction of Social Reality. The Free Press, New York (1995)

14. Singh, M.P.: Commitments in multiagent systems: some history, some confusions, some controversies, some prospects. The Goals of Cognition. College Publications, London (2012)

15. Vasconcelos, W., Kollingbaum, M., Norman, T.: Resolving conflict and inconsistency in norm-regulated virtual organizations. In: AAMAS (2007)

16. Vasconcelos, W., Kollingbaum, M., Norman, T.: Normative conflict resolution in multi-agent systems. JAAMAS **19**(2), 124–152 (2009)

17. Zimmermann, A., Lorenz, A., Oppermann, R.: An operational definition of context. In: Kokinov, B., Richardson, D.C., Roth-Berghofer, T.R., Vieu, L. (eds.) CONTEXT 2007. LNCS (LNAI), vol. 4635, pp. 558–571. Springer, Heidelberg (2007)

Institutions

Emotions and Norms in Shared Spaces

Mónica Sara Santos and Jeremy Pitt[(✉)]

Department of Electrical and Electronic Engineering, Imperial College London,
Exhibition Road, London SW7 2BT, UK
{monica.santos,j.pitt}@imperial.ac.uk

Abstract. Open-plan offices are working environments which require
people to share a common space. However, violation of conventional
rules (norms) can cause instances of incivility which, if untreated, can
cause further problems: escalating retaliation, demoralised or demotivated workforce, staff turnover, etc. In this paper, we envision the common space as a *common pool resource* which we seek to manage
according to the institutional design principles of Elinor Ostrom. We
describe the design and implementation of an *affective conditioning system*, which detects a violation of office norms and deterioration of (positive) affective (emotional) state of the office occupants, and seeks to
restore a homeostatic equilibrium using self-regulation and forgiveness.
We suggest that this convergence of normative, affective and adaptive
computing demonstrates the possibilities for self-regulatory platforms
for successful collective action in such communal situations.

1 Introduction

Open-plan offices, using assigned seating, or unassigned seating with (hoteling)
or without (hot-desking) reservation are typical interior design arrangements for
clerical and technical work in modern organisations. These workplaces require
people to share a common space, where violation of (implicitly or explicitly
stated) conventional rules, or social norms, can cause instances of incivility [20].
Such workplace incivility, characterised as a low-intensity form of workplace
deviance, can be difficult to detect and resolve, but is also very harmful for
both people and organisations [14]. However, if nothing is done to avoid or
ameliorate such incivility, bad feeling can lead to diminished productivity of
and cooperation between demoralised or demotivated personnel, and, in the
long-term, to more serious problems, such as escalatory retaliation, aggressive
conflict, and/or increased staff turnover [12].

Therefore, it is a pressing problem in ergonomics and workplace design to
find ways in which to reduce the negative side-effects of workplace incivility. The
technological solution we propose for addressing the workplace incivility problem, is MACS (M—s Affective Conditioning System): a system that attempts
to avoid, reduce and/or resolve incivility in the workplace, before an incivility
episode escalates into a higher-intensity workplace deviance situation, e.g. conflict or aggression. MACS is intended to emphasise stakeholder engagement and

T. Balke et al. (Eds.): COIN 2013, LNAI 8386, pp. 157–176, 2014.
DOI: 10.1007/978-3-319-07314-9_9, © Springer International Publishing Switzerland 2014

empower collective choice: firstly by avoiding micro-management, as the main idea is that incivility episodes are resolved between stakeholders (i.e. the office occupants themselves), and only as a last resort is there need to involve higher management; and secondly by providing social support, through a network of communication and mutual obligations, via the collective selection, monitoring and enforcement of the stakeholders' own social norms and pro-social processes such as forgiveness [25].

Our approach is based on two premises: firstly, conceptually, that if "offices are open systems" [7], then open-plan offices are common-pool resource management systems; and secondly, technologically, that aspects of the normative, affective and adaptive computing paradigms can be converged in the implementation and visualisation of such systems.

On the first premise, we envision the common workspace as a *common pool resource* which we seek to manage according to the institutional design principles of Elinor Ostrom [15]. In this respect, the metaphor we are pursuing is that the (intangible) 'office atmosphere' is a pooled resource which the office occupants can deplete by anti-social behaviour and re-provision by pro-social behaviour. Furthermore, what is (and is not) anti-social behaviour is determined by the occupants themselves – a specific instantiation of Ostrom's third principle (that those affected by collective choice arrangements participate in their selection).

On the second premise, we contend that aspects of affective computing [17] can provide theories which can be used to detect affective state from physiological signals; normative computing offers the basis for representation of and reasoning with office rules, especially conventional rules with permissions, prohibitions, obligations, etc. [2]; and adaptive computing can support the mechanisms by which office occupants can propose, select, configure and de-select the rules. When faced with incivility, most people's coping strategy is to disengage. They try to change their own behaviours, or the endure the situation, and very seldom choose to confront the instigator. Adaptive computing can instead empower people by a process of definition and adaptation of social norms.

This paper is structured as follows. Section 2 reviews and analyses the literature in workplace incivility from an inter-disciplinary perspective, describes some experiments indicating that a technological solution to workplace incivility can be developed from a convergence of affective, adaptive and normative, computing, and presents in more detail Ostrom's institutional design principles for enduring common-pool resource management. On the basis of this analysis, we specify the system requirements for and describe the implementation of MACS in Sect. 3, concentrating particularly on the forgiveness mechanism. Section 4 presents the interface design and development, showing the visualisation of social norms, social standing and social processes. Section 5 provides some preliminary evaluation results derived from usability testing, which leads onto a consideration of some further and related research in Sect. 6. We summarise and conclude in Sect. 7, in particular arguing that this convergence of normative, affective and adaptive computing demonstrates the potential for self-regulatory platforms for successful collective action in such communal situations.

2   Background and Rationale

In this section, we review the background research on workplace incivility and explain the rationale for the development of MACS. We start by considering the psychology and sources of workplace incivility to identify what are the main signals and what mechanisms are required to resolve them. We then describe some background experiments which give an indication that these signals can be detected and how the mechanisms can be automated. We then consider how these can be situated in a formal framework for self-organisation.

2.1   The Psychology of Workplace Incivility

Today's organisations are characterised by fast-paced relationships between co-workers, often mediated by high-tech, asynchronous communications [16]. All these can be facilitators for employees' mistreatment of one another, which can take various forms – bullying, abuse, conflict, aggression, mobbing, social undermining and incivility – but with a common ground: They all share expressions of disrespect among people who work together. Leiter [11] considers incivility to be a contemporary workplace crisis, and the entry level form of workplace mistreatment.

The prevailing and costly effects of workplace deviance are considered to be among the most serious problems organisations face today [3]. Workplace incivility is a kind of deviance that although occurring regularly in many organisations, is not easily recognisable and addressed [16]. The offender's intent to harm is ambiguous, as it may be perceived differently from different perspectives – that of the offender, the victim and other observers. And the instigator might be violating norms without intent to do so. The fact that the intent is ambiguous is very relevant to the definition of incivility, as it distinguishes incivility from more serious forms of workplace deviance, such as verbal aggression or bullying. Workplace incivility has therefore been defined as "a low-intensity deviant behaviour with ambiguous intent to harm the target, in violation of workplace norms for mutual respect. Uncivil behaviours are characteristically rude and discourteous, displaying a lack of regard for others" [1].

Given its low-intensity quality and the fact it's not illegal, many companies fail to recognise incivility and most managers are ill-equipped to deal with it. Employees are trained to recognise and deal with other forms of mistreatment, organisations have policies and mechanisms to address them and laws back them up, but the same does not happen for incivility [16].

However, when an incivility episode occurs it might not be an isolated incident. A series of incivility episodes, each of which is minor on its own, might accumulate to become a more substantial problem. There are three potential outcomes for the people involved such a series: They may continue to be uncivil to each other through other acts of incivility; they may increase the intensity of the offence; or one of the parties may choose to walk away [16]. If the choice is to increase the intensity of offences, each round of disrespect may become more dramatic and aggressive, leading to what can be defined as an incivility spiral [1].

The occurrence of the first violation of a norm creates negative affect and a feeling of perceived unfairness, and motivates the victims to reciprocate [9]. And the most common means of releasing negative affect in this kind of situation is to reciprocate with further unfairness [9]. The incivility spiral might only stop when one of the parties involved chooses to stop retaliating, or when one of the parties apologises, denies intent to harm and/or offers an excuse [1].

2.2 Experiments in QoE, Affect and Forgiveness

The previous section has identified the types of activity that constitute workplace incivility, the negative effects it can have on individuals, and the behaviours that it can induce. However, the activity in itself is not illegal. Moreover, persistent low-grade deviance, which has an adverse affect on individuals, tends only to be of significant concern to those directly impacted by it. As a result higher management are reluctant to intervene, as the intervention of external authorities and imposition of top-down rules are inconsistent with an open, collegiate, inclusive working environment supposedly promoted by having an open-plan office in the first place.

Therefore we propose to develop an automated solution using ICT (information and communication technologies) that can address the problem of workplace incivility in a 'self-contained' manner.

The first issue with such a proposal is that the aim of the system is, in essence, to enhance the *quality of experience* (QoE) of the office occupants. This is a supra-functional system requirement, in the sense that it relates to the system's impact on its users (which goes beyond the usual concept of functional or non-functional requirements which specify system behaviour or operational parameters).

In previous work [19], we observed that public collections (like museums and art galleries) were under pressure to maintain visitor numbers. We proposed one way was to use ICT to enhance the QoE of visitors, by saturating the physical space (i.e. the exhibits) with sensors and displays and streaming information directly to the visitors' own devices. To investigate the enhancement of QoE using ICT, we built a usability lab that was a microcosm of an exhibition space in the Science Museum, London, called *iCars*. The iCars exhibition involved a sensor-saturated environment, including several traditional and non-traditional exhibits, one of which was a fully-interactive model car loaded with touch sensors, micro-switches, compass, a 3-axis accelerometer and Bluetooth wireless communication. Policies were used to personalise the exhibit by using intelligent decision-making to adapt its behaviour and customise the content streamed directly to the visitor's device, based on their behaviour and the profile. Our experiments showed that subjects had longer interaction with, and greater recall of information presented by, the fully-interactive exhibit.

This is, we believe, prima facie evidence that QoE can be side-effected by embedded systems of this kind. The next question is how to replicate this for office environments and workplace incivility. This breaks down into addressing three related issues:

- how to detect an adverse affective reaction to an instance of a workplace incivility;
- how to defuse an adverse reaction to a workplace incivility before it can spark an incivility spiral; and
- how to define (and who defines) what constitutes a workplace incivility in a particular context.

For detecting affective state, the AffectiveWare system has been developed [6], which consisted of sensors to read galvanic skin response (either rings, or a mouse covered in conductive paint), a wireless communication protocol to communicate signals, and a central server that interpreted the signals as emotions using fuzzy logic.

One experiment with AffectiveWare used three female teenage subjects, and had two parts. In the first part of the experiment, the subjects held four pieces of iconic branded fashion garments whilst reading the company's promotional information downloaded from the official web site, and the subject's galvanic skin response was measured. In the second part, the same subjects were shown same garments but with brief explanation of a sustainable issue in the public domain connected to each item, relative to clothing supply chains consumption and disposal. Galvanic skin response was again measured. A measurable physiological response was observed while holding the iconic items, and the response was different if the subjects were reading company PR as opposed to factual information about sustainable issues. It was concluded that while it was not possible to infer an *actual* emotive state from the recoded signals (we could not tell if the signals indicated, joy, disgust, surprise, sorrow, etc.), but it was possible to infer a *change* of state [5].

For defusing workplace incivility, we note a similarity with trust breakdowns found in various forms of computer-mediated communication, in particular e-commerce and online social networks.

Some online auction and market companies rely on reputations, fed by feedback mechanisms from transactions, to establish trust between buyers and sellers. A reputation system "collects, distributes, and aggregates feedback about participants' past behaviour" [21]. There is a high correlation between buyer and seller feedback, for example, which suggests they reciprocate when giving reputation ratings [10,22]. They can also retaliate: one negative rating could initiate a spiral of negative ratings, marked by the inability to escape the mutual tit-for-tat being exacerbated by a lack of cues to do so. There were also other curious features that one negative rating would spark others (stoning [8]).

These reputation systems have, therefore, taken little provision to encourage the repair of trust breakdowns, mostly because reputation is part of the trust decision and not part of the punishment or (better) reparation mechanism. There is a psychological mechanism associated with such human-human interaction though: forgiveness. Forgiveness is a pro-social motivational change in someone who has incurred a transgression [13]. It implies giving up resentment and desire to punish someone. When people forgive, they become motivated to engage in relationship-constructive, rather than relationship-destructive, actions towards the offender. Forgiveness is influenced by psychological processes such as empathy for the transgressor, attributions and appraisals, and rumination about the transgression [13].

In various experiments, it has been shown that interface cues can be used to simulate self-awareness and activate self-conscious emotions, which in turn motivate the reversal of offensive behaviour [25], and that a computational model of the forgiveness process can be implemented using fuzzy inference [23].

In the next section, we consider an appropriate context for detecting, defusing and defining workplace incivility.

2.3   Self-Organising, Norm-Governed Institutions

Hewitt [7] defined offices as open systems, in which it could be assumed there was a common language, but not necessarily a common goal and no central controller. Pursuing this metaphor, we envision open-plan offices as common-pool resource management systems, in which there is still no common interest and no central controller, but a group of actors have to collectivise their resources and would prefer to sustain the resource in the long-term.

We propose to consider the 'office atmosphere', from which the occupants derive their quality of experience, as the common pool resource, which the occupants provision to and appropriate from according to their behaviour. Instances of anti-social behaviour, such as workplace incivility, appropriate from the resource by diminishing the 'atmosphere', while instances of pro-social behaviour, like apologising for a workplace incivility, provision to the 'atmosphere'.

Now the answer to the question – what constitutes a workplace incivility? – is: it depends on what the office occupants themselves mutually deem to be anti-social behaviour which causes (them) adverse affective reactions and by extension diminishes the office atmosphere. Then the mutually agreed, conventional rules which prohibit certain forms of anti-social behaviour are, in this envisionment, a set of collective choice rules which office occupants themselves can propose, select, configure and de-select. It is, in effect, an institution; i.e. a set of working rules which permit or prohibit certain forms of behaviour in a particular context.

There is one outstanding tradition of common-pool resource management through institutions of this sort, due to Ostrom [15]. For long-enduring institutions, of the kind that we want for shared environments like workspaces, Ostrom identified eight institutional design principles. Of these, one was that those affected by provision and appropriation rules should participate in their selection; another, that there should be fast and efficient mechanisms for conflict prevention and resolution. Norm-governed systems provide the basis for representing and reasoning with norms, especially in an institutional content where permissions, obligations, prohibitions and (institutionalised) power are concerns, and for defining protocols which specify how to change norms and resolve conflicts [2]. Processes for participatory selection and adaptation of the collective choice arrangements, i.e. the definition of workplace incivility rules, and conflict resolution mechanisms based on forgiveness, are therefore primary functional requirements of the system that has been developed, as described in the next section.

3   MACS: System Architecture and Implementation

3.1   System Architecture

MACS was designed and implemented as a web-based system, to obviate the need to instal any software on a user's computer. It comprises a 3-layer architecture:

- the front-end Interface layer (written in HTML, CSS, PHP and JavaScript): accessible by a web browser and the only point of communication between the user and MACS (see Sect. 4);
- the middle layer, comprising seven modules (all written in PHP) that work together to compute the process and outcome of each episode of incivility, from the moment it is *flagged*, to the moment it's closed;
- the back-end database handler (written in PHP and SQL), which provides access between the database and the middle layer, so that all communications with a MySQL database are made through this module.

Figure 1 shows the UML Components Diagram of MACS's architecture. The top layer is the interface and it communicates with all other modules. All users only interact with the interface when accessing MACS. The several modules, described in the following sections, communicate between themselves, the interface component, and the database handler. Finally, the database handler is used as an interface between the database and all other components of MACS.

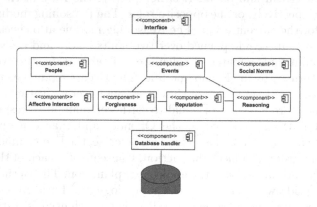

Fig. 1. UML Components Diagram of the MACS's architecture.

In the next sub-section, we describe how an event is processed by MACS. Following that, we examine in detail the operation of the Forgiveness module, and briefly consider the Social Norms module, leading to a detailed presentation of the design and implementation of the interface layer.

3.2   Event Processing

MACS provides a computer-mediated interaction between everyone in the workplace, especially between people (the *victims*) who are affected by an instance of workplace incivility (an *event*), and the person who behaved in a way that upset other people in the workplace (an *offender*).

The basic sequence of operation is that a user or users (victims) *flags* an event through the web interface, and the event is validated through the Event, Reasoning and Reputation modules. If the event is validated as an instance of workplace incivility by some violation of the agreed social norms (stored in the Social Norms module), then the Event and Forgiveness modules combine to elicit an apology from the offender (or other act of reparation) and recommend (or not) forgiveness from the victim.

An event in MACS is an atomic episode of incivility, committed by an offender, in violation of a social norm, and flagged by a single victim. The same episode of incivility might be flagged by multiple people, but for each one of the victims, a new event is created. Whenever a person flags a violation of norms in MACS, the Events module receives inputs from the Interface to create a new event: victim, offender, social norm, date/time, and some (optional) additional information entered by the victim. When it creates a new event, it consults the Reasoning module for recent events with matching details, and if it finds one, it joins them together in an event group. An event/event group has a status which can be either created (0), validated (1), apologised (2), and either forgiven (3) or ignored (4).

When an event is created, the Events module makes the first call to the Reasoning module, sending it data about the current event and previous events regarding both victim and offender, either playing the roles of the victim and the offender, respectively, or the opposite roles. The Reasoning module returns a partial score for the current event. The Reasoning module also checks for events or event groups that have happened over two hours before and are waiting for a score, and when it finds a match, it calculates a final score for the event or event group, and returns it to the Events module. The Events module can then either activate the event or event group, or close it without ever activating it, depending on whether the score is higher or equal to, or lower than 50 %, respectively.

The event is then presented to the Offender and they can apologise and explain their behaviour. Should an offender apologise, the Events module updates the event/event group to reflect that action. Consequently each of the victims is notified, on the Interface, about the apology/explanation. The victims can, then, individually, decide whether to accept the apology and forgive the offender, or ignore their apology. These actions are reflected on each event's status. A scheduled task will check, every 15 min, for events that are ready to be closed, and when it finds one, it calls the Events module for this final update.

3.3   Forgiveness Module

The Forgiveness module has two main components, one on the side of the offender – the apology/explanation, and the other on the side of the victim(s) – the

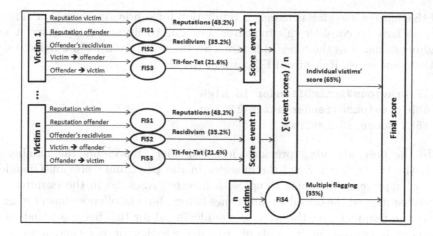

Fig. 2. Fuzzy inference system for calculating event group score in MACS.

forgiveness. These components are connected as forgiveness only happens if it's preceded by an apology.

Several fuzzy inference systems (FIS$_i$) are used in the calculation of the scores. Figure 2 shows the whole process of calculation of an event group's score, based on **n** victims. Here, the first calculation of an event's score, for each of the victims, is presented on the further left area of the figure. For each of the victims, three fuzzy inference systems calculate the event's score, which will later be combined with other scores to calculate the final event group score. FIS1 deals with the reputations of the victim and the offender. Its result weighs 43.2 % in the final individual victim's score, for Victim 1. It calculates the score based on rules that state the highest the victim's reputation and the lowest the offender's are, the highest the score will be. Rules regarding this FIS are of the kind:

```
IF reputationVictim IS positive
AND reputationOffender IS negative
THEN score IS likely
```

FIS2 deals with a single variable, the offender's recidivism, i.e., the number of times the offender has violated the social norm in question for the current event. In this case, the highest the number of times the norm has been broken by this person, the highest the impact in the event's score will be. This result weighs 35.2 % on the event's score.

Finally, FIS3 analyses situations of "tit-for-tat", i.e., it tries to find situations where each of the parties have been involved in an event in the past, either where the victim has flagged the offender's behaviour, or the offender has flagged the victim's behaviour. Although several previous entries involving both parties might only mean both people break the norms frequently, and they both flag norm violations often, it might also mean that there is an issue between them, and this current flagging is merely a retaliation for a previous situation. Therefore, we have to consider this indicator, but due to its ambiguity, have it not weighing as much as the other indicators. So the result from FIS3 weighs 21.6 % on the event score. Rules from FIS3 are of the kind:

```
IF previousVictimOffender IS high
AND previousOffenderVictim IS low
THEN score IS neutral
```

In the previous rule, "previousVictimOffender" represents the number of times the victim has flagged the offender in the past, and "previousOffender-Victim" represents the same thing, with inverted roles. So in the example the victim has flagged the offender many times before, but the offender hasn't flagged the victim frequently, in the past, so the likelihood for this being a situation of tit-for-tat is neutral, as it's difficult to infer whether or not there's an issue between the parties, based on these variables.

FIS4 is based on the number of people who have flagged the same episode of incivility, and the highest the number of victims, the more likely it is the event is valid. All partial scores from each of the events, calculated from FIS1, FIS2 and FIS3, are summed and divided by n, the number of events, and the resulting value is added with 65 % weight to 35 % of the score coming from FIS4.

This means the final score is always based on 35 % of the value for multiple flagging and 65 % for the individual events, regardless of how many they are. This decision was made because we believe the factor that should weigh the most should always be multiple people being affected by the incivility episode. Also, if multiple people flag a situation, it's more likely they're doing it seriously, and not e.g. out of personal problems with the offender, or because they're having a bad day and have decided to take it out on a co-worker, or even because they're a bully and this is their idea of an innovative bullying tool.

3.4   Social Norms Module

The Social Norms module is concerned with everything related to social norms, including creation, change, disabling, votes and suggestion of new norms.

An example of a social norm would be:

Social norm: "Keep the mobile phones in silent or vibrating mode".
Description: "Mobile phones should be kept in silent or vibrating mode at all times.
Category: Noise.
Severity: Critical.

MACS implements a voting system for social norms, which allows for everyone (and only those ones) in a particular office to vote positively or negatively for a norm. It also allows people to suggest new norms, as the dynamic nature of offices might mean there is a constant need to change norms, so MACS should provide flexible ways of either changing norms frequently, or settling for a set of norms and abiding by them permanently.

The visualisation of the social norms, and other interaction, affordances and displays, are presented in the next section.

4   MACS: Interface Development and Visualisation

This section presents figures of the interfaces displayed and interactions in configuring MACS and processing an event. One primary design decision was to use avatars rather than real photos to represent the users for three reasons:

- avatars make the interface look lighter and more fun, counter-balancing the issue that confronting incivility is potentially delicate and sensitive;
- vatars are less intrusive, and as people are already putting themselves in a position where their co-workers are more aware of their actions, they would be more willing to participate if they felt less exposed; and
- avatars, when created with similarity to the physical image of the person they're portraying, still create self-awareness [24].

The victim and offender roles are played by the same type of user, so those two roles and activities are blended into the same interface. This is presented as the regular user's interface, as described in Sect. 4.1. There is also a separate set of interfaces for function provided to the 'office manager' (Sect. 4.2).

4.1   Regular User Interface

Figure 3(a) depicts the first screen displayed for a user, right after a successful login to MACS. The navigation bar, on top, and the footer bar, at the bottom of the screen, are constant throughout MACS. The navigation bar provides direct access to the home screen presented in Fig. 3, the social norms screen (see later) and the historical information about events where the logged-in user has been involved in, as an offender. The footer bar is used to logout from MACS.

Right below the navigation bar, is the set of avatars representing all the people the logged used shares the workplace with. By hovering on each of the avatars the text "Flag *person's name*'s violation of norms" shows up, where *person's name* is replaced by the chosen person's name. By clicking on an avatar, the user is taken to the flagging screen, where they can create a new event, by flagging a violation of norms by the person they chose.

At the bottom left area of the screen there are two different items regarding the logged user: Their current reputation and its evolution graph for the previous 10 days, and their avatar and name.

On the list of people at the top of the screen, some people have a "forbidden" sign next to their avatar. People who have this sign have requested not to be interrupted. This "busy" status can be toggled on and off by the logged user, by clicking on their own avatar to swap the current status.

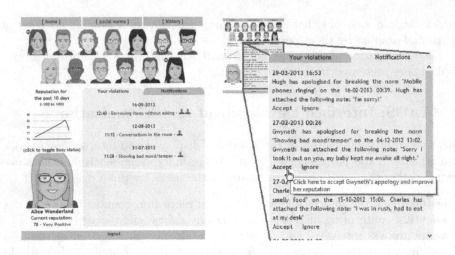

Fig. 3. Regular user: (a) Start screen; (b) "Notifications" screen

The right area of the screen, below the list of avatars, always starts with the "Your Violations" tab selected, and presents all open events where the user is an offender, ordered by date, from the most recent to the most ancient. The user can see the time and date of the offence, the social norm they have allegedly broken and how many people have flagged each event, but not specifically who has flagged it. If the event text is black, this means they have apologised. If it's blue, it's a link and they can click on it to go to the event details screen, where they can apologise and explain what happened, or say they didn't do what they're being accused of.

If they have notifications from MACS, the "Notifications" tab's text is printed in dark-red, with a counter of open notifications in brackets. Otherwise, the tab's text has the same colour as the "Your violations" tab.

Figure 3(b) shows a zoomed-in extract of the "Notifications" screen. This screen is accessible by clicking on the "Notifications" tab on the home screen (see Fig. 3). These notifications are either about open events where the user was the victim, or information about the closing of events where the user has apologised for breaking a norm. Notifications are listed by update date. Notifications about events where someone has apologised show the date of apology and respective apologies/explanations. The "Accept"and "Ignore" links are self-explanatory: If the user wants to forgive the offender and improve their reputation, they should click "Accept". Otherwise, they should press "Ignore".

Finally, a core function of MACS is to keep the users informed about the social norms they must abide by. Besides being able to check the norms at all times, users must also be able to vote for them, positively or negatively, and to suggest new norms.

Figure 4(a) displays the "Social Norms" screen. Here all norms are presented, ordered by severity level, from the most to the least critical. Each norm is printed

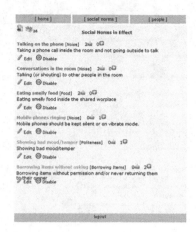

Fig. 4. Social norms interface: (a) regular user's view; (b) manager's view. (Color figure online)

in the colour code that reflects its severity. Red means the norm is very critical, orangey-red means critical, orange means average, and finally yellow means minor. In this case, there aren't any minor severity norms to be displayed. In front of each norm, in square brackets, is its category. Categories are "noise", "privacy" "food", "environment", "politeness" and "borrowing items". Below each norm is its description. And finally by each norm are an approve (thumbs up) and a disapprove (thumbs down) buttons, which can be used to vote positively, or negatively, respectively, for the norm.

At the bottom of the list of norms is the suggestion box, where the user may suggest a new norm for their workplace. The manager has access to suggested norms, and if they want to turn a suggested norm into an active norm, they must suggest it to every user, and only create the norm if at least the majority of people agrees with it.

4.2   Manager's Interface

The manager is someone who has some sort of administration privileges over the users sharing the workplace MACS is installed in. However, their responsibility is only in configuration and not in participation of the norms, so we expect the manager role in the system to be taken by an administrator, rather than a line-manager in the 'real' organisation.

On login, the manager is taken to the "Open Events" screen, presented in Fig. 5(a), ordered by social norm. This screen, as the title indicates, displays all open events for the given workplace. As it happened for the regular user's interface, the manager's interface also has a constant navigation bar on top and a footer bar for logging out, at the bottom.

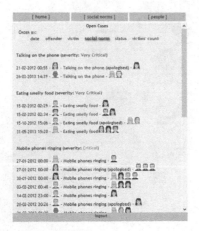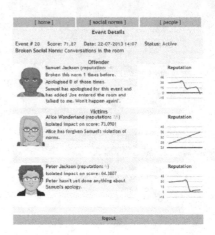

Fig. 5. (a) Starting screen for the manager's interface, presenting all open events, ordered by social norm; (b) Manager's view of the details of an open event.

Open events are all events that require action from either the offender (to apologise and explain what happened) or the victim(s) (to forgive the offender or ignore their apology). Each event is presented on a line, which shows, in order, the time of the offence, the avatar of the offender, the broken social norm (with "apologised" in brackets, if the offender has apologised for this event), and the avatars of the victims. All avatars throughout the manager's interface are clickable to display the details of the person they represent.

The default order by which open events are presented is date, but the manager can change the order field, so open events are ordered by offender, victim, social norm, status (either waiting for an offender's or victims' action), and victims' count, i.e. the number of people who have flagged the same event. Figure 5 shows the list of events ordered by social norm, giving an overview about which social norms are being violated the most, at a given time.

Figure 4(b) displays the manager's view of social norms. Whereas regular users can only read, vote for, and suggest new social norms, the manager has a wider range of options regarding the norms. In this screen the norms are presented ordered by their severity level. The title of the norm is printed in the colour that reflects its severity – red for very critical, orangey-red for critical, orange for medium and yellow for minor. In front of the title are counters for positive and negative votes, respectively, and a description of the norm. And finally below it, are links for editing and disabling the norms. If a norm is disabled, it will be presented below all active norms, with an option to enable it. On the top left of the "Social Norms" screen are a button to create a new norm, and a button to check the suggested norms.

The manager interface also provides access to the People module, but these interface displays are omitted here for space constraints.

5   Evaluation Results

MACS is a conceptually innovative system which has just completed its first phase of development, and has reached the point where in can be deployed in field trials to test the hypothesis that a 'socially intelligent ICT can address problems of workplace incivility and improve QoE in working environments'. Those trials are in progress, so here we report on two other aspects of evaluation: the first being lab-based usability testing, and the second being a heuristic evaluation of the visualisation of Ostrom's institutional design principles [15].

5.1   Usability Testing

MACS' user experience (UX) has been studied throughout its design and development. The initial prototypes were evaluated by colleagues, and a preliminary version of MACS was installed in a room with 14 PhD students. The feedback from this installation was used to validate some design choices, e.g. user representation by avatars rather than photos, and to modify others, e.g. we used flagging events by users, rather than trying to identify them automatically using signal processing applied to sound or vision feeds. These studies were used to inform the final interface and interactions. MACS' 'final' version went through a UX user study to produce the version that is ready for being used in field trials.

The UX testing involved 6 people in the study, who all had have different sorts of jobs, from accounting to working in a biology lab. The common ground they share is they all need to share workspaces and/or equipment in their everyday work life.

The subjects were given a script to follow on MACS. They were filmed while going through the script and thinking-aloud. Before they started the test they were given a briefing about what MACS is intended to achieve; how social norms in MACS have to be defined by people who share the workplace, rather than management; and what the situation they're trying to test is, i.e. they were told every person in the workplace is represented by an avatar, and to imagine they share a workplace with the 13 people presented in the MACS test version.

The script presented 15 instructions or questions that were meant to test all of MACS's features, without coaching subjects into achieving their goals. So rather than saying, e.g., "Please click on *social norms* to view all the norms you should abide by", it asked "What are the social norms in your workplace?".

The functionality that was tested included:

- flagging a co-worker's violation of norms;
- reputations;
- apologising for a violation of the social norms;
- notifications and forgiveness;
- social norms;
- "busy" status; and
- historical information

The intended work-flow and user interfaces to support the smooth passage of the work-flow have been validated by the UX user testing. There wasn't any task the test subjects couldn't perform, and the issues we found were mostly related to a first-time usage lack of hints for some situations. All test subjects said they found MACS to be very easy and intuitive to use. Nevertheless MACS has been 'fine tuned' based on the feedback from the UX study.

However, there is one caveat to the interpretation of results, there was a personal connection between the evaluator and the test subjects, and the evaluator was in the room, so there is a slight possibility that the evaluator was interfering with the test conditions. However, a visible and audible emotive reaction was observed when people read the apology, which indicated the apology had elicited an empathic response. After that, all test subjects were instructed to either forgive or ignore the apology, and they all decided to forgive the offender.

On the other hand, one conclusion from UX testing is to draw up a set of 'design guidelines' as they specifically relate to the social norms:

- secure agreement on social norms from everyone who must abide by them;
- ensure the social norms are visible to everyone;
- allow for participatory adaption of social norms over time;
- provide ways for people to solve situations of incivility amongst themselves, without the need for micro-management;
- ensure awareness of, and enforcement of, graduated sanctions for repeated violation of norms;
- offer positive feedback for people who consistently abide by the social norms.

5.2   Heuristic Evaluation Against Ostrom's Principles

Heuristic evaluation is a common evaluation method used in human-computer interaction. The idea is that interfaces are designed according to a set of principles, so one way to evaluate the interface is for the evaluator to walk through a series of screens and checking that the design principles have been observed.

Also from human-computer interaction, the concept of visualisation tries to ensure that interfaces make information that is conceptually important is made perceptually accessible.

In the case of MACS, we have been motivated by the idea of a self-organising, norm-governed institution based on the eight institutional design principles of Elinor Ostrom, and the visualisation of those in and through the user interface. We have therefore applied a sort of heuristic evaluation to MACS from the perspective of visualising Ostrom's design principles. The results are as follows.

Principle 1: Clearly defined boundaries (of membership and resources). MACS is built to be used by people who share an open-space. People outside the open-space have no saying in the social norms definition and modification, and the office occupants resolve incivilities amongst themselves. In this sense, MACS defines clear group boundaries.

Principle 2: Congruence between appropriation and provision rules and local conditions. People who are going to use the common goods are the ones defining the social norms, so these rules should reflect ways of using the common goods. However, MACS can't guarantee they do, because it has no saying in the social norms defined for a workplace. But we believe by giving the power to create the norms to the people who will abide by them, they can and will decide on their ideal way of sharing common goods.

Principle 3: Self-determination of collective-choice arrangements. This principle states "individuals affected by the operational rules can participate in modifying the operational rules" [15] and this is one of the principles MACS is grounded on. With its participatory definition and adaptation of social norms, MACS fits the principle that those affected by the rules can participate in defining and modifying them.

Principle 4: Effective monitoring by monitors who are part of or accountable to the appropriators. MACS provides community members with a system for monitoring members' behaviour. It's intended to be used by people who share a workplace, and they all have the same kind of access to the system. They define the norms they're going to abide by and adapt them over time, through a voting system. Norm compliance is monitored by the members, as they're the ones flagging other people's violations of the social norms.

Principle 5: Graduated sanctions for resource appropriators who violate communal rules. Graduated sanctions progress incrementally based on severity of the violation and recidivism. MACS provides the tools for grounding graduated sanctions on, as it keeps historical data about violations of norms and the following actions, e.g. how many times someone has broken a specific norm, whether or not the offenders apologise, and whether or not the victims forgive the offenders.

Two of our proposed guidelines are relevant to this principle: "Making people aware of the graduated sanctions applicable for repeated violation of norms" and "Enforcing graduated sanctioning for repeated violation of norms".

Principle 6: Mechanisms for conflict resolution that are cheap and of easy access. This principle is the *sine qua non* for MACS: the entire event processing loop and forgiveness modules are predicated on effective conflict resolution, and indeed, by heightening awareness, of effective conflict prevention. Not only does MACS allow for people to flag violations of norms, it also lets offenders know their actions have violated the norms (many times people don't realise they've done something wrong until they're informed of it). Then MACS promotes dispute resolution, by allowing offenders to apologise and explain what happened, and victims to accept the offenders' apologies and forgive them.

Principle 7: Self-determination of the community recognised by higher-level authorities. MACS's social norms are defined by those who will abide by them, and only by them. This means even if management thinks they'd like to impose a social norm, the only thing they can do about that is to suggest it to the employees. That social norm will be inserted in MACS, only if everyone who would abide by it, agrees with it.

Principle 8: Nested enterprises, from the lowest level up to the entire interconnected system. This principle is the only one that is completely not applicable, as it's meant for a whole organisation, rather than a workplace.

6   Further Work and Related Research

There are undoubtedly a number of limitations of the current system and opportunities for improvement and further work. These include:

- Positive flagging and feedback. By analysing reputations and historical data, MACS could, from time to time, provide positive feedback to users who have good reputations and users whose reputations have been consistently evolving positively for some time.
- Affective interaction. It has been shown affective dissonance, i.e. a change in the physiological signals, can be derived by using devices for measuring galvanic skin response [5]. A new version of MACS could integrate such devices and look for affective dissonance at (or close to) the time the victim claims there was a violation of norms.
- Event recognition. MACS relies on its users to indicate whenever a social norm is broken, but doesn't integrate any event recognition. Whenever an event is flagged, a social norm is implicated. One way of confirming whether or not that norm was, as claimed, broken, would be to use environment sensors and event handlers. This requires that the violation of the norm is capable of being measured in some way, for example it might be possible to use sensors to verify violations of noise and temperature-related norms; detecting the consumption of 'smelly' food during office hours might be harder;
- Privacy. All three of these developments raise a question of privacy, and whether people are willing to undergo 'sous-veillance' of this kind, even for a participatory sensing application where the data is guaranteed to go no further than the four office walls.

There are three directions for further research. The first is the relationship between the design method of MACS and what is called *design contractualism* [18]. Design contractualism is the idea that that designers make legal, moral or ethical judgements and then literally code them into the computer system. In some ways, the implementation of Ostrom's design principles in MACS are a kind of 'social contract' between the system developers, the employees, and the office occupants, and it would be interesting in subsequent field trials to evaluate this delegated model of self-governance.

The second direction concerns the nature of intelligent infrastructure. In other work, we have been exploring the contribution of intelligent agents in assisting with resource allocation, for example the SmartMeter in SmartGrids [4]. In the current instantiation of MACS, for example, the Forgiveness module works reactively as a decision-support system. It would be interesting to explore the potential of more pro-active computational intelligence in the system.

Finally, there are new efforts to make what might be considered to be platforms for more equitable social networking applications: see for example the Open Mustard Seed (OMS) initiative of the Institute for Data Driven Design (ID3: idcubed.org). It would be extremely interesting to re-imagine and re-engineer MACS as an application running on OMS and test it in multiple different communal spaces.

7   Summary and Conclusions

In this paper, we have considered a substantial problem in today's knowledge economy – with numerous pressures from specific social, cultural and organisational directions, instances of workplace incivility are on the increase. Although low-grade, cumulatively it is becoming a significant problem for organisations and workforce alike.

The solution we have proposed is based on envisioning a shared working environment as common-pool resource, and trying to leverage Ostrom's concepts of long-enduring, self-organising, norm-governed institutions as a way of managing such a resource. This envisionment has been realised in the system MACS, whose architecture and interfaces have been presented. Particular features of MACS are participatory adaptation in the selection of the office norms, the visualisation of Ostrom's institutional design principles in the interface, and restoration of a homeostatic equilibrium through an autonomic mechanism based on forgiveness.

It could be said sardonically, given our recent track-record in formalising Ostrom's theories, that "if the only tool you have is an Ostrom-shaped hammer, then every problem you see is a collective action-shaped nail". We would counter-argue that, just because our tool is an Ostrom-shaped hammer, it doesn't mean the problem isn't a collective action-shaped nail. We would maintain that treating workplace incivility as a collective action problem through the medium of Ostrom's institutional design principles achieves two goals. Firstly, it is successful step in converging norm-governed systems with pervasive, adaptive and affective computing; and secondly it demonstrates the possibilities for self-regulatory platforms for successful collective action in such communal situations.

Acknowledgements. This paper is based on an Invited Talk at the COIN Workshop at PRIMA, Dunedin, 2013, presented by the second author. We are very grateful to the organisers of the workshop for the opportunity to present this work, and to the participants of the workshop for their helpful questions and discussion.

References

1. Andersson, L., Pearson, C.: Tit for tat? the spiraling effect of incivility in the workplace. Acad. Manag. Rev. **24**(3), 452–471 (1999)
2. Artikis, A.: Dynamic specification of open agent systems. J. Logic Comput. **22**(6), 1301–1334 (2012)
3. Bennett, R.J., Robinson, S.L.: The past, present, and future of workplace deviance research. In: Greenberg, J. (ed.) Organizational Behavior: The State of the Science, 2nd edn, pp. 235–268. Lawrence Erlbaum, Mahwah, NJ (2003)
4. Bourazeri, A., Pitt, J., Almajano, P., Rodríguez, I., López-Sánchez, M.: Meet the meter: visualising smartgrids using self-organising electronic institutions and serious games. In: SASO Workshops, pp. 145–150 (2012)
5. Farrer, J., Goulev, P., Pitt, J.: Emotive episode: an investigation into user response to sustainable issues in fashion/textiles and affective computing. In: Proceedings of the Sustainable Innovation 06: Global Challenges, Issues and Solutions, pp. 54–60 (2006)

6. Goulev, P., Mamdani, E.: Utilizing real time affectivesensors to incorporate emotions into human computer interactions. In: International Workshop on Wearable and Implantable, Body Sensor Networks, London, pp. 6–7 (2004)
7. Hewitt, C.: Offices are open systems. Trans. Inf. Syst. **4**(3), 271–287 (1986)
8. Khopkar, T., Li, X., Resnick, P.: Self-selection, slipping, salvaging, slacking, and stoning: the impacts of negative feedback at eBay. In: Proceedings of the 6th ACM Conference on Electronic Commerce, pp. 223–231. ACM (2005)
9. Kim, S., Smith, R.H.: Revenge and conflict escalation. Negot. J. **9**(1), 37–43 (1993)
10. Klein, T.J., Lambertz, C., Spagnolo, G., Stahl, K.O.: The actual structure of eBay's feedback mechanism and early evidence on the effects of recent changes. Int. J. Electron. Bus. **7**(3), 301–320 (2009)
11. Leiter, M.: Analyzing and Theorizing the Dynamics of the Workplace Incivility Crisis. Springer, New York (2013)
12. Lim, S., Cortina, L., Magley, V.: Personal and workgroup incivility: impact on work and health outcomes. J. Appl. Psychol. **93**(1), 95–107 (2008)
13. McCullough, M.E.: Forgiveness: who does it and how do they do it? Curr. Dir. Psychol. Sci. **10**(6), 194–197 (2001)
14. Miner, K.N., Settles, I.H., Pratt-Hyatt, J.S., Brady, C.C.: Experiencing incivility in organizations: the buffering effects of emotional and organizational support. J. Appl. Soc. Psychol. **42**(2), 340–372 (2012)
15. Ostrom, E.: Governing the Commons: The Evolution of Institutions for Collective Action. Cambridge University Press, Cambridge (1990)
16. Pearson, C., Porath, C.: On the nature, consequences and remedies of workplace incivility: no time for 'nice'? think again. Acad. Manag. Executive **19**(1), 7–18 (2005)
17. Picard, R.W.: Affective Computing. MIT Press, Cambridge (1997)
18. Pitt, J.: Design contractualism for pervasive/affective computing. IEEE Technol. Soc. Mag. **31**(4), 22–29 (2012)
19. Pitt, J., Bhusate, A.: Enhancing quality of experience in public collections. In: Trillas, E., Bonissone, P.P., Magdalena, L., Kacprzyk, J. (eds.) Combining Experimentation and Theory. STUDFUZZ, vol. 271, pp. 271–286. Springer, Heidelberg (2011)
20. Porath, C., Pearson, C.: The price of incivility. Harvard Bus. Rev. **91**(1–2), 114 (2013)
21. Resnick, P., Kuwabara, K., Zeckhauser, R., Friedman, E.: Reputation systems. Commun. ACM **43**(12), 45–48 (2000)
22. Resnick, P., Zeckhauser, R.: Trust among strangers in Internet transactions: empirical analysis of eBay's reputation system. Adv. Appl. Microeconomics **11**, 127–157 (2002)
23. Vasalou, A., Pitt, J., Piolle, G.: From theory to practice: forgiveness as a mechanism to repair conflicts in CMC. In: Stølen, K., Winsborough, W.H., Martinelli, F., Massacci, F. (eds.) iTrust 2006. LNCS, vol. 3986, pp. 397–411. Springer, Heidelberg (2006)
24. Vasalou, A., Joinson, A.N., Pitt, J.: Constructing my online self: avatars that increase self-focused attention. In: Proceedings of the SIGCHI Conference on Human Factors in Computing Systems, pp. 445–448. ACM (2007)
25. Vasalou, A., Pitt, J.: Reinventing forgiveness: a formal investigation of moral facilitation. In: Herrmann, P., Issarny, V., Shiu, C.S.K. (eds.) iTrust 2005. LNCS, vol. 3477, pp. 146–160. Springer, Heidelberg (2005)

Analysis of the Use of Events and States as Brute Facts in Modelling of Institutional Facts

Maiquel de Brito[1](✉), Jomi Fred Hübner[1], and Rafael H. Bordini[2]

[1] Federal University of Santa Catarina, Florianópolis, SC, Brazil
maiquel.b@posgrad.ufsc.br, jomi.hubner@ufsc.br
[2] FACIN–PUCRS, Porto Alegre, RS, Brazil
r.bordini@pucrs.br

Abstract. Although the institutional dimension of a multi-agent system can be affected directly by the actions of the agents, it can be also affected by facts originating in the environment or even in the institution. In previous work, we proposed a model, language and its interpreter to specify the institutional consequences of both events and states from environment and institution. This paper analyses this twofold approach, looking for a better understanding about the performance of the interpreter and about the design differences between using event and states. The contributions of this work are (i) the evaluation of some aspects of a proposed and implemented language, (ii) guidelines to choose between events and states to model count-as rules, and (iii) an initial benchmark to evaluate further improvements to the interpreter and the performance of similar proposals.

Keywords: Institutional facts · Constitutive rules · Environment · Institution · Events · States

1 Introduction

In open multi-agent systems (MAS), the autonomous behaviour of the agents can endanger the achievement of system goals [3,5,15]. To deal with this issue, the use of an institutional dimension is a usual approach [10]. That dimension can be formed by several kinds of mechanisms, such as norms, roles, sanctions, etc.[1]. While the *state* of the institutional dimension can be affected directly by the actions of the agents, it can be also affected by facts originating in the environment or even in the institution itself. For instance, the detection, through a camera [13], of an agent running through a red traffic light is a fact triggered by an environmental artifact (the camera) originating from the action of the agent in the environment. This fact means, in the institutional dimension, a norm violation.

---

[1] Besides agents and institution, this work considers the environment as a first-class abstraction, composed by non autonomous elements that encapsulate functionalities and services to support agent activities [16].

T. Balke et al. (Eds.): COIN 2013, LNAI 8386, pp. 177–192, 2014.
DOI: 10.1007/978-3-319-07314-9_10, © Springer International Publishing Switzerland 2014

The specification of the institutional meaning of facts occurred in environment and institution has been addressed in the MAS research literature [1,3, 8,9,15,19], most of them inspired by the *count-as* theory proposed by John Searle [18]. According to the literature, either events or states from environment and institution are *brute facts* that can have a meaning in the institutional level. The aforementioned example of an agent running through a red traffic light is an *event* with institutional meaning. To illustrate the institutional meaning of a *state*, we can consider that the fact of an agent situated into a classroom means, in institutional dimension, that the agent has the duties and the rights of a student.

While most of models focus on a specific kind of brute fact, in an earlier work [7] we proposed a programming language and its interpreter where *count-as rules* model the institutional meaning of both events and states. The aim of this double approach was (i) to fit the proposal in environmental and institutional models that give access both to events and states, (ii) to allow the modelling of the count-as rules where a specific kind of brute fact is more suitable and (iii) give more flexibility in allowing the designer to choose a particular kind of brute fact when events and states are interchangeable. This double approach, however, raises the following questions that are addressed in this paper: (i) is the use of both events and states really needed in the same model? (ii) in situations where both events and states are applicable, what are the aspects to be taken into account to choose a specific approach (considering both performance and design aspects)?

To address these questions, this paper evaluates both the event- and the state-based approaches from our previous work. This evaluation is twofold, focusing on (i) performance and (ii) design aspects. The design analysis, described in Sect. 4, investigates when a particular approach is more suitable (or even mandatory) regardless of performance aspects. By evaluating the performance, in Sect. 3, we analyse the behaviour of the interpreter in evaluating events and states by taking into account some aspects such as the amount of events and state changes of the system and the size of the rule set. The design analysis help us to answer the first question, verifying situations where either events or states are mandatory. Moreover, the design analysis and the performance analysis help us to answer the second question regarding performance and design aspects that influence a better choice between events and states. The main contributions of this work are (i) an evaluation of the performance of an implemented interpreter for a language to program count as rules, (ii) an evaluation of both event- and state-based approach for specification of institutional facts, (iii) guidelines for design of count-as rules taking into account both performance and functional aspects and (iv) an initial framework for benchmarking the language and interpreter proposed in [7] and similar work.

2   Background

In this paper, the focus is on the use of both events and states as the brute fact (i.e. the activation condition) of count-as rules, that are based on the theory of

John Searle [18]. Searle observed that, in human societies, the facts occurring in institutional level (*institutional facts*) are a correspondence of more concrete ones, named *brute facts*. This correspondence is described by *constitutive rules* (or *count-as rules*) that have the form X *count as* Y *in* C where: (i) X is a brute fact; (ii) Y is an institutional fact that is consequence of the brute fact X and (iii) C is the context where X *count as* Y. For instance, a priest performing a ceremony (X) *count as* an act of marriage (Y) if there is a sufficient number of witnesses (C).

In MAS, some works investigate how brute facts (agent interaction, agent actions in the environment, events occurred in the environment, etc.) may have meaning in institutional level (pointing to a correspondence to the Searle's theory) [2,3,7–9,15,19]. Events are brute facts in [15,19]. States are brute facts in [9]. Actions of the agents are brute facts in [1,3,8].

The model proposed in our previous work [7] considers an MAS as a system where agents, environment, and institution are first-class abstractions [20]. Environment and institution have *observable* events and states[2]. Charles Hamblin points that events are of two types: (i) deeds, which are performed by the agents and (ii) happenings, which are world effects [11,14]. The events, in this work, are happenings[3]. We use E to refer to the set of all observable events in the environment and institution. A state is characterized by a set of properties that can be observed in environment and institution. We use P_e to refer to the set of all observable properties of the environment (a particular environmental state s_e is a subset of P_e). Similarly, P_i refers to the set of all observable properties of institution (a particular institutional state s_i is a subset of P_i). We use $P = P_e \cup P_i$ to refer to the set of all environmental and institutional observable properties. In our model both observable events and observable states from environment and institution can lead to changes in the observable state of the institution. This dynamics is modelled in a *count-as program* composed by two kinds of *count-as rules*: (i) *event-count-as rules*, that deal with events and (ii) *state-count-as rules* that deal with states. Formally, both *event-count-as rules* and *state-count-as rules* are a tuple $\langle x, y, c \rangle$ where:

- x is a brute fact. In *event-count-as rules*, $x \in E$. In *state-count-as rules*, x is a logical formula composed of predicates belonging to P which point to the observable state of the environment and institution; the formula must be true for the rule to apply;
- $y \in 2^{P_i}$ is a set of institutional properties that become true in the institution through the application of the rule. Since y is a set or properties instead of an event, a count-as rule defines how the institution *must to be* rather than what it *must to do*.
- c is a logical formula composed of predicates belonging to P which point to the observable state of the environment and institution; the formula must be true for the rule to apply.

---

[2] About the unobservable portion, its existence is assumed but is not of our concern.
[3] Although some happenings are effects of agents' actions, our focus is just on the effect regardless the agents' action.

The interpreter for the count-as program, named *Count-as Engine*, is placed side by side with the environmental and institutional platforms. It is constantly informed by these platforms about events and new states and, as the result of the application of some count-as rule, the interpreter sends to the institutional platform what should be its next state. The operational semantics is given as a transition system where a particular state of the system is represented by a *configuration* as formally defined below.

Definition 1. *A configuration of the transition system is a tuple* $\langle R_e, R_s, D, \mathcal{E}, \mathcal{N}, \mathcal{I}, \mathcal{T} \rangle$, *where:*

- R_e *is a set of* event-count-as *rules provided by (the parsing of) the count-as program;*
- R_s *is a set of* state-count-as *rules provided by the count-as program;*
- D *is a set of* domain knowledge *predicates provided by the count-as program;*
- $\mathcal{E}$ *is a queue of events* $e \in E$ *provided by the environment and institution platforms;*
- $\mathcal{N}$ *is a set of predicates representing the observable state of the environment as provided by the environment platform;*
- $\mathcal{I}$ *is a set of predicates representing the observable state of the institution as provided by the institution platform;*
- $\mathcal{T}$ *is a queue of properties that are the result of the interpretation of the rules and must become true of the institution.*

The initial configuration is $\langle R_e, R_s, D, \emptyset, \emptyset, \emptyset, \emptyset \rangle$. As the interpreter runs, and events and states are informed by the platforms, this configuration evolves as defined by transition rules explained in Sects. 2.1 and 2.2[4].

2.1   Event Processing

Let $\mathsf{head}(\mathcal{E})$ be a function that returns the head of a list, $\mathsf{tail}(\mathcal{E})$ be a function that returns the tail of a list, and θ be a substitution of all variables of the brute fact in the rule. The Count-as Engine constantly checks the queue $\mathcal{E}$. If there is an *event-count-as* rule where $x\theta$ is equal to the event given by $\mathsf{head}(\mathcal{E})$, the term c is a logical consequence of the state of environment and institution, and the count-as consequence y does not belong to the current state of the institution, then the rule fires. As a result, the properties expressed by y will be added to the result queue $\mathcal{T}$.

$$\frac{\langle x, y, c \rangle \in R_e \qquad x\theta = \mathsf{head}(\mathcal{E}) \qquad \mathcal{N} \cup \mathcal{I} \cup D \models c \qquad y \notin \mathcal{I}}{\langle R_e, R_s, D, \mathcal{E}, \mathcal{N}, \mathcal{I}, \mathcal{T} \rangle \longrightarrow \langle R_e, R_s, D, \mathsf{tail}(\mathcal{E}), \mathcal{N}, \mathcal{I}, \mathcal{T} \cup y \rangle}$$

---

[4] In this paper we present the most relevant transition rules for the language semantics. The complete operational semantics is presented in [7].

2.2 State Processing

When the environmental or the institutional platforms inform changes in their states, the Count-as Engine starts an evaluation cycle. In an evaluation cycle, all state-count-as rules are evaluated. Each *state-count-as* rule $r_s \in R_s$ whose brute fact x and context c are logical consequences of the state of the environment and institution is triggered and its properties expressed by y are added to the result queue $\mathcal{T}$.

$$\frac{\langle x, y, c \rangle \in R_s \qquad \mathcal{N} \cup \mathcal{I} \cup D \models x \qquad \mathcal{N} \cup \mathcal{I} \cup D \models c \qquad y \notin \mathcal{I}}{\langle R_e, R_s, D, \mathcal{E}, \mathcal{N}, \mathcal{I}, \mathcal{T} \rangle \longrightarrow \langle R_e, R_s, D, \mathcal{E}, \mathcal{N}, \mathcal{I}, \mathcal{T} \cup y \rangle}$$

3 Performance Analysis

This section analyses the performance of the Count-as Engine evaluating states and events. This analysis aims to understand how the behaviour of Count-as Engine is affected by the number of (i) events, (ii) state changes, and (iii) rules. A clear understanding about these points is suitable (i) to guide the choice between the use of event- or state-count-as rules (when both approaches are interchangeable) and (ii) to guide and evaluate further improvements in the interpreter.

A simple MAS composed by agents, environment, and institution has been designed for the analysis. In this MAS, the institution drives the system to the achievement of its goal: to process all integer numbers ranging from 1 to an upper bound. The numbers are informed by the agents to an environmental artifact that accepts any number. The institution, however, expects that the numbers are informed consecutively in ascending order. Thus, the institution recognizes only the successor of the last informed number. For instance, if the last number recognized by the institution is 9, the institution will accept only the number 10 and will ignore any other (Fig. 1). Thus, in this scenario, it is possible to state that *the filling of a number counts as a correct filling if the filled number is the successor of the number last computed by the institution.*

In the experiment, the agents, coded in *Jason* [6], act in an environment implemented with CArtAgO [17]. The environment artifact provides the operation *fill_number*(X) that allows the agents to inform a number. When completed, the operation triggers the event fill_number(X) and updates the observable property last_filled(X). Figure 2 shows an event-count-as rule stating the institutional meaning of the event and an state-count-as rule stating the institutional meaning of the state. The rules are similar as, while the event-count-as rule has one event in *term x*, the state-count-as rule has only 1 property in *term x* and, in addition, *term y* and *term c* are identical in both rules. Although the scenario is simple, it is suitable to our analysis. The institution drives the system to achieve its overall goal. This achievement depends on the agents: they are the elements that act informing the numbers. To inform the numbers, the agents need an environmental resource. The agents focus on acting in the environment and are not concerned about the institution. In the Sects. 3.1 and 3.2 this scenario is used

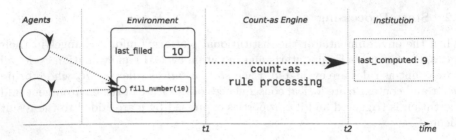

Fig. 1. Agents fill in the number 10, that will be computed by the institution.

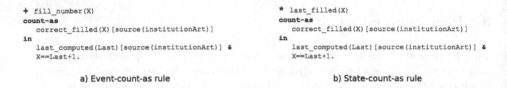

a) Event-count-as rule   b) State-count-as rule

Fig. 2. Count-as rules for performance analysis

for the performance analysis. The performance is evaluated considering the time that the CE takes to process a count-as rule. In Fig. 1, this time corresponds to the period between the instant $t1$ and $t2$. The measured time, however, is the time taken by a complete execution of the system, from the starting of the execution to the processing, by the institution, of the last expected number[5]. Although the performance analysis takes into account the execution time, our focus is on the variation of the time rather than the absolute time. While the absolute time is affected by aspects such as computational resources, features of the count-as rules and features of the application, the focus here is to observe how the performance of evaluation of similar rules is affected by change of some variables (number of events, number of rules, etc.) using similar computational resources in the same application.

3.1   Performance Against the Number of Events and State Changes

The first analysis verifies the performance of the Count-as Engine when the number of events and state changes is increased. For each kind of rule, 10 rounds of experiments were executed. Each round increases the number of agents by 10. The first round has 11 agents and the 10th round has 101 agents. In every round of the experiment, the agents inform 100 integer numbers to the environmental artifact, ranging from 1 to 100. As all agents concurrently perform actions

---

[5] Although the complete execution time is influenced by factors other than the CE (e.g. the time taken by an agent acting in the environment, the time that the environmental artifact takes to process an action, etc.), the comparisons are made considering these factors as equals, changing only the factors under evaluation.

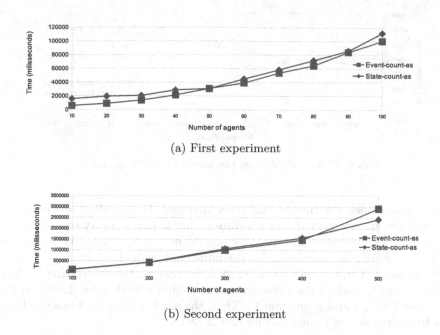

(a) First experiment

(b) Second experiment

Fig. 3. Performance when the number of events and state changes increases

in the environment, the increasing of the number of agents implies increasing of the number of observable events. This implies also a more dynamic change of the observable state of the environment, as the actions change its observable properties. A second experiment was performed where the number of agents ranges from 100 to 500.

We observe that the execution time increases almost linearly with the increasing in the number of events and state changes (Fig. 3). Although the execution time of event- and state-count-as rules was different over the different rounds, the behaviour of two kinds of rules is similar. We observe that, while event-count-as rules were faster in some rounds, state-count-as rules were faster in other rounds. These differences seems related to external factors, introduced by the experiment environment. Taken from a bird's eye view, both kinds of rules seem to have a similar growing trend.

3.2   Number of Rules

The second analysis verifies how the number of count-as rules of a count-as program affects the performance of the rule evaluation. In the experiment, 10 agents inform 100 integer numbers to the environmental artifact, ranging from 1 to 100. For each kind of rule, 11 rounds were executed. Each round increases the number of rules in 2000. The first round has one rule and the 11th round has 20001 rules. Figure 4 displays the result of the experiment. It is possible to observe that, with event-count-as rules, the performance is stable and with

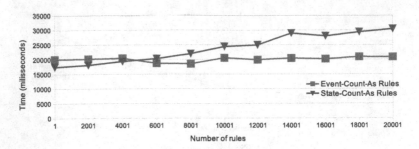

Fig. 4. Performance when the number of rules increases

state-count-as rules, the time of execution increases. This result is related to the
way the rules are interpreted. In each state evaluation cycle, every state-count-as
rule need to be evaluated (see Sect. 2.2 and Algorithm 2). Thus, the increasing
in the number of rules increases also the number of evaluations in a cycle. Let r
be the number of state-count-as rules, then the cost of state processing is $O(r)$.
In the event evaluation, the rules are selected from a hash table based on the
event (see Sect. 2.1 and Algorithm 1). Thus, the number of evaluations is related
only to the number of events and its cost is $O(1)$.

Algorithm 1. Algorithm for event processing

---

1 **when** event e happened
2   **if** $\exists \langle x, y, c \rangle \in R_e : x\theta = e$ **then**
3   **if** $\mathcal{N} \cup \mathcal{I} \cup D \models c$ **then**
4   the institution should have y
5   **end**
6   **end**
7 **end_when**

Algorithm 2. Algorithm for state processing

---

1 **when** observable state changed
2   **foreach** $\langle x, y, c \rangle \in R_s$ **do**
3   **if** $\mathcal{N} \cup \mathcal{I} \cup D \models x$ **then**
4   **if** $\mathcal{N} \cup \mathcal{I} \cup D \models c$ **then**
5   the institution should have y
6   **end**
7   **end**
8   **end**
9 **end_when**

---

4 Design Analysis

The choice between to write an event- or a state-count-as rule can be influenced by aspects such as designer's knowledge, models of environment and institution, implementation of institutional and environmental platforms and features of the system. In this section, we analyze some situations where, taking these aspects into account, (i) a particular kind of rule is mandatory, (ii) both kinds of rules are available but one of them is more suitable or (iii) both kinds of rules are interchangeable.

To illustrate some points of the analysis, we use the *Build-a-House* example [4]. The example concerns a MAS representing the inter-organizational work-flow involved in the construction of a house. An agent called Giacomo owns a plot and wants to build a house on it. In order to achieve this overall goal, first Giacomo will have to hire various specialized companies (the *contracting phase*) and then ensure that the contractors coordinate and execute the various required tasks required to build a house (the *building phase*). For each company, there is a *company* agent participating in the contracting phase and then, possibly, in the building phase too. In [7], the original example was extended using count-as rules. In this paper the example is extended again and the institutional specification defines also the resource management of the house building. For instance, the institutional goal *resources_for_floor* must be achieved before the achievement of the goal *floors_laid*. In the functional specification of the example (Fig. 5), the overall goal *house built* is decomposed in subgoals. Some subgoals must to be achieved in sequence and other can be achieved in parallel.

4.1 Undefined Relation Between Events and States

Besides the knowledge about the institutional meaning of events and states, the design of count-as rules is influenced by the relation between events and their consequent state changes *inside* the dimensions (from the designer perspective).

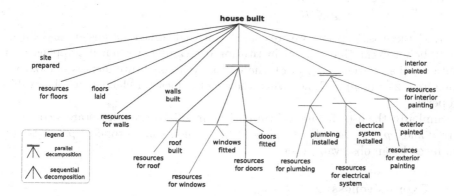

Fig. 5. Functional specification of the *Build-a-House* example (according to the Moise model [12]).

We assume that this relation can be unknown, i.e., we assume that some events do not change any known observable property and that some observable properties can be raised only by unobservable events. The undefined relation may be related to:

- **Partial knowledge about environmental and institutional models.** As the relation between event and state is taken here from the designer perspective we assume the possibility of incomplete knowledge about the institutional and environmental models we are dealing with. It is possible then that the system designers do not know all the events that produce some particular state and they have to write count-as rules using states. Conversely, designers may not know the complete system states generated after some relevant events, so they have to write count-as rule using events as triggers instead.
- **Absence of relation between events and states in environmental and institutional models.** Even if the observable portions of environment and institutional models are fully known, it could be the case that there is not relation between some events and states. Some reasons for this absence or relation are (i) features of the application and (ii) features of the environmental and institutional platforms.

In the *Build-a-House* example, the event *build_walls*, triggered when the building walls is done, does not change any observable state. This is a feature of the original implementation. Thus, the institutional meaning of the walls being done has to be described by an event-count-as rule. State-count-as rules are mandatory when properties are changed by unobservable events. The institutional model of the example has the goal *resources_for_floor* that is achieved when all resources needed for the floor laying are available. If it is not possible to observe the events that make the resources available, then the achievement of the goal has to be modelled by a state-count-as rule.

Formally, let $\mathcal{R} \subseteq E \times 2^P$ be the relation between events and its consequent state changes. We admit that:

- $\exists e \in E \; \forall p \in 2^P : (e, p) \notin \mathcal{R}$
- $\exists p \in P \; \forall e \in E : (e, p) \notin \mathcal{R}$

With these assumptions we are considering that some relations are undefined. Let e be an event that has an institutional meaning y when it happens in a context c (i.e., e *count-as* y *in* c), the use of events as brute facts is mandatory when $\forall p \in 2^P : (e, p) \notin \mathcal{R}$, i.e., when the event e does not change any observable property.

Similarly, the use of state as brute fact is mandatory when a state s count-as y in c and $\exists p \in s \;\; \forall e \in E : (e, p) \notin \mathcal{R}$, i.e., when some property $p \in s$ is not produced by an observable event.

4.2   Expressiveness

Even when the designer knows the relations between events and states, there are cases where either state based or event based rules are preferred. For instance,

```
/* Rule #1 */
* stock_of_brick(Brick)[source(stockArt)] & Brick>=10000 &
  stock_of_cement(Cement)[source(stockArt)] & Cement>=10 &
  stock_of_floorTile(FloorTile)[source(stockArt)] & floor_tile>=200 &
  water_supply[source(stockArt)]&
  electric_power[source(stockArt)]
count-as
  goalState(bhsch,resources_for_floors,Ag,Ag,satisfied)[source(bhsch)]
in
  play(Ag,house_owner,_)[source(hsh_group)].
```

(a) State-count-as rule

```
/* Rule #2 */
+ buy_brick(Brick)[artifact(stockArt)] & Brick>=10000
count-as
  goalState(bhsch,resources_for_floors,Ag,Ag,satisfied)[source(bhsch)]
in
  play(Ag,house_owner,_)[source(hsh_group)] &
  stock_of_cement(Cement)[source(stockArt)] & Cement>=10 &
  stock_of_floor_tile(FloorTile)[source(stockArt)] & FloorTile>=200 &
  water_supply[source(stockArt)]&
  electric_power[source(stockArt)]
```

(b) Event-count-as rule

```
/* Rule #3 */
+ buy_cement(Cement)[artifact(stockArt)] & Cement>=10
count-as
  goalState(bhsch,resources_for_floors,Ag,Ag,satisfied)[source(bhsch)]
in
  play(Ag,house_owner,_)[source(hsh_group)] &
  stock_of_brick(Brick)[source(stockArt)] & Brick>=10000 &
  stock_of_floor_tile(FloorTile)[source(stockArt)] & FloorTile>=200 &
  water_supply[source(stockArt)]&
  electric_power[source(stockArt)]
```

(c) Event-count-as rule

```
/* Rule #4 */
+ buyResourcesForFloors[artifact(stockArt)]
count-as
  goalState(bhsch,resources_for_floors,Ag,Ag,satisfied)[source(bhsch)]
in
  play(Ag,house_owner,_)[source(hsh_group)].
```

(d) Event-count-as rule

Fig. 6. Count-as rules

in particular cases, the combination of properties produced by n events (where $n > 1$) can *count-as* a new institutional state. While this can be expressed by a single state-count-as rule, n event-count-as rules are required. In the *Build-a-House* example, we can consider that the goal *resources_for_floor* is achieved when 5 properties hold and each property is produced by a different event. In this case, a single state-count-as rule (Fig. 6(a)) replaces 5 event-count-as rules (Figs. 6(b) and (c) illustrate two of them).

A state-count-as rule replaces n event-count-as rules if (i) every property in s is produced by just one event and (ii) at least two events are needed to produce s. Formally, a state-count-as rule is more expressive under the following conditions:

$$(i) \ \forall p \in s \ \exists e \in E \ \neg \exists e' \in E : (e,p) \in \mathcal{R} \wedge (e',p) \in \mathcal{R}$$

$$(ii)\ \exists p \in s\ \exists p' \in s\ \exists e \in E : (e,p) \subset \mathcal{R} \wedge (e,p') \notin \mathcal{R}$$

Figure 7 illustrates examples where a state s is composed by the properties $p1$, $p2$ and $p3$. In Fig. 7(a), a single state-count-as rule (Fig. 8 - rule 1) replaces three event-count-as rules (Fig. 8 - rules 2–4). In Fig. 7(b), although the property $p2$ can be produced by two events ($e1$ and $e2$), a single state count-as rule (Fig. 8 - rule 5) replaces two event-count-as rules (Fig. 8 - rules 6 and 7). It seems to be inconsistent to our previous claim that every property in s must be produced by just one event. But, if $p1$ or $p3$ holds, $p2$ necessarily also holds. Thus, we can even ignore $p2$. The Fig. 7(c) illustrates an example where it is not possible to replace several event-count-as rules with a single state-count-as rule, as when $p2$ or $p3$ holds, it is not possible know what event happened ($e2$ or $e3$).

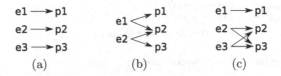

Fig. 7. Expressiveness cases

```
rule 1:   * p1 & p2 & p3 count-as y.
rule 2:   + e1 count-as y in p2 & p3.
rule 3:   + e2 count-as y in p1 & p3.
rule 4:   + e3 count-as y in p1 & p2.
rule 5:   * p1 & p3 count-as y.
rule 6:   + e1 count-as y in p3.
rule 7:   + e2 count-as y in p1.
```

Fig. 8. Rules for expressiveness cases

The contrary is not truth: if a single event produces n properties ($n \geq 1$), it is possible to use both event- and state-count-as rules. Considering that the state s counts as y in c, the use of state-count-as rule or event-count-as rule is equivalent if (i) all properties of s are produced by the same event e (ii) every property in s is produced only by e. Formally, event- and state-count-as rules are equivalent if:

$$\exists e \in E\ \neg \exists e' \in E\ \forall p \in s : (e,p) \in \mathcal{R} \wedge (e',p) \in \mathcal{R}$$

Let's suppose that the event *buyResourcesForFloors* changes the properties *stock_of_brick*, *stock_of_cement*, *stock_of_floorTile*, *water_supply*, and *electric_power*. In this case, the rules of Fig. 6(a) and (d) are equivalent.

5   Results

The explicit representation of both events and states provides flexibility to the model. With event-count-as rules it is possible to model institutional consequences to *what happens* in the environment and institution. With state-count-as rules it is possible to model institutional consequences to *how are* environment and institution. Another advantage of this twofold approach is the robustness against unpredicted changes in the environmental and institutional applications. The relation between events and their consequent states ($\mathcal{R}$) may change along the time. Assuming an external perspective, the designer may not predict changes in the environment and institution. The choice between events and states can cover unpredicted changes.

Although the performance of both kinds of rules is similar under equal conditions, the performance for state-count-as rules is influenced by the number of rules in a count-as program. Thus, it is worth taking into account an upper bound λ for the number of state-count-as rules. The bound λ is specific to the particular application. In our experiment, λ is around 5000 rules (Fig. 4).

Besides the performance, some design aspects influence the choice for a specific kind of rule. The designer can choose a particular approach accordingly to his knowledge about the platforms. Besides, if the platforms do not give access to observable events or observable states, a specific approach may be mandatory. Finally, in some cases, if there is some relation between events and the properties that it produces, there is some guidelines to be observed in order to do a suitable choice between events and states.

When there is no relation between events and states inside the dimensions, a specific kind of rule is mandatory (Sec. 4.1). For the cases where this relation exists, it is possible to state the following guidelines to choose between events and states as brute facts in count-as rules:

1. If the number of state-count-as rules is equal or higher than λ then the use of events seems a better choice.
2. If the number of state-count-as rules is lower than λ then
   (a) If s is a state such that (i) every property in s is produced by just one event and (ii) at least two events are needed to produce s, then the use of state is a better choice;
   (b) If s is a state and all properties $p \in s$ are produced only by the same event e then both event and state will produce one count-as rule.

We point that the use of events *seems* suitable when the number of state-count-as rules is equal or upper than λ (item 1) because other factors rather than λ can be considered. For example, if n is a very high number, (i) the writing of n event-count-as rules can be hard and (ii) the amount of computational resources for processing a higher number of rules can be unavailable.

5.1   Limitations of the Approach

There are some points related to the interpreter that must be considered when evaluating events and states. All observable events from the environment and

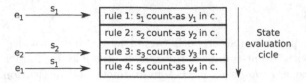

Fig. 9. State evaluation cycle

institution are stored in the Event Queue for further evaluation (Sect. 2). This is an advantage in the sense that all observable events will be eventually evaluated. A drawback of this approach, however, is the possibility that the context c of the rule, that was true when the event happened, does not hold when the event is evaluated. This implies that the rule will not be fired. Considering again a scenario where an agent runs through a traffic light in a context where the red light is on, the event is placed on the event queue for further evaluation. But, if during its evaluation, the context has already changed and the red light is not on anymore, the norm violation is not detected even though it actually happened. A way to deal with this issue would be to attach to each event a snapshot of the state that holds when the event occurs. The cost of getting the snapshot, however, seems to be significant (although it remains future work to systematically evaluate this).

Regarding state-based rules, they are all evaluated in an *evaluation cycle* that starts when the observable state changes. A drawback of this approach is the possibility of changes in the observable state during an evaluation cycle. Again, a rule that should be triggered when the state changes, might not be triggered when is evaluated. Figure 9 illustrates this issue in a scenario where an event e_i produces the state s_i (considering $1 \leq i \leq 4$) with a count-as program with 4 state-count-as rules that define institutional consequences for states s_1, s_2, s_3, s_4. The evaluation order is $\{rule1, rule2, rule3, rule4\}$. In the figure, the run $\{e_1, e_2, e_1\}$ occurs during a state evaluation cycle and e_2 occurs after the evaluation of $rule2$. As state s_2 starts to hold after the evaluation of $rule2$, this rule is not fired.

6   Conclusion and Future Work

This paper analysed the use of events and states as brute facts in count-as rules from the perspective of the language and interpreter proposed in [7]. The analysis focuses in performance and in design aspects of using both kinds of rules.

At the end of this paper, it is possible to answer the questions proposed at the beginning. First, the twofold approach proposed in [7] is appropriate since it accounts for the undefined relation between events and its consequent state changes inside environment and institution. Second, the main aspects to be taken into account to choose a specific kind of rule (when both events and states are applicable) are the (i) relation between events and their consequent states and (ii) the number of state-count-as rules of the count-as program.

The contributions of this work include an evaluation of the performance of an implemented interpreter, a design evaluation of the use of events and states as brute facts, some guidelines to choose between a particular approach, an initial benchmark for performance analysis and the identification of some drawbacks of the evaluated approach.

In future work, we plan to address some drawbacks raised from present evaluation, such as the evaluation of an event in a context that does not hold any more and the evaluation of states that hold and ceases to hold during a state evaluation cycle. We plan also to improve the current analysis with new experiments, evaluating other points of the use of events and states as brute facts in count-as rules.

Acknowledgments. Maiquel de Brito is financed by CAPES. Jomi Fred Hübner and Rafael H. Bordini acknowledge the partial financial support for this work given by CNPq (grant numbers 306301/2012-1 and 308095/2012-0).

References

1. Aldewereld, H., Álvarez-Napagao, S., Dignum, F., Vázquez-Salceda, J.: Making norms concrete. In: van der Hoek, W., Kaminka, G.A., Lespérance, Y., Luck, M., Sen, S. (eds.) Proceedings of the 9th International Conference on Autonomous Agents and Multiagent Systems, vol. 1, pp. 807–814, Toronto, Canada (International Foundation for Autonomous Agents and Multiagent Systems) (2010)
2. Aldewereld, H., Alvarez-Napagao, S., Dignum, F., Vázquez-Salceda, J.: Engineering social reality with inheritance relations. In: Aldewereld, H., Dignum, V., Picard, G. (eds.) ESAW 2009. LNCS (LNAI), vol. 5881, pp. 116–131. Springer, Heidelberg (2009)
3. Artikis, A., Pitt, J., Sergot, M.: Animated specifications of computational societies. In: Proceedings of the First International Joint Conference on Autonomous Agents and Multiagent Systems Part 3 - AAMAS '02, pp. 1053–1062. ACM Press, New York (2002)
4. Boissier, O., Bordini, R.H., Hübner, J.F., Ricci, A., Santi, A.: Multi-agent oriented programming with jacamo. Sci. Comput. Program. **78**(6), 747–761 (2013)
5. Boissier, O., Hübner, J.F., Sichman, J.S.: Organization oriented programming: from closed to open organizations. In: O'Hare, G.M.P., Ricci, A., O'Grady, M.J., Dikenelli, O. (eds.) ESAW 2006. LNCS (LNAI), vol. 4457, pp. 86–105. Springer, Heidelberg (2007)
6. Bordini, R.H., Hübner, J.F., Wooldridge, M.J.: Programming Multi-Agent Systems in AgentSpeak Using Jason. Wiley, Chichester (2007)
7. de Brito, M., Hübner, J.F., Bordini, R.H.: Programming institutional facts in multi-agent systems. In: Aldewereld, H., Sichman, J.S. (eds.) COIN 2012. LNCS (LNAI), vol. 7756, pp. 158–173. Springer, Heidelberg (2013)
8. Campos, J., López-Sánchez, M., Rodríguez-Aguilar, J.A., Esteva, M.: Formalising situatedness and adaptation in electronic institutions. In: Hübner, J.F., Matson, E., Boissier, O., Dignum, V. (eds.) COIN 2008. LNCS (LNAI), vol. 5428, pp. 126–139. Springer, Heidelberg (2009)

9. Dastani, M., Tinnemeier, N., Meyer, J.-J.: A Programming Language for Normative Multi-agent Systems, Chap. XVI. Information Science Reference, Hershey (2008)
10. Esteva, M., Rosell, B., Rodríguez-Aguilar, J.A., Arcos, J.L.: AMELI: An Agent-Based Middleware for Electronic Institutions. In: AAMAS'2004, pp. 236–243 (2004)
11. Hamblin, C.L.: Imperatives/C.L. Hamblin; Foreword by Nuel Belnap. Basil Blackwell, New York (1987)
12. Hübner, J.F., Sichman, J.S., Boissier, O.: Developing organised multiagent systems using the moise+ model: programming issues at the system and agent levels. Int. J. Agent-Oriented Softw. Eng. 1(3/4), 370–395 (2007)
13. Liu, Y., Payeur, P.: Robust image-based detection of activity for traffic control. J. Electr. Comput. Eng. Can. 28(2), 63–67 (2003)
14. Norman, T.J., Reed, C.: Delegation and responsibility. In: Castelfranchi, C., Lespérance, Y. (eds.) Intelligent Agents VII. LNCS (LNAI), vol. 1986, pp. 136–149. Springer, Heidelberg (2001)
15. Piunti, M.: Designing and programming organizational infrastructures for agents situated in artifact-based environments. Ph.D. thesis, Universit' di Bologna (2009)
16. Ricci, A., Piunti, M., Viroli, M.: Environment programming in multi-agent systems: an artifact-based perspective. Auton. Agent Multi-Agent Syst. 23(2), 158–192 (2011)
17. Ricci, A., Piunti, M., Viroli, M., Omicini, A.: Environment programming in CArtAgO. In: Fallah-Seghrouchni, A.E., Dix, J., Dastani, M., Bordini, R.H. (eds.) Multi-Agent Programming. Springer, New York (2009)
18. Searle, J.: The Construction of Social Reality. Free Press, New York (1995)
19. Stratulat, T., Ferber, J., Tranier, J.: MASQ: towards an integral approach to interaction. In: Sierra, C., Castelfranchi, C., Decker, K.S., Sichman, J.S. (eds.) AAMAS (2), pp. 813–820 IFAAMAS (2009)
20. Weyns, D., Omicini, A., Odell, J.: Environment as a first-class abstraction in multiagent systems. Auton. Agent. Multi-Agent Syst. 14(1), 5–30 (2007)

Norms

We Ought To; They Do; Blame the Management!

A Conceptualisation of Group Norms

Huib Aldewereld[1](✉), Virginia Dignum[1], and Wamberto Vasconcelos[2]

[1] Delft University of Technology, Delft, The Netherlands
{H.M.Aldewereld,M.V.Dignum}@tudelft.nl
[2] University of Aberdeen, Aberdeen, UK
wvasconcelos@acm.org

Abstract. Norms are used to represent desirable behaviours that software agents should exhibit in sophisticated multi-agent solutions. Although we now enjoy a body of research on norms, research has, so far, largely ignored a formal treatment of norms aimed at *groups of individuals*. Depending on the interpretation, group norms may be intended to effect all, each or some members of the group, sometimes requiring coordination among the members of the group to ensure norm-compliance. In this paper, we map out the various groups which might be involved, and use these groups to sketch a taxonomy of group norms. We also propose a formal representation of group norms using simple set expressions, and provide its semantics. To do so, we introduce a simple notion of power and formally represent the various cases of group norms of our taxonomy.

1 Introduction

The need for ever more sophisticated computing solutions requires distributed systems comprising of hundreds of individual components which may appear and disappear (i.e., systems are *open*). Moreover, the components themselves may have been developed by distinct parties, using disparate technologies (i.e., systems are *heterogeneous*). Norms have been used to represent, in compact ways, desirable behaviour components should have (alternatively, undesirable behaviour they should not have), so as to provide guarantees for distributed, open, and heterogeneous computing solutions.

Research on norms has tackled important issues, ranging from logic-theoretic aspects (e.g., [20]), to more pragmatic concerns (e.g., [15]). We have, however, detected an important gap in the literature – research has hitherto largely ignored a formal treatment of norms aimed at *groups of individuals*. Some examples of the kind of norms we mean here are:

1. "Program Committee members must return their reviews before the deadline";
2. "Project team members must file in a meeting report within 48 h after the meeting";

T. Balke et al. (Eds.): COIN 2013, LNAI 8386, pp. 195–210, 2014.
DOI: 10.1007/978-3-319-07314-9_11, © Springer International Publishing Switzerland 2014

3. "Groups of more than 3 school kids are prohibited from entering the shop".

These examples all refer to normative behaviour of groups of individuals. However, the intended effect of the norm varies: e.g., while in the first example, each PC member is obliged individually to return his/her review, in the second example, if one participant in the project team meeting files in the report, the obligation for the whole team is satisfied. The third example require coordination of activities between the group members. These examples show that group norms (i.e., norms referring or applying to a group, in opposition to norms applying to a single individual) are more than a mere aggregation of individual norms.

Although previous work has tackled related issues such as collective agency [6,7,28], and, even closer to our concern here, collective obligations [16], our research has uncovered various distinct groups which norms should formally account for, in order to properly capture our examples above, and others which occur in real-life. We formally represent three distinct groups, namely, (i) the group which the norm is addressed to (the addressees), (ii) the group responsible for the norm, and (iii) the group whose behaviours are affected by the norm. We provide a semantics for our group norms – since we differentiate acting from responsibility, we formally relate groups utilising a simple notion of power (akin to those notions developed in, for instance, [19,21]).

In the next section we present and motivate a taxonomy of group norms. This study provided us with information requirements for our formalisation, presented in Sect. 3 – we use a set-based language to represent our groups, and provide a formal definition for group obligations and prohibitions, together with their semantics; in that section we also put forth a simple definition of individual and group power. In Sect. 4 we formally represent group norms for the examples used to illustrate our taxonomy (Sect. 2). In Sect. 5 we discuss how our formalisation fits within organisation-based approaches to multi-agent systems engineering, and practical normative reasoning of individual agents. We contrast our research with related work in Sect. 6, and in Sect. 7 we draw conclusions, discuss relevant issues, and give avenues for future investigation.

2   A Taxonomy of Group Norms

One of the challenges with applying normative theories is that of describing observations and practices using the formal concepts offered by the theories. Our perception is that there is a distinct gap between the normative statements used in everyday practice and those that can be expressed in most (formal) normative modelling frameworks.

In everyday practice, norms can be seen as linguistic statements that prescribes, permits, or obliges actions or outcomes for actors (both individual and collective) [27]. This definition includes norms of collective nature, while most formal frameworks only allow the specification of role-oriented individual norms, that is individual norms that are specified in a generic way: e.g., "Program Committee members are obliged to return their reviews before the deadline." or "Project Team members must file a meeting report within 48 h after the end of the meeting." While these norms are stated more generically than, e.g., "Agent 0x0FF must return its review before the deadline", the first example is of a similar (individual) nature; each agent enacting the program committee role has to return its review(s) before the deadline. The second norm is different, however, since of all agents enacting the 'Project Team member' role, only one has to file a meeting report for all agents to be compliant with the norm. In the following we sketch a taxonomy of the different types of group norms, which we then formalise in Sect. 3.

Before we start to analyse what differentiates the various types of norms shown as examples above and in the introduction, let us first discuss the requirements for a formalism to express group norms. A normative formalism for the expression of collective/group norms in agent-based organizations should at least include the following elements:

- Deontic modality – necessary to represent and differentiate obligation, prohibition and permission (*how* the norm is influencing behaviours);
- Group representation – necessary to identify those to whom the norm applies (*who* the norm is influencing);
- Action/state representation – necessary to define what behaviour(s) the norm is influencing (*what* the norm is influencing).

Moreover, the formalism should comply with usual desirable properties of formalisation: compact, precise, machine-processable, and clear semantics.

Norms are a natural way of allocating tasks to groups and individuals. For example, if one wants that agent i achieves outcome φ, then one can stipulate that $O_i\varphi$. In the case of an individual agent, interpretation is straightforward, but in the case of a group, things get more complicated. For instance, by saying that "group G should achieve outcome φ", it is not clear who in the group should actually perform the actions that lead to φ and who is blamed if the outcome is not achieved. In order to grasp the meaning of this difference, we consider, for example, the obligation for children under the age of 16 to attend school. While the norm addresses children under the age of 16, who are also the ones who must perform the task, the responsibility and blame lays with their parents/guardians. Another example is a removal company, which is obliged by contract to move the contents of someone's house, including a piano. Given that the moving of the piano requires specialised qualifications, even though the removal company is the addressee of the obligation, the company is not able to act on it itself and must delegate the task.

Therefore, besides identifying who is addressed by the norm, two other important groups that can affect, or be affected, by a group norm, and must be included in the norm specification, are (i) responsibility, and (ii) fulfilment, or actorship. We distinguish three types of groups that are affected by a normative statement:

- **Addressees** describe who is addressed by the normative statement; i.e. to whom the normative statement applies
- **Actors** describe who should achieve the goal or action of the statement that the norm refers to

- **Responsibles** describe who takes care that the norm is upheld, and can be sanctioned if the norm is violated.

In the example about school attendance above, the children are both the addressee and the actor, and the parents are the responsible party. In the piano removal example, the removal company is the addressee and the responsible party, and the subcontractor is the actor. We notice that the concept of addressee is similar to that of attribute in the ADICO grammar for institutions introduced by Ostrom (cf. [27]).

In our view, *responsibility* expresses who gets the blame when the norm is violated (i.e., obligations that are not acted upon, or performing forbidden actions). This aspect of norms was already investigated in [16], with respect to (collective) obligations. It is also similar to the notion of "backward looking" responsibility, as defined in [8]. A limitation in the approaches of [8,16] is that they only consider obligations and collective action. Moreover, responsibility can be viewed on several levels in respect to collective norms: (a) individuals are each responsible for their part in the norm (*individual responsibility*), (b) the whole group is held accountable for failures of the group (*collective responsibility*), or (c) a representative is responsible for the failures of a group (*representative responsibility*); that is, an (previously) appointed member is held accountable for failures of the group.

Next to responsibility, we differentiate norms in terms of fulfilment, or *actorship*, that is, looking at who should fulfil the norm. This is similar to the notion of "forward looking" responsibility, which according to [8] accounts for task allocation and achievement. In some cases, each group member has to do their part in fulfilling the norm (that is, *individual actorship*). In other cases, it might be required that the group performs a collective action together (that is, *collective actorship*). While, in most formalisms, these are considered the same (as collective actions are assumed to be decomposable into individual parts), they have a distinct coordination difference. In the latter all the individual parts (namely, the single agent contributes with parts of the collective action) have to be performed in synchrony to be successful, while in the former, each agent can decide on its own when to perform the required individual action; one should compare, for instance, lifting a table (which is necessarily done together) with submitting a review (which has less stringent coordination restrictions[1]). There is a third case, where it might be that a single group member (or a select subset of the group) fulfilling the norm is sufficient, e.g., as in the filing of a meeting report example mentioned above; we call this latter type *representative actorship*.

This analysis of norms along these two directions, namely, responsibility and fulfilment, can be summarised by the matrix of options shown in Table 1.

---

[1] The only coordination aspect of submitting paper reviews is that they are all performed before a particular deadline, instead of them being done simultaneously at a same time.

Table 1. Taxonomy of group norms, based on responsibility and fulfilment.

	Individual responsibility	Representative responsibility	Collective responsibility
Individual actorship	(1,1) Individual norm specified in a generic (role-based) way: "PC members are obliged to return their reviews before the deadline."	(1,2) Individual action, appointed blame: "Employees are obliged to do task, but if task goes wrong blame management."	(1,3) Individual action, collective blame: "Each project member must file a meeting report within 48 h after the meeting."
Representative actorship	(2,1) Appointed action, individual blame: "Group leader must submit report by 12am, otherwise each student in the group fails the course."	(2,2) Appointed action, appointed blame: "Every meeting ought to have public minutes. The chairman is responsible for correct minutes being taken by secretary."	(2,3) Appointed action, collective blame: "An appointed project member must file a meeting report within 48 h after the meeting."
Collective actorship	(3,1) Collective action, individual blame: "Groups of more than 3 kids are not allowed to enter the shop together."	(3,2) Collective action, appointed blame: "All PhD students must pack the supervisor stuff for the department move, otherwise, the supervisor will be blamed."	(3,3) Group action, group blame: "The procedure must be carried out by a team of experts."

3 Formalisation

In this section we formalise group norms to capture all the different cases of our taxonomy from the previous section. First we start by introducing a language of set definitions required to precisely establish the various groups of our norms. After that we introduce group norms and provide their semantics via temporal logic.

3.1 Set Definitions

We propose a compact way to represent groups as set definitions and operations. We assume the existence of a non-empty and finite universal set $Agents = \{\alpha_1, \ldots, \alpha_n\}$ consisting of the unique identifier of each agent in our society.

Definition 1 (Set Definition). *A set definition Σ is as below*

$$\Sigma ::= \Sigma \cup \Sigma \mid \Sigma \cap \Sigma \mid \Sigma \setminus \Sigma \mid \Sigma^C \mid S$$
$$S ::= \{a_1, \ldots, a_n\} \mid \{x : P(x)\}$$

The grammar captures some of the common operations of naïve set theory [17], namely, union, intersection, difference, and absolute complement (with respect to the universal set *Agents*). The S stands for an actual set, and it can be represented as an extensive (finite) listing $\{\alpha_1, \ldots, \alpha_m\} \subseteq$ *Agents* of the elements of the set, or an intensional definition $\{x : P(x)\}$, standing for $\forall x \in$ *Agents*. $P(x)$, that is, all those elements of the universal set who fulfil some property P.

We extend the language of set definitions $\mathcal{L}_\Sigma$ to represent more sophisticated scenarios. It is common for certain norms to address groups with size restrictions, as in "gatherings of more than 5 people are prohibited". We can formalise such requirements as $|\Sigma| \circ n$, where $\circ$ is a comparison operator $>, <, \geq, \leq, =$, or $\neq$ and $n \in \mathbb{N}$ (a natural number). These set definitions can be seen as *constrained sets* and they restrict which sets can be built. For instance, if *Agents* $= \{a, b, c, d\}$ the definition $|\{x : \top\}| = 3$ (where $\top$ stands for "true", that is a property which is vacuously true for everyone) stands for all subsets of *Agents* with 3 elements, that is, all groups of three agents.

We formally define the value of a set definition Σ with respect to the universal set *Agents*, denoted as $value(\Sigma, Agents) \subseteq Agents$, as follows:

Definition 2 (Set Definition Value).

1. $value(\Sigma' \cup \Sigma'', Agents) = value(\Sigma', Agents) \cup value(\Sigma'', Agents)$
2. $value(\Sigma' \cap \Sigma'', Agents) = value(\Sigma', Agents) \cap value(\Sigma'', Agents)$
3. $value(\Sigma' \setminus \Sigma'', Agents) = value(\Sigma', Agents) \setminus value(\Sigma'', Agents)$
4. $value(\Sigma^C, Agents) = Agents \setminus value(\Sigma, Agents)$
5. $value(\{a_1, \ldots, a_n\}, Agents) = \{a_1, \ldots, a_n\}$
6. $value(\{x : P(x)\}, Agents) = \{a_0, \ldots, a_n\}, \forall i, 0 \leq i \leq n, a_i \in Agents \wedge P(a_i)$
7. $value(|\Sigma| \circ n, Agents) = value(\Sigma, Agents) \; s.t. \; |value(\Sigma, Agents)| \circ n$

Cases 1–4 "decompose" a set definition into its sub-parts, recursively obtaining their value, which then get combined, using the corresponding set operations – this is a straightforward mapping of our notation to the usual semantics of sets. Cases 5 and 6 are the "base cases": a set tabulation is itself, and an intensional definition gives rise to every possible sub-set whose elements satisfy property P. Case 7 generically defines the meaning of constrained sets – these are the values of the set definition which satisfy their constraints.

We assume a reference set *Agents* in our discussions, and since we are chiefly interested in what the set definitions actually are, we will simply use the set definitions Σ, meaning $value(\Sigma, Agents)$.

3.2 Group Norms and Their Semantics

We formally capture three different groups as sets expressions Σ, as introduced in the previous sub-section, as well as the usual [15,20] parts of norms, namely, the deontic modality and the target of the norm.

We make use of a set of propositions $\mathcal{P}$, which can be used to construct sentences using the usual propositional operators $\neg, \wedge, \vee, \rightarrow, \leftrightarrow$. We use variables like p, q, r to represent atomic propositions, and variables φ, δ, ψ to indicate propositional formulas. The set of well-formed propositional formulas is denoted as $\mathcal{L}_\mathcal{P}$. We define group norms as follows:

Definition 3 (Group norms). *Group norms are of the form* ${}^A\mathbf{O}^R_G \, \varphi < \delta$ *(a group obligation) or* ${}^A\mathbf{F}^R_G \, \varphi < \delta$ *(a group prohibition), where A, R and G are set definitions (from the language $\mathcal{L}_\Sigma$ of Definition 1), and φ, δ are propositional formulae from $\mathcal{L}_\mathcal{P}$.*

Intuitively, the annotations A, R and G of the deontic modalities $\mathbf{O}$ and $\mathbf{F}$ correspond to, respectively, the *actors* (those agents whose behaviours are affected by the norm), those *responsible* for the norm and the *addressees* of the norm. The construct $\varphi < \delta$ informally states "φ before δ", a temporal constraint which enables us to capture deadlines (of obligations) and periods (of prohibitions). Some examples of group norms and their informal meaning are:

- ${}^{|Kids'|>3}\mathbf{F}^{\{Kid\}}_{Kids} \ inShop < \bot$ – groups of more than 3 kids are forbidden to be in the shop; the norm is addressed (G) at the group of all kids, the actors (A) are groups of kids with 3 or more members, and each individual kid is responsible (R) for norm violation/compliance.
- ${}^{\{secretary\}}\mathbf{O}^{\{chair\}}_{Meeting} \ circulateMinutes < deadline$ – the chairperson of a meeting is obliged to have the secretary circulating the minutes before a deadline; the norm is addressed (G) at all members of the meeting, the actor (A) is the secretary and the responsible party (R) is the chairperson.

We provide the semantics of our group norms via a temporal logic based on CTL* [12]. Our temporal logical language $\mathcal{L}_{T\mathcal{P}}$ extends our propositional logic $\mathcal{L}_\mathcal{P}$ by adding path operators A (all paths), E (some paths), and state operators X (next), G (always), F (sometime), U (until). The language is further enriched with *stit*, $stit(x,\varphi)$ meaning x "sees to it that" φ [3] and expressing individual action, and $stit(G,\varphi)$ meaning that group G together "sees to it that" φ, for collective action. The semantics of this logic is constructed in the typical manner from the semantics of CTL* [12] combined with *stit* [3].

Following the formalisations of [10], our semantics of the deontic modalities are handled via an Anderson's reduction [2] of the modality to the reserved $viol(G, A, R, \varphi)$ construct indicating that a violation has happened of G's norm on φ by (in)action of A under the responsibility of R. We define the meaning of group obligations as follows:

Definition 4 (Semantics of Obligation).
$$
{}^A\mathbf{O}^R_G \, \varphi < \delta \stackrel{def}{=} \mathsf{AF}\, \delta \wedge \mathsf{A}\left[\left(\begin{array}{c}\neg\delta \wedge \neg stit(A,\varphi)\wedge \\ \neg viol(G,A,R,\varphi)\end{array}\right) U \right.
$$
$$
\left.\left(\left(\begin{array}{c}\neg\delta \wedge stit(A,\varphi)\wedge \\ \mathsf{X}(\mathsf{AG}\, \neg viol(G,A,R,\varphi))\end{array}\right) \vee \left(\delta \wedge viol(G,A,R,\varphi)\right)\right)\right]
$$

Intuitively, this definition expresses that the deadline δ will occur at some point in time and for all paths *either* φ is achieved by the actors ($stit(A, \varphi)$), in which case no violation of the obligation will ever occur ($\mathsf{X}(\mathsf{AG}\neg\ viol(G, A, R, \varphi))$), *or* the state is not achieved, the deadline occurs, and a violation happens ($\delta \wedge viol(G, A, R, \varphi)$). Similarly, we define the meaning of group prohibitions:

Definition 5 (Semantics of Prohibition).
$$^A\mathbf{F}_G^R\ \varphi < \delta \stackrel{def}{=} \mathsf{A}\left[\begin{pmatrix} \neg\delta \wedge \neg stit(A, \varphi) \wedge \\ \neg viol(G, A, R, \varphi) \end{pmatrix} U \right.$$
$$\left.\left(\begin{pmatrix} \neg\delta \wedge stit(A, \varphi) \wedge \\ viol(G, A, R, \varphi) \end{pmatrix} \vee (\delta \wedge \mathsf{AG}\ \neg viol(G, A, R, \varphi))\right)\right]$$

Group prohibitions are similar to group obligations, except that the deadline δ is better seen as a deactivation of the prohibition (and may, therefore, not actually occur in the future states, meaning the prohibition is not deactivated). So, until *either* a violation is triggered by seeing to it that the prohibited state is achieved before the deactivation ($\neg\delta \wedge stit(A, \varphi) \wedge viol(G, A, R, \varphi)$), *or* the prohibition is deactivated (after which no violation can occur any more; i.e. $\delta \wedge \mathsf{AG}\ \neg viol(G, A, R, \varphi)$), no violations should occur.

With these definitions of the meaning of group norms, when $G = A = R$ and they all refer to a role specification (in an organisation), we capture norms as explored in, for instance, [5,10] – all those agents adopting a role (hence belonging to the group) are simultaneously actors, addressees and responsible parties. For simplification and without loss of generality, in the rest of our discussion we may drop the deadline component of our norms.

To formally relate the responsible party and the actors of a group norm, we must formalise a notion of power[2], as explored in, for instance, [19,21,26], and more recently (and closer to our approach) in [11]. However, we do so in a simple fashion – ours is a minimalist definition which is sufficient for our purposes:

Definition 6 (Power). *Power* $\preccurlyeq \subseteq 2^{Agents}$ *is a reflexive* ($\forall x \in Agents.x \preccurlyeq x$) *and transitive* (($x \preccurlyeq y \wedge y \preccurlyeq z$) $\to x \preccurlyeq z$) *and anti-symmetric* (($x \preccurlyeq y \wedge y \preccurlyeq x$) $\to (x = y)$) *relation on the set of agents. If* $\alpha_1 \preccurlyeq \alpha_2$ *we say that* α_2 *has power over* α_1.

When an agent α_2 "has power over" another agent α_1 then α_2 may delegate tasks to α_1 – the *stit* operator might involve "passing down the buck" along a chain of pairs/delegations (hence the transitivity requirement), but all agents may consider themselves as potential actors (hence the reflexive requirement).

We extend the power relation to cater for sets of agents, that is, the value of groups, as follows:

Definition 7 (Group Power). *Given two sets of agents* $Agents_1, Agents_2 \subseteq Agents$, *and a power relation* $\preccurlyeq \subseteq 2^{Agents}$ *(cf. Definition 6) we say that* $Agents_2$

---

[2] We note that we address *social power* (*viz.*, a relation among individuals of a society, establishing who has authority or control over others [14]), as opposed to *institutional power* (*viz.*, whereby members of an institution are empowered to perform certain deeds [9,19]).

has power over Agents$_1$, denoted as Agents$_1 \preccurlyeq$ Agents$_2$, if, and only if, $\forall x \in$ Agents$_1.\exists y \in$ Agents$_2 : x \preccurlyeq y$, that is, every member of Agents$_1$ is power-related with at least one member of Agents$_2$.

Group power exploits the transitivity property of the underlying (individual) power relation.

4   Representing Group Norms

Using the formal definitions introduced in Sect. 3, we present here the formal specification of the different types of group norms described in Sect. 2. Depending on the membership of the different groups (addressees, actors and responsible) the 'scope of influence' of the group norm is different.

Table 2 provides the formalization of the different types of group norms described in Sect. 2, as follows. Concerning responsibility, individual responsibility is defined as assigning responsibility to each member of the Addressee set, i.e. norm responsibility is distributed to each of the Addresses, $\forall x \in G : R = \{x\}$, and in collective responsibility, the Responsible set R is the same as the Addressee set, $R = G$. Representative responsibility is more complex. As seen in some of the examples above, in some cases those who are responsible for upholding a norm (and getting the blame if not) are not those addressed by the norm (e.g. parents are responsible for the obligation for children to attend school). However, in order to be able to enforce responsibility, a power relation must exist between the Responsible group and the Actor group, i.e. $A \preccurlyeq R$.

Actorship is dealt with in a similar way. In the individual case, each member of the Addressee set is the Actor of the norm, $\forall x \in G : A = \{x\}$, and in the collective case, all Addressees must act together on the norm, $A = R = G$. Again, in the Representative Actorship case, a power relation is required between the Addressees and the Actors, $A \preccurlyeq G$.

Table 2. Formal characterisation of the different types of group norms.

	Individual responsibility	Representative responsibility	Collective responsibility
Individual actorship	$\forall x \in G : A = R = \{x\}$	$\forall x \in G : A = \{x\}$, $A \preccurlyeq R$	$\forall x \in G : A = \{x\}$, $R = G$
Representative actorship	$A \preccurlyeq G$, $\forall x \in G : R = \{x\}$	$A \preccurlyeq G$, $A \preccurlyeq R$	$A \preccurlyeq G$, $R = G$
Collective actorship	$A = G$, $\forall x \in G : R = \{x\}$	$A = G$, $A \preccurlyeq R$	$A = R = G$

The different interpretations of group norms above, also reflect on the target of the norm, i.e. the action being influenced by the norm. In all types of actorship, we assume that the members of the Actor set have the capabilities to act on the target. We are aware that this is a very strong assumption, and that the matter of linking capabilities to action is an open research issue which is out of the scope of this paper[3]. For the moment, we interpret the target of the different types of group norms as follows.

- **Individual Actorship:** the target φ is an individual action, i.e. $\forall x \in A : stit(x, \varphi)$
- **Collective Actorship:** the target φ is a collective action of the whole Addressee group, i.e. $stit(G, \varphi)$
- **Representative Actorship:** the target φ can be either an individual or a collective action. That is, if the actor set a singleton, i.e. $A = \{x\}$, then φ is such that $stit(x, \varphi)$; if the actor set is composed of more than one agent, i.e. $|A| > 1$, then φ is such that $stit(A, \varphi)$

In the following, we briefly demonstrate the applicability of the formalism, by providing the formal representation of the examples described in Table 1:

Case (1,1) Individual Responsibility, Individual Actorship
  PC members are obliged to return their reviews before the deadline, is formalised as:
  $\forall x \in PCM : {}^{\{x\}}\mathbf{O}_{PCM}^{\{x\}}$ *return_review < deadline*

Case (1,2) Representative Responsibility, Individual Actorship
  Employees are obliged to do task, but if task goes wrong blame management, is formalised as:
  $\forall x \in Employees, x \preccurlyeq Mngt : {}^{\{x\}}\mathbf{O}_{Employees}^{Mngt}$ *task*

Case (1,3) Collective Responsibility, Individual Actorship
  Each project member must file a meeting report within 48 h after the meeting, is formalised as:
  $\forall x \in ProjM, {}^{\{x\}}\mathbf{O}_{ProjM}^{ProjM}$ *file_report < 48h*

Case (2,1) Individual Responsibility, Representative Actorship
  Group leader must submit report by 12am, otherwise each student in the group fails the course, is formalised as:
  $\forall x \in Std : leader \in Std, leader \preccurlyeq Std, {}^{\{leader\}}\mathbf{O}_{Std}^{\{x\}}$ *submit < 12am*

Case (2,2) Representative Responsibility, Representative Actorship
  Every meeting ought to have public minutes. The chairman is responsible for correct minutes being taken by secretary, is formalised as:
  $secr \in Meeting, secr \preccurlyeq chair, {}^{\{secr\}}\mathbf{O}_{Meeting}^{\{chair\}}$ *take_minutes*

Case (2,3) Collective Responsibility, Representative Actorship
  An appointed project member must file a meeting report within 48 h after the meeting, is formalised as:
  $appMemb \in M, appMemb \preccurlyeq M, {}^{\{appMemb\}}\mathbf{O}_M^M$ *file_report < 48h*

Case (3,1) Individual Responsibility, Collective Actorship
  Groups of more than 3 kids are not allowed to enter the shop together, is formalised as:
  $\forall x \in Kids : {}^{|Kids'|>3}\mathbf{F}_{Kids}^{\{x\}}$ *enter_shop_together*

---

[3] We refer the interested reader to, e.g. [11].

Case (3,2) Representative Responsibility, Collective Actorship

All PhD students must pack the supervisor's stuff for the department move, otherwise, the supervisor will be blamed, is formalised as:

$$PhD \preccurlyeq prof, \quad {}^{PhD}\mathbf{O}_{PhD}^{\{prof\}} \ pack\_stuff$$

Case (3,3) Collective Responsibility, Collective Actorship

The procedure must be carried out by a team of experts, is formalised as:

$${}^{Experts}\mathbf{O}_{Experts}^{Experts} \ procedure$$

5 Group Norms in Practice

Norms aimed at groups of individuals require that groups are clearly defined and, very importantly, that individuals are aware of the groups they belong to. Human societies have natural groups (e.g., females over a certain age and with two children), as well as groups artificially created via institutions (e.g., students of a particular university, firemen, and so on). However, group norms are more useful when individuals have formal and/or explicit relationships, as those found in organisations.

Indeed, our research is best exploited within organisation frameworks such as OperettA [1,25], MOISE [18] or MOChA [23]. Within (formally specified) organisations, individuals have their relevant features represented (e.g., unique identity, capabilities, roles, and so on), as well as their contextual relations (e.g., power, responsibilities, and so on). These features allow designers (at design time) and individuals/agents (at run time) to factor consequences of group norms in the individual and organisation as a whole.

More specifically, we plan to equip designers with mechanisms to check for desirable properties in organisations, given some group norms. Given a group norm ${}^{A}\mathbf{O}_{G}^{R} \varphi$ and an organisation specification, one may want to check, for instance, if G has (the potential to have) any members (so as to ensure that the norm will be applicable to someone), and if it does, what we can say about R and A – to what extent these sets overlap, and which individuals in R have power over those in A.

More formally, given a group obligation ${}^{A}\mathbf{O}_{G}^{R} \varphi$ and a set of agents *Agents* populating an organisation, we want to alert the designer when the following situations arise:

- $|A| = 0$, that is, there is no-one to act on an obligation, which makes it doomed to be violated.
- $|R| = 0$, that is, the norm does not have anyone responsible for it, which means no-one is accountable for the norm being violated (alternatively, no-one will merit any rewards associated with fulfilling the norm). In practice, this renders a norm useless as no-one has any incentive to act on it.
- $|G| = 0$, that is, the norm has no addressees and actorship is impaired, especially in the cases where the norm translates into individuals.
- $|R \cap A| \leq n$, for some threshold value n, that is, the norm favours agents who are responsible for a norm, but who delegate (via their power relation) to actors.

5.1 Group Norms and Individual Agents

Individuals/agents also need run-time mechanisms to enable group norms to be factored in during their participation in an organisation enactment. By an "enactment" we mean the (static) organisation being populated at run-time by invidual agents, and interacting/acting to achieve individual and organisational goals. We thus consider the following sequence of steps for organisation enactment:

1. An organisation specification is made available to software and human agents (in some machine-processable format, such as OperettA's Extensible Markup Language (XML[4]) representation [1])
2. Software and human agents join the organisation, taking up roles, and associated rights, duties and power relations. By joining an organisation, agents' behaviours may change as they now need to operate within the constraints imposed.
3. The organisation is finally enacted, whereby agents act and interact – they perform individual and collective actions, send messages to one another (to coordinate/agree on who is to do what and when), with a view to achieving organisational goals (as well as fulfilling their own individual goals)

The group norms in the organisation specification influence steps 2 and 3 above, in interesting ways.

Agents should be aware of the consequences of joining an organisation (step 2), because norms will prevent them from or force them to behave in particular ways. Agents should consider their own goals, as well as any norms they might already have prior to joining the organisation, and they decide if they indeed want to join the organisation and, if so, in what role(s). A reasoning mechanism should allow agents to work out what values the sets of each group norm will have, considering those agents who currently joined the organisation. The mechanism could be used to alert the agent about norms which will give them more responsibility (the agent is a member of R), more to do (the agent is a member of A) or more to worry about (the agent is a member of G). Another mechanism will help agents decide how to join the organisation if they do not want to be in the set R, A or G of specific norms. A third interesting mechanism should allow the agent to work out how to join the organisation so as to avoid being grouped together with other agents (forcing it, for instance, to perform collective actions with team-mates the agent does not like).

During the enactment (step 3), even though the organisation restricts actions/behaviours from agents, agents still have choices of what to do, when to do it, and who they do it with. We envisage rational and autonomous agents building plans for joint action, and in doing so they factor in group norms applicable to them as addressees G, actors A and/or responsible parties R. For instance, given a group obligation $^A\mathbf{O}_G^R\varphi$, if an agent is in R, it might decide to create a sub-plan to achieve φ, roping in actors A under her power, and alerting

---

[4] http://www.w3.org/XML/

the addressees G of her intention; in doing so the agent might need to coordinate with other members of R. Likewise, a group prohibition $^A\mathbf{F}^R_G\,\varphi$ should cause agents in R to liaise among themselves about monitoring agents A to ensure they do not violate the norm (distributing members of A among members of R) and informing G about this.

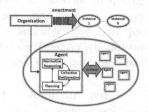

Fig. 1. Architecture: components and how they relate

We illustrate in Fig. 1 a reference architecture and how components fit together. An organisation specification gives rise, through a process of *enactment* (represented as the fragmented arrow), to many *instances* of the organisation – instances are best described as populations of individual (autonomous and rational) agents, joining an organisation with a view to pursue individual and organisational goals. The organisation specification is available to agents, who use it as input in its individual reasoning, communication and coordination. In the diagram, we "zoom in" one agent, showing three basic mechanisms together:

- *Normative reasoning* – mechanisms to allow agents to factor in norms during their activities.
- *Planning* – a planning mechanism (necessary for agents to decide on what they will do) which is combined with normative reasoning and collective deliberation.
- *Collective deliberation* – means for agents to collectively decide on joint courses of action, considering individual preferences as well as group norms.

6 Related Work

In addition to the various pieces of research work discussed previously, in this section we address other related work. The concept of *roles* has been explored in research on electronic institutions [13] and organisations [10,18,23,28]. Roles describe collections of *stereotypical* individuals who, by adopting a role, become subject to any norms associated with that role. We note that norms addressing roles are a useful shorthand for specialised norms addressing individuals, that is, they stand for "anyone who has adopted role r is subject to norm ν". For instance, a norm such as "Soldiers are forbidden to enter area (x,y)" and given agents $a_1, \ldots, a_n$ who have taken up the *soldier* role, stands for "Agent a_i is forbidden to enter area (x, y)", for each $i, 1 \leq i \leq n$. Very importantly, in the existing research role norms do not influence the joint behaviour of individuals and do not require coordination.

Work on collective agency (e.g., [6,7,28]) and collective obligations (e.g., [16]) have addressed similar concerns. These approaches represent norms over actions, also establishing a group of agents to whom the norm apply. Some approaches regard group norms as a shorthand for a norm which applies to all/some members of the group (e.g. [7]), whereas other approaches (e.g. [16]) regard group norms (more specifically, collective obligations) as a shared complex action requiring individual contributions (i.e., simpler actions) from those individuals of the group.

We are also aware of research on joint action and coalitions (e.g., [4,22,29]). This line of investigation is very relevant as it looks into individual deliberation when coordination is required. Work exploring aspects in delegation (e.g., [11,24]) sheds light on how norms can be transferred among individuals and groups. When agents join organisations they will need to consider the implications of taking up roles, since these will determine which groups agents will ultimately belong, and consequently, which norms will be applicable, as well as how power and delegation will impact on the agents' choices.

7   Conclusions, Discussion and Future Work

In this paper we have explored the concept of norms targetting groups. Our main contributions are (i) a taxonomy of group norms, making a case for the need to explicitly refer to three groups of concerned parties; (ii) a formal representation of group norms and a semantics; (iii) an expressiveness analysis in which we formally represent the various cases of our taxonomy; (iv) a sketch of how group norms fit within organisation-oriented engineering of multi-agent systems.

We are aware of many important issues our research raises. Initially, checking for membership (as in an agent checking if it belongs to a group and hence a norm may be relevant to it) can be a costly process, which might, in the worst case, lead to the exhaustive search of an exponential number of possibilities. For instance, a set expression $\Sigma_1 \cap \Sigma_2$ requires the computation of every value for Σ_1 and Σ_2, so that one can compute their intersection, and each element of the universe set of agents will be considered in turn, that is, $2^{|Agents|}$ possibilities.

We have a minimalist information model which we can use in different mechanisms. We are currently investigating reasoning mechanisms to enable agents carry out strategic reasoning when taking up roles (by allowing agents to check which norms will influence their behaviour and how). We are also formally connecting group norms with power and the *stit* operator to propose an operational semantics of delegation through group norms, factoring the various groups involved. Finally, we are investigating design- and run-time mechanisms for checking properties of organisations under group norms, so as to ensure, for instance, that a group norm will be eventually acted upon or, if it is violated, someone or some group will be responsible for it.

References

1. Aldewereld, H., Dignum, V.: OperettA: organization-oriented development environment. In: Dastani, M., El Fallah Seghrouchni, A., Hübner, J., Leite, J. (eds.) LADS 2010. LNCS, vol. 6822, pp. 1–18. Springer, Heidelberg (2011)
2. Anderson, A.: A reduction of deontic logic to alethic modal logic. Mind **67**, 100–103 (1958)
3. Belnap, N., Perloff, M.: Seeing to it that: a canonical form for agentives. Theoria **54**(3), 175–199 (1988)
4. Borgo, S.: Coalitions in action logic. In: Proceedings of the IJCAI 2007, USA. Morgan Kaufmann (2007)
5. Broersen, J., Dignum, F., Dignum, V., Meyer, J.-J.C.: Designing a deontic logic of deadlines. In: Lomuscio, A., Nute, D. (eds.) DEON 2004. LNCS (LNAI), vol. 3065, pp. 43–56. Springer, Heidelberg (2004)
6. Carmo, J.: Collective agency, direct action and dynamic operators. Logic J. IGPL **18**(1), 66–98 (2010)
7. Carmo, J., Pacheco, O.: Deontic and action logics for organized collective agency, modeled through institutionalized agents and roles. Fundam. Inform. **48**(2–3), 129–163 (2001)
8. de Lima, T., Royakkers, L., Dignum, F.: A logic for reasoning about responsibility. Logic J. IGPL **18**(1), 99–117 (2010)
9. Demolombe, R., Louis, V.: Norms, institutional power and roles: towards a logical framework. In: Esposito, F., Raś, Z.W., Malerba, D., Semeraro, G. (eds.) ISMIS 2006. LNCS (LNAI), vol. 4203, pp. 514–523. Springer, Heidelberg (2006)
10. Dignum, V.: A model for organizational interaction: based on agents, founded in logic. Ph.D. Thesis, Universiteit Utrecht, The Netherlands (2004)
11. Dignum, V., Dignum, F.: A logic of agent organizations. Logic J. IGPL **20**, 283–316 (2011)
12. Emerson, E.: Temporal and modal logic. In: van Leeuwen, J. (ed.) Handbook of Theoretical Computer Science, vol. B, pp. 955–1072. MIT Press, Cambridge (1990)
13. Esteva, M., Rodríguez-Aguilar, J.-A., Sierra, C., Garcia, P., Arcos, J.-L.: On the formal specification of electronic institutions. In: Sierra, C., Dignum, F.P.M. (eds.) AgentLink 2000. LNCS (LNAI), vol. 1991, pp. 126–147. Springer, Heidelberg (2001)
14. Friedkin, N.E.: A formal theory of social power. J. Math. Sociol. **12**(2), 103–126 (1986)
15. García-Camino, A., Noriega, P., Rodríguez-Aguilar, J.-A.: Implementing norms in electronic institutions. In: Proceedings of the AAMAS 2005. ACM (2005)
16. Grossi, D., Dignum, F., Royakkers, L.M.M., Meyer, J.-J.C.: Collective obligations and agents: who gets the blame? In: Lomuscio, A., Nute, D. (eds.) DEON 2004. LNCS (LNAI), vol. 3065, pp. 129–145. Springer, Heidelberg (2004)
17. Halmos, P.: Naive Set Theory. Van Nostrand (1960). Reprinted by Springer-Verlag, Undergraduate Texts in Mathematics (1974)
18. Hannoun, M., Boissier, O., Sichman, J.S., Sayettat, C.: MOISE: an organizational model for multi-agent systems. In: Monard, M.C., Sichman, J.S. (eds.) IBERAMIA-SBIA 2000. LNCS (LNAI), vol. 1952, pp. 156–165. Springer, Heidelberg (2000)
19. Jones, A.J.I., Sergot, M.J.: A formal characterisation of institutionalised power. Logic J. IGPL **4**(3), 427–443 (1996)
20. Lomuscio, A., Sergot, M.: On multi-agent systems specification via deontic logic. In: Meyer, J.-J.C., Tambe, M. (eds.) ATAL 2001. LNCS (LNAI), vol. 2333, pp. 86–99. Springer, Heidelberg (2002)

21. López y López, F.: Social power and norms: impact on agent behaviour. Ph.D. Thesis, University of Southampton, UK (2003)
22. Ågotnes, T., Alechina, N.: Reasoning about joint action and coalitional ability in K_n with intersection. In: Leite, J., Torroni, P., Ågotnes, T., Boella, G., van der Torre, L. (eds.) CLIMA XII 2011. LNCS, vol. 6814, pp. 139–156. Springer, Heidelberg (2011)
23. McCallum, M., Vasconcelos, W.W., Norman, T.J.: Organisational change through influence. Auton. Agents Multi-Agent Syst. **17**(2), 157–189 (2008)
24. Norman, T.J., Reed, C.: A logic of delegation. Artif. Intell. **174**, 51–71 (2010)
25. Okouya, D., Dignum, V.: OperettA: a prototype tool for the design, analysis and development of multi-agent organizations. In: Proceedings of the AAMAS. IFAA-MAS (2008)
26. Oren, N., Luck, M., Miles, S.: A model of normative power. In: Proceedings of the AAMAS, pp. 815–822. IFAAMAS (2010)
27. Ostrom, E.: Understanding Institutional Diversity. Princeton University Press, Princeton (2005)
28. Pacheco, O., Carmo, J.: A role based model for the normative specification of organized collective agency and agents interaction. Auton. Agent. Multi-Agent Syst. **6**, 145–184 (2003)
29. Royakkers, L.: Combining deontic and action logics for collective agency. JURIX. Front. Artif. Intell. Appl., vol. 64, pp. 135–146. IOS Press, Amsterdam (2000)

Modelling Institutions Using Dynamic Deontics

Christopher Frantz[1]([✉]), Martin K. Purvis[1],
Mariusz Nowostawski[2], and Bastin Tony Roy Savarimuthu[1]

[1] Department of Information Science, University of Otago, Otago, New Zealand
christopher.frantz@otago.ac.nz
[2] Faculty of Computer Science and Media Technology, Gjøvik University College,
Gjøvik, Norway

Abstract. We have developed a refined institutional scheme derived from Crawford and Ostrom's *Grammar of Institutions* (also referred to as ADICO) that has been adapted for the detailed representation of conventions, norms, and rules. In this work we apply this schema to model the emergence of norms. While previous work in the area of normative agent systems largely represents obligation and prohibition norms by discrete deontic primitives (e.g. 'must', 'must not', 'may'), we propose the concept of dynamic deontics to represent a continuous perspective on emerging institutions. This supports the expression of norm salience based on the differentiated internal representation among participants.

To demonstrate how it can be operationalised for dynamic modelling of norms in artificial societies, we apply nADICO to a simple agent-based simulation. Our intention is to arrive at a dynamic modelling of institutions in general, facilitating a movement beyond the artificial boundaries between different institution types, while making the institutional grammar purposeful for a wide range of application domains.

Keywords: Dynamic deontics · Institutions · Norms · Grammar of institutions · Nested ADICO · nADICO · Reinforcement learning · Social learning · Norm enforcement · Multi-agent systems

1 Introduction

Crawford and Ostrom's *Grammar of Institutions* [5] (GoI) is an approach to express social organisation (institutions) of different kinds, such as shared strategies (or *conventions*), *social norms*, and *codified rules*, using a unified grammar that not only integrates those different perspectives but supports the discrimination between those different institution types. To do so, the grammar consists of five components, *Attributes*, *Deontic*, *AIm*, *Conditions* and an *Or else* – ADICO in short – that are necessary to specify rules. By restricting constitutive components to a minimum, this syntax affords a wide scope for the expression of various institutional statements, such as norms and conventions, which we refer to as institution types for the remainder of the paper.

T. Balke et al. (Eds.): COIN 2013, LNAI 8386, pp. 211–233, 2014.
DOI: 10.1007/978-3-319-07314-9_12, © Springer International Publishing Switzerland 2014

The generality of ADICO enables researchers to express various institutional views, including *institutions as equilibria* [15] (championed in the area of economic analysis), *institutions from a normative perspective* [28] (which concentrates on the behavioural perspective and is favoured by many researchers in the field of multi-agent systems (e.g. [2,29])), and *institutions as rules*, e.g. [17] (which is favoured by the New Institutional Economics movement [5,17]).

Previous approaches, such as Ghorbani et al.'s [8] work as well as Crawford and Ostrom's conceptualisation, use the original grammar for a comprehensive description of *existing* institutions along with the social entities that shape and abide to them.

Notwithstanding the grammar's attempt to represent institutions in a comprehensive manner, in this work we review central limitations of the grammar in its current state and discuss a refined formalisation of the grammar we have proposed in previous work [6]. In this paper we develop a more dynamic perspective on the grammar's prescriptive component that is geared towards facilitating the bottom-up *emergence and establishment* of institutions we observe in human societies.

Accordingly the key element is our use of a *continuous notion of deontics* as an alternative to rigid deontic primitives, such as **must**, **must not**, and **may**, that are often associated with the use of deontic logic [31]. Our modification allows for less rigid and more fuzzy representations of institutions across individuals, while allowing the representation of fluid change over time. Along with this increased scope of expression, dynamic deontics can be used as an indicator of relevance offering the capability of weighing and prioritising potentially conflicting norms. This aspect allows for the modelling of the dynamic emergence of norms and their evolution over time, along with the representation of the important characteristic of stability that institutions exhibit.

In the next section (Sect. 2) we review Crawford and Ostrom's grammar and its adoption in different fields. Then in Sect. 3 we present Nested ADICO (nADICO), which extends the feature set of the existing grammar and allows for a more detailed representation of institutions, including characteristics particular to institutions themselves (such as institutional regress). Following this, in Sect. 4, we introduce the notion of dynamic deontics that further refines the institutional grammar to enable the modelling of dynamic institutional environments. We demonstrate an executable agent-based model that uses the extended institutional grammar to dynamically generate institutional statements in Sect. 5. In Sect. 6 we summarise and contextualise this work and provide directions for future work.

2   The Institutional Grammar

2.1   Overview

The original ADICO grammar consists of five components. Those include:

- *Attributes* – describe the attributes and characteristics of social entities (which can be individuals or groups) that are subject to the institutional statement (e.g. convention, norm, rule). If not specified explicitly, all individuals (or members of a group/society) are implied.

- **Deontics** – a deontic primitive that describes either an *obligation* (e.g. represented as **must**), *permission* (**may**), or a *prohibition* (**must not**). In Crawford and Ostrom's conception [5] it captures the aspects of deontic logic.
- **AIm** – describes an action or outcome associated with the institutional statement.
- **Conditions** – capture the circumstances under which the statement applies. This can include spatial, temporal, and procedural elements. If not further constrained, conditions default to "at all times and in all places" [5].
- **Or else** – describes consequences that are associated with the violation of the institutional statement, i.e. the combination of all other components used in that statement.

Crawford and Ostrom not only specify the components of the grammar; as indicated in the first section, the particular power of the grammar lies in its ability to satisfy different views on institutions, expressed as conventions, norms, and rules.

Using these three statement types, one can construct institutional rules of increasing prescriptiveness.

For a shared strategy (AIC), or convention, we can say:[1]

> **Drivers (A) hand their driver's license to the police officer (I) when stopped in traffic control (C).**

It effectively reflects a description of drivers' commonly observable behaviour when facing the request to hand over their license. From a normative perspective, this can be interpreted as a descriptive norm.

In the GoI, a norm would extend a shared strategy with a prescription (and thus be equivalent to an injunctive norm), expressed as ADIC:

> **Drivers (A) *must (D)* hand their driver's license to the police officer (I) when stopped in traffic control (C).**

This represents an unambiguous instruction to the driver who (if taking a strictly deontological perspective) perceives it as his duty to present his driver's license, independent of any threatening consequences.

Finally, a rule (ADICO) would introduce consequences for non-compliance:

> **Drivers (A) must (D) hand their driver's license to the police officer (I) when stopped in traffic control (C), *or else the police officer must enforce it based on traffic law (O).***

---

[1] In the following examples, we put in brackets the respective grammar component that represents the preceding fragment of the encoded institutional statement (e.g. 'Drivers' representing the *Attributes* component of the institutional statement).

Here the driver faces explicit consequences, which, depending on the nature of his refusal, can result in material (e.g. fines) or physical sanctions (e.g. arrest).

2.2   Application Fields, Refinements and Limitations

The ADICO grammar provides a semi-formal description of operational institutional rules that make them accessible for institutional analysis [18] and structured policy coding [26]. In the area of multi-agent simulation, Smajgl et al. [27] have used the grammar to model endogenous changes of ADICO rule statements in the context of water usage. Significant recent contributions that use the grammar in more depth include Ghorbani et al.'s MAIA framework [8], which represents a comprehensive attempt to translate Ostrom's Institutional Analysis and Development Framework [18] into an agent-based meta-model. Earlier, Ghorbani et al. [7] explored the notion of shared strategies as a fundamental statement type and differentiated their application across common, shared, and collective strategies.

Apart from a wide range of uses, the grammar has attracted some suggestions for refinement [22]. Our own work in this area is driven by the interest to make the grammar more flexible and dynamic. In this context we wish to highlight two key issues of concern, the first of which has been addressed and discussed in previous work [6].

First, the existing ADICO differentiation between shared strategies, norms, and rules (differing grammar components are used in those separate contexts) seems to limit the grammar's ability to capture the notion of a norm in its full extent. In original ADICO terms, rules are assumed to have sanctions, whereas norms do not – at least not specified ones [5]. A further limitation is the lack of an ability to model the direct dependency of institutions in a specified systematic manner, i.e. the rules another rule depends on for its enforcement, such as 'sanctioning the sanctioners' in case of non-compliance, which we think is crucial to provide an authentic representation of codified rules/formal institutions in particular, but also offers alternative means to differentiate norms and rules (see Subsect. 3.2).

Second, in ADICO the notions of prohibition and obligation norms are mapped into a "boolean" [9] perspective. Other authors have already pointed out this limitation and argued for a more continuous perspective, both for the ADICO grammar [22] and for social norms in general [9]. Particularly when conceiving institutions as emergent properties of societies (as opposed to intentionally constructed), modelling the progression from individual behaviour to social behaviour across differing institutional types requires more flexibility in specifying norms, beyond the discrete **may**s, **must**s, and **must not**s; if not prescribed by some social authority (e.g. leader), the rigid prescriptive deontics are an unlikely starting point of institutional development. In practice, more flexible boundaries are desirable to support continuous adaptation so that a new and different norm may gradually emerge from an existing one or simply gain salience and replace a norm that reached the end of its life cycle. Given the interpretation of norms as implicitly shared representations, they are subject to subjective perception and evaluation by norm participants, an aspect we can observe in the daily use of language (e.g. use of 'should' instead of 'must'). In that context particularly the permissive primitive **may** is of limited value when describing behavioural regularities. Apart from constituting the right to take an action [5,24], its concrete meaning relies on internal individual utility evaluations (e.g. Crawford and Ostrom's deltas) and is often insufficient to express observable social norms.

Attributing stronger descriptive power of norms by offering a more fluid representation is in line with demands raised by institutional scholars [12]. The selective use of Dynamic Deontics emphasises the general nature of the institutional grammar, beyond the refinements offered by Nested ADICO.

3   Nested ADICO (nADICO)

This section provides a brief overview of the refinements suggested as part of Nested ADICO (nADICO). Earlier [6], we discussed those refinements in more detail.

To address the limited expressiveness and unbalanced representation of different institution types in the GoI, we refine the GoI by introducing the following three central amendments:

- Representation of Sanctions for Norms
- Systematic Nesting of Institutional Statements
- Refined Differentiation between Norms and Rules

3.1   Nesting Capabilities

Crawford and Ostrom's grammar uses the 'Or else' component, which is used to express sanctions, including a notion of nesting of institutional statements. However, the unstructured manner of the sanction component limits the computational representation, but also does not exploit the grammar's potential. To extend the comprehensiveness of the grammar (in particular with respect to norms), opening it for a more dynamic perspective and improving its computational accessibility, we can back institutional statements with statements that bear the same structural components (an aspect that was considered by Crawford and Ostrom [5], but not systematically explored).[2] This entails developing a nesting structure of institutional statements consisting of the ADIC components of the original GoI. Extending the example from Sect. 2, we can thus capture consequences associated with a given rule breach, and do so for an arbitrary number of nesting levels, reflecting the notion of institutional regress.

---

[2] In the context of normative multi-agent systems, the nesting of norms based on their function (e.g. substantive norm backed by check norm) has been discussed by Grossi et al. [10].

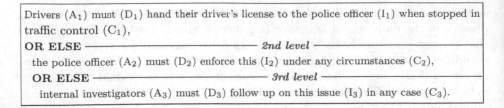

Drivers (A_1) must (D_1) hand their driver's license to the police officer (I_1) when stopped in traffic control (C_1),

OR ELSE ———————————————— *2nd level* ————————————————

the police officer (A_2) must (D_2) enforce this (I_2) under any circumstances (C_2),

OR ELSE ———————————————— *3rd level* ————————————————

internal investigators (A_3) must (D_3) follow up on this issue (I_3) in any case (C_3).

Vertical Nesting – Given the introduction of different levels that are activated upon institution violation on the preceding level, we call this nesting type *vertical nesting*. Using the grammar primitives, we can express this structure as `ADIC(ADIC(ADIC))`, where the respective leading statement represents the *monitored statement* (obligation of drivers to hand over license) that activates a *consequential statement* (police officer's obligation to enforce it). In this case, the 'drivers' (A_1) are potential first-order violators, and the police officer is first-order sanctioner (A_2). Looking at extended nesting levels, the police officer is likewise a potential second-order violator, and internal investigators (A_3) represent second-order sanctioners, and so on. In equivalence, the first-order consequential statement is likewise second-order monitored statement, etc.

Horizontal Nesting – Apart from facilitating the representation of institutional regress, nADICO further introduces a notion of *horizontal nesting*. The purpose of this is to provide more detailed modelling capabilities by avoiding a strict 1:1 assignment of monitored and consequential statements. One can imagine a variety of different gradual sanctions imposed upon the individual (e.g. speeding may result in an instant fine as well as an increment in demerit points), which may be applied in conjunction or alternatively. Especially for the normative case, in which consequences may not be formally specified, sanctions can be unpredictable, e.g. sanctions for observing a jaywalker may extend from scolding to physical abuse, or none may be applied. For this purpose, nADICO introduces different logical operators that allow the expression of statement combinations. The operators include logical conjunction (*and*), inclusive disjunction (*or*) and exclusive disjunction (*xor*). Their use allows the expansion of simple `ADIC` statements into statement combinations such as `(ADIC and ADIC)` on a given level, which could likewise be nested (e.g. `(ADIC and (ADIC xor ADIC))`) to express complex institutional constructs.

Expanding the previous example into the structure `ADIC((ADIC and (ADIC xor ADIC))ADIC)`, we could express:[3]

---

[3] Note that we extend the index indicating the nesting levels along with letters that associate grammar components with the respective consequential statement(s) on that level. In this example, the second level comprises three statements (a, b and c), all of which share a common sanctioner A_2, expressed as $A_{2a/b/c}$, but only b and c share the same *Conditions* ($C_{2b/c}$) and so on.

Drivers (A_1) must (D_1) hand their driver's license to the police officer (I_1) when stopped in traffic control (C_1),

OR ELSE ———————————————— *2nd level* ————————————————

the police officer ($A_{2a/b/c}$) must (D_{2a}) enforce this (I_{2a}) under any circumstances (C_{2a}) **and**,

depending on severity ($C_{2b/c}$), must ($D_{2b/c}$)

either fine the driver (I_{2b})

or arrest him (I_{2c}),

OR ELSE ———————————————— *3rd level* ————————————————

internal investigators (A_3) must (D_3) follow up on this issue (I_3) in any case (C_3).

Note that horizontal nesting can likewise occur in monitored and consequential statements (which is consequent, knowing that monitored statements can be consequential statements with respect to different institutional statement levels).

Figure 1 visualises the nesting capabilities of nADICO in an exemplified manner. An extended description of nADICO along with its formalisation can be found in [6].

3.2   Refined Differentiation Between Norms and Rules

The introduction of sanction specifications for norms requires a revised grammar interpretation, as we lose the ability to syntactically differentiate norms and rules purely based on the existence of sanctions. However, by introducing nested institutional statements we gain the ability to inspect the characteristics of respective nested statements. A characteristic of norms is their generally distributed enforcement and the associated nature of the norm monitor (and potential sanctioner), an entity that is not represented in the original GoI. Monitors can be internal (e.g. unconscious self-monitoring), self-assigned or informally assigned, and beyond that, particularly for less salient norms, it can be hard to know who monitors the given norm after all, and if so, what the nature of the sanctions associated with a violation is. Expressing norms in nADICO, we would expect a fuzzy representation of the sanctioner and likewise sanctions. To express the varying application of sanctions, the introduced logical operators can facilitate the differentiation between different institution types, with the 'inclusive or' (*or*) implying some fuzziness as to which one(s) and how many concrete sanctions out of a selection may be applicable in a given situation.

On the other hand, the existence of a well-specified formally assigned monitor is a characteristic for rules.[4] Given that the specification clarity is a key differentiation criterion between norms and rules, the nature of rules can be further associated with the use of *and* and *xor* operators if horizontal nesting is

---

[4] For a detailed overview of potential monitor types and their association to institution types, refer to [6]. Also note that, beyond the differentiation mechanisms discussed here, and in line with the original ADICO grammar, nADICO relies on the meta-norm of collective action to constitute rules.

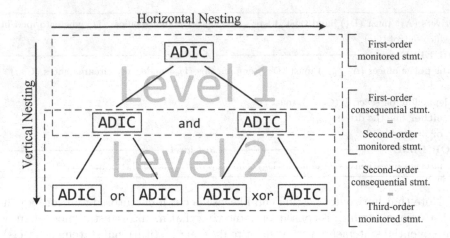

Fig. 1. Nesting characteristics of nADICO

applied, inasmuch as those allow an unambigious specification of sanctions in contrast to *or*.

An important aspect the original GoI does not consider is the *differentiation between rule monitor and sanctioner/enforcer*. In nADICO we introduce not only the clear specification of the sanctioner, but, where applicable and possible, the explicit specification of sanctioner and monitor. From an operational perspective, this can, again, be facilitated using horizontal nesting of statements that allow the specification of duties for both the monitor and sanctioner on a given nesting level.

Table 1 summarizes the discussed differentiation mechanisms. Note that the differentiation highlighted here smoothens the crisp boundaries between norms and rules and may not capture all imaginable cases, but offers a more detailed and realistic encoding of institutional complexity.

Table 1. Differentiating characteristics for norms and rules in nADICO

Characteristic	Norms	Rules
Specification of monitor	Unspecified/fuzzy	Clear specification
Specification of sanctioner	Unspecified/fuzzy	Clear specification
Assignment of monitor/sanctioner	Informal	Formal
Relationship between monitor/sanctioner	Often unified entity, not explicitly specified	Unified or separated, clear specification
Nature of monitor	See monitor types specified in [6]	
Combination operators	*or*	*and*, *xor*

4   Dynamic Deontics

4.1   Concept and Characteristics

As mentioned in Sect. 2.2, the restriction to three deontic primitives is not sufficient to represent the mechanisms by which institutions evolve and the way
they change over time. This rigidity is primarily due to the discrete primitives
must and **must not** that represent obligations and prohibitions, which reflect
commonly accepted notions of social norms [9,23], particularly in the context of
normative multi-agent systems (e.g. [2]). In contrast to those two strict injunc-
tions stands the permissive primitive **may**, which remains imprecise concerning
its associated duties.[5] We introduce three aspects that are central to a more continuous notion of deontics, before discussing underlying conceptual implications.

Continuous Notion of Deontics – Instead of relying on a strict tripartite
structure of deontics, we believe that a more straightforward way to deal with
this consistency issue is to allocate deontic values on a continuous scale (an
aspect von Wright [30] was already aware of), delimited at the extremes by a
prescription (obligation, i.e. **must**) and a proscription (prohibition, i.e. **must
not**) advocating a gradual understanding of norms, a schematic visualization of
which with respect to an aim (i.e. an action or an outcome in the sense of the
ADICO syntax) is provided in Fig. 2. At the extremes we allocate **must** and
must not, with more permissive points in between, effectively capturing the
omissible and *promissible* to a varying extent[6]. This approach underlies the
assumption that an institutional statement is associated with a valence that
drives it either towards prescription or proscription, irrespective of whether it
ever reaches one of those two extremes.

Stability – Using this continuous-scale perspective depicted in Fig. 2, we can
model institutional emergence and also identify the relative importance of various institutions. In addition, we can use this scheme to represent stability, a
key aspect of prohibition and obligation norms. Norms that have reached the
extremes of the normative scale tend to show strong change resistance – thus
once settled on a **must** or **must not** (e.g. prohibition of homosexuality), they
often become stubbornly entrenched. We can represent this 'stickiness' of prohibition and obligation statements by introducing tolerance regions around the
deontic extremes, denoted by t_{Pr} and t_{Ob} in Fig. 2, which are associated with
conditions that prevent the rapid change of extreme deontic values. One could
likewise introduce a notion of friction or viscosity to constrain the movement and
thus have uniform or differing stability characteristics along the deontic scale.

---

[5] These incongruencies of the deontics were recognised by Crawford and Ostrom [5],
in particular the contrast between the semantics of permission and those of a prescription of duty [25].

[6] The *omissible* describes an obligation from which we can deviate in exceptional cases;
under *promissible* we understand a prohibition which we can exceptionally deviate
from.

220   C. Frantz et al.

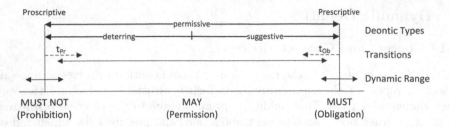

Fig. 2. Dynamic deontic scale

Dynamic Deontic Range – Measures of extremes are taken from an individual utilitarian viewpoint. The width of the range is thus based on the personal experience of the agent along with preimposed moral dictate based on family, culture or religion. With experience, one's moral views evolve, and his or her subjective range between **must**s, **may**s, and **must not**s will be adjusted. A relatively inexperienced agent may have a narrow deontic range and have many attitudes lodged at the extreme positions that have been imposed, e.g. by preimposed religious beliefs. But as one is exposed to a wider range of experiences (e.g. in the case for attitudes concerning homosexuality, one is exposed to a wider range of views and backgrounds on this issue), adjusted experiences may lead to an expanded or more nuanced deontic scale that captures a more refined viewpoint. We suggest that this dynamic deontic scale can expand and contract throughout an individual's lifetime, both based on reinforced or subsiding external stimuli as well as adopted viewpoints.

4.2   Discussion

At this stage, we wish to elaborate on the philosophical underpinnings that motivate dynamic deontics[7]. When analysing norms in a given society, those are conventionally assumed stable [23] and objectified using a unified representation (e.g. All agents think: 'An agent must not cheat') that allows their explicit sharing and unambiguous understanding. Utilizing a varying degree of salience for different norms [4], individuals then decide whether to comply with such norms depending on their situational disposition. In this view the assumption of a unified understanding is a generally accepted convenient modelling abstraction, but it does not take into account the different nature of individuals based on their background[8] and experience, an aspect the concept proposed here captures by incorporating a dynamic deontic range. By respecting the fluidity and nuanced nature of norms, we can leverage norms as artifacts that describe the society they act in.

---

[7] Note that the concept of dynamic deontics is not to be confused with dynamic deontic logic [16], which formalises norms over action as opposed to norms over states, an aspect pointed out by one of the anonymous reviewers.

[8] Henrich [11] describes the varying emotions associated with the perception of obligation and prohibition in different cultures.

The concept of Dynamic Deontics adopts this perspective and does not assume (but permits) the explicit communication of norms but allows the development of subjective norm understanding based on experience (see e.g. Savarimuthu et al.'s work on norm learning [21]) that relaxes the assumption of a unified norm understanding (e.g. Agent 1 thinks: 'An agent *must not* cheat.'; Agent 2 thinks: 'An agent *should not* cheat.'), which, in the light of differing exposure of individuals in open societies, hardly seems realistic. Instead we can conceive norms as inherently distributed in their nature, which includes the subjective understanding within individuals. Accepting the individualised understanding of norms by assigning varying deontics along a deontic range, the norm in the society can then be described as the aggregate of the individual norm perceptions, i.e. the collective understanding of what the norm is. The level of agreement on that norm within a society then is a property of that particular norm instance (i.e. the norm in the context of the society it acts in) itself, which, over longer time frames, allows the representation of fluidity of social norms.

It is important to note that the individualised understanding of norms is not to be confused with the individuals' attitudes towards that norm. Individuals do not autonomously align norms and their attitudes towards them unless they have the power to do so (e.g. by influencing others); instead the individualised norm understanding (and in principle also representation) is subject to modification based on social norm transmission processes (e.g. norm enforcement, social learning) individuals are exposed to. In addition to the "boolean" mode of the deontic primitives, the modelling of norms in a more fluid (or viscous) nature, as demanded by various institutional scholars [12], makes a norm's specific nature (including aspects such as the aggregate understanding across as well as diverging understanding within a society) a characteristic of the society it describes.

5 Simulation

5.1 Model

Using the nADICO grammar, we introduce an agent-based simulation model that demonstrates how agents could leverage some of the nADICO characteristics and dynamic deontics, in coordination with reinforcement learning (RL) [32] based on the reward from the environment and social learning [3] (i.e. based on the rewards obtained from others). Doing so, we take a consequentialist perspective on norms, thus suggesting the adoption of norms based on experience, as opposed to the conventionally assumed deontological ethics perspective in which individuals act with respect to a known 'Right' (as opposed to 'Wrong'), which requires the existence of preimposed norms. However, the operationalisation proposed here assumes a greenfield approach without pre-existing norms.

In this experiment each agent in the model has a set of actions it can perform (its *action pool*) as well as a set of reactions to other agents' actions (rewards/punishments – *reaction pool*). The operation of the model employs a simple trade metaphor. Imagine that two agents, A and B, get together for a

Table 2. Action sanction feedback

Action-reaction combinations		Utility from actions	
Action (Agent B)	Reaction (Agent A)	For Agent B	For Agent A
Trade fair	Don't pay commission	−0.5	1
Trade fair	Fire	−1	−0.5
Trade fair	Retaliate family	−1.5	−0.5
Trade fair	Pay commission	0.5	0.5
Withhold profit	Don't pay commission	0.5	−0.5
Withhold profit	Fire	−0.5	0
Withhold profit	Retaliate family	−1.5	1
Withhold profit	Pay commission	1	−1

transaction. A can hire B to sell some of his goods for a commission. B in this scenario has two options: it can return the cash it received to A (*trade fairly*) or cheat A out of the money (*withhold profit*). In response to either of these actions, A can choose one of the following rewards/punishments (reactions) for B: a) Pay the commission to B, b) Refuse to pay commission to B, c) Fire (dismiss) B from further employment, d) Retaliate against B's family. The respective utilities for these actions and reactions are given in Table 2.[9]

Each agent maintains its own memory instance (here: Q-Learning). Since the assembled agents can act as both actors and reactors, the utility response from actions is fed into a combined RL instance structure, which is used for both the choice of actions and reactions. Since agents don't have intrinsic knowledge about the value of their actions ex ante, the model uses RL and/or social learning to build social norms to guide behaviour.

Agent Strategies – At the beginning of each simulation round, based on the exploration probability, agents choose to

- *exploit* (engage directly in trade by interacting with another agent), or
- *explore* (learn more about its environment for future benefit by observing other agents).

When an agent is in *exploitation* mode, it chooses reward-maximizing actions and reactions based on what it has learned from past experiences. In this mode the agent can also be assigned by the modeller to engage in third-party norm enforcement. In this case the third-party agent observes the action of another agent (which is involved in an interaction with some other agent), and it carries out its own reaction (reward or punishment) on this observed agent, irrespective of whatever reaction the observed agent received from its own trading partner. To facilitate this operation, the modelling environment has each agent display its most recent action and the reaction it received, along with how the agent considered that received reaction (expressed as a valence of −1, 0, or +1).

---

[9] To facilitate the interpretation, we only introduce two actions for this simulation.

When an agent is in *exploration mode*, the agent randomly chooses an action to see if it "works". The reaction it receives from this randomly chosen action will be remembered for future learning purposes. In this exploration mode, the agent can also observe action-reaction activities from randomly chosen other agents and thereby learn about consequences. Actions are expressed as ADIC statements, with the deontic component (D) set to zero, which implies a neutral perception towards the action (which is the center of the deontic scale in Fig. 2). In terms of the deontic triad, we can interpret this as a **may**. Action-reaction combinations are then ADIC(ADIC). Observing agents use the valence (-1, 0, or $+1$) associated with the visible action-reaction combination to approximate what the observed agent received as a reaction and thereby learn from the observation.

Operationalising Dynamic Deontics With Reinforcement Learning – Although in a fixed social world the deontic value range could be held static, we are interested in environments where deontic values can change over time. Under these circumstances each agent maintains min and max values that may vary. We offer a sample semantic mapping: at the extremes (i.e. at min. and max.) we associated **must** (max.) and **must not** (min.); between those extreme values we associate the values **should**, **may**, **may not**, and **should not** (which could be allocated along the scale in Fig. 2). For this initial operationalisation we put emphasis on simplicity and assume the compartments of the respective deontics to be of equal size and symmetric along the deontic scale.

In the present context, the min and max values are based on the agent's Q-values stored in its memory. Using a sliding window approach, the mean of a fixed-length history of highest Q-value defines the prescriptive end; likewise the mean of the lowest Q-value history specifies the proscriptive boundary of the deontic range. In this case, RL operationalises both the expansion as well as the reduction of the deontic range (based on the reinforcement and discounting of Q-values at the end of each round). The Q-values are collected for action-reaction combinations, with experienced consequences combined using the *or* operator[10]. Transforming RL memory entries to institutional statements, action-reaction sequences are aggregated by action using nADICO's horizontal nesting capabilities (see Sect. 3). Let us assume, that $stmt_l$ indicates a statement on l^{th} level, and $stmt_{l+1,i}$ indicates i^{th} statement on $(l+1)^{th}$ level, $count_l$ indicates the number of statements on l^{th} level, and $c_{deonticRange}$ is the center of the deontic range. The deontic of the leading monitored statement $stmt_l$ ($d(stmt_l)$) is then derived by aggregating the consequential statements and depends on the logical connection of the consequential statements on a given nesting level, i.e. all the $stmt_{l+1,i}$ statements.

For *or* and *xor* combinations, the monitored deontic is the value of the consequential statement whose individual deontic shows the greatest deviation

---

[10] Note that this simulation takes the greenfield approach, i.e. individuals do not know about action effects. No collective action process takes place; no rules are specified ex ante.

(extremal) from the center of the deontic range towards the direction indicated by the sum of all consequential deontics (*deontic bias*), i.e.

$$extremeDeontic(stmt_l) := [(\sum_{i=0}^{count_{(l+1)}} d(stmt_{(l+1),i})) > c_{deonticRange}] \begin{cases} \text{true,} & max(d(stmt_{(l+1)})) \\ \text{false,} & min(d(stmt_{(l+1)})) \end{cases}$$

However, the extreme deontic is only applied if the sum of the consequential deontics is not located at the deontic range center $c_{deonticRange}$, in which case the deontics of the nested statements cancel each other. In that case, the deontic range center itself describes the statement's deontic (which, under the assumption of a symmetric deontic range, resolves to **may**), i.e.

$$d(stmt_l) := [(\sum_{i=0}^{count_{(l+1)}} d(stmt_{(l+1),i})) = c_{deonticRange}] \begin{cases} \text{true,} & c_{deonticRange} \\ \text{false,} & extremeDeontic(stmt_l) \end{cases}$$

Reason for choosing the extreme deontic is the assumed application of only one sanction at a time. The modelled agents are modelled as pessimistic and expect the most extreme individual sanction for a given action when interpreting the action.

For *and* combinations, the monitored deontic is the sum of all the consequential statements' deontic values as agents can assume the co-occurrence of sanctions combined by *and* operators, i.e.

$$d(stmt_l) := (\sum_{i=0}^{count_{(l+1)}} d(stmt_{(l+1),i}))$$

The resulting deontic value for the aggregated action is then the agent's valuation of this action (irrespective of a potential reaction) in terms of its own system. Since the Q-value reflects both, qualitative feedback and frequency (i.e. probability of occurrence), the use of the maximum Q-value is well-suited for this purpose.

In an effort to reflect the experience that social norms (particularly at the extremal ends of the scale) tend to be enduring, even after they no longer reflect their original purposes, we have also incorporated a 'stickiness' mechanism in our simulation to be associated with the extremal (min and max) ends of the deontic scale. Thus associated with those two ends of the deontic scale are occurrence thresholds that determine whether an institution is worthy of being designated as an obligation or a prohibition norm based on the deontic range allocation. We operationalise this by tracking the number of rounds a deontic value reaches into the tolerance zone around an extreme deontic (t_{Pr} and t_{Ob}). This transition is parameterised using a stability threshold ($th_{establish}$) as well as a destruction threshold ($th_{destruct}$).

Algorithm 1 summarises the agents' execution cycle. The parameter set of the model is presented in Table 3.

Algorithm 1. Agent Execution Cycle

Pick <u>two</u> random other agents;
Decide whether to *explore* or *exploit* in this round;
if *exploring* **then**
> Pick random action from action pool;
> **if** *social learning activated* **then**
> > Observe action of <u>first</u> randomly chosen agent and internalize action-sanction combination along with valence (not actual reward value);

else
> Pick action with highest Q-value from action pool;
> **if** *norm enforcement activated* **then**
> > Sanction action taken by <u>first</u> randomly chosen agent using sanction with highest Q-value;
> > Memorize feedback from sanction choice;

end
Execute picked action and apply to <u>second</u> randomly chosen agent;
Memorize reaction and make action-reaction combination (with valence representation of feedback) visible to other agents;
Update deontic range;
Check for stability of nADICO sequences as well as shifts from/to obligation or prohibition norms;

5.2   Results

The simulation runs comprised the following four configurations based on the combination of different social actions:

- No social learning, no norm enforcement (Scenario 1)
- Social learning, no norm enforcement (Scenario 2)
- No social learning, norm enforcement (Scenario 3)
- Social learning, norm enforcement (Scenario 4)

In all cases, agents receive direct feedback for their actions and likewise sanction others (positively or negatively) for actions imposed on them. In some simulation configurations, secondary indirect social interactions – norm internalising (social learning) and socialisation (norm enforcement) – were included. The simulation environment is based on our own simulation platform that uses the Mason

Table 3. Simulation parameters

Parameter	Value
Number of agents	100
Tolerance zone around extreme deontics (t_{Pr}, t_{Ob})	0.1 of deontic range amplitude
Norm stability threshold $(th_{establish})$	100 rounds
Norm destruction threshold $(th_{destruct})$	200 rounds
Deontic range history length	100 rounds
Memory discount factor	0.99
Exploration probability	0.4

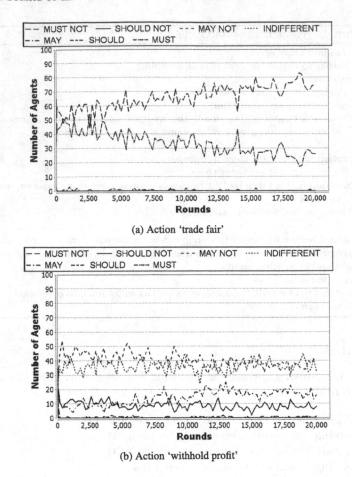

(a) Action 'trade fair'

(b) Action 'withhold profit'

Fig. 3. Emerging norms in Scenario 1 (no social learning, no norm enforcement)

simulation toolkit [13] for scheduling and visualisation support. We repeatedly ran each simulation configuration 30 times for 20,000 rounds to validate the outcomes, but given the explorative nature of this simulation, we describe the outcome of a representative simulation run. In the results shown in the following figures, we present the learned behaviour from the perspective of the role of Agent B (the hired trader). However, during the course of the simulation, agents can take both roles repeatedly and integrate their normative understanding towards those actions from both perspectives.

In the scenario that avoids any indirect social action (Scenario 1; Fig. 3), all indirect social actions were excluded.[11] Throughout these simulation runs, agents gradually developed the "understanding" that it is most beneficial to

---

[11] Each figure consists of two subfigures (one for each action), visualising the distribution of the different deontic terms towards that action in the agent society.

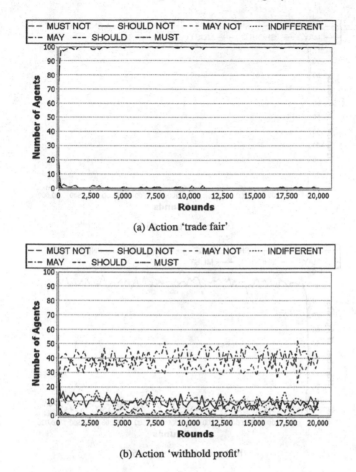

(a) Action 'trade fair'

(b) Action 'withhold profit'

Fig. 4. Emerging norms in Scenario 2 (social learning, no norm enforcement)

cheat (i.e. **must not** trade fair), a tendency that reached to 70–80 % of the agents during the execution. There was a complementary, declining portion of agents that thought they **must** trade fairly. A less visible norm that arose included the suggestion that agents **may** withhold profit, while a significant number of agents maintain the understanding that they **may not**, and to a lesser extent, **should not** withhold profit. Overall, the graph in Fig. 3 shows a diversity of views in the community with tendency to non-cooperation.

For Scenario 2 (Fig. 4), for which social learning was incorporated, we can observe its significant effect on behaviour. Agents "mimic" other agents' behaviours, and given that unfair trading dominates in the previous scenario that does not employ any social learning (Scenario 1), the performance of the community converges towards clear and extreme norms. The perception of unfair trading (**must not** trade fair) ranges at around 100 %; Agents increasingly think they **may** withhold profit (reaching 40–50 %), complemented by gently declining

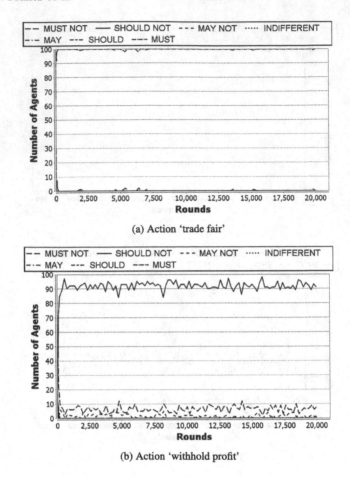

(a) Action 'trade fair'

(b) Action 'withhold profit'

Fig. 5. Emerging Norms in Scenario 3 (no social learning, norm enforcement)

percentages of agents feeling merely that one **may not** and (on a lower level) **should not** trade fair. The benefit here from the combined use of RL and social learning is compatible with previous findings (see e.g. [20]).

For Scenario 3 (Fig. 5), which incorporated indirect norm enforcement by third parties but not social learning, an entirely different pattern from that of Scenario 2 emerged. Given that any additional social reaction here is based on previous actions on the part of an observed agent, norm enforcers act from the perspective of a hiring agent, thus rewarding fair trading and punishing unfair trading. As a result the obligation norm of fair trading (**must**) dominates and is increasingly supported by the complementary understanding not to withhold profits ('**should not** withhold profit' at around 90 %); less than 10 % believe they **must not** withhold profit. At this stage it is important to note that although both mentioned actions ('trade fair', 'withhold profit') are seemingly complemen-

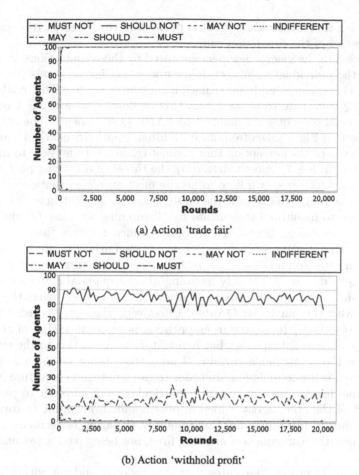

(a) Action 'trade fair'

(b) Action 'withhold profit'

Fig. 6. Emerging norms in Scenario 4 (social learning, norm enforcement)

tary, their reinforcement (both positive and negative experiences) depends on the agents' situational choice, which during the course of the simulation (driven by the pay-offs defined in Table 2 and the fact that agents integrate the experience from both perspectives, both as acting (hired) agent and reacting agent) drives towards the dominant choice of the action 'trade fair'. Consequently, the normative reinforcement of this action exceeds that of 'withhold profit'.

The final scenario (Scenario 4; Fig. 6) explores the combined use of social learning and norm enforcement. The outcome here enhances the effect of norm enforcement shown in Scenario 3, but improves the convergence by incorporating social learning effects. As a result, agents develop more extreme normative understandings (all agents believe they **must** trade fair; the number of agents thinking they **should not** withhold profit is increasingly replaced by the extreme understanding that withholding profit is prohibited (**must not**), reaching up to 20 % at the end of the simulation run).

In addition to the macro view demonstrated by these simulations, it is useful to look at the individual agents' evolving understanding of norms (the emerging nADICO sequences and the situational deontic range). This enables one to see how Q-values are translated from this reinforcement learning-based approach into social consequences mapped to nADICO statements. The situational extract shown in Fig. 7 taken from an individual agent of Scenario 4 shows how the agent develops the perception that it must trade fair (refer here to nADICO "Statement 1" in Fig. 7), mostly driven by the threat of not being paid its wage (commission), which is shown here to be the most extreme deontic value in the agent's deontic range. Recall that the ADICO syntax is constructed to sanction nonadherence to monitored statements by threatening with an 'Or else'. However, the deontic values, here derived from Q-values, imply a "because" or "on the grounds that" relationship (e.g. 'I *must* trade fairly, *because* my employer *must* pay me my commission.'). In order to establish this semantic translation from Q-values to subjectively meaningful consequential statements, which includes a shift in perspective from subject to sanctioner, we invert the deontic associated with the particular Q-value. Effectively, the agent is using its own experience (Q-values) to engage in empathetic perspective-taking of the other observed agent, and anticipates what it might do as a reaction to the evaluated action. Thus the agents might surmise, 'I must trade fairly, *or else* my employer *must not* pay me my commission.' In order to carry out that conjecture, we need to *invert* the deontic associated with a particular value in order to place it in the context of the other agent, which implies a shift from **must** to **must not**, **should** to **should not** and so on. Consequently, the agent bases its understanding on the negative consequences of being fired, not being paid wage, and family retaliation.

"Statement 2" in Fig. 7 indicates that the trader should not withhold profit, or else retaliation against family may ensue as well as the other consequences. This example highlights the differentiated perceived threats when mapped to human-readable deontics. Note in this figure that while retaliation appears to be a dominating sanction ('**should**'), other sanctions are associated with weaker prescriptions ('**mays**').

6   Discussion and Future Work

This paper discusses the introduction of dynamic deontics into nADICO, a refined 'Grammar of Institutions', with the intent to extend its capabilities to express the dynamic aspects of institutions, such as their emergence and change over time (continuity of deontics) as well as stability (establishment/destruction thresholds), while reflecting individual participants' differentiated understanding of institutions (individual dynamic deontic ranges). We operationalised nADICO with dynamic deontics to model the establishment and change of norm understanding over time based on different scenarios that incorporated reinforcement learning, social learning, and norm enforcement as mechanisms to socialise

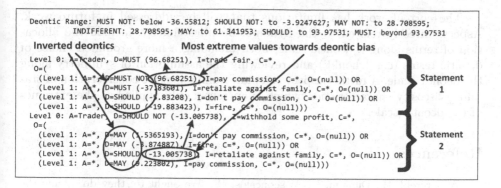

Deontic Range: MUST NOT: below -36.55812; SHOULD NOT: to -3.9247627; MAY NOT: to 28.708595; INDIFFERENT: 28.708595; MAY: to 61.341953; SHOULD: to 93.97531; MUST: beyond 93.97531

Inverted deontics   Most extreme values towards deontic bias

```
Level 0: A=Trader, D=MUST (96.68251), I=trade fair, C=*,
   O=(
   (Level 1: A=*, D=MUST NOT (96.68251), I=pay commission, C=*, O=(null)) OR
   (Level 1: A=*, D=MUST (-37.83601), I=retaliate against family, C=*, O=(null)) OR
   (Level 1: A=*, D=SHOULD (-9.83208), I=don't pay commission, C=*, O=(null)) OR
   (Level 1: A=*, D=SHOULD (-19.883423), I=fire, C=*, O=(null)))
Level 0: A=Trader, D=SHOULD NOT (-13.005738), I=withhold some profit, C=*,
   O=(
   (Level 1: A=*, D=MAY (1.5365193), I=don't pay commission, C=*, O=(null)) OR
   (Level 1: A=*, D=MAY (-3.874887), I=fire, C=*, O=(null)) OR
   (Level 1: A=*, D=SHOULD (-13.005738), I=retaliate against family, C=*, O=(null)) OR
   (Level 1: A=*, D=MAY (9.223802), I=pay commission, C=*, O=(null)))
```

} Statement 1

} Statement 2

Fig. 7. Situational deontic range and generated nADICO statements

norm understanding. The experiments described in this work take a greenfield approach and trade the strictly deontological perspective on social norms for a consequentialist perspective, in which agents develop an understanding of conduct by individual learning, observation, but also via norm enforcement by others, instead of relying on preimposed norms to regulate their behaviour. Existing institutional environments characterised by preimposed norms and rules can be represented by modification of the 'stickiness' behaviour but also the specification of predefined deontic ranges (both described in Sect. 4), an aspect left for future work. Particularly the 'stickiness' aspect is important to simulate the 'lock-in' effect of norms, i.e. the adoption and persistence of suboptimal norms, but also to model conflicting behaviour in culturally diverse environments.

In the area of normative multi-agent systems we can find a variety of approaches to model norms im/emergence and sanction-based enforcement (e.g. Andrighetto et al. [2]). Our simulation exemplifies an approach of dynamic sanctioning, but unlike Mahmoud et al.'s approach [14], it does not base its reaction on individual norm-compliance but only on aggregate experience. Villatoro et al. [29] propose a more complex model of dynamically adjusted sanctioning based on a heuristic that, in addition to violation behaviour, incorporates sanctioning cost. Reflecting on work produced in the context of this volume, our approach shares intentions with and complements other contributions, such as Panagiotidi et al.'s [19] attempt to bridge the gap between norm formalisation and operationalisation as well as Aldewereld et al.'s [1] conceptualisation of group norms whose elements could be expressed using the nADICO grammar.

However, to date we have not seen approaches employing a continuous notion of deontics to represent a more fluid understanding of norms as displayed in this work. We believe that our approach is not only useful to represent norm emergence, but also to model long-term adaptation of social institutions, such as transitions between conventions, norms and rules. In this context, note that with its emphasis on different institution types, the approach explored here assumes a higher level perspective on institutions in general, instead of concentrating on specific institution types.

The current work has limitations that will be addressed in future work. Aspects directly related to the dynamic deontics concept include the allocation of terms along a deontic scale, both including a more grounded choice of deontic terms (e.g. 'should') and reviewing the assumption of symmetry along the deontic scale. A further aspect is a more comprehensive consideration of stability/viscosity characteristics, which is currently only applied at the extremes of the deontic scale.

References

1. Aldewereld, H., Dignum, V., Vasconcelos, W.: We ought to; they do; blame the management! - a conceptualisation of group norms. In: Balke, T., Dignum, F., van Riemsdijk, M.B., Chopra, A.K. (eds.) COIN 2013. LNCS (LNAI), vol. 8386, pp. 195–210. Springer, Heidelberg (2014)
2. Andrighetto, G., Villatoro, D., Conte, R.: Norm internalization in artificial societies. AI Commun. **23**(4), 325–339 (2010)
3. Bandura, A., Ross, D., Ross, S.: Transmission of aggressions through imitation of aggressive models. J. Abnorm. Soc. Psychol. **63**, 575–582 (1961)
4. Cortell, A.P., Davis Jr, J.W.: Understanding the domestic impact of international norms: a research agenda. Int. Stud. Rev. **2**(1), 65–87 (2000)
5. Crawford, S.E., Ostrom, E.: A Grammar of Institutions. In: Ostrom, E. (ed.) Understanding Institutional Diversity (Chapt. 5), pp. 137–174. Princeton University Press, Princeton (2005)
6. Frantz, C., Purvis, M.K., Nowostawski, M., Savarimuthu, B.T.R.: nADICO: A Nested Grammar of Institutions. In: Boella, G., Elkind, E., Savarimuthu, B.T.R., Dignum, F., Purvis, M.K. (eds.) PRIMA 2013. LNCS (LNAI), vol. 8291, pp. 429–436. Springer, Heidelberg (2013)
7. Ghorbani, A., Aldewereld, H., Dignum, V., Noriega, P.: Shared strategies in artificial agent societies. In: Aldewereld, H., Sichman, J.S. (eds.) COIN 2012. LNCS (LNAI), vol. 7756, pp. 71–86. Springer, Heidelberg (2013)
8. Ghorbani, A., Bots, P., Dignum, V., Dijkema, G.: MAIA: a framework for developing agent-based social simulations. J. Artif. Soc. Soc. Simul. **16**(2), 9 (2013)
9. Ghose, A., Savarimuthu, T.B.R.: Norms as objectives: revisiting compliance management in multi-agent systems. In: Aldewereld, H., Sichman, J.S. (eds.) COIN 2012. LNCS (LNAI), vol. 7756, pp. 105–122. Springer, Heidelberg (2013)
10. Grossi, D., Aldewereld, H., Dignum, F.P.M.: *Ubi Lex, Ibi Poena*: designing norm enforcement in E-Institutions. In: Noriega, P., Vázquez-Salceda, J., Boella, G., Boissier, O., Dignum, V., Fornara, N., Matson, E. (eds.) COIN 2006. LNCS (LNAI), vol. 4386, pp. 101–114. Springer, Heidelberg (2007)
11. Henrich, J.: Does culture matter in economic behaviour? Ultimatum game bargaining among the Machiguenga of the Peruvian Amazon. Am. Econ. Rev. **90**(4), 973–979 (2000)
12. Kinzig, A.P., Ehrlich, P.R., Alston, L.J., Arrow, K., Barrett, S., Buchman, T.G., Daily, G.C., Levin, B., Levin, S., Oppenheimer, M., Ostrom, E., Saari, D.: Social norms and global environmental challenges: the complex interaction of behaviors, values, and policy. Bioscience **63**(3), 164–175 (2013)
13. Luke, S., Cioffi-Revilla, C., Panait, L., Sullivan, K., Balan, G.: MASON: a multi-agent simulation environment. Simulation **81**(7), 517–527 (2005)

14. Mahmoud, S., Griffiths, N., Keppens, J., Luck, M.: Efficient norm emergence through experiential dynamic punishment. In: ECAI'12, pp. 576–581 (2012)
15. Menger, C.: Problems in Economics and Sociology. University of Illinois Press, Urbana (1963)
16. Meyer, J.-J.C.: A different approach to deontic logic: deontic logic viewed as a variant of dynamic logic. Notre Dame J. Formal Logic 29, 109–136 (1988)
17. North, D.C.: Institutions, Institutional Change, and Economic Performance. Cambridge University Press, Cambridge (1990)
18. Ostrom, E.: Understanding Institutional Diversity. Princeton University Press, Princeton (2005)
19. Panagiotidi, S., Alvarez-Napagao, S., Vázquez-Salceda, J.: Towards the norm-aware agent: bridging the gap between deontic specifications and practical mechanisms for norm monitoring and norm-aware planning. In: Balke, T., Dignum, F., van Riemsdijk, M.B., Chopra, A.K. (eds.) COIN 2013. LNCS (LNAI), vol. 8386, pp. 346–363. Springer, Heidelberg (2014)
20. Savarimuthu, B.T.R., Arulanandam, R., Purvis, M.: Aspects of active norm learning and the effect of lying on norm emergence in agent societies. In: Kinny, D., Hsu, J.Y., Governatori, G., Ghose, A.K. (eds.) PRIMA 2011. LNCS (LNAI), vol. 7047, pp. 36–50. Springer, Heidelberg (2011)
21. Savarimuthu, T., Cranefield, S., Purvis, M.A., Purvis, M.K.: Obligation norm identification in agent societies. J. Artif. Soc. Soc. Simul. 13(4), 3 (2010)
22. Schlüter, A., Theesfeld, I.: The Grammar of Institutions: the challenge of distinguishing between strategies, norms, and rules. Ration. Soc. 22, 445–475 (2010)
23. Scott, W.R.: Approaching adulthood: the maturing of institutional theory. Theory Soc. 37, 427–442 (2008)
24. Searle, J.R.: Speech Acts: An Essay in the Philosophy of Language. Cambridge University Press, London (1969)
25. Shimanoff, S.B.: Communication Rules: Theory and Research. Sage Publications, Beverly Hills (1980)
26. Siddiki, S., Weible, C.M., Basurto, X., Calanni, J.: Dissecting policy designs: an application of the institutional grammar tool. Policy Stud. J. 39, 79–103 (2011)
27. Smajgl, A., Izquierdo, L., Huigen, M.G.A.: Rules, knowledge and complexity: how agents shape their institutional environment. J. Model. Simul. Syst. 1(2), 98–107 (2010)
28. Ullmann-Margalit, E.: The Emergence of Norms. Clarendon Library of Logic and Philosophy. Clarendon Press, Oxford (1977)
29. Villatoro, D., Andrighetto, G., Sabater-Mir, J., Conte, R.: Dynamic sanctioning for robust and cost-efficient norm compliance. In: IJCAI'11, pp. 414–419. AAAI Press (2011)
30. von Wright, G.H.: An Essay in Modal Logic. North Holland Publishing Company, Amsterdam (1951)
31. von Wright, G.H.: Norm and Action: A Logical Enquiry. Routledge & Kegan Paul, London (1963)
32. Watkins, C.: Learning from delayed rewards. Ph.D. thesis, Cambridge University (1989)

Agents and Expectations

Stephen Cranefield[✉]

Department of Information Science, University of Otago, Dunedin, New Zealand
scranefield@infoscience.otago.ac.nz

Abstract. This paper discusses the role that expectations have in agent reasoning, and focuses on the author's previous work on modelling and monitoring expectations with a complex temporal structure, and its application to expectation monitoring in virtual worlds. It also presents a proposal for a new extension of this work by integrating it with the event calculus to simplify the definition of institutions with actions that create expectations. It is shown how this "expectation event calculus" could provide a uniform basis for reasoning about various types of expectation, and commitments and norms in particular.

1 Introduction

As we interact with the world, in any given situation we do not choose our actions in isolation from our previous experiences. Rather, our choices are influenced by knowledge of our physical and social environment gained through experience and knowledge we have been previously gained. In particular, we develop expectations about events that may (or may not) occur in the future. As Gärdenfors states [21, pp. 1–2]:

> "... expectations are ubiquitous, although they are not often made explicit. You expect there to be a floor when you enter a room; you expect a door handle not to break when you press it; you expect your morning newspaper to arrive on time; and you don't expect Sears to assemble a lawn mower. ... expectations play a crucial role in everyday reasoning."

Provided that our expectations are well founded, it is rational to consider the likelihood and consequences of these expectations being fulfilled or violated when choosing our actions. For example, Piunti et al. argue that "expectations are directly involved at various level[s] in goal deliberation, planning, intention reconsideration, learning and action control" [32].

Expectations may be inferred based on observed regularities in the world, but can also arise explicitly from our social context, e.g. commitments made and received, social norms and laws, organisational policies, and team tactics.

Castelfranchi et al. [8] have analysed the nature of expectations and contrasted them with forecasts, hypotheses, and predictions about the future state of the world:

T. Balke et al. (Eds.): COIN 2013, LNAI 8386, pp. 234–255, 2014.
DOI: 10.1007/978-3-319-07314-9_13, © Springer International Publishing Switzerland 2014

"Expectations in our ontology are not indifferent hypothesis, forecasts or predictions. They imply a subjective concern in the realization of p."

Here, p is the state of the world that is expected to hold in the future. Castelfranchi et al. classify expectations into *hopecasts* and *fearcasts*. These are modelled formally as conjunctions of (i) a belief that p has a greater than 50 % chance of holding in the future, and (ii) a goal stating (for a hopecast) that p will hold in the future or (for a fearcast) that p will not hold. They use these notions to argue that in cognitive agents there is an intrinsic tendency for a belief about the future action of another agent (e.g. due to the existence of a convention) to progress to an expectation about that action (which includes a goal that the action should happen or not happen), then to the adoption of an "influencing goal" to induce the other agent to perform the action, a subsequent goal to request (tacitly or explicitly) the desired behaviour, and finally a normative belief that the other agent is obliged to do the action.

In later work, Castelfranchi [9] adds an additional component to his account of expectations: as well as a predictive belief about a future state of affairs p and a goal that p should hold or not hold, he adds an epistemic goal expressing that the agent X has an active interest in knowing whether or not p comes to pass:

"X has the Goal to know whether the predicted event or state really happens (epistemic goal). She is 'waiting for' this; at least for curiosity. This concept of 'waiting for' and of 'looking for' is necessarily related to the notion of expecting and expectation, but not to the notion of prediction.

Either X is actively monitoring what is happening and comparing the incoming information (for example perception) to the internal mental representation; or X is doing this cyclically and regularly; or X will in any case at the moment of the future event or state compare what happens with her prediction"

This paper discusses how this active interest in expectations has been addressed by multi-agent systems researchers to date, with a particular focus on the author's logic of expectations and its application to expectation monitoring in virtual worlds. Section 2 presents a brief overview of computational problems related to expectations (mostly in specialised forms, such as norms), before Sect. 3 discusses the author's approach to modelling and monitoring expectations with a complex temporal structure. Section 4 describes some alternative computational accounts of expectations. Two applications of expectation monitoring to agents in virtual worlds are presented in Sect. 5. Finally, Sect. 6 proposes an integration of the logic of expectations with the event calculus to allow simpler specifications of institutions with actions that create expectations, and it is shown how this "expectation event calculus" could provide a uniform basis for reasoning about various types of expectation, and commitments and norms in particular.

2   Computing with Expectations

Researchers have investigated a number of computational problems related to expectations, although most of this work has had a specific focus on particular types of expectations such as norms and commitments. Problems of interest include the following:

Verifying fulfilment of expectations from system specifications
> Given the specification of the agents in a multi-agent system (or the protocols they must follow to interact), how can a designer ensure that all norms or generated commitments will be complied with [1,43]? This problem assumes that the agents' design or code is known or that they can be relied on to follow a specified protocol, and is therefore more applicable to closed systems than open ones.

Run-time detection of fulfilment and violation
> Based on observations of a multi-agent system (either by a central authority or an individual agent), what norms are fulfilled and violated? This has been the focus of the author's research on expectations to date. Cranefield et al. [16] discuss some of the research in this area, including work using the following approaches:
> - Abductive inference
> - Model checking a path
> - Forward chaining rule execution
> - Temporal projection using the event calculus
> - Automaton execution

Making practical reasoning architectures expectation-aware
> How can an agent use expectations to guide its own planning? Particular aspects of this problem include:
> - Integrating expectation monitoring with BDI agents [36]
> - Planning or plan selection while subject to expectations [3,17,22,25,28,30]
> - Planning informed by an agent's expectations of others. The author is not aware of any existing work on this problem.

Generating an agent's expectations from experience
> Given an agent's observations and experience, what should its expectations of others be? In particular, this has been investigated in the context of acquiring norms [37,38].

Acquiring expectations from humans
> How can non-technical humans communicate expectations to software? Some preliminary work in this area has been done by Winikoff and Cranefield, using positive and negative examples [48].

Designing expectations at the system level
> How can expectations be designed and provided to an entire MAS in order to improve its efficiency? In particular, this has been addressed in the context of automated norm synthesis [26].

3   Logical Modelling and Monitoring of Rules of Expectation

A wide variety of formalisms have been proposed for representing different types of expectation and the mechanisms that give rise to them, especially for norms, contracts and commitments. The author's work has focused on the logical modelling and run-time monitoring of the expectations with a complex temporal structure, with a focus on providing a logical account of expectation fulfilment and violation.

Figure 1 gives an example of a temporally complex rule of expectation modelled using the hyMITL$^{\pm}$ expectation logic [12]. This encodes a service offer made by the publisher of a monthly periodical: once the consumer has made the appropriate payment, each month during the next year, that month's issue will be sent to the consumer. Other examples of temporally rich expectations are presented in Sect. 5.

A detailed explanation of the hyMITL$^{\pm}$ logic is beyond the scope of this paper, but key features are the use of both past- and future-oriented temporal logic operators, possibly qualified by time intervals over which they apply (using ISO 8601 notation[1] for time points and periods, e.g. "P1W" for the period of one week), and hybrid logic concepts extended to suit a metric interval temporal logic. The example uses the temporal operators A for "in all paths", G^+ for "always in the future", X^- for "in the previous state", and F^+ for "some time in the future". The hybrid logic constructs used are the "binder" $\downarrow^{unit}_{tz} v$, which binds the variable v to the time of the current state in the time zone tz, rounded down to the precision indicated by $unit$, and time interval formulae that evaluate to true if the current state is within the interval. Time arithmetic (a time point plus a period) is necessarily qualified by a time zone by writing "$| tz$", and Z refers to "Zulu" time, i.e. the zero meridian, more commonly known as UTC or GMT.

Monitoring expectations in hyMITL$^{\pm}$ was implemented procedurally, and the semantics of the logic did not include explicit notions of expectation, fulfilment and violation. To investigate these semantic issues, Cranefield and Winikoff [15] defined a simplified (unnamed) version of the logic based on a propositional linear temporal logic and without the use of time intervals and a human-friendly time scale. The following formula illustrates the features of this logic[2]:

$$\mathsf{Fulf}(\neg ex1\_achieved \wedge in\_zone1 \wedge dribbling\_downfield$$
$$\wedge \neg \ominus (in\_zone1 \wedge dribbling\_downfield),$$
$$dribbling\_downfield \ \mathsf{U} \ (in\_zone2 \wedge kick \wedge \downarrow x. \diamondsuit (\exists_{goal(y)} @_x y))$$

The meaning of this formula will be explained in Sect. 5; here we focus on explaining the syntax of the logic. The temporal operators used in the formula are $\ominus$ (in the previous state), U (the subformula on the left must hold *until* the one

---

[1] http://www.iso.org/iso/catalogue_detail?csnumber=40874

[2] This paper includes some minor modifications to the syntax introduced by Cranefield et al. [16].

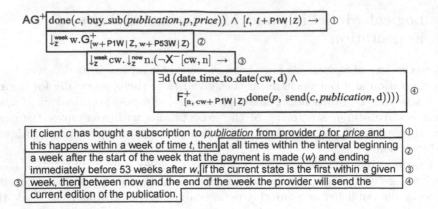

In other words, once the payment is made, the publication will be sent every week for 52 weeks.

Fig. 1. Example expectation in hyMITL$^\pm$ [13]

on the right holds) and $\Diamond$ (the subformula that follows must hold *eventually*). The logic retains some features of hybrid logic: the binder $\downarrow$ binds a variable to the nominal (unique name) for the current state, and $@_x$ evaluates the formula that follows in the state identified by the binding of x. Aside from propositions, states may also contain "state-referencing propositions", which can take as an argument a nominal or a variable bound to a state. These allow relationships between states to be expressed.

The logic includes operators Exp, Fulf and Viol representing the existence of expectations, and their fulfilments and violations. Rather than having a separate rule base recording the rules of expectation, we use formulae that are *hypothetical*: a formula $\mathsf{Exp}(\lambda, \rho, n, \phi)$ is true if ϕ would be a current expectation due to the firing of a rule of expectation with condition λ and the resulting (initial) expectation ρ. The rule may have fired in a prior state, with the expectation remaining unfulfilled since then. In that case, ρ is *progressed* over a sequence of intervening states to result in the current residual expectation ϕ. The state in which the rule fired is recorded using the nominal n. Fulf and Viol formulae have the same argument structure and represent current (hypothetical) expectations that are fulfilled and (respectively) violated in the current state.

Clearly there are an infinite number of Exp formulae that are true in any state n, e.g. $\mathsf{Exp}(true, \phi, n, \phi)$ holds for any ϕ. However, in our model checking approach to expectation monitoring (described below), only Exp, Fulf and Viol formulae that are of interest to the application are monitored.

An expectation ϕ is a temporal logic formula that is expressed from the context of the current state (and it may include nested Exp, Fulf and Viol formulae [16]). Formula progression involves partially evaluating it given what is known in the current state, and re-expressing the remaining expectation from the viewpoint of the next state [5]. For example, if p holds in the current state, then $p \wedge \bigcirc q$ progresses to q in the next state. We use the formula $\mathsf{Progress}(\phi, \psi)$ to state that ϕ, when considered in the current state, progresses to ψ in the next state.

We consider that an expectation cannot be fulfilled or violated based on future information. Suppose a friend makes a commitment to me on a certain day d that he will meet me for lunch the next day, but he does not. While the commitment was made on d, the violation of the commitment occured on the day after d. Therefore, the semantics of Fulf and Viol formula incorporate an operator TruncS[3] that evaluates its argument without considering any future states. The 'S' indicates that it uses the "strong semantics", i.e. that it is pessimistic. A formula that cannot be evaluated without future information (e.g. $\bigcirc p$) evaluates to false within a TruncS operator.

The semantics of expectation, fulfilment and violation can then be defined by the following axioms:

$$\mathsf{Exp}(\lambda, \rho, n, \phi) \Longleftrightarrow (n \wedge \mathsf{TruncS}\,\lambda \wedge \phi \equiv \rho) \vee$$
$$\exists \psi \ominus (\mathsf{Exp}(\lambda, \rho, n, \psi) \wedge$$
$$\neg \mathsf{TruncS}\,\psi \wedge \neg \mathsf{TruncS}\,\neg \psi \wedge \mathsf{Progress}(\psi, \phi))$$
$$\mathsf{Fulf}(\lambda, \rho, n, \phi) \Longleftrightarrow \mathsf{Exp}(\lambda, \rho, n, \phi) \wedge \mathsf{TruncS}\,\phi$$
$$\mathsf{Viol}(\lambda, \rho, n, \phi) \Longleftrightarrow \mathsf{Exp}(\lambda, \rho, n, \phi) \wedge \mathsf{TruncS}\,\neg \phi$$

The first axiom specifies that an expectation arises either by a rule of expectation firing in the current state, or by progressing an expectation that was not fulfilled or violated in the previous state. The second and third axioms define the conditions for fulfilment and violation of an expectation: an expectation that evaluates to true without considering future information is fulfilled, and one whose negation evaluates to true without considering future information is violated.

The problem of monitoring expectations expressed using this logic for their activation (when a rule of expectation fires), fulfilment and violation can be viewed as the problem of "model checking a path" [24], where the model is a sequence of observed states. A formula labelling technique has been developed [15] to determine the truth of formulae in the logic given a model. We also define existentially quantified versions of the Exp, Fulf and Viol operators, e.g. $\mathsf{Exp}(\lambda, \rho) \equiv \exists n, \phi\, \mathsf{Exp}(\lambda, \rho, n, \phi)$. Monitoring formulae of these types determines whether there are *any* active expectations, fulfilments or (respectively) violations of the rule of expectation with condition λ and resulting expectation ρ. If there are, the model checker returns, for each state s, a list of *witnesses* (n, ϕ) specifying the state n in which the rule fired, and the residual formula that is expected, fulfilled or violated in state s.

---

[3] This is a simplified form of an operator defined by Eisner et al. [19].

4   Other Computational Accounts of Expectations

Besides the prior work discussed in the previous sections, a number of researchers have investigated the general concept of expectation using different computational frameworks. This sections presents a brief summary of some of these other approaches.

Gärdenfors [21] investigates the relationship between expectations and non-monotonic reasoning, and proposes a treatment of expectations as defeasible premises for an argument, with varying degrees of defeasibility. He also presents an account of the "core meaning" of the linguistic pattern "α but β" as an indication that β violates our expectations in conjunction with α.

Alberti et al. [2] consider the application of expectations to the run-time monitoring of agents' compliance with a protocol. In this work, an abductive proof procedure is used to generate expectations about agent behaviour, and this process is informed by "social integrity constraints", which formally encode protocol rules such as "if a request has occurred, either an accept or refuse is expected within τ time units". The abductive proof procedure also allows the generated expectations to be monitored at run time.

Nickles et al. [27] propose the use of explicit representations of agent expectations in both the agent design process and the agents' run-time execution. Their *expectation-oriented modelling* approach involves specifying agent interactions using a graph-based formalism called *expectation networks*. Nodes in these networks represent event occurrences and edges are annotated to encode information about how the occurrence of events result in expectations of other subsequent events.

Wallace and Rovatsos [45] present an approach for defining and implementing an agent's practical social reasoning in terms of expectations. They model an expectation as a conditional belief associated with a test condition that will (eventually) confirm or refute the expectation. The social context of the agent is encoded by defining how positive and negative test results will result in the activation and deactivation of expectations. This allows an "expectation graph" to be derived, with sets of expectations as nodes and edges representing the possible transitions between these sets of expectations. A set of rules specifies when agents should perform actions based on the agents' current beliefs and properties of the expectation graph.

Vo and Li [44] extend the notion of normal form games in game theory with an explicit notion of agent expectations. In their approach, each agent in a normal form game maintains a set of its expectations about the other agents' probabilities of choosing each possible action, and has a decision function to select a mixed strategy based on these expectations. A technique is proposed for agents to correlate their expectations, to ensure that the agents expect to reach the same equilibrium.

Van Ditmarsh et al. [18] define an extension of epistemic models that includes a function assigning to each state a set of expected sequences of action observations. A dynamic logic with knowledge operators is used to reason about how an agent's observations match its expectations. The role of epistemic protocols as the source of agents' expectations is investigated, and it is shown how the logic allows reasoning about agents' knowledge based on their observations and the protocols followed.

5 Applications of Expectation Monitoring in Virtual Worlds

Virtual worlds such as Second Life[4] are increasingly being seen as an attractive testbed environment for testing artificial intelligence techniques [41, 46]. They provide a physics simulation engine, tools for creating in-world content, and a large community of users who have developed a wide range of simulated environments. Provided that a virtual world provides some mechanism for software to control avatars and to sense the simulated environment symbolically, AI researchers can develop and test virtual agents that aim to exhibit some level of intelligent behaviour in the virtual world without needing sophisticated vision and other real-world sensing systems. Furthermore, virtual worlds provide the opportunity for humans and software agents to interact, e.g. in the context of "serious games" [47], or to deploy social reasoning techniques to enhance human user's awareness of their social context in the virtual world.

To this end, our research group has applied the logic of expectations and the expectation monitor outlined above to support the development of socially aware agents in Second Life, or to provide social monitoring services to human users [14, 34, 35]. In this section we give an overview of two application domains we have applied our techniques to: the Second Life Football System[5] and the Otago Virtual Hospital [6].

The Second Life Football System comprises association football (soccer) pitch and ball objects that can be instantiated within Second Life, as well as a head-up display that can be incorporated into the Second Life viewer to control an avatar to kick the ball, run, etc. This is a challenging simulation for the integration of agents to Second Life as it is fast moving and agents need to be able to perceive their environment and react quickly. An infrastructure was developed to interconnect a Second Life client library with Jason agents, the Esper complex event recognition engine[6] and the expectation monitor described above [35, 36].

Figure 2 shows two football-related scenarios involving monitoring expectations. The scenario in Fig. 2a was presented previously as a hypothetical example [15], and has not been implemented (although it now could be with our virtual agent infrastructure [33, 35]). It involves a human player performing a training exercise that his coach requires him to complete. Rather than personally monitoring the player's completion of this expectation, the coach delegates this duty to a monitor service. The exercise proceeds as follows:

---

[4] http://secondlife.com
[5] http://secondfootball.com
[6] http://esper.codehaus.org

Starting in a certain region of the field ("zone 1"), the player must dribble the ball while advancing continuously down the field until another region ("zone 2") is reached. The player must then attempt to kick the ball into the goal from within zone 2. The exercise finishes if a goal is scored from this kick, and the monitoring service adds the proposition *ex1_achieved* to the current state to assert that this "Exercise 1" has been completed.

The Fulf formula containing a rule encoding the coach's expectation is shown in the figure, and the rule always results in an active expectation if the exercise is not in progress or completed. The expectation monitor checks for the truth of this formula in all states. The last part of the formula needs some explanation: the binder ($\downarrow$) binds x to a nominal referencing the current state, in which a kick is known to have occurred (due to the conjunct preceding the binder). The rest of the formula requires that eventually there exists some state (s say) in which the state-referencing proposition $goal(y)$ holds for some y, and x and y are the same state (expressed by the formula $@_x y$: at state x the nominal y is true). A formula of the form $goal(y)$ will be added by the complex event detection engine when a kick in a previous state y has resulted in the ball crossing the goal line in the current state. In summary, the subformula beginning with $\downarrow$ means that the current state (in which a kick occurred) is eventually followed by a state in which that kick results in a goal being scored.

The football scenario in Fig. 2b (which has been implemented [35]), involves two members of a team who are beginning the "give and go" tactic. Give and go involves one player (Player 1 in the figure) passing the ball to another player (Player 2). Player 2 then expects Player 1 to run down the field to an advantageous position (in this case, near the opposition team's goal-mouth), so that the ball can be passed back to him. Once Player 2 recognises that Player 1 has initiated the tactic (e.g. through context and agreed team strategy), he needs to detect either the future fulfilment or violation of his expectation about Player 1's behaviour. Once the expectation is fulfilled, he must pass the ball to Player 1. If it is violated (e.g. Player 1 slips and is no longer advancing towards the opposition goal), he must plan a new tactic to follow, such as a solo run towards the goal. However, as Player 2 will now be the subject of attempted tackles from the opposition, he needs to focus his attention on maintaining possession of the ball. Therefore he requests an expectation monitoring service to notify when either of the formulae shown becomes true: one expressing the fulfilment of the expectation, and one expressing its violation. The first argument in these formulae (*state97*) is a nominal naming the state in which the expectation was created (and evaluating to true only in that state). The intention is that the rule of expectation is fired exactly once—in that state.

Note that the angle brackets in Fig. 2b are used to encode an internal structure to the propositions. These have no meaning in the logic, but are replaced by brackets when sending fulfilment or violation notifications to an agent from the expectation monitor.

Another application domain that we have applied our work to is the training of medical students in a virtual hospital. The Otago Virtual Hospital (OVH) [6]

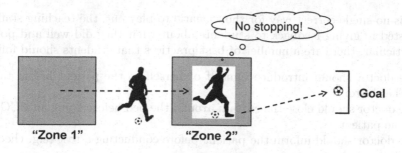

$$\mathsf{Fulf}(\neg ex1\_achieved \land in\_zone1 \land dribbling\_downfield$$
$$\land \neg \ominus(in\_zone1 \land dribbling\_downfield),$$
$$dribbling\_downfield \ \mathsf{U} \ (in\_zone2 \land kick \land \downarrow x. \Diamond(\exists_{goal(y)} @_x y))$$

(a) A training exercise [15]

$$\mathsf{Fulf}(state97, advanceToOppGoal\langle player1 \rangle \ \mathsf{U} \ nearOppGoal\langle player1 \rangle)$$
$$\mathsf{Viol}(state97, advanceToOppGoal\langle player1 \rangle \ \mathsf{U} \ nearOppGoal(player1))$$

(b) The give and go tactic [35, 33]

Fig. 2. Two Second Life Football scenarios and their monitored formulae

is a virtual hospital in which medical students practice their patient interview and diagnosis skills. In a simulation run, one or more students play the role of a junior doctor interviewing a patient, performing or requesting virtual tests to be performed, prescribing medication, admitting the patient to hospital, etc., with the aim of diagnosing and treating the patient's illness. All communication (between doctor and patient, between doctors, and between doctors and nurses) is done via text chat in the public chat channel. The user playing the role of the patient has a script to follow, outlining the patient's history and symptoms, and how they should be exhibited (e.g. a patient who is continually thirsty may repeatedly ask for drinks). The aim of the OVH is to give the students experience with open-ended clinical cases in a realistic hospital setting. However, while there is no single correct way for the scenario to play out, the teaching staff are interested in giving feedback to students about what they did well and poorly. In particular, there are a number of best practices that students should follow:

- The doctor should introduce himself or herself to the patient before taking his/her history
- The doctor should close the curtain around the bed before doing an ECG test on the patient
- The doctor should inform the patient before conducting a test (e.g. checking his/her pulse)
- The doctor should conduct a certain set of tests indicated by the scenario

After defining the salient event patterns to be recognised by the complex event processor, and implementing a technique for the recognition of domain-specific high-level communication acts (such as "inform_illness") from chat messages, these expectations were encoded in the expectation logic and could be recognised by the expectation monitor [33].

6   Towards the Expectation Event Calculus

Researchers in artificial intelligence have long been interested in automating reasoning about how the performance of actions affects the state of the world, e.g. to compute the consequences of a given sequence of events, to plan sequences of actions that will produce a desired outcome (planning), or to induce the effects of actions based on a history of events and world states. A popular formalism used in these areas of research is the *event calculus* (EC) [23,39][7]: a logical theory that defines how events change the state of the world based on descriptions of the effects of events, the initial state of the world, and when events occur.

6.1   Specifying Institutions Using the Event Calculus

In the area of multi-agent systems, the EC has been widely used to model the social consequences of actions. Yolum and Singh [49] used the EC to model the social semantics of agent interaction protocols in terms of commitments, and to generate the possible execution paths of the protocol in which all pending commitments are resolved. Farrell et al. [20] used the EC to model and monitor the state of contracts. Chesani et al. [10] also defined commitment-based semantics for agent interaction protocols using the EC, but focused on run-time monitoring of commitments. Artikis and Sergot [4] used the EC for specifying and tracking the normative states of multi-agent systems based on the notions of obligation, power and permission. Cliffe et al. [11] presented an approach for modelling norms using an action description formalism related to the EC, and applied answer set programming to perform queries about possible traces that satisfy

---

[7] The event calculus was originally developed by Kowalski and Sergot [23], but the discussion in this section is based on a later version presented by Shanahan [39].

Clearly defined boundaries

- Those with rights or entitlements to appropriate resources are clearly defined
- EC protocol for role-based access control

$apply(A, I)$ initiates $applied(A, I, member) = true$ at $T \leftarrow$
  $pow(A, apply(A, I)) = true$ holdsAt T
$pow(A, apply(A, I)) = true$ holdsAt $T \leftarrow$
  $role\_conditions(A, I, member) = true$ holdsAt T
$include(C, A, I)$ initiates $role\_of(A, I, member) = true$ at $T \leftarrow$
  $pow(C, include(C, A, I)) = true$ holdsAt T
$pow(C, include(C, A, I)) = true$ holdsAt $T \leftarrow$
  $role\_of(C, I) = gatekeeper$ holdsAt $T \wedge$
  $applied(A, I, member) = true$ holdsAt T

Collective choice arrangements

- The agents affected by the operational rules participate in the selection and modification of those rules
  - Voting protocol and the notion of enfranchisement
    - Right aspect: being empowered (as a member) to vote
    - Entitlement aspect: vote counted/result declared correctly

$vote(A, X, M, I)$ initiates $votes\_cast(M, I) = [X | L]$ at $T \leftarrow$
  $votes\_cast(M, I) = L$ holdsAt $T \wedge$
  $pow(A, vote(A, X, M, I)) = true$ holdsAt T
$pow(A, vote(A, X, M, I)) = true$ holdsAt $T \leftarrow$
  $status(M, I) = open$ holdsAt $T \wedge$
  $role\_of(A, I) = member$ holdsAt $T \wedge$
  $voted(M, I) = L$ holdsAt $T \wedge$ not $in\_voted(A, L)$

The entitlement aspect in EC

- Suppose the motion M is the resource allocation method
- Given a narrative of votes cast for the choice of method
- The chair counts the votes and declares the result

$declare(C, W, M, I)$ initiates $M(I) = W$ holdsAt $T \leftarrow$
  $pow(C, declare(C, W, M, I)) = true$ holdsAt T
$obl(C, declare(C, W, M, I)) = true$ holdsAt $T \leftarrow$
  $role\_of(C, I) = head$ holdsAt $T \wedge$
  $status(M, I) = closed$ holdsAt $T \wedge$
  $votes\_cast(M, I) = Votelist$ holdsAt $T \wedge$
  $win\_det\_meth(M, I) = WDM$ holdsAt $T \wedge$
  $winner\_determination(WDM, Votelist, W)$

Monitoring

- Monitoring, of both state conditions and appropriator behaviour, is by appointed agencies, who are either accountable to the appropriators or are appropriators
- Introduce role of monitor
  - Sense environment, report findings (formalise element of Principle 2, important when monitoring has a cost)
  - Observe appropriations, empowered to report

$pow(B, report(B, A, R, I)) = true$ holdsAt $T \leftarrow$
  $role\_of(B, I) = monitor$ holdsAt $T \wedge$
  $role\_of(A, I) = member$ holdsAt T

- Accountability
  - The head can remove an agent from the role if it 'misbehaves' (cf. Principle 6)

Fig. 3. Encoding of Ostrom's principles for enduring institutions [29] using the event calculus by Pitt et al. [31] (partial extract). Figure adapted from a presentation by Jeremy Pitt and used with permission.

properties of interest. Visara et al. [40] used a distributed implementation of an object-based variant of the EC to enable agents to query the normative state of a norm-governed multi-agent system. Pitt et al. [31] used the EC to provide an axiomatization of six of Ostrom's principles for designing *enduring* institutions for the management of common-pool resources (see Fig. 3). Alrawagfeh [3] modelled norms using the event calculus and presented a BDI agent architecture modified to take potential norm violation penalties into account when selecting a plan.

The event calculus consists of a set of predicates used to encode information about time periods in which dynamic properties of world state (*fluents*) hold and events occur (see Table 1), and a set of axioms that relate these predicates (see Fig. 4). In particular, given the specification of an institution or normative multi-agent system using logical rules and the EC ontology (such as the one by Pitt et al. [31] in Fig. 3), the EC axioms can be used to deduce the institutional state in each time point of an observed history that records the initial state of the world and the occurrence of actions at specific time points. This process is illustrated in Fig. 5. In particular, note how the institution specification in Fig. 3 contains two types of rules: those defining when an action *initiates* the value of a fluent (referred to as the action theory in Fig. 5), and those defining when a

Table 1. The event calculus ontology (based on Shanahan [39, Tables 1 and 2])

Formula	Meaning
$Initiates(a, f, t)$	Fluent f starts to hold after action a at time t
$Terminates(a, f, t)$	Fluent f ceases to hold after action a at time t
$Initially_P(f)$	Fluent f holds from time 0
$Initially_N(f)$	Fluent f does not hold from time 0
$t_1 < t_2$	Time point t_1 is before time point t_2
$Happens(a, t)$	Action a occurs at time t
$Happens(a, t_1, t_2)$	Action a starts at time t_1 and ends at time t_2
$HoldsAt(f, t)$	Fluent f holds at time t
$Clipped(t_1, f, t_2)$	Fluent f is terminated between times t_1 and t_2
$Declipped(t_1, f, t_2)$	Fluent f is initiated between times t_1 and t_2
$Releases(a, f, t)$	Fluent f is not subject to inertia after action a at time t

$$HoldsAt(f, t) \leftarrow Initially_P(f) \land \neg Clipped(0, f, t)$$

$$HoldsAt(f, t_3) \leftarrow Happens(a, t_1, t_2) \land Initiates(a, f, t_1) \land t_2 < t_3 \land \neg Clipped(t_1, f, t_3)$$

$$Clipped(t_1, f, t_4) \leftrightarrow \exists a, t_2, t_3 \, [Happens(a, t_2, t_3) \land t_1 < t_3 \land t_2 < t_4 \land$$
$$[\, Terminates(a, f, t_2) \lor Releases(a, f, t_2)\,]\,]$$

$$\neg HoldsAt(f, t) \leftarrow Initially_N(f) \land \neg Declipped(0, f, t)$$

$$\neg HoldsAt(f, t_3) \leftarrow Happens(a, t_1, t_2) \land Terminates(a, f, t_1) \land t_2 < t_3 \land$$
$$\neg Declipped(t_1, f, t_3)$$

$$Declipped(t_1, f, t_4) \leftrightarrow \exists a, t_2, t_3 \, [Happens(a, t_2, t_3) \land t_1 < t_3 \land t_2 < t_4 \land$$
$$[\, Initiates(a, f, t_2) \lor Releases(a, f, t_2)\,]\,]$$

$$Happens(a, t_1, t_2) \rightarrow t_1 \leq t_2$$

Fig. 4. Event calculus axioms (from Shanahan [39])

certain fluent value *holds at* a time point based on other fluent values holding at that time (referred to as state constraints or derived fluent definitions in Fig. 5)[8].

6.2 Adding Expectations to the Event Calculus

EC specifications of institutions and normative multi-agent systems often define actions that initiate fluents that have a natural interpretation as future expectations. For example, Artikis and Sergot [4] define the effect of a consumer accepting an online merchant's quote as the initialisation of an *obl* (obligation) fluent, which has arguments recording the consumer's identity and the action it is obliged to do: to send an electronic payment order to an 'intermediation

---

[8] There are minor differences in the syntax used in Figs. 3 and 5, the most significant being that Fig. 3 uses a variant of the EC in which fluents can take non-Boolean values.

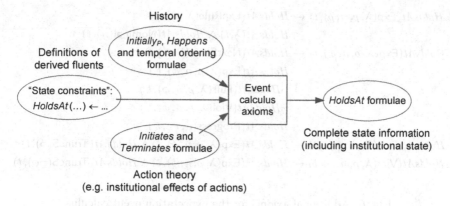

Fig. 5. Deducing institutional state using the event calculus (modified from Shanahan [39, Fig. 2])

server'. There is an implicit deadline, the expiry of which is represented by a *timeout* event. A separate rule is needed to terminate the obligation fluent when the payment event occurs, and the deadline monitoring and the generation of the timeout event appear to be handled by some mechanism external to the EC logic.

This section proposes an alternative way to handle expectations in EC domain specifications: by equipping the EC with additional semantics that incorporate the notions of expectation, fulfilment and violation, and an expectation progression mechanism. While this would add complexity to the EC engine, it would enable specifications of institutions involving the creations of norms, contracts, commitments and other forms of expectation to be shorter and more declarative in nature. In the example above, the effect of accepting the quote could then be specified as the creation of an Exp fluent with an argument stating the constraint that the payment should be made before a certain time (such as the current time plus some fixed period)[9]. More generally, it would be desirable if EC rules could introduce fluents expressing the existence of conditional rules of expectation. The consequences of fulfilment and violation of expectation would then be defined by rules with conditions of the form $HoldsAt(\mathsf{Fulf}(\ldots),t)$ and $HoldsAt(\mathsf{Viol}(\ldots),t)$, respectively.

Implementing this proposal requires finding a way to augment the event calculus so that a new rule of expectation can be dynamically introduced by an EC rule, and this rule can then trigger an expectation when its condition is satisfied. Furthermore, once an expectation exists in a state (represented by a $HoldsAt(\mathsf{Exp}(\ldots),t)$ fluent), the expectation should be iteratively progressed and recorded in its progressed form in subsequent states (using $HoldsAt$), until the

---

[9] Using real-time deadlines would require using a logic of expectations based on a metric temporal logic, such as that used in Fig. 1. However, the approach proposed here still has benefits if a simpler logic of expectations is used.

$$HoldsAt(\mathsf{Exp}(\lambda,\rho,n,\rho),t) \leftarrow HoldsAt(\mathsf{ExpRule}(\lambda,\rho),t) \wedge$$
$$HoldsAt(\lambda,t) \wedge HoldsAt(\mathsf{Nominal}(n),t)$$
$$HoldsAt(\mathsf{Exp}(\lambda,\rho,n,\psi),t) \leftarrow HoldsAt(\mathsf{NextState}(t),t') \wedge$$
$$HoldsAt(\mathsf{Exp}(\lambda,\rho,n,\phi),t') \wedge$$
$$\neg HoldsAt(\mathsf{Fulf}(\lambda,\rho,n,\phi),t') \wedge$$
$$\neg HoldsAt(\mathsf{Viol}(\lambda,\rho,n,\phi),t') \wedge$$
$$HoldsAt(\mathsf{Progress}(\phi,\psi),t')$$
$$HoldsAt(\mathsf{Fulf}(\lambda,\rho,n,\phi),t) \leftarrow HoldsAt(\mathsf{Exp}(\lambda,\rho,n,\phi),t) \wedge HoldsAt(\mathsf{TruncS}(\phi),t)$$
$$HoldsAt(\mathsf{Viol}(\lambda,\rho,n,\phi),t) \leftarrow HoldsAt(\mathsf{Exp}(\lambda,\rho,n,\phi),t) \wedge HoldsAt(\mathsf{TruncS}(\neg\phi),t)$$

Fig. 6. Additional axioms for the expectation event calculus

semantics of expectations indicate that it is fulfilled or violated. The fulfilment or violation must also be recorded in the appropriate state using *HoldsAt*.

Figure 6 illustrates some additional EC axioms needed to handle expectations in the manner outlined above. These correspond to the semantics of expectations shown in Sect. 3. The first axiom creates a new expectation from a current expectation rule if its condition holds in the current state. It is the role of the institution's action theory to define which expectation rules hold in which states. The fluent Nominal(n) reflects a particular assumption that our logic of expectations makes: each state is identified by a unique 'nominal' proposition that is true only in that state.

The second axiom accounts for the progression of unfulfilled and non-violated expectations from one state to the next (the states are assumed to form a linear sequence of discrete states so that each state has a unique successor, represented by the NextState(t) fluent). The last two rules state when fulfilment and violation fluents hold.

As the fluents Progress and TruncS are temporal operators (see Sect. 3), these must be evaluated in the context of the entire history of past states. For this reason, rather than modifying an EC reasoner to include temporal reasoning, we propose an alternative approach: linking an event calculus reasoner with an expectation monitor that incorporates the semantics of expectations, such as an enhancement of the one discussed in Sect. 3. This is illustrated in Fig. 7.

In this approach, the history supplied to the EC reasoner is passed to the monitor: a *HoldsAt*(p,t) formula causes p to be added to the state at time t in the model, and a *Happens*(a,t) formula causes *Happ*(a) to be added at time t[10]. NextState and Nominal fluents are also passed to the monitor, and these are directly encoded in the history structure.

The current expectation rules are sent to the monitor as ExpRule fluents, and one-off unconditional expectations can also be sent as Exp fluents. These types

---

[10] A propositional naming convention can be used to encode this if a propositional expectation logic is used in the monitor.

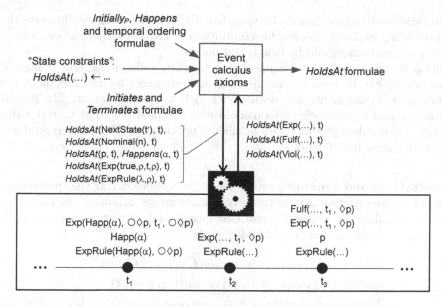

Fig. 7. Connecting an expectation monitor to an event calculus reasoner (the upper section of the figure is modified from Shanahan [39])

of fluent may contain formulae with temporal operators referring to the future and/or past, depending on the form of expectation logic used. In an extension to the model checking approach to expectation monitoring described in Sect. 3, the one-off expectations and expectation rules present in each state are not treated as fluents, but rather give rise to corresponding Exp, Fulf and/or Viol formulae to be checked in that state (this detail is not shown in the figure). As the monitor detects active fulfilments and their fulfilments and violations, these are passed to the EC reasoner using *HoldsAt* assertions.

If necessary, fluents can be divided into two categories: those that may appear within expectations and should be passed to the expectation monitor, and those that cannot. This would be useful, for example, when using a logic of expectations based on a propositional temporal logic. Non-propositional fluents could still be used within an institution's EC rules, but these would not be able be used in expectations. The following section illustrates two EC theories for which this distinction would be useful, as they use predicates to encode commitments and norms, which are defined in terms of expectations.

6.3 Defining Commitments and Norms in the Expectation Event Calculus

Above, we suggested that an institution's action theory should specify which expectation rules should apply in which states. In this section we propose that institutions could instead refer to fluents representing specific types of expectation defined by domain-independent EC theories, and we illustrate this by presenting example theories for commitments introduced by messages in an agent communication, and by rule-based norms.

This section briefly (and somewhat informally) illustrates how a logic of expectations can be used to provide common semantics for the fulfilment and violation of commitments and norms with rich temporal content. The presentation is based on the logic of Cranefield and Winikoff [15]. The material that follows in this subsection has been published previously[11] [7], and is reproduced here with minor modifications.

Expectations and Commitments. We begin by considering the specification of agent communication acts in terms of commitments, following the ideas (but not the formalism) of Verdicchio and Colombetti [42]. A partial specification in terms of the event calculus might look like this:

$$Initiates(inform(x, y, \phi), comm(t, x, y, \phi), t) \tag{1}$$

$$Initiates(request(x, y, \phi), precomm(t, x, y, \phi), t) \tag{2}$$

$$Terminates(accept(x, y, \phi, t_1), precomm(t_1, x, y, \phi), t_2) \tag{3}$$

$$Initiates(accept(x, y, \phi, t_1), comm(t_1, x, y, \phi), t_2)$$
$$\leftarrow HoldsAt(precomm(t_1, x, y, \phi), t_2) \tag{4}$$

$$Terminates(refuse(x, y, \phi, t_1), precomm(t_1, x, y, \phi), t_2) \tag{5}$$

This states that the sending of an inform message from x to y with content ϕ (a formula in linear temporal logic) establishes a fluent expressing that a commitment holds from x to y that ϕ is true. A request initiates a precommitment, which is terminated when the request is accepted or refused (the *request* and *refuse* communicative acts include the time that the precommitment was established in order to disambiguate different requests with the same content). If the request is accepted, a commitment is established. The time at which the commitment (or precommitment, if applicable) was established is recorded in the *comm* fluent. This is important for linking commitments (with their additional social context, x and y) to expectations.

We now model the relationship between commitments and expectations:

$$HoldsAt(\mathsf{Exp}(true, \phi, t, \phi), t) \leftarrow HoldsAt(comm(t, x, y, \phi), t) \tag{6}$$

$$HoldsAt(fulf\_comm(t_1, x, y, \phi), t_2)$$
$$\leftarrow HoldsAt(comm(t_1, x, y, \phi), t_2) \land HoldsAt(Fulf(true, \phi, t_1, \_), t_2) \tag{7}$$

$$HoldsAt(viol\_comm(t_1, x, y, \phi, \psi), t_2)$$
$$\leftarrow HoldsAt(comm(t_1, x, y, \phi), t_2) \land HoldsAt(Viol(true, \phi, t_1, \psi), t_2) \tag{8}$$

Clause 6 states that a one-off unconditional expectation is established when a commitment is created. Clauses 7 and 8 state that a commitment is fulfilled

---

[11] © the authors [7]. Licence: CC-BY (http://creativecommons.org/licenses/by/3.0/).

(respectively violated) if it currently exists (having been established at some time t_1) and the corresponding unconditional rule of expectation would have resulted in a current fulfilment (respectively violation) if it had fired at time t_1. The predicate *viol_comm* has an additional final argument (compared to *fulf_comm*) that encodes the residual formula ψ that was violated in the current state. This is likely to differ from the original commitment after partial evaluation and progression across a number of states occurring between t_1 and the present.

Expectations and Norms. In this section we show how the logic of expectations can also be used to define the fulfilment and violation of conditional rule-based norms. We assume that norms are encoded by fluents of the form $norm(\lambda, \rho, sanction)$, where λ is the condition under which the norm holds, ρ is a linear temporal logic formula encoding the norm as a constraint on the present and future states of the world, and *sanction* encodes a sanction to be applied if the norm is violated. Norms may be static and introduced by $Initially_P$ in a normative multi-agent system's EC theory, or they may be dynamic and created and removed by that theory using *Initiates* and *Terminates*. The sanction in the norm fluent is an example of the additional contextual information that might be associated with a norm in contrast to the strictly temporal focus of an expectation.

$$HoldsAt(\mathsf{Exp}(\lambda, \rho, t, \rho), t)$$
$$\leftarrow HoldsAt(norm(\lambda, \rho, sanction)) \wedge HoldsAt(\mathsf{TruncS}(\lambda), t) \quad (9)$$
$$HoldsAt(fulf\_norm(\lambda, \rho, t_1, sanction), t_2)$$
$$\leftarrow HoldsAt(norm(\lambda, \rho, sanction)) \wedge HoldsAt(\mathsf{Fulf}(\lambda, \rho, t_1, \_), t_2) \quad (10)$$
$$HoldsAt(viol\_norm(\lambda, \rho, t_1, \phi, sanction), t_2)$$
$$\leftarrow HoldsAt(norm(\lambda, \rho, sanction)) \wedge HoldsAt(\mathsf{Viol}(\lambda, \rho, t_1, \phi), t_2) \quad (11)$$

These clauses state that when a conditional norm is triggered, a corresponding expectation is triggered. The fulfilment or violation of an expectation that corresponds to a triggered norm results in the fulfilment or violation of the norm. Note that the time the norm was triggered serves to distinguish different fulfilments or violations of the same norm—it appears as the third argument in *fulf_norm* and *viol_norm*. As in the commitments case, we add an additional argument (ϕ) to the predicate *viol_norm* to record the residual violated formula derived from the right hand side of the norm after partial evaluation and progression since the norm was triggered.

7   Conclusion

This paper has discussed the use of expectations in agents' practical reasoning. A overview of the author's work on modelling and monitoring of expectations with a complex temporal structure was given, and applications of this work in the area of expectation monitoring in virtual worlds were described.

An extension of the event calculus incorporating first-class notions of expectation, fulfilment and violation was proposed, and it was shown how this would allow institution and normative MAS specifications in the event calculus to directly refer to commitment and norm fulfilment and violation, by using an intermediate domain-independent event calculus theory defining these notions in terms of commitments. Future work in this area includes implementing the proposal and investigating its applications.

References

1. Ågotnes, T., van der Hoek, W., Rodríguez-Aguilar, J.A., Sierra, C., Wooldridge, M.: On the logic of normative systems. In: Proceedings of the 20th International Joint Conference on Artificial Intelligence, pp. 1175–1180. AAAI Press (2007)
2. Alberti, M., Gavanelli, M., Lamma, E., Chesani, F., Mello, P., Torroni, P.: Compliance verification of agent interaction: a logic-based software tool. Appl. Artif. Intell. **20**(2), 133–157 (2006)
3. Alrawagfeh, W.: Norm representation and reasoning: a formalization in event calculus. In: Boella, G., Elkind, E., Savarimuthu, B.T.R., Dignum, F., Purvis, M.K. (eds.) PRIMA 2013. LNCS, vol. 8291, pp. 5–20. Springer, Heidelberg (2013)
4. Artikis, A., Sergot, M.: Executable specification of open multi-agent systems. Logic J. IGPL **18**(1), 31–65 (2010)
5. Bacchus, F., Kabanza, F.: Using temporal logics to express search control knowledge for planning. Artif. Intell. **116**(1–2), 123–191 (2000)
6. Blyth, P., Loke, S.K., Swan, J.: Otago Virtual Hospital: medical students learning to notice clinically salient features. In: Proceedings of the 27th Annual Ascilite Conference, pp. 108–112. Australasian Society for Computers in Learning in Tertiary Education (2010)
7. Broersen, J., Cranefield, S., Elrakaiby, Y., Gabbay, D., Grossi, D., Lorini, E., Parent, X., van der Torre, L.W.N., Tummolini, L., Turrini, P., Schwarzentruber, F.: Normative reasoning and consequence. In: Andrighetto, G., Governatori, G., Noriega, P., van der Torre, L.W.N. (eds.) Normative Multi-Agent Systems, Dagstuhl Follow-Ups, vol. 4, pp. 33–70. Schloss Dagstuhl-Leibniz-Zentrum für Informatik, Dagstuhl (2013). http://drops.dagstuhl.de/opus/volltexte/2013/399
8. Castelfranchi, C., Giardini, F., Lorini, E., Tummolini, L.: The prescriptive destiny of predictive attitudes: from expectations to norms via conventions. In: Proceedings of the 25th Annual Meeting of the Cognitive Science Society, pp. 222–227 (2003)
9. Castelfranchi, C.: Mind as an anticipatory device: for a theory of expectations. In: De Gregorio, M., Di Maio, V., Frucci, M., Musio, C. (eds.) BVAI 2005. LNCS, vol. 3704, pp. 258–276. Springer, Heidelberg (2005)
10. Chesani, F., Mello, P., Montali, M., Torroni, P.: Commitment tracking via the reactive event calculus. In: Proceedings of the 21st International Joint Conference on Artificial Intelligence, pp. 91–96. Morgan Kaufmann (2009)
11. Cliffe, O., De Vos, M., Padget, J.: Modelling normative frameworks using answer set programing. In: Erdem, E., Lin, F., Schaub, T. (eds.) LPNMR 2009. LNCS, vol. 5753, pp. 548–553. Springer, Heidelberg (2009)
12. Cranefield, S.: A rule language for modelling and monitoring social expectations in multi-agent systems. In: Boissier, O., Padget, J., Dignum, V., Lindemann, G., Matson, E., Ossowski, S., Sichman, J.S., Vázquez-Salceda, J. (eds.) ANIREM and OOOP 2005. LNCS (LNAI), vol. 3913, pp. 246–258. Springer, Heidelberg (2006)

13. Cranefield, S.: Modelling and monitoring social expectations in multi-agent systems. In: Noriega, P., Vázquez-Salceda, J., Boella, G., Boissier, O., Dignum, V., Fornara, N., Matson, E. (eds.) COIN 2006 Workshops. LNCS (LNAI), vol. 4386, pp. 308–321. Springer, Heidelberg (2007)

14. Cranefield, S., Li, G.: Monitoring social expectations in second life. In: Padget, J., Artikis, A., Vasconcelos, W., Stathis, K., da Silva, V.T., Matson, E., Polleres, A. (eds.) COIN 2009. LNCS (LNAI), vol. 6069, pp. 133–146. Springer, Heidelberg (2010)

15. Cranefield, S., Winikoff, M.: Verifying social expectations by model checking truncated paths. J. Logic Comput. **21**(6), 1217–1256 (2011)

16. Cranefield, S., Winikoff, M., Vasconcelos, W.: Modelling and monitoring interdependent expectations. In: Cranefield, S., van Riemsdijk, M.B., Vázquez-Salceda, J., Noriega, P. (eds.) COIN 2011. LNCS, vol. 7254, pp. 149–166. Springer, Heidelberg (2012)

17. Criado, N., Argente, E., Botti, V.: Normative deliberation in graded BDI agents. In: Dix, J., Witteveen, C. (eds.) MATES 2010. LNCS, vol. 6251, pp. 52–63. Springer, Heidelberg (2010)

18. van Ditmarsch, H., Ghosh, S., Verbrugge, R., Wang, Y.: Hidden protocols: modifying our expectations in an evolving world. Artif. Intell. **208**, 18–40 (2014)

19. Eisner, C., Fisman, D., Havlicek, J., Lustig, Y., McIsaac, A., Van Campenhout, D.: Reasoning with temporal logic on truncated paths. In: Hunt Jr, W.A., Somenzi, F. (eds.) CAV 2003. LNCS, vol. 2725, pp. 27–39. Springer, Heidelberg (2003)

20. Farrell, A.D.H., Sergot, M.J., Sallé, M., Bartolini, C.: Using the event calculus for tracking the normative state of contracts. Int. J. Coop. Inf. Syst. **14**(2 & 3), 99–129 (2005)

21. Gärdenfors, P.: The role of expectations in reasoning. In: Masuch, M., Pólos, L. (eds.) Knowledge Representation and Reasoning Under Uncertainty. LNCS, vol. 808, pp. 1–16. Springer, Heidelberg (1994)

22. Kollingbaum, M.J., Norman, T.J.: Norm adoption in the NoA agent architecture. In: Proceedings of the Second International Joint Conference on Autonomous Agents and Multiagent Systems, pp. 1038–1039. ACM (2003)

23. Kowalski, R., Sergot, M.: A logic-based calculus of events. New Gener. Comput. **4**, 67–95 (1986)

24. Markey, N., Schnoebelen, P.: Model checking a path. In: Amadio, R.M., Lugiez, D. (eds.) CONCUR 2003. LNCS, vol. 2761, pp. 251–265. Springer, Heidelberg (2003)

25. Meneguzzi, F., Luck, M.: Norm-based behaviour modification in BDI agents. In: Proceedings of the 8th International Conference on Autonomous Agents and Multiagent Systems, pp. 177–184. IFAAMAS (2009)

26. Morales, J., Lopez-Sanchez, M., Rodríguez-Aguilar, J.A., Wooldridge, M., Vasconcelos, W.: Automated synthesis of normative systems. In: Proceedings of the International Conference on Autonomous Agents and Multi-agent Systems, pp. 483–490. IFAAMAS (2013)

27. Nickles, M., Rovatsos, M., Weiss, G.: Expectation-oriented modeling. Eng. Appl. Artif. Intell. **18**, 891–918 (2005)

28. Oren, N., Vasconcelos, W., Meneguzzi, F., Luck, M.: Acting on norm constrained plans. In: Leite, J., Torroni, P., Ågotnes, T., Boella, G., van der Torre, L. (eds.) CLIMA XII 2011. LNCS, vol. 6814, pp. 347–363. Springer, Heidelberg (2011)

29. Ostrom, E.: Governing the Commons: The Evolution of Institutions for Collective Action. Cambridge University Press, Cambridge (1990)

30. Panagiotidi, S., Vázquez-Salceda, J.: Towards practical normative agents: a framework and an implementation for norm-aware planning. In: Cranefield, S., van Riemsdijk, M.B., Vázquez-Salceda, J., Noriega, P. (eds.) COIN 2011. LNCS, vol. 7254, pp. 93–109. Springer, Heidelberg (2012)

31. Pitt, J., Schaumeier, J., Artikis, A.: Axiomatization of socio-economic principles for self-organizing institutions: concepts, experiments and challenges. ACM Trans. Auton. Adapt. Syst. **7**(4), 39:1–39:39 (2012)

32. Piunti, M., Castelfranchi, C., Falcone, R.: Surprise as shortcut for anticipation: clustering mental states in reasoning. In: Proceedings of the 20th International Joint Conference on Artificial Intelligence, pp. 507–512 (2007)

33. Ranathunga, S.: Improving awareness of intelligent virtual agents. Ph.D. thesis, University of Otago (2013)

34. Ranathunga, S., Cranefield, S.: Improving situation awareness in intelligent virtual agents. In: Dignum, F., Brom, C., Hindriks, K., Beer, M., Richards, D. (eds.) CAVE 2012. LNCS, vol. 7764, pp. 134–148. Springer, Heidelberg (2013)

35. Ranathunga, S., Cranefield, S., Purvis, M.: Identifying events taking place in Second Life virtual environments. Appl. Artif. Intell. **26**(1–2), 137–181 (2012)

36. Ranathunga, S., Cranefield, S., Purvis, M.: Integrating expectation monitoring into BDI agents. In: Dennis, L., Boissier, O., Bordini, R.H. (eds.) ProMAS 2011. LNCS, vol. 7217, pp. 74–91. Springer, Heidelberg (2012)

37. Savarimuthu, B.T.R., Cranefield, S., Purvis, M., Purvis, M.K.: Obligation norm identification in agent societies. J. Artif. Soc. Soc. Simul. **13**(4), 3 (2010)

38. Savarimuthu, B.T.R., Cranefield, S., Purvis, M., Purvis, M.K.: Identifying prohibition norms in agent societies. Artif. Intell. Law **21**(1), 1–46 (2013)

39. Shanahan, M.: The Event Calculus Explained. In: Veloso, M.M., Wooldridge, M.J. (eds.) Artificial Intelligence Today. LNCS (LNAI), vol. 1600, pp. 409–430. Springer, Heidelberg (1999)

40. Urovi, V., Bromuri, S., Stathis, K., Artikis, A.: Initial steps towards run-time support for norm-governed systems. In: De Vos, M., Fornara, N., Pitt, J.V., Vouros, G. (eds.) COIN 2010. LNCS, vol. 6541, pp. 268–284. Springer, Heidelberg (2011)

41. Veksler, V.D.: Second Life as a simulation environment: rich, high-fidelity world, minus the hassles. In: Proceedings of the 9th International Conference on Cognitive Modeling, pp. 420–425 (2009)

42. Verdicchio, M., Colombetti, M.: Communication languages for multiagent systems. Comput. Intell. **25**(2), 136–159 (2009)

43. Viganò, F., Colombetti, M.: Symbolic model checking of institutions. In: Proceedings of the 9th International Conference on Electronic Commerce, pp. 35–44. ACM Press (2007)

44. Vo, Q.B., Li, M.: On the role of expectations in multi-agent reasoning and decision making. In: Proceedings of the IEEE/WIC/ACM International Conferences on Web Intelligence and Intelligent Agent Technology, vol. 2, pp. 162–169. IEEE (2012)

45. Wallace, I., Rovatsos, M.: Bounded practical social reasoning in the ESB framework. In: Proceedings of the 8th International Conference on Autonomous Agents and Multiagent Systems, pp. 1097–1104. IFAAMAS (2009)

46. Weitnauer, E., Thomas, N.M., Rabe, F., Kopp, S.: Intelligent agents living in social virtual environments – bringing Max into Second Life. In: Prendinger, H., Lester, J.C., Ishizuka, M. (eds.) IVA 2008. LNCS (LNAI), vol. 5208, pp. 552–553. Springer, Heidelberg (2008)

47. Westra, J., van Hasselt, H., Dignum, F., Dignum, V.: Adaptive serious games using agent organizations. In: Dignum, F., Bradshaw, J., Silverman, B., van Doesburg, W. (eds.) Agents for Games and Simulations. LNCS (LNAI), vol. 5920, pp. 206–220. Springer, Heidelberg (2009)

48. Winikoff, M., Cranefield, S.: Eliciting expectations for monitoring social interactions. In: Purvis, M., Savarimuthu, B.T.R. (eds.) ICCMSN 2008. LNCS, vol. 5322, pp. 171–185. Springer, Heidelberg (2009)

49. Yolum, P., Singh, M.: Reasoning about commitments in the event calculus: an approach for specifying and executing protocols. Ann. Math. Artif. Intell. **42**, 227–253 (2004)

Norm Conflict

An Algorithm to Identify Conflicts
Between Norms and Values

Karen da Silva Figueiredo[1](✉) and Viviane Torres da Silva[2]

[1] Computer Science Department, Universidade Federal do
Mato Grosso (UFMT), Cuiabá, MT, Brazil
karen@ic.ufmt.br
[2] Computer Science Department, Universidade Federal Fluminense (UFF),
Niterói, RJ, Brazil
viviane.silva@ic.uff.br

Abstract. Norms and values are part of the organizational culture. While the
values support the agent's autonomy by representing its character and helping
to make decisions and execute actions, the norms are used by the system to
cope with the autonomy of the agents by regulating their behavior and the
execution of actions. One of the main challenges faced by agents at runtime is
the conflicts that may arise between the systems norms and their values. The
goals of this paper are to point out the conflict cases between norms and values
and to propose an algorithm to help the agent to identify those conflict cases.

Keywords: Norm · Value · Conflict · Identification · Algorithm

1 Introduction

Culture can be seen as a social accepted collection of behavior patterns learned, shared
and transmitted with the aim of adapt the individuals of a group [1, 2]. These behavior
patterns are expressed by the group in many forms of cultural mechanisms, such as
norms and values.

Norms are used to regulate the behavior of the agents by describing the actions
they must (or must not) execute in specific situations in order to cope with the
heterogeneity, autonomy and diversity of interests of those agents. On the other hand,
values are used to help the agents to evaluate and decide what to do based on what
they believe is right to themselves and to their group [3]. The actions executed by the
agents will promote or demote their values. Thus, the agents will always prefer to
execute the actions that promote more values (or demote fewer values).

Since norms are used to regulate the actions of an agent and its values are promoted or demoted due to execution of such actions, conflicts can arise between the
norms and its values. For instance, a norm can prohibit the agent to execute an action
that promotes one of its values. Although there are several works proposing solutions
for the checking of conflicts between norms [4–11] and between norms and some
agents' elements, such as goals [12] and plans [13], there is a need for an approach to
check for conflicts between norms and values. In this paper we point out the conflict

T. Balke et al. (Eds.): COIN 2013, LNAI 8386, pp. 259–274, 2014.
DOI: 10.1007/978-3-319-07314-9_14, © Springer International Publishing Switzerland 2014

cases that may arise between norms and values and propose an algorithm to identify those conflict cases.

As far as we know, this is the first MAS work that investigates the identification of this kind of conflicts. The identification of the conflicts between the system's norms and the agents values is an important issue, because by identifying and solving the conflicts the agents are able to decide, for instance: (i) whether or not enter an organization once they realize if the organization's norms are coherent or not with their values; and (ii) which actions they will execute and, as consequence, which norms they will fulfill or violate.

The reminder of this paper is organized as follows. In Sect. 2 we provide some background material about norms (Sect. 2.1), values (Sect. 2.2) and the specification notation adopted (Sect. 2.3) for the understanding of this work. Section 3 is the core of this paper, where we discuss the norms and values relation, address the conflict cases between them (Sect. 3.1), present the proposed algorithm to identify these conflict cases (Sect. 3.2) and show an example (Sect. 3.3). To finish, Sect. 4 presents some related work and Sect. 5 concludes the paper with final remarks and discusses future work.

2 Background

In this section some background material for the understanding of this work is presented. We introduce the basic concepts about norms and values in Sects. 2.1 and 2.2, respectively, in order to support the conflicts discussion of Sect. 3. In Sect. 2.3 we summarize the Z language that was used to write the algorithm to identify conflicts between norms and values proposed in this work.

2.1 Norms

Norms are mechanisms used to regulate the behavior of the agents by describing the actions that can be performed (*permissions*), actions that must be performed (*obligations*), and actions that cannot be performed (*prohibitions*). They represent a way for agents to understand their responsibilities and the responsibilities of the other agents in the system.

A norm can be described by several elements, the main elements that compose a norm are [4]: the *deontic concept* (i.e. obligation, prohibition and permission) that designate the behavior restrictions for the agents; the *involved entities* who have their behavior restricted by the norm; the *actions* being regulated by the norm; the *activation constraints* that limit the period during while the norm is active; the *sanctions* to be applied when the norm is violated or fulfilled; and the *context* that determines the area of application of the norm.

Due to the dynamics of MAS, conflicts may arise between the system norms and other system elements as goals, e.g. [12], plans, e.g. [13], values and even other norms, e.g. [4–11]. The agents must be able to cope with these conflicts, identifying and solving them at running time in order to make decisions, select intentions and execute actions. In this paper we focus on the identification of conflicts between the system's norms and the agent's values (see Sect. 3).

2.2 Values

In this work we address the definition of value of the Schwartz Value Theory (SVT) [14] because it is the state-of-the-art theory about value [15] and it has been previously adopted in MAS research [11, 16]. Values are described by SVT as concepts about desirable end states or behaviors that transcend specific situations used to guide the selection or evaluation of behavior and events that are ordered by relative importance [14]. Let's discuss this definition in parts.

Values are concepts about desirable end states or behaviors. Values are represented in the agent's mind as major guidelines that say what is good or bad, right or wrong and worth to achieve or not. They somehow define the character of the agent. *Ambition*, *honesty* and *social recognition* are some examples of values [17]. Each agent has its set of values (called values system). So, an agent may think that to have *ambition* is good while another agent may not. An agent may think that act with *honesty* is right while another agent may not consider it. An agent may think that is important to pursue *social recognition* while another agent may not care about it.

Values transcend specific situations. Different from other representations as goals and norms that are applied to specific situations and contexts, values work as general principles that are independent of time, place and objects [18]. For example, an agent that has *honesty* as an important value will act with honesty in every situation, because that is a priority to it.

Values guide the selection or evaluation of behavior and events. Similar to goals, we can say that values are reached by the execution of certain actions. Though, a value is not something that can be achievable [3]. How can we achieve *ambition*? How we can we say that we have enough *social recognition*? So, we say that a value is something that can be *promoted* or *demoted*[1] by certain actions and attitudes[2].

An agent will always prefer to execute an action or show a behavior that promotes its values. In the same way an agent will not intend to execute an action or show a behavior that demotes its values. In face of a choice, the agent will use its values system to evaluate the best option, i.e. which option will promote more and demote fewer values. Suppose that an agent who has the values *honesty* and *social recognition* finds a suitcase with a great amount of money. The agent will decide to return the suitcase to its owner, because not returning it would demote its *honesty* value. Then, the agent has two ways to return the suitcase: anonymously and non-anonymously.

---

[1] A value can be promoted or demoted in many levels and the measurement of the intensity of the promotion or demotion is out of the scope of this paper because it is still an open question to Psychology [14].

[2] Some values can also be indirectly promoted/demoted by the promotion/demotion of other values [14, 16], but the discussion of the post-effects of the promotion/demotion of values is out of the scope of this paper.

The agent will choose to return the suitcase non-anonymously because, in addition to promote the *honesty* value, it will also promote the *social recognition* value.

Values are ordered by relative importance. Although an agent can have a set of values, some values are more important to it than others, i.e. the priority of a value can be higher than another. Each value in an agent's values system receives a relative importance that helps the agent reasoning to evaluate events and make decisions.

Consider that an agent who has the values *ambition* and *honesty* finds a suitcase with a great amount of money as in the previous example. If the agent returns the suitcase, then it will promote its *honesty* value and demote its *ambition* value. But, if it does not return the suitcase, then the *ambition* value will be promoted and the *honesty* value will be demoted. In cases like this, the importance of each value will be used to make the decision. If the importance of the *ambition* value is greater than the importance of the *honesty* value, the agent will not return the suitcase even knowing that this action will demote its *honesty* value.

When agents cohabit they share and discuss their values [16]. The common values of the majority of agents of one organization are part of the organizational culture [19] and are transmitted to the agents that inhabit such organization.

2.3   The Z Language

There are several languages and formal techniques available to specify properties of software systems [20]. In this work we choose to do the specification using the Z language [21]. Z is a model-oriented formal specification language based on set theory and first-order logic. By choosing the Z language we adopt a language that is extremely expressive, elegant and more accessible than many other formalisms because it is based on existing elementary components such as first order predicates and set theory. Moreover, Z is being used both in industry [22, 23] and academia, including MAS researches [9, 24]. It is also supported by a large array of books [25] and tools for type checking, testing and animating operations [26, 27].

The key syntactic element of Z is the *schema*, which allows specifications to be structured into manageable modular components. Z schemas consist of two parts: the upper declarative part, which declares variables and their types, and the lower predicate part, which relates and constrains those variables. If we allow d to stand for a set of declarations, p to be a set of predicates and S to be the name of a schema we have the basic notation for a schema as follows:

$$
\begin{array}{|l}
\hline
\_S\ \underline{\hspace{6cm}} \\
\hline
d \quad \{set\ of\ declarations\} \\
\hline
p \quad \{set\ of\ predicates\} \\
\hline
\end{array}
$$

Declarations and predicates are composed by expressions using the elements of the Z language's notation. A summary of the Z notation that is used in this paper is given in Fig. 1. More details about Z and its formal semantics can be found elsewhere [21].

Definitions		Logic	
a ::= b | ...	Free type definition	true	Logical true constant
[a]	Introduction of a given set	false	Logical false constant
		p ∧ q	Logical conjunction, *and*
Sets, functions and expressions		p ∨ q	Logical disjunction, *or*
Ø	Empty set	p ⇒ q	Logical implication
P A	Power set	p ⇔ q	Logical equivalence
A ∩ B	Set intersection	∀ X • q	Universal quantification
A ∪ B	Set union	∃ X • q	Existential quantification
A × B × ...	Cartesian product	**Schema**	**Axiomatic definition**
A → B	Total functions	S	
x = y	Equality		d
x ≠ y	Inequality	d	
m ≤ n	Less than or equal		
m < n	Less than		p
m ≥ n	Greater than or equal	p	
m > n	Greater than		
if p then x else y	Conditional expression		

Fig. 1. Summary of Z notation.

3 Norms and Values Conflicts

Both norms and values are part of the organizational culture. On one hand the values support the agent's autonomy by representing its character and helping the agent to take its own decisions and execute actions based on what it thinks it's important and on its preferences. On the other hand the norms are used by the system to cope with the autonomy of the agents by regulating their behavior in order to promote the system order.

As stated before in Sect. 2, agents prefer to execute actions that promote their values and not execute actions that demote their values. Since norms may prohibit or oblige agents of execute actions, conflicts between the system's norms and the agent's values may arise. For instance, if a norm prohibits the execution of an action that promotes a value or obligates the execution of an action that demotes a value, such norm is in conflict with the values of the agent.

The identification of the conflicts between the system's norms and the values is important to the agent when deciding, for instance: (i) whether or not to enter an organization once it realizes that the organization's norms are coherent or not with its values; and (ii) which actions it will execute and, as consequence, which norms it will violate or fulfill.

The identification of conflicts between norms and values *at runtime* is an important because new conflicts may arise at any time. First the norms change due to the dynamic of the MAS environments, and, second, the agent's values may also change due to the living together and cultural influences [3, 14].

In Sect. 3.1 we discuss in which cases the norms and values are in conflicts. In the next sections we present the algorithm proposed to identify these conflict cases (Sect. 3.2) and an example of the application of this algorithm (Sect. 3.3). In our work we consider that the agent knows its values system, which actions promote and demote its values and which norms are applied to it.

3.1 Conflict Cases

Norms regulate the execution of actions by describing obligations, prohibitions and permissions to the agents. The actions to be executed by the agents can promote and demote some of their values. So, the actions are the central element linking norms to values, as shown in Fig. 2.

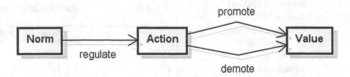

Fig. 2. Norm, action and value relationships

There may be norms that describe the actions that must be executed (obligations), the actions that cannot be executed (prohibitions), and the actions that can be executed (permissions). The agents will prefer to execute actions that promote their values and they will not intend to execute actions that demote their values. Considering this, we can point the two main conflict cases between norms and values, which are:

1. *The norm states an obligation to the agent to execute an action that demotes an important value to the agent*;
2. *The norm states a prohibition to the agent to execute an action that promotes an important value to the agent.*

In both cases the norm defines a behavior that is against the personal interests of the agent. Norms that state permissions to execute actions will not be in conflicts with the agent's values, because even if the action regulated to the norm demotes an important value to the agent, it can simply choose to not execute the action or to not join the group that states the permission of the action.

Despite the identification of conflicts between norms and values seems simple, it may be complicate to identify the conflicts when a norm and a value do not mention exactly the same action, but related actions. When a norm regulates an action and a value is promoted/demoted by another action, a simple conflict checker would conclude that the norm and the value are not in conflict since they do not mention the same action. However, if these actions are related, the conflict may arise. In the next sections we detail the identification of conflict cases when one action is the specialization of another (items 3.1 and 3.2) and when one action is a part of another action (items 4.1 and 4.2). These relationships between actions are necessary to describe complex actions and they have been previously used on MAS researches, e.g. [5, 10, 28].

3.1.1 Action Refinement

If the refinement relationship is defined between two actions, it means that there is an action called subaction that is more specific than another action called superaction. The states that should be achieved by executing the superaction are a subset of the states achieved by executing the subaction. If there is more than one subaction for a given superaction, it is necessary to execute only one subaction in order to achieve the goal of executing the superaction.

Norm: If the norm applied to the superaction is an obligation, it means that at least one subaction must be executed in order to fulfill the obligation. On the other hand, if the norm applied to the superaction is a prohibition, it means that if one subaction is executed the norm will be violated.

Value: The values promoted and demoted by a superaction are also promoted and demoted by all subactions. But each subaction can promote and demote new values. The relation between the action refinement relationship and its sets of promoted and demoted values are described in Fig. 3a.

So, if a norm regulates the execution of a superaction, there will be conflicts in the following cases:

3.1. *The norm states an obligation to the agent to execute a superaction and all its subactions demote an important value to the agent.* An obligation to execute a superaction means an obligation to execute one of its subactions. If all subactions demote an important value to the agent, then the agent will not be able to choose an action to fulfill the obligation without be in conflicts with its values system;

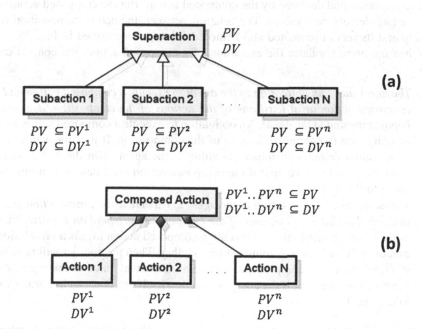

Fig. 3. The Promoted and Demoted Value Sets of Actions – Let the set of promoted values of an action be PV and the set of demoted values of an action be DV. The set of values promoted/demoted by a superaction is included in the set of values promoted/demoted by each of its subactions. And the set of values promoted/demoted by a composed action includes all the sets of values promoted/demoted by the actions of the composition.

3.2.   *The norm states a prohibition to the agent to execute a superaction and at least one of its subactions promotes an important value to the agent.* The prohibition to execute a superaction means a prohibition to execute each of its subactions. One subaction that promotes an important value to the agent is enough to establish a conflict between the norm and the values of the agent.

3.1.2   Action Composition

If the composition relationship is defined between two actions, it means that there is an action that is a part of another action called composed action. The states that should be achieved by executing the action that is part of the composition are a subset of the states achieved by executing the composed action. If there is more than one action in a given composition, it is necessary to execute all of them in order to achieve the goal of executing the composed action.

Norm: If the norm applied to the composed action is an obligation, it means that all actions of the composition must be executed in order to fulfill the obligation. On the other hand, if the norm applied to the composed action is a prohibition, it means that only if all actions of the composition are executed together the norm will be violated.

Value: The values promoted and demoted by an action that is part of a composition are also promoted and demoted by the composed action. But the composed action can promote and demote new values. The relation between the action composition relationship and its sets of promoted and demoted values are described in Fig. 3b.

When the norm regulates the execution of a composed action, the conflict cases are:

4.1.   *The norm states an obligation to the agent to execute a composed action and the composed action or at least one of the actions of the composition demotes an important value to the agent.* An obligation to execute a composed action means an obligation to execute all actions of the composition. If just one action of the composition demotes an important value to the agent, then there is a conflict. Also, there will be a conflict if the composed action itself demotes an important value to the agent;

4.2.   *The norm states a prohibition to the agent to execute a composed action and the composed action or all actions of the composition promote an important value to the agent.* A prohibition to execute a composed action means a prohibition to execute all actions of the composition together. Then the conflict will arise only if all actions of the composition demote an important value to the agent. Also, there will be a conflict if the composed action itself promotes an important value to the agent.

Just like the norms that regulate simple actions, there are no conflicts between values and permission norms that regulate superactions and composed actions.

3.2 An Algorithm to Identify the Conflicts

In this section we propose an algorithm to verify if a norm is in conflicts with the agent values by checking every case of conflict described in the previous section. The algorithm and its input elements (norm, value and action) are written in Z as functions and schema definitions[3].

Values are represented by the *Value* schema where *identifier* indicates the value identifier symbol from the set [*ValueSym*], i.e. the name of the value, and *importance* indicates the relative importance associated by the agent with that value. If *importance* = 0 then the value is not important to the agent and if *importance* > 0 then the agent consider the value important.

$$\begin{array}{|l}
\hline
Value \underline{\hspace{10cm}} \\
\quad identifier : ValueSym \\
\quad importance : \mathbb{N} \\
\hline
\end{array}$$

The actions are described by the *Action* schema where: *identifier* indicates the action identifier symbol from the set [*ActionSym*], i.e. the action's name; *subactions* specifies the subactions set of the action, if there are any; *compositeactions* specifies the actions set of the composition, if the action is a composed action; *promotes* indicates the values set promoted by the action; and *demotes* indicates the values set demoted by the action. For consistence reasons, an action cannot be part of its own subactions or composite actions set. Also, an action cannot both promote and demote a given value.

$$\begin{array}{|l}
\hline
Action \underline{\hspace{10cm}} \\
\quad identifier : ActionSym \\
\quad subactions : \mathbb{P}\ Action \\
\quad compositeactions : \mathbb{P}\ Action \\
\quad promotes : \mathbb{P}\ Value \\
\quad demotes : \mathbb{P}\ Value \\
\hline
\quad self \cap subactions = \emptyset \\
\quad self \cap compositeactions = \emptyset \\
\quad promotes \cap demotes = \emptyset \\
\hline
\end{array}$$

Finally, norms are represented by the *Norm* schema where *identifier* indicates the norm identifier symbol from the set [*NormSym*]; *deonticconcept* indicates if the norm states an obligation, a prohibition or a permission as shown by *DeonticConcept* definition; and *action* indicates the action regulated by the norm. Although norms are usually composed by all the elements described in Sect. 2.1, we are only interested to address here the elements that affect the conflicts verification.

---

[3] The specification presented in this section can be considered as a preliminary extension of the specification of the BDI agent proposed in [9] to include values in the agent reasoning process.

DeonticConcept ::= *OBLIGATION* | *PROHIBITION* | *PERMISSION*

Norm _____

| *identifier* : *NormSym*
| *deonticconcept* : *DeonticConcept*
| *action* : *Action*
_____

The algorithm that we propose is divided in two parts or two functions: the *checkNormValueMainConflicts* and the *checkNormValueAllConflicts*. The first function verifies only the conflict cases 1 and 2 which just analyze the values promoted and demoted by a specific action regulated by the norm. The second function includes the first function and also covers the 3.1, 3.2, 4.1 and 4.2 conflict cases by analyzing all the values promoted and demoted by the subactions and composite actions of the structure of the action regulated by the norm.

| *checkNormValueMainConflicts* : (*Norm* × *Action*) → *Boolean*

| 1 : ∀ n : *Norm*; a : *Action* • *checkNormValueMainConflicts*(n, a) ⇔
| 2 :   (((n. *deonticconcept* = *OBLIGATION*) ∧
| 3 :   (∃ *demotedvalue* : a.*demotes* | *demotedvalue.importance* > 0))
| 4 :   ∨ ((n. *deonticconcept* = *PROHIBITION*) ∧
| 5 :   (∃ *promotedvalue* : a.*promotes* | *promotedvalue.importance* > 0)))

The *checkNormValueMainConflicts* function maps a norm and its action to a boolean that indicates whether or not exists a conflict between the norm and the values promoted and demoted by the action of the norm. This function returns true if the deontic concept of the norm is obligation and at least one of the values demoted by the action of the norm has an importance greater than 0 (conflict case 1 – lines 1–3) or if the deontic concept of the norm is prohibition and at least one of the values promoted by the action of the norm has an importance greater than 0 (conflict case 2 – lines 4 and 5).

The *checkNormValueAllConflicts* is the main function. It is the function that must be called in order to check all the conflict cases between a norm and the values of the agent. The *checkNormValueAllConflicts* function maps a norm and its action to a boolean that indicates whether or not exists a conflict between the norm and the values promoted and demoted by the action of the norm and its subactions and composite actions.

$checkNormValueAllConflicts : (Norm \times Action) \rightarrow Boolean$

1 : $\forall n : Norm;\ a : Action\ |\ checkActionsUnification(a, n.action)$ •
2 :   if $a.subactions \neq \emptyset$ then
3 :   if $((n.deonticconcept = OBLIGATION\ \wedge$
4 : $(\forall subaction : a.subactions\ |\ checkNormValueAllConflicts(n, subaction)))$
5 : $\vee\ (n.deonticconcept = PROHIBITION\ \wedge$
6 : $(\exists subaction : a.subactions\ |\ checkNormValueAllConflicts(n, subaction))))$
7 :   then $checkNormValueAllConflicts(n, a) = true$
8 :   else $checkNormValueAllConflicts(n, a) = false$
9 :   else if $a.compositeactions \neq \emptyset$ then
10 :   if $checkNormValueMainConflicts(n, a)$
11 :   then $checkNormValueAllConflicts(n, a) = true$
12 :   else if $((n.deonticconcept = OBLIGATION\ \wedge$
13 : $(\exists compositeaction : a.compositeactions\ |$
14 : $checkNormValueAllConflicts(n, compositeaction)))$
15 : $\vee\ (n.deonticconcept = PROHIBITION\ \wedge$
16 : $(\forall compositeaction : a.compositeactions\ |$
17 : $checkNormValueAllConflicts(n, compositeaction))))$
18 :   then $checkNormValueAllConflicts(n, a) = true$
19 :   else $checkNormValueAllConflicts(n, a) = false$
20 :   else $checkNormValueAllConflicts(n, a) = checkNormValueMainConflicts(n, a)$

First, the function verifies if the action inputted is really the action of the norm before proceed the conflict identification (line 1)[4]. Then the function confirms if the action of the norm has subactions (line 2) in order to check recursively all the subactions and its values (lines 2–8). The function returns true (i) if the deontic concept of the norm is obligation and a conflict was identified while checking all the subactions of the norm action (conflict case 3.1 – lines 3 and 4) or (ii) if the deontic concept of the norm is prohibition and a conflict was identified while checking at least one subaction of the norm action (conflict case 3.2 – lines 5 and 6).

After that, the function verifies if the action of the norm is a composed action (line 9) in order to check the action of the norm itself (line 10) and recursively verify all the actions of the composition and its values (lines 9–19). The function returns true (i) if a conflict was identified while checking the action of the norm with the *checkNorm-ValueMainConflicts* function, (ii) if the deontic concept of the norm is obligation and a conflict was identified while checking at least one action of the composition of the norm action (conflict case 4.1 – lines 12–14) or (iii) if the deontic concept of the norm is prohibition and a conflict was identified while checking all the actions of the composition of the norm action (conflict case 4.2 – lines 15–17).

---

[4] The function *checkActionsUnification* applies the unification between two actions as in [9, 24] and was omitted here due to the lack of space. It can be seen in http://www.ic.uff.br/~kfigueiredo/values/normvalueconflictsidentification.pdf together with the complete specification presented in this work.

To conclude, if the action of the norm is not a superaction or a composition, the function calls the *checkNormValueMainConflicts* function and returns its result, applying the verification of the two main conflict cases to the single action and its values (conflict cases 1 and 2 – line 20).

The next section presents an example to illustrate our approach of conflicts identification between norms and values.

3.3 Running Example

Let's consider an agent who has the values *security* and *agility*, both with *importance* = *1*, i.e. both values are important to the agent. Suppose that exists a norm that obligates this agent to go from X to Y. Figure 4 illustrates the paths the agent can use to go from point X to Y.

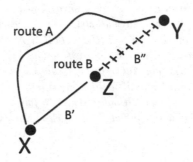

Fig. 4. Example illustration

The agent can go from X to Y via route A or via route B passing by Z. The route A is longer than route B, but the subroute B″ that connects Z to Y has some obstacles. On one hand, going through route A demotes the *agility* value since it is the longest path and going through route B promotes *agility*. On the other hand, going through route B″ demotes its *security* value because of the obstacles.

The following structure describes the values, actions and norm of this scenario example according to the specification of the previous section:

security(1)
agility(1)

goFromXtoY({goFromXtoYViaA, goFromXtoYViaB}, {}, {}, {})
goFromXtoYViaA({}, {}, {}, {agility})
goFromXtoYViaB({}, {goFromXtoZ, goFromZtoY}, {agility}, {})
goFromXtoZ({}, {}, {}, {})
goFromZtoY({}, {}, {}, {security})

norm1(OBLIGATION, goFromXtoY)

To check if *norm1* is in conflict with the values of the agent, first the algorithm identifies that the action regulated by *norm1*, *goFromXtoY*, is a superaction. Since the norm is an *obligation*, the algorithm starts by analyzing all its subactions: *goFromXtoYViaA* and *goFromXtoYViaB* (checking conflict case 3.1).

The action *goFromXtoYViaA* is a simple action, so the algorithm verifies if this action demotes any value that is important to the agent (checking conflict case 1). In this case the action *goFromXtoYViaA* demotes the *agility* value, so the *obligation* of *goFromXtoYViaA* is in conflicts with the agent's values (conflict case 1 identified).

Then, the algorithm identifies that the action *goFromXtoYViaB* is a composed action and starts to analyses each action of the composition: *goFromXtoZ* and *goFromZtoY* (checking conflict case 4.1). Both are simple actions and the algorithm verifies if any of them demotes a value important to the agent (checking conflict case 1). The action *goFromXtoZ* does not demote any value of the agent, but the action *goFromZtoY* demotes the *security* value due to the obstacles (conflict case 1 identified). So, the *obligation* of *goFromXtoYViaB* is in conflicts with the agent's values because the agent would demote its *security* value in order to execute the composite action *goFromZtoY* (conflict case 4.1 identified).

As both obligations *goFromXtoYViaA* and *goFromXtoYViaB* are in conflicts with the agent's values, **the** *obligation* **of** *norm1* **to execute** *goFromXtoY* **is also in conflicts with the agent's values** because the agent is not able to fulfill the obligation without demote any of its values (conflict case 3.1 identified). The presented example covered the algorithm execution and three conflict cases between norms and values pointed out in this paper.

4 Related Work

Although there are several works in MAS that discuss the values of agents and organizations, e.g. [29, 30], as far as we know, this is the first research to point out the conflicts between norms and values.

In [11, 16, 29–33] we can see extensions of the BDI architecture that include values in the deliberation process of the agent, but they do not make reference to norms. The values are just used to filter options in order to select goals and intentions. In another paper [31], the necessity of a BDI architecture that study norms and values is mentioned but conflicts between these elements are not part of the discussion.

In [16, 32] argumentation frameworks that include values are presented. However, in [16] the framework does not include norms and in [32] the paper only considers norms already adopted that are mapped into agent's goals.

In a close related work to ours [11], the authors present series of simulations involving norms and values. They show how values can influence in norm acceptance in scenarios with personal, social and legal norms. The simulations were constructed assuming that the agents will prefer to execute actions that are consistent to their values preferences, but the paper does not address the specific question about conflicts between norms and values.

In [33] each type of norm (personal, social and legal) is related to a value (integrity, conformity and compliance) and, according to the values preferences of the agent, the values are used to filter out conflicting norms for the generation of agent's goals and subsequent plans of action, but once again, the conflicts between norms and values are not discussed.

5 Conclusion and Future Work

In this paper we presented the conflict cases that can arise between the system's norms and the values of the agents. We have also provided an algorithm that can identify these conflicts and support the different relationships between norms, values and action types. The algorithm proposed can be used together with any normative MAS framework[5], e.g. [4, 9, 10], because the elements of the norm description are general and elementary enough. As far as we know, this is the first MAS work that investigates the identification of conflicts between norms and values.

The identification and resolution of the conflicts between the system's norms and the values are important to the agents in their decision making process. The agents can choose the actions to execute, the norms to fulfill or violate and the groups to join.

This research is not complete and it is the beginning of a process. In this paper we covered the conflict cases involving norms that restrict actions, but there are also norms that restrict states to be achieved. By adapting the present approach to include states, we can also define the conflict cases between values and a norm fulfillment, a norm violation and sanctions.

The next steps of this work consist of develop ways to help the agents to solve the norms-values conflicts (for instance, by using the importance value to support the decisions as in the last example of Sect. 2.2) and make a full extension of the BDI agent architecture proposed in [9, 24] in order to include values with norms and their influences in the agent's reasoning process.

References

1. Keesing, R.M.: Theories of culture. Ann. Rev. Anthropol. **3**, 73–97 (1974)
2. Linton, R.: The Tree of Culture. Knopf, New York (1955)
3. Schwartz, S., Bilsky, W.: Toward a universal psychological structure of human values. J. Pers. Soc. Psychol. **53**(3), 550–562 (1987)
4. Figueiredo, K.: Modeling and validating norms in multi-agent systems. Master's Thesis, Universidade Federal Fluminense, Instituto de Computação (2011)
5. Kollingbaum, M.J., Vasconcelos, W.W., García-Camino, A., Norman, T.J.: Conflict resolution in norm-regulated environments via unification and constraints. In: Baldoni, M., Son, T.C., van Riemsdijk, M., Winikoff, M. (eds.) DALT 2007. LNCS (LNAI), vol. 4897, pp. 158–174. Springer, Heidelberg (2008)
6. Oren, N., Luck, M., Miles, S., Norman, T.J.: An argumentation inspired heuristic for resolving normative conflicts. In: Proceedings of the International Workshop on Coordination, Organizations, Institutions and Norms in Agent Systems (COIN@AAMAS 2008), pp. 41–56. Estoril, Portugal (2008)
7. Vasconcelos, W., Kollingbaum, M., Norman, T.: Resolving conflict and inconsistency in norm-regulated virtual organizations. In: Proceedings of the 6th International Joint Conference on Autonomous Agents and Multiagent Systems, ACM (2007)

---

[5] Some adaptations may be needed, according to the chosen framework.

8. Kagal, L., Finin, T.: Modeling conversation policies using permissions and obligations. Auton. Agent. Multi-Agent Syst. **14**(2), 187–206 (2007)
9. dos Santos Neto, B.F., da Silva, V.T., de Lucena, C.J.: An architectural model for autonomous normative agents. In: Barros, L.N., Finger, M., Pozo, A.T., Gimenénez-Lugo, G.A., Castilho, M. (eds.) SBIA 2012. LNCS, vol. 7589, pp. 152–161. Springer, Heidelberg (2012)
10. da Silva, V.T., Zahn, J.: Normative conflicts that depend on the domain. In: Balke, T., Dignum, F., van Riemsdijk, M.B., Chopra, A.K. (eds.) COIN 2013. LNCS (LNAI), vol. 8386, pp. 311–326. Springer, Heidelberg (2014)
11. Dechesne, F., Di Tosto, G., Dignum, V., Dignum, F.: No smoking here: values, norms and culture in multi-agent systems. Artif. Intell. Law **21**(1), 79–107 (2013)
12. Modgil, S., Luck, M.: Argumentation based resolution of conflicts between desires and normative goals. In: Rahwan, I., Moraitis, P. (eds.) ArgMAS 2008. LNCS, vol. 5384, pp. 19–36. Springer, Heidelberg (2009)
13. Toniolo, A., Norman, T., Sycara, K.: An empirical study of argumentation schemes for deliberative dialogue. In: ECAI (2012), pp. 756–761 (2012)
14. Schwartz, S.: Universals in the content and structure of values: theoretical advances and empirical tests in 20 countries. Adv. Exp. Soc. Psychol. **25**(1), 1–65 (1992)
15. Rohan, M.: A rose by any name? The values construct. Pers. Soc. Psychol. Rev. **4**(3), 255–277 (2000)
16. van der Weide, T.L., Dignum, F., Meyer, J.-J.C., Prakken, H., Vreeswijk, G.A.W.: Practical reasoning using values. In: McBurney, P., Rahwan, I., Parsons, S., Maudet, N. (eds.) ArgMAS 2009. LNCS, vol. 6057, pp. 79–93. Springer, Heidelberg (2010)
17. Rokeach, M.: The Nature of Human Values. Free Press, NY (1979)
18. Antunes, L.: Towards a model for value-based motivated agents. In: Proceedings of MASTA97 (1997)
19. Hofstede, G., Hofstede, G., Minkov, M.: Cultures and Organizations. McGraw-Hill, London (1991)
20. Hayes, I., Flinn, B.: Specification Case Studies. Prentice Hall Professional Technical Reference, Uk (1992)
21. Spivey, J.M.: Understanding Z: A Specification Language and Its Formal Semantics. Cambridge University Press, New York (1988)
22. Craigen, D., Gerhart, S.L., Ralston, T.: An international survey of industrial applications of formal methods. In: Proceedings of the Z User Workshop, pp. 1–5. Springer, London (1992)
23. Wezeman, C.D.: Using Z for network modelling: an industrial experience report. Comput. Stand. Interfaces **17**(5–6), 631–638 (1995)
24. D'Inverno, M., Kinny, D., Luck, M., Wooldridge, M.: A formal specification of dMARS. In: Singh, M.P., Rao, A., Wooldridge, M.J. (eds.) ATAL 1997. LNCS, vol. 1365, pp. 155–176. Springer, Heidelberg (1998)
25. Bowen, J.P.: Formal Specification and Documentation Using Z: A Case Study Approach. International Thomson Computer Press, London (1996)
26. Hewitt, M.A., O'Halloran, C., Sennett, C.T.: Experiences with PiZA, an animator for Z. In: Till, D., Bowen, J.P., Hinchey, M.G. (eds.) ZUM 1997. LNCS, vol. 1212, pp. 37–51. Springer, Heidelberg (1997)
27. Saaltink, M.: The Z/EVES system. In: Till, D., Bowen, J.P., Hinchey, M.G. (eds.) ZUM 1997. LNCS, vol. 1212, pp. 72–85. Springer, Heidelberg (1997)

28. García Camino, A., Noriega, P., Rodríguez-Aguilar, J.-A.: An algorithm for conflict resolution in regulated compound activities. In: O'Hare, G.M., Ricci, A., O'Grady, M.J., Dikenelli, O. (eds.) ESAW 2006. LNCS (LNAI), vol. 4457, pp. 193–208. Springer, Heidelberg (2007)
29. Atkinson, K., Bench-Capon, T., McBurney, P.: Computational representation of practical argument. Synthese 152(2), 157–206 (2006)
30. Antunes, L., Faria, J.C., Coelho, H.: Improving choice mechanisms within the BVG architecture. In: Castelfranchi, C., Lespérance, Y. (eds.) ATAL 2000. LNCS (LNAI), vol. 1986, pp. 290–304. Springer, Heidelberg (2001)
31. Di Tosto, G.: Using values in normative multi-agent systems. Dagstuhl Seminar 12111, Dagstuhl Reports, vol. 2, no. 3 (2012)
32. Burgemeestre, B., Hulstijn, J., Tan, Y.-H.: Value-based argumentation for justifying compliance. In: Governatori, G., Sartor, G. (eds.) DEON 2010. LNCS, vol. 6181, pp. 214–228. Springer, Heidelberg (2010)
33. McBreen, J., Di Tosto, G., Dignum, F., Hofstede, G.: Linking norms and culture. In: 2011 Second International Conference on Culture and Computing (Culture Computing), pp. 9–14. IEEE (2011)

Re-checking Normative System Coherence

Thomas Christopher King[(✉)], Virginia Dignum, and M. Birna van Riemsdijk

TU Delft, Delft, The Netherlands
{t.c.king-1,m.v.dignum,m.b.vanriemsdijk}@tudelft.nl

Abstract. Sets of related norms (normative systems) are likely to evolve due to changing goals of an organization or changing values of a society, this may introduce incoherence, such as the simultaneous prohibition and obligation of an action or a set of deadlocked duties. This paper presents a compositional framework that may be used for detecting whether normative systems are coherent by analysing traces of actions and their legality. Unlike other mechanisms for checking normative system coherence, the framework makes it possible to re-check just those parts of the system that have changed, without re-checking the entirety.

1 Introduction

Increasingly, Multi-Agent Systems (MAS) are applied to solving a diverse range of problems, benefiting from available heterogeneous agents by providing an open system to which they may join. Although agents may be asked to do one thing, their autonomy can lead to behaviour different from what is desired [14]. Consequently, organisations are used to direct and constrain agents into achieving particular goals, by giving them social norms that specify what an agent ought to do in a given context and sanctions to deter them from disobeying.

It is difficult to design sets of norms (normative systems) where satisfying some norms does not cause agents to violate others (known as coherence), hence the extensive research on identifying incoherent normative systems [1,2,4,7,10–13].

Normative systems may also change and evolve over time (through the addition, deletion and/or modification of norms). This can be due to changed goals of an organisation, changed values of society or existing norms being shown to be inadequate (e.g. first introducing a speed limit and then later increasing or decreasing the limit). So, it is also important to re-check them for coherence.

Yet, it is undesirable to do completely new checks on normative systems if only a small part has changed. For this reason, this paper focuses on a structured and compositional means of re-checking just those parts of normative systems that have changed.

It is assumed that the validity of the compositional semantics presented here depends on the expressiveness of the framework. Re-checking has not been specifically examined before, so this paper proposes the following concepts that are interesting enough to, at a minimum, have the expressiveness required to argue the compositional semantics are useful:

T. Balke et al. (Eds.): COIN 2013, LNAI 8386, pp. 275–290, 2014.
DOI: 10.1007/978-3-319-07314-9_15, © Springer International Publishing Switzerland 2014

- *Logical relationships* between norms, for example in many cases it may be required to stipulate that an agent ought to do *a* or ought to do *b*.
- Norms with a *condition, consequence* and/or *deadline* that may be the condition, consequence and/or deadline of other norms. First described by López and Luck as *interlocking norms* [8], their existence means incoherence may arise due to deadlock. This complicates the check for coherence. Frameworks which consider interlocking norms include those proposed by López, Luck et al. [8,9] and later by Jiang et al. [6].
- Secondary norms that may act as a *sanction* for "fixing" the violation of a primary norm. Sanctions express what ideally and sub-ideally ought to be done. For example 'a person ought not steal' may be what ideally ought to be done and 'if someone steals, they ought to pay a fine' is a sanction for violating the primary norm.

The results of this paper make it possible to determine if a normative system is coherent in a compositional way that may make use of checks on previous versions of a normative system. This is especially useful for checking changes to a normative system before they are implemented, that is, before run-time. The approach taken is to first formally define the key concepts in a conceptual framework, such as the legality of actions and how norms may be structured (Sect. 2). Section 3 is the main contribution of a framework for compositionally determining what may and may not be legally done with respect to a given normative system, it is here that one possible semantics of norms is also given. In Sect. 4 the framework examples are given for illustrating checking and re-checking a system, using a running example on a shoplifting offence with a potential fine. The results from using the compositional semantics may be used to check the coherence of a normative system, what makes a coherent normative system is discussed in Sect. 5. Section 6 gives the relevant work surrounding efficient norm coherence checking. In Sect. 7, conclusions and directions for future work are presented.

2   The Normative Conceptual Framework

This section follows the conceptual normative framework of Jiang et al. [6] with some minor syntax changes. The conceptual framework gives an abstract representation of social norms, the relationships between social norms and the legality of actions.

In the following, let the set A be the set of all agents with typical element a and Act be the set of all actions with typical element φ.

A normative trace is an alternating sequence of zero or more agent/action pairs and the legal state of the sequence up until that point (denoting the legality of the preceding agent/action pairs). For simplicity it is assumed each agent/action pair occurs at most once, consequently if A and Act are finite sets then the set of all possible traces for $(A \times Act)$ is also finite. The legal states stipulate whether the preceding sequence is compliant (c) but with the possibility for there to be a violation in the future, in violation (v) but may or may not

become completely compliant (*cnd*) in the future, or completely compliant with
no possibility of there being a violation in the future (*cnd*). Formally:

Definition 1 *(Normative Trace).* *A normative trace nt is a finite sequence of
alternating elements of the form:* $[l_0, (a, \varphi)_1, l_1, ..., (a, \varphi)_n, l_n]$ *where* $l_i \in \{cnd, c,$
$v\}$, $(a, \varphi) \in (A \times Act)$ *and* $(a, \varphi)_j \neq (a, \varphi)_k$ *for* $0 \leq i \leq n$, $1 \leq j < k \leq n$.

From here on the variables X, Y and Z will be used to denote agent/action
pairs s.t. $X, Y, Z \in (A \times Act)$ and the variables g and l will be used to denote
legal states s.t. $g, l \in \{cnd, c, v\}$.

Norms in a normative system have a deontic modality indicating whether
they are an obligation or prohibition, permissions are not considered for
simplicity:

Definition 2 *(Deontic Types).* *A deontic type d is a member of the set of deontic
types* $D = \{O, F\}$ *where:*

- *O - Means that it is* obligatory *to carry out the action to which it applies.*
- *F - Means that it is* prohibited *to carry out the action to which it applies.*

Given the definition of deontic types, a norm may express that an agent is
either obligated or forbidden to carry out an action under some (pre)condition
before a deadline, if there is no (pre)condition or deadline, 'null' is used:

Definition 3 *(Norm).* *Let* $d \in D$, $\rho \in (A \times Act)$, $\delta, \sigma \in (A \times Act) \cup \{null\}$ *a
norm is* $n = (d(\rho) \leq \delta/\sigma)$ *where:*

- ρ *is the agent/action pair which is obligatory or forbidden.*
- δ *is the non-temporal deadline of the norm.*
- σ *is the precondition of the norm.*

Norms may be related to other norms, in a norm net, via a logical connective.
Such a relation is defined as a norm net in [6] and defined similarly here. This
makes it possible to express different conditions of when a sequence of actions
is legal with respect to two child nodes of a norm net:

- The sequence should be legal with both (*AND*) child nodes (you ought to do
  this and you ought to do that).
- The sequence should be legal with just one child node (*OR*) (you ought to do
  this or you ought to do that).
- The sequence either should be legal with the primary legislature or else (*OE*)
  it should be legal with the sanctioning legislature, but never both (ideally you
  ought to do this, if and only if you are not then you ought to do that).

Definition 4 *(Norm Net).* *Let* n *be a norm, a norm net NN is a formula in
the following BNF grammar:*

$$NN ::= n \mid AND(NN, NN) \mid OR(NN, NN) \mid OE(NN, NN)$$

Norm nets are used to formalize an example of shoplifting where two agents are considered, a person and a security guard:

Example 1 $OE(n_1, n_2)$. A person ought not shoplift, $n_1 = F((p, shoplift) \leq null/null)$. If a person tries to shoplift, then a security guard ought to give them a fine before they let them go $n_2 = O((s, fine) \leq (p, let\_go)/(p, shoplift))$.

3   Compositional Semantic Framework

We define the semantics of a norm net as a set of normative traces. Coherence of a norm can then be defined as a property of this set of traces, e.g., at least one of the normative traces in the set has 'compliant' as its final legality, expressing that there is a way to satisfy all norms such that one ends up in a compliant state. In this section we define how to generate this set of traces.

The basic idea of how to generate the set of traces is to follow the compositional tree structure of norm nets. That is, we first define the semantics for obligations and prohibitions as a set of normative traces, which form the leaves of the tree (Sect. 3.1). Then we compose these sets of traces according to the tree structure of the norm net, taking into account the normative connectives in the nodes. For this we need to combine (i.e., interleave) the traces in the respective sets, computing the legality of the combined traces by combining the legality states of the constituent traces according to the normative connectives. We define how to combine legalities in Sect. 3.2 and define how to compose traces informally in Sect. 3.3 and formally in 3.4.

3.1   Norm Semantics

The general idea behind the framework as a whole is to produce a set of normative traces, $traces(NN)$, that expresses all those actions a norm net commands agents to do or not do and stipulates the legality of doing them. For example, given the norm that a security guard should fine a shoplifter before letting them go, $O((s, fine) \leq (p, let\_go)/(p, shoplift))$, a possible set of normative traces is:

$$\{[c, (p, shoplift), c, (s, fine), cnd, (p, let\_go), cnd]$$
$$[c, (p, shoplift), c, (p, let\_go), v, (s, fine), v], [c]\}$$

However, these traces would suggest a norm is commanding the agent p to shoplift or do nothing, this is clearly not the case because shoplifting is a condition and not a consequence. We would not expect a security guard to fine someone unless the shoplifting offence occurred and we may therefore only wish to test whether fining is legal if we believe shoplifting ought to occur or will occur.

Therefore, from now on agent/action pairs which are things there is no reason to believe ought to be done, will be marked with $-$ as in $(a, \phi)^-$. We also introduce the concept that two agent/action pairs from different traces are loosely equal, $\approx$, if one agent/action is the same as the other regardless of if there is a marking. Furthermore, the concept of an agent/action pair being a member, $\in$, of a normative trace is also given.

Definition 5 *(Agent/Action Markings, Loose Equality, Membership and Ordering).*

- *X may have a marking $^-$ s.t. $X = (a, \phi)^-$ denotes that X is only found in the condition of a norm.*
- *$X \approx Y$ holds if $(X = (a, \phi)^-$ and $Y = (a, \phi)^-)$ or $(X = (a, \phi)^-$ and $Y = (a, \phi))$ or $(X = (a, \phi)$ and $Y = (a, \phi)^-)$ or $(X = (a, \phi)$ and $Y = (a, \phi))$.*
- *$X \not\approx Y \leftrightarrow \neg(X \approx Y)$*
- *Given a normative trace nt let $X \in nt$ denote that there is a Y in the normative trace nt s.t. $X \approx Y$.*
- *$X \notin nt \leftrightarrow \neg(X \in nt)$*
- *Given a normative trace nt and two agent action pairs X and Y let $X <_{nt} Y$ denote $X, Y \in nt$ and X occurs before Y in nt.*

The general idea behind producing the set of traces for an obligation is that if there is a condition then we give the traces where the condition is met and we also give the possibility of doing nothing ($[c]$), because we do not believe the condition ought to be met and consequently no duties ought to arise. The set of traces should also convey the other possibilities, which are, carrying out the duty before any deadline that there may be (as ought to be done) or the deadline occurring before the duty is carried out (as ought not be done). Therefore, the set of traces for an obligatory norm n are:

Definition 6 *(Traces for Obligation).* Let $n = (O(\rho) \le \delta/\sigma)$

If $\delta \ne null$ and $\sigma \ne null$ then :
$$traces(n) = \{[c], [c, \sigma^-, c, \rho, cnd, \delta, cnd], [c, \sigma^-, c, \delta^-, v, \rho, v],$$
$$[c, \delta^-, c, \sigma^-, v, \rho, v], [c, \delta, c, \rho, c, \sigma^-, v],$$
$$[c, \rho, cnd, \sigma^-, cnd, \delta^-, cnd], [c, \rho, cnd, \delta^-, cnd, \sigma^-, cnd]\}$$
If $\delta = null$ and $\sigma \ne null$ then :
$$traces(n) = \{[c], [c, \sigma^-, c, \rho, cnd], [c, \rho, cnd, \sigma^-, cnd]\}$$
If $\delta \ne null$ and $\sigma = null$ then :
$$traces(n) = \{[c, \rho, cnd, \delta^-, cnd], [c, \delta^-, v, \rho, v]\}$$
If $\delta = null$ and $\sigma = null$ then :
$$traces(n) = \{[c, \rho, cnd]\}$$

Like obligations, if a prohibition has a condition then the set of traces for it also includes doing nothing. Where prohibition differs is that we wish to generate traces that convey the prohibited action ought not be done. That is, the subject either ought to do nothing (in the case of no deadline) or see to it that a deadline occurs first.

We also note the following is true $(O(\rho) \leq \delta/\sigma) \equiv (F(\delta) \leq \rho/\sigma)$. This means the previous shoplifting example may be rephrased as "if someone shoplifts the security guard ought not let them go before giving them a fine". Formally, the traces for a prohibition n are:

Definition 7 *(Traces for Prohibition). Let $n = (F(\rho) \leq \delta/\sigma)$*

If $\delta \neq null$ and $\sigma \neq null$ then :

$$traces(n) = \{[c], [c, \sigma^-, c, \rho^-, v, \delta, v], [c, \sigma^-, c, \delta, cnd, \rho^-, cnd],$$
$$[c, \delta, cnd, \sigma^-, cnd, \rho^-, cnd], [c, \delta, cnd, \rho^-, cnd, \sigma^-, cnd],$$
$$[c, \rho^-, c, \sigma^-, v, \delta, v], [c, \rho^-, c, \delta, c, \sigma^-, v]\}$$

If $\delta = null$ and $\sigma \neq null$ then :

$$traces(n) = \{[c], [c, \sigma^-, c, \rho^-, v], [c, \rho^-, c, \sigma^-, v]\}$$

If $\delta \neq null$ and $\sigma = null$ then :

$$traces(n) = \{[c, \rho^-, v, \delta, v], [c, \delta, cnd, \rho^-, cnd]\}$$

If $\delta = null$ and $\sigma = null$ then :

$$traces(n) = \{[c], [c, \rho^-, v]\}$$

3.2 Connective Semantics

The general idea is that the legality of a sequence of actions with respect to a norm net may be composed from the legality with the norm net's child nodes using the semantics for the connectives defined here. OR and AND follow their counterparts in boolean logic. OE is given semantics for expressing, possibly cascading, sanctions. Sanctions 'fix' violations, e.g. given "a person ought not shoplift, or else you must pay a fine before a deadline.", paying a fine 'fixes' a shoplifting offence.

The semantics of sanctions gives rise to a three-valued legality system of compliance with no outstanding duties (cnd), compliance (c) and violation (v). The two compliance states distinguish between when there is compliance (c) with a sanction because the deadline has not passed (e.g. when we are waiting for a fine to be paid) or when there is compliance and no further duties (cnd) because it has been fulfilled (e.g. paying a fine before the deadline).

Given the aforementioned descriptions, the semantics for the connectives are defined in terms of the legality function and the following tables for each connective (to be interpreted in the same way as truth tables for a logic):

Definition 8 *(Legality Semantics). Let $g, l \in \{cnd, c, v\}$, conn $\in \{AND, OR, OE\}$ the following tables give the results of the function $leg(conn, g, l)$:*

$conn = AND$		l	
	cnd	c	v
cnd	cnd	c	v
g c	c	c	v
v	v	v	v

$conn = OR$		l	
	cnd	c	v
cnd	cnd	cnd	cnd
g c	cnd	c	c
v	cnd	c	v

$conn = OE$		l	
	cnd	c	v
g cnd	v	c	cnd
c	v	c	c
v	cnd	v	v

The OE connective should be used in a particularly way. Firstly, the sanctioning norm should have a condition if we do not wish to consider the sanction may occur before the violation. Secondly, if the secondary norm is a prohibition used to 'fix' the primary norm then it should have a deadline.

Without a deadline for a sanctioning prohibition, compliance with it will not fix the primary norm because the subject of the prohibition may yet violate it. For example, if someone steals and consequently they ought not visit a shop again, but there is no deadline on the shopping ban, then there is no way of telling whether by not visiting the shop they have fixed the shoplifting offence or they are merely postponing violating the ban (and so the shoplifting offence would never be fixed by observing the ban). As Governatori et al. put it, legislators need to use deadlines for sanctions to be enforced and to represent a hierarchy of what ought to be done [3].

3.3 Informal Compositional Semantics

Previously, the set of traces that express what an individual norm stipulates should and should not be done were defined. When combining individual norms through a connective, the set of traces for the resulting norm net should describe those things that the norm net as a whole says should and should not be done.

Interleaving traces. The basic idea of combining two sets of normative traces through a connective is to do a pairwise interleaving of the traces in the two sets and compute the legality of the resulting traces by applying the connective semantics on the legality of the constituent traces. That is, we compute interleavings for all combinations of traces from the two sets (preserving the ordering of agent/action pairs), where after a sequence of agent/action pairs each legal state in an interleaved trace is composed from the legal state of each contributory trace that comes after the same sequence agent/action pairs and before any agent/action pairs yet to occur in the interleaving. For example, consider two normative traces $[c, (p_1, eat), v, (p_1, think), v]$ and $[c, (p_1, work), cnd, (p_1, rest), cnd]$ and assuming we want to combine them through an OR connective. Then we get the following set of interleaved traces:

$$\{[c, (p_1, eat), v, (p_1, think), v, (p_1, work), cnd, (p_1, rest), cnd],$$
$$[c, (p_1, eat), v, (p_1, work), cnd, (p_1, think), cnd, (p_1, rest), cnd],$$
$$[c, (p_1, eat), v, (p_1, work), cnd, (p_1, rest), cnd, (p_1, think), cnd],$$
$$[c, (p_1, work), cnd, (p_1, eat), cnd, (p_1, think), cnd, (p_1, rest), cnd],$$
$$[c, (p_1, work), cnd, (p_1, eat), v, (p_1, rest), cnd, (p_1, think), cnd],$$
$$[c, (p_1, work), cnd, (p_1, rest), cnd, (p_1, eat), cnd, (p_1, think), cnd]\}$$

The resulting set expresses what should and should not be done in the composed system.

Minimality. In the example above, the agent/action pairs occurring in the traces are disjoint. If these are (partly) overlapping, we need to take several additional considerations into account when composing the traces. We start by considering the case of one overlapping agent/action pair as in the following example:

Example 2 $NN = AND(n_1, n_2)$. A person ought to eat before they go out $n_1 = O((p, eat) \leq (p, go\_out)/null)$ and they ought not drink before they eat $n_2 = F((p, drink) \leq (p, eat)/null)$.

$$traces(n_1) = \{[c, (p, eat), cnd, (p, go\_out), cnd], [c, (p, go\_out), v, (p, eat), v]\}$$
$$traces(n_2) = \{[c, (p, eat), cnd, (p, drink), cnd], [c, (p, drink), v, (p, eat), v]\}$$

We can see that both $traces(n_1)$ as well as $traces(n_2)$ refer to p eating. Thus both of these sets have something to say about whether eating could lead to a violation: the traces of $traces(n_1)$ express that eating before going out is okay, but they state nothing about drinking, whilst the traces for norm n_2 stipulate that eating leads to a compliant state if it is before drinking.

We interleave traces with an overlapping agent/action pair such that the ordering of agent/action pairs is preserved, and the overlapping pair occurs only once in the trace, in accordance with the definition of normative traces. Intuitively, we strive for a kind of "minimality" of traces that still allows us to derive conclusions concerning coherence of the norm net. Thus when composing traces from $[c, (p, eat), cnd, (p, go\_out), cnd]$ and $[c, (p, eat), cnd, (p, drink), cnd]$, the resulting set of traces is:

$$\{[c, (p, eat), cnd, (p, go\_out), cnd, (p, drink), cnd],$$
$$[c, (p, eat), cnd, (p, drink), cnd, (p, go\_out), cnd]\}$$

The legality of the first trace after eating is composed from the legality after eating in the contributing traces. Whilst the last legality is composed from the legality after eating and going out in the first contributory trace and the legality after eating and drinking in the second contributory trace.

Compatibility. Now we consider the case of composing two traces that have multiple overlapping agent/action pairs, which induces a second aspect to take into consideration. These overlapping pairs are either in the same order or in a different order in the two traces. If they are in a different order, they consider different cases. For example, $[c, (p, eat), cnd, (p, go\_out), cnd]$ and $[c, (p, go\_out), v, (p, eat), v]$. Intuitively, these traces express properties of different situations that cannot be considered jointly, i.e., the traces are not *compatible*. Thus we do not compute interleavings for incompatible traces.

Maximality. Finally we identify one more case in which we do not compute interleavings. Take the following example:

$$S1 = \{[c, W, cnd, X, v], [c, W, cnd]\} \quad S2 = \{[c, W, cnd, X, cnd, Y, cnd]\}$$

In identifying traces in S1 with which we can combine the trace $[c, W, cnd, X, cnd, Y, cnd]$ from S2, one may expect that this trace should be combined with all traces from S1. However, if it is combined with $[c, W, cnd]$ then although the resulting trace would take into account what S1 says about performing W, it would not take into account what it says about performing W and then X, therefore the result would not be composed of all of the 'facts' stated by S1. Thus, the idea is to take only "maximal" traces, where maximal means that a trace should only be combined with another if there does not exist another trace in the same set that says more about the trace with which it is being combined.

3.4 Formal Compositional Semantics

The formal semantics are given in terms of the informal requirements outlined in the previous section. We wish to only interleave those traces with the same ordering of agent/action pairs, a symmetric relation $compatible(nt^1, nt^2)$ is defined for traces that meet the **compatibility** requirement:

Definition 9 *(Compatible Normative Traces). For two normative traces nt^1 and nt^2, compatible(nt^1, nt^2) holds iff:*

$$\forall X \forall Y (X <_{nt^1} Y) : X <_{nt^2} Y$$

The idea behind the semantics of interleaving compatible traces is to first create a triple, $\langle nt^1, nt^2, result \rangle$, of two compatible normative traces nt^1 and nt^2 and an empty trace, $result$, that will become an interleaving of the two. Then, a system of transition rules is repeatedly applied to this triple, taking the first elements off nt^1 and nt^2, adding them to the result. After an action is added to the result, so is a legal state composed from the legal states of the last actions added from nt^1 and nt^2. This is done until nt^1 and nt^2 are empty and thus the trace $result$ is an interleaving of the two.

To meet the requirement of **minimality** the transition system should 'merge' agent/action pairs from the traces if they are the same, rather than add the same agent/action pair twice. However, agent/action pairs may be the same yet have different markings. An operation is defined to only maintain markings signifying an action is a condition if both agent/action pairs have the marking:

Definition 10 *(Composing Markings). Let X and Y be two agent/action pairs with the same agent and action (a, ϕ). The function $comp(X, Y)$ is defined as:*

$$comp(X, Y) =$$
$$(a, \phi)^-, iff\ X = (a, \phi)^-\ and\ Y = (a, \phi)^-$$
$$(a, \phi), otherwise$$

Each of the following rules of the transition system are just for a single step of the interleaving operation. Traces are merged with respect to a connective, thus the transition rules include a connective in their definitions $c \in \{AND, OR, OE\}$.

The following transition rule defines how to progress with the interleaving if the next agent/action pair in both traces being interleaved is the same (as in the first condition). We do this by merging the agent/action pairs and adding them with the correct markings to the result (performed by the second condition). The last condition expresses that the new legal state is composed from the legalities that occur in each trace after the agent/action pair that is being added.

$$\frac{\langle [l_0, X_1, l_1, left\_seq], \; [g_0, Y_1, g_1, right\_seq], \; [result] \rangle \quad X_1 = Y_1 \quad Z = comp(X_1, Y_1) \quad l' = leg(c, l_1, g_1)}{\langle [l_1, left\_seq], \; [g_1, right\_seq], \; [result, Z, l'] \rangle} \; Merge$$

The next transition rule defines how to progress if the next agent/action pairs in the left and right traces are different (stipulated by the first condition) and thus a choice must be made to add one of them to the interleaving result (this rule is for choosing the agent/action pair from the left trace). The second condition states that this choice can only be made if the next action in the left trace is not found somewhere else in the right, this stops the same agent/action pair being added again (preserving **minimality**). The final rule composes the new legal state for the interleaving from the legality of the agent/action pair in the left trace being added and the legality of the last agent/action pair added from the right trace. Thus, the new legality takes into account what both traces being interleaved say about the sequence of actions up until that point.

$$\frac{\langle [l_0, X_1, l_1, left\_seq], \; [g_0, Y_1, g_1, right\_seq], \; result \rangle \quad X_1 \not\approx Y_1 \quad X_1 \notin right\_seq \quad l' = leg(c, l_1, g_0)}{\langle [l_1, left\_seq], \; [g_0, Y_1, g_1, right\_seq], \; [result, X_1, l'] \rangle} \; Arbitrary \; Choice \; 1$$

The final transition rule defines how to progress if one trace only contains a legal state (in which case we wish to add the remaining agent/action pairs from the other trace). This may be because a normative trace $[c]$ is being interleaved with a longer trace, or because all of the agent/action pairs from one trace have been added. Here the rule is given for when the right trace only has a legal state, where the first and only condition composes the new legality state in the same way as the aforementioned arbitrary choice rule.

$$\frac{\langle [l_0, X_1, l_1, left\_seq], \; [g_0], \; result \rangle \quad l' = leg(c, l_1, g_0)}{\langle [l_1, left\_seq], \; [g_0], \; [result, X_1, l'] \rangle} \; Exhausted \; Choices \; 1$$

The transition system $\Sigma(c)$ where $c \in \{AND, OR, OE\}$ is defined as consisting of the rules above, the rule symmetric to the rule 'Arbitrary Choice 1', the rule symmetric to the rule 'Exhausted Choices Trace 1' (left out for brevity) and the variable c in each rule substituted with the value of c in $\Sigma(c)$.

The set of traces for a norm net NN, $traces(NN)$, may be composed from the sets of traces for the child nodes of NN. The idea is to take all those compatible pairs of traces for the child nodes and produce all interleavings of them by applying the rules of $\Sigma(c)$ until all possibilities are exhausted. However, the requirement for **maximality** should be observed such that a trace on the left side should not be interleaved with a trace on the right if there is another trace on the right with more information for the resulting interleaved trace and vice versa. We approach this problem by defining the concept of subsumption and only interleave those traces that are not subsumed by others. If given three compatible traces nt^1, nt^2 and nt^3, nt^1 has all of the agent action pairs in nt^2 and some additional pairs found in nt^3, we say nt^1 subsumes nt^2 with respect to nt^3. A predicate $subsume(nt^1, nt^2, nt^3)$ is defined for such a relationship:

Definition 11 *(Normative Trace Subsumption). Let:*
nt^1, nt^2 and nt^3 *be normative traces.* $subsume(nt^1, nt^2, nt^3)$ *holds iff:*

$$compatible(nt^1, nt^2) \wedge compatible(nt^1, nt^3) \wedge compatible(nt^2, nt^3)$$
$$\wedge \, \forall X \in nt^2, nt^3, \exists Y \in nt^1 : X \approx Y$$
$$\wedge \, \exists X \in nt^1, nt^3, \forall Y \in nt^2 : X \not\approx Y$$

For two sets of normative traces NT^1 and NT^2, the pairs of normative traces that are compatible but not subsumed by other traces in the same set are in the set $maximal(NT^1, NT^2)$:

Definition 12 *(Maximality Set). Let* NT^1, NT^2 *be two sets of normative traces. The set of pairs of traces* $maximal(NT^1, NT^2)$ *is defined as:*

$$maximal(NT^1, NT^2) = \{\langle nt^1, nt^2 \rangle : (\exists nt^1, \forall nt^{1\prime} \in NT^1, \exists nt^2, \forall nt^{2\prime} \in NT^2)$$
$$[compatible(nt^1, nt^2) \wedge \neg subsume(nt^{1\prime}, nt^1, nt^2)$$
$$\wedge \neg subsume(nt^{2\prime}, nt^2, nt^1)]\}$$

Performing the interleavings for an entire tree produces the full set of traces for a norm net (see Algorithm 1). If the traces for a particular node are already computed (i.e. cached), then they may be re-used so long as the node has not changed. Thus *re-checking* of a norm net avoids a check on the entire structure.

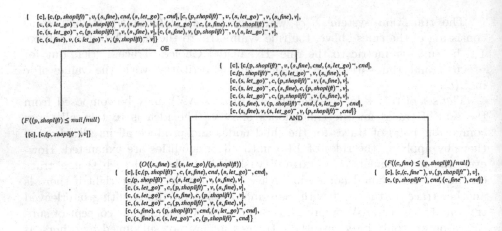

Fig. 1. The results of a compositional computation on a normative system for a shoplifting offence

---

Algorithm 1. ComputeTraces(*NormNet*)

Require: *NormNet* is a norm net in the grammar of *NN*
Ensure: The set of all traces for *NormNet*
  if *NormNet* is a norm **then**
    traces ← *traces*(*NormNet*)
  else *NormNet* is a norm net $c(NN_1, NN_2)$ where $c \in \{AND, OR, OE\}$
    if the traces of *NormNet* are cached **then**
      traces ← *cached*(*NormNet*)
    else
      LT ← ComputeTraces(NN_1)
      RT ← ComputeTraces(NN_2)
      traces ← ∅
      for all $\langle lt, rt \rangle \in maximal(LT, RT)$ **do**
        traces ← *traces* ∪ all possible values for *result* produced by applying
            $\Sigma(c)$to$\langle lt, rt, result \rangle$
      end for
    end if
  end if
  return traces

---

4 Examples

The framework is illustrated by formalising Example 3, an extended version of the example on shoplifting and a security guard's responsibilities.

Example 3 (Shoplifting). If a person *p* shoplifts, they should be fined by a security guard *s* before the shoplifter leaves the shop. The security guard should not fine the person p before they shoplift. This is formalised as a norm net $NN_1 = OE(n_1, NN_2)$, where $n_1 = F((p, shoplift) \leq null/null)$, $NN_2 = AND(n_3, n_4)$, $n_3 = O((s, fine) \leq leave_-/null)$ and $n_4 = F((s; fine) \leq (p, shoplift)/null)$

We see in Fig. 1 that compliance is possible with the system. Using Example 4 we demonstrate that a partial re-check on the system may also be performed if the norm net is revised. In this example, we assume the duties of two criminals are expressed as obligations and criminals in the organisation's norm net structure, this assumption is made so that we can illustrate the system.

Example 4 (Criminals). As before, shoplifters should be fined, the agents p and s are governed by the norm net NN_1 from the previous shoplifting norm net with an OE connective. However, both the person p and the security guard s are now criminals working together, we may represent this as norms in the system (in reality such information would be private), $NN_3 = AND(NN_1, NN_4)$, $NN_4 = AND(n_5, n_6)$, $n_5 = O((p, shoplift) \leq null/null)$ and $n_6 = F((s, fine) \leq null/null)$.

The norm net NN_3 in the new example gives us the traces:

$$\{[c, (p, shoplift), c], [c, (s, fine)^-, v, (p, shoplift), v],$$
$$[c, (p, shoplift), c, (s, fine)^-, v]\}$$

Now we may take the traces computed for the previous version of the normative system and re-use them for computing the result of conjoining these new norms for a norm net $AND(NN_1, textit{NN}_3)$. As a consequence it is clear that the person p and the security guard s cannot carry out both their duties as employees and as criminals:

$$\{[c, (p, shoplift), v, (s, let_-go)^-, v, (s, fine), v]$$
$$[c, (p, shoplift), v, (s, fine), v, (s, let_-go), v], ...\}$$

Furthermore, it appears that there is no opportunity to do nothing, in all cases something has been commanded and in all cases it is also prohibited.

The previous example is on a straightforward conflict between an obligation and a prohibition, but using Example 5 we can also see that the formalism is sufficient for detecting deadlock:

Example 5 $AND(n_1, n_2)$. Consider two people (p_1 and p_2) and the norm that you ought to be the first to apologise, $n_1 = O(p_1, apologise) \leq (p_2, apologise)/null)$ and $n_2 = O(p_2, apologise) \leq (p_1, apologise)//null)$.

The set of traces for this example show that it is not possible for both people to comply with the system, because it obligates one thing to be done before another whilst also obligating the opposite of this:

$$\{[c, (p_1, apologise), v, (p_2, apologise), v], [c, (p_2, apologise), v, (p_1, apologise), v]\}$$

These examples show the framework can be used to detect conflicts between obligations and prohibitions and deadlock, and for a norm net to be re-checked for these properties.

However, we note that in one example there was a marking signifying that we do not expect the security guard to let someone go before fining them because they have not been told to. Whether this is a good notion to have in the trace is unclear, it does not seem harmful but nor is it particularly useful. We also note a drawback of this approach, namely that the ordering of actions is irrespective of whether they can really happen, thus, it would be advisable to ignore traces that consist of a sequence of events that are impossible.

5   What is a Coherent Norm Net?

We say there is coherence if a certain level of compliance is possible under some conditions, but what level of compliance and the conditions that should be assumed to be true is not necessarily clear. We do not aim to solve the problem of giving a 'one size fits all' definition, but instead give the general notion and argue the framework supports many definitions, for brevity we leave out formal definitions of the properties.

In terms of the problems in defining coherence, many are the same as those presented by Hansen et al. [5]. These are not repeated here for reasons of brevity, but generally they encompass the problem of determining what elements of a normative system should be assumed to be in the same context, the facts that should be simultaneously assumed (affecting what duties are simultaneously active) and whether conditions should be considered for conflict with consequences.

Another problem is determining what level of compliance a normative system requires to be deemed coherent, particularly given that sanctions may fix violations. It may be the case that a system is coherent if there is at least one trace that ends up being compliant. This would imply the legislator considered sanctions to be mitigating costs for the violation of a norm. In such a case violations are allowable if they can always be 'fixed'.

Alternatively, it may be the case that sanctions merely act to deter too many malign agents from violating norms that are costly to the organization, but not so costly to the point of discouraging too many agents from joining the organization (as may be the case if they are mitigating costs).

6   Related Work

In the area of checking normative systems for particular properties, this paper appears to be the first to examine the *re-checking* of normative systems. Therefore, there is little directly relevant work.

The most relevant work is that from which the semantic framework is derived, loosely the work of López, Luck et al. on interlocking norms [8,9]. More specifically, the work of Jiang et al. [6] which focuses on a normative framework and in particular different contexts for norms. In their work, they provide a conceptual normative framework for interlocking norms. The conceptual framework does not have semantics, instead these are given when norms expressed in the framework are mapped to Coloured Petri Nets, operationalising the system in the process. Their Coloured Petri Nets produce compliance traces that are similar to the normative traces in this paper.

Outside of this, there is some relevant work on the efficient checking (but not re-checking) of normative system coherence. A common approach is to use first-order unification, where conflict is detected if two norms with the same consequence may be unified and they have opposing modalities (i.e. obligation and prohibition) [7,10–13]. This is a suitable mechanism if efficient algorithms are used, but it does not consider the advantages of using previous checks for re-checking. Furthermore, such work has not considered the increased computational complexity interlocking norms would cause.

Finally, since the efficiency of checking and re-checking a normative system depends on its structure, loosely related research on efficient structuring follows the same motivation as this paper. In their work on Defeasible Deontic Logic, Governatori and Rotolo [4] provide rewrite rules for placing normative systems in a normal form, removing redundancies in the process and identifying conflicts thereafter. Although normal forms are not directly relevant to the work in this paper, it is important for the general goal of efficient coherence checks and checking for changes in normative systems (where normal forms may aid in equivalence checks).

7   Conclusions

This paper has given a novel, compositional, approach to checking the coherence of a normative system. This was achieved by giving the semantics to norms with terms of normative traces, connectives in terms of their legality and semantics for interleaving normative traces compositionally such that the full set of traces to be checked may be generated.

This is not applied to a system of unrelated norms, but instead systems of interlocking norms which increase the complexity. Thus, this paper argues that the framework is particularly invaluable for such complex systems of interrelated norms. Not just for the checking of normative system's coherence, but re-checking any changes made by making use of cached traces of previous checks. We leave a formal analysis of the time complexity of the proposal for future work that may give algorithms for all of the operations defined.

Two topics for future work are identified, namely examining the definition of coherence further and defining how to change a normative system and how to apply the work here to just those parts of a system have changed, such that it is re-checked efficiently. The topic of coherence has been discussed already, in terms of system change we expect it to be in a similar vein to that of Governatori et al. [4] on optimal structures of normative systems and normal forms that may be used for equivalence checks.

References

1. Boella, G., Pigozzi, G., van der Torre, L.: Normative framework for normative system change. In: Proceedings of AAMAS 2009, pp. 169–176 (2009)
2. Governatori, G., Giusto, P.D.: Modifying is better than deleting: a new approach to base revision. AI* IA 99, pp. 145–154 (1999)
3. Governatori, G., Hulstijn, J., Riveret, R., Rotolo, A.: Characterising deadlines in temporal modal defeasible logic. In: Orgun, M.A., Thornton, J. (eds.) AI 2007. LNCS (LNAI), vol. 4830, pp. 486–496. Springer, Heidelberg (2007)
4. Governatori, G., Rotolo, A.: How do agents comply with norms? In: Dagstuhl Seminar Proceedings, pp. 488–491. IEEE (2009)
5. Hansen, J., Pigozzi, G., van der Torre, L.: Ten philosophical problems in deontic logic. In: NORMAS, Dagstuhl, Germany (2007)
6. Jiang, J., Aldewereld, H., Dignum, V., Tan, Y.-H.: Norm contextualization. In: Aldewereld, H., Sichman, J.S. (eds.) COIN 2012. LNCS, vol. 7756, pp. 141–157. Springer, Heidelberg (2013)
7. Kollingbaum, M.J., Vasconcelos, W.W., García-Camino, A., Norman, T.J.: Managing conflict resolution in norm-regulated environments. In: Artikis, A., O'Hare, G.M.P., Stathis, K., Vouros, G.A. (eds.) ESAW 2007. LNCS (LNAI), vol. 4995, pp. 55–71. Springer, Heidelberg (2008)
8. López, F.L.y., Luck, M.: Modelling norms for autonomous agents. In: Proceedings of The Fourth Mexican Conference on Computer Science, pp. 238–245. IEEE Computer Society (2003)
9. López, F.L., Luck, M., D'Inverno, M.: A normative framework for agent-based systems. Comput. Math. Organ. Theor. 12(2–3), 227–250 (2006)
10. Lupu, E., Sloman, M.: Conflicts in policy-based distributed systems management. IEEE Trans. Software Eng. (-) Spec. Issue Inconsistency Manag. 25(6), 852–869 (1999)
11. Uszok, A., Bradshaw, J., Jeffers, R., Suri, N., Hayes, P., Breedy, M., Bunch, L., Johnson, M., Kulkarni, S., Lott, J.: KAoS policy and domain services: toward a description-logic approach to policy representation, deconfliction, and enforcement. In: Proceedings of IEEE Policy 2003, Los Amitos, CA, pp. 93–98. IEEE Computer Society (2003)
12. Uszok, A., Bradshaw, J.M., Lott, J., Breedy, M., Bunch, L., Feltovich, P., Johnson, M., Jung, H.: New developments in ontology-based policy management: increasing the practicality and comprehensiveness of KAoS. in: 2008 IEEE Workshop on Policies for Distributed Systems and Networks, pp. 145–152, June 2008
13. Vasconcelos, W., Kollingbaum, M.J., Norman, T.J.: Resolving conflict and inconsistency in norm-regulated virtual organizations. In: Proceedings of AAMAS '07, vol. 5, pp. 632–639, ACM Press, New York (2007)
14. Wooldridge, M.: An Introduction to Multi-Agent Systems. Wiley, Chichester (2002)

Changing Commitments Based on Reasons and Assumptions

Diana Marosin[1,2(✉)] and Leendert van der Torre[3]

[1] CRP Henri Tudor, Luxembourg, Luxembourg
[2] Radboud University Nijmegen, Nijmegen, The Netherlands
[3] University of Luxembourg, Luxembourg, Luxembourg
diana.marosin@tudor.lu, leon.vandertorre@uni.lu

Abstract. Intention reconsideration is a central challenge in BDI (Belief-Desire-Intention) theory. The intention reconsideration models of the early nineties focus on *when* a commitment may be reconsidered, for example when it has been achieved, when it is no longer achievable, or when the associated goal has been dropped. In this paper, we create an abstract framework in which we add the "reasons" and the "assumptions" that form the base of those commitments. Reasons are an abstract category of cognitive attitudes that motivate something else, including goals, principles, norms, intentions, and actions. To make our mechanism widely applicable, we introduce an abstract approach and 10 requirements from both early and more recent approaches, such as the model of Icard *et al.*, focusing on the interaction between beliefs and changing commitments. Moreover, we do not focus only on an intention's reconsideration, but also on the *effects*. To that end, we introduce an intention reconsideration mechanism with algorithms satisfying the requirements, using only the dichotomy between assumptions and reasons.

Keywords: Group planning agreements · Distributed decision making · Coordination · Intention and commitment · Logics for agreement

1 Introduction

Intention reconsideration is a central challenge in BDI theory. The models of the early nineties developed by Cohen and Levesque [8] and by Rao and Georgeff [20] focus on *when* an intention may be reconsidered. We are interested in intentions that may be reconsidered when the reasons for the intention are no longer valid, or when the associated assumptions are violated. Previous work [3,8,18–20,24] in the field of belief revision is lacking the relation between multiple intentions.

In human behaviour we see that a goal, a norm, an intention or action can lead to another intention, while in formal models of intention reconsideration we talk only about goals that can generate commitments. Therefore our scope for this paper is to investigate the link among the reasons of intentions. Also, in social sciences and real life scenarios we see people forming commitments based

T. Balke et al. (Eds.): COIN 2013, LNAI 8386, pp. 291–310, 2014.
DOI: 10.1007/978-3-319-07314-9_16, © Springer International Publishing Switzerland 2014

on assumptions formulated a priori. One presumes certain background information (e.g. domain knowledge, environment, stakeholders) in order to define the requirements of a system under discussion. This information can be referred to as "assumptions" or "rationales". An assumption is a notion related to "beliefs", defined as "an act or statement (as a proposition, axiom, postulate, or notion) taken for granted" [2,6]. There is a distinction between assumptions and constraints [1]. Constraints are "items that will limit the developer's options" (e.g. regulatory policies, reliability requirements, criticality of the applications safety and security considerations), while assumptions are "factors that affect the requirements stated" (e.g. one makes assumptions about the fact that a specific operating system will be available on the hardware designated for the software product).

These features are missing in the existing intention reconsideration models. Therefore, our main research question is:

How to change commitments based on reasons and assumptions?

There has already been a lot of work on intention reconsideration, using a variety of formalisms. For example, the early approaches use modal temporal logics, such as modal predicate logic [8] or BDI$_{CTL}$ [20]. A more recent approach, by Icard *et al.*, uses belief revision [14]. We take as starting point those formalisms and in order to make our model generally applicable, we introduce an abstract approach, accommodating reasons and assumptions. The research questions are answered in three parts:

1. What are requirements for intention reconsideration based on reasons and assumptions?
2. How to define an abstract formal framework to accommodate reasons and assumptions?
3. How to define algorithms for changing commitments, based on reasons and assumptions?

Our approach is based on three ideas. First, if an assumption is violated, then we have to reconsider all intentions based on the assumption. Second, if an intention is retracted, then we have to find new intentions to satisfy the reasons. However, in general, when intentions have to be reconsidered, there can be many reasons for this change. In order to be able to change the assumptions and intentions we introduce the notion of an explained event. Third, an explained event does not contain only the assumptions which are violated and the intentions which are reconsidered, but also the reasons for the violations and reconsiderations.

We explain the model with an extended scenario of the house robot Willie, from Cohen and Levesque [8]. We do not fully automate the change of intentions. Instead, our logical abstract framework for intention reconsideration provides a setting to define actual procedures (definitions and algorithms).

This paper is structured after the research questions. In Sect. 2 we survey existing intention reconsideration mechanisms. We define ten requirements for an intention reconsideration mechanism in Sect. 3. We introduce our running example in Sect. 4. In Sect. 5 we define the abstract formal framework, give examples and properties, and explain how our framework satisfies four requirements. In Sect. 6 we introduce two intention reconsideration algorithms based on assumptions and reasons and show how the algorithms satisfy the other six requirements. Related work is described in Sect. 7. Furthermore, we apply our framework on a case study from the field of enterprise architecture in Sect. 8. In the last section we conclude our work and we present our future research focus.

2   Intention Reconsideration

The BDI approach is one of the major approaches for building agents and multiagent systems. It was inspired by philosophy (theory of mind) and folk psychology, and as the name implies, the key here is to build agents using symbolic representations of their beliefs, desires, and intentions. The main idea is that an autonomous agent should act on its intentions, not in spite of them, adopt intentions it believes are feasible and forget those believed to be infeasible, keep or commit to intentions, but not forever, discharge those intentions believed to be satisfied, alter intentions when relevant beliefs change and adopt subsidiary intentions during plan formation.

To specify what it means for an agent to have an intention, one needs to describe how that intention affects the agent's web of beliefs, commitments to future actions or other independent intentions [8]. Cohen and Levesque define intentions in terms of temporal sequences of an agent's beliefs and goals, using the operators $BEL, GOAL$ and $INTEND$. The agent fanatically commits to its intentions and will maintain its goals until either they are believed to be fulfilled or to be impossible to achieve. Rao and Gerogeff [20] identify three commitment strategies. A *blindly* committed agent maintains its intentions until it actually believes that they were achieved. If an agent intends that ϕ be eventually true, then the agent will inevitably maintain its intentions until it believes ϕ. A blind-commitment strategy is very strong, as the agent will eventually come to believe it achieved its intentions or keep them forever. A weakening of the requirements leads us to defining a *single-minded* commitment, in which the agent maintains its intentions as long as it believes they are still options. As long as an agent believes its intentions are still achievable, a *single-minded* agent will not drop the intentions (and its committed goals). This requirement can be relaxed further, as an *open-minded* commitment. In this case, the agent maintains its intentions as long as these intentions are still its goals.

An alternative perspective is given by Shoham's database approach [14, 22]. In addition to atomic facts, the agent has beliefs about what the preconditions and postconditions of actions are and about which sequences of actions might be possible. From the perspective of a planner, the postconditions of intended actions are justifiable beliefs merely by the fact that the agent has committed to completing the action. In this way, these beliefs are contingent on the success of the agent's plans. The preconditions, on the other hand, are believed even if they are not directly justified by any future intended action. These kinds of beliefs might also be called "optimistic" beliefs, since the agent assumes the success of the action without ensuring the preconditions hold.

We believe that Shoham's approach is suitable to describe plans and in general the decision making process. Each commitment to a goal or action has an associated belief about the world, and has the role to support that commitment. We call those beliefs "assumptions." Assumptions by definition do not necessary need to be true, but the agent makes commitments assuming they are. This is what makes the preconditions in Shoham's model similar to assumptions in our model and such assumptions are the key starting point of our framework.

3   Intention Reconsideration Requirements

In this section we present and motivate ten requirements for a mechanism of intention reconsideration.

The first requirement derives from the fact that existing models use a variety of formalisms, either to describe an intention reconsideration mechanism, or properties of such mechanisms, such as temporal logic methods (Cohen and Levesque [8], Rao and Georgeff [20]), or belief revision methods (Icard et al. [14]). The first requirement implies that our mechanism has to be applicable more generally, independently of the used formalism.

Requirement 1. The intention reconsideration mechanism should be defined in an abstract model covering existing models, in particular both the BDI logic approach, and the belief revision based approach.

The following requirements state that our mechanism should be able to model key features of existing models. Existing models distinguish blindly committed, simple - minded commitment and open - minded commitment. This says *when* an intention may be reconsidered, for example when it has been achieved, when it is no longer achievable, or when the associated goal has been dropped.

Requirement 2. The mechanism must be able to represent that intentions are reconsidered when the agent believes that they are no longer achievable.

Requirement 3. The mechanism must be able to represent that intentions are reconsidered when the agent believes that the associated goal is dropped.

Icard et al. [14] study the relation between belief revision and intention revision. An important relation between the two is that belief revision may trigger intention revision, but not vice versa. If intention revision would trigger belief revision we might come across inconsistent results. By imposing that intention revision does not trigger belief revision we avoid *wishful thinking* [5]. For example, Bob intends to drive his car to work, based on the belief that the car works. What if a colleague offers to drive Bob to work and he drops the intention of driving himself? This should not generate a revision process concerning the belief that Bob's car is functional.

Requirement 4. Belief revision may trigger intention revision, but not vice versa.

The first extension we consider is that intentions are based on assumptions, and when the assumptions turn out false, then the intention is reconsidered. Also, there can be many reasons to form an intention. In classical models [8, 14, 20], the only reasons considered are goals. But, intentions can be based for example on norms, such that if norms are no longer in force, then the intention is reconsidered.

Requirement 5. The model of the mechanism associates assumptions with intentions, such that if belief revision leads to a violation of assumptions, then the related intentions are reconsidered.

Requirement 6. The model of the mechanism associates reasons such as goals and norms with intentions, such that if the reason disappears, then the intention is reconsidered.

From an architectural point of view, intentions need to be translated in a way such that their impact on the system can be described directly, in order to be incorporated into the system. We adopt Grossi's [13] abstract and concrete norms and apply them to intentions. Abstract intentions can be decomposed into several more concrete intentions. For example, the intention to "go to the cinema" can be decomposed into the intentions to "finish work early", "buy a ticket", and "travel to the cinema."

Requirement 7. The model of the mechanism associates new intentions with existing ones, such that if the latter are reconsidered, also the former must be reconsidered.

Existing models seem to focus on when an intention can be reconsidered. However, it is less often discussed how the reconsideration of an intention can affect other intentions and how to elaborate alternatives in case is not longer possible to commit to an intention.

Considering that an agent commits based on its assumptions about the current state of the world, we formulate the following requirement:

Requirement 8. The intention reconsideration mechanism should be such that if an intention is reconsidered because an assumption is violated, then other intentions based on the same assumption must also be reconsidered.

Given the human nature of the world, we argue that agents may commit to something based on previously made commitments. For example, Bob commits to "read a book", goes to the store in order to "buy a book" and commits also to "pay the book" based on a previously made commitment of "respecting the law." Considering Bob does not have his wallet with him, he should not just drop his goal of "reading" or his commitment to "respect the law", but he should find an alternative (e.g. "borrow a book" or "return home for money").

Requirement 9. The intention reconsideration mechanism should be such that if an intention is reconsidered while the reason[1] of this intention is still valid, then, if possible, another intention should be created to address this reason.

The description of the mechanism has to focus on the intention revision, and should not go into details less relevant for the mechanism.

Requirement 10. The model of the mechanism should be as simple as possible, in the sense that it does not introduce more concepts than necessary.

4   Running Example

We have the scenario by Cohen and Levesque as a starting point, describing Willie [8], the household robot. We explain how introducing reasons and assumptions can fix Willie's attitude problems.

We represent Willie's goal to provide beer to his owner (and *enable the owner to drink the beer*) and the plan he follows (deprecated in intentions and actions). He is committing to his goal, and two other commitments follow (*get the beer* and *bring a bottle opener*). Bringing the beer raises the option of getting it *from the fridge* or *from the table*. We mark the "and" relation between two nodes with an arc, while for the "or" relations we use two unconnected arrows. In Fig. 1 we also associate each intention/commitment/goal (square nodes) with the underlying assumptions (rounded nodes). For example, the intention to get the beer from the table is made based on the assumption that *there is beer on the table* and the robot *can reach the table*.

For this paper we use a simple example in order to illustrate our abstract framework and reconsideration mechanisms. The mechanism can be applied to more complicated structures; reasons can incorporate norms, goals, other intentions, commitments, actions. In this example we use all distinct elements of our framework. The example can be expanded further to any level or abstraction, or applied to different domains of interest.

5   Formal Framework

In this section we introduce a formal abstract framework for intention reconsideration based on reasons and assumptions. In Fig. 2 we abstractly represent the plan of robot Willie.

A reason is valid at a time moment if and only if all reasons that influence it are valid at that time. We say a reason holds at a time moment if it has not been invalidated, either by a false assumption or an influence reason. We say that if an upper node has his children in an "and" relation, all of the children need to be valid in order for the parent to be valid. If children are in an "or" relation, the parent needs at least one valid child in order to be valid.

---

[1] Note that we call norms, goals, other intentions, commitments or actions "reasons for a commitment". Our driving hypothesis is that "everything is a reason for something else."

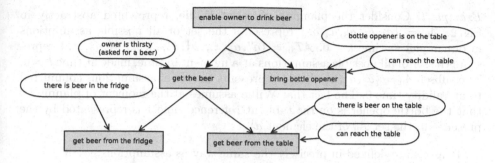

Fig. 1. Robot Willie's plan extended with reasons and assumptions

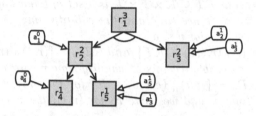

Fig. 2. Abstract representation of Robot Willie's plan

5.1 Definitions

A standard distinction in temporal models is the distinction between *validity time* and *reference time*. If we assume today that it will rain tomorrow, then today is the validity time and tomorrow the reference time. We write a^t or (a, t) for an assumption a with reference time t, and we write A_v for all assumptions with validity time v. We also write $\mathcal{A}_v$ for all possible untimed assumptions at validity time v, and $\mathcal{AT}_v$ for all possible timed assumptions at validity time v. We assume that the set of assumptions can increase over time, as new concepts may be introduced, and we thus have $\mathcal{A}_v \subseteq \mathcal{A}_w$ and thus $\mathcal{AT}_v \subseteq \mathcal{AT}_w$ if $v \leq w$.

Definition 1 (Assumptions). *Let* $\mathcal{T} \subset \mathcal{N}$ *be a set of natural numbers expressing time moments, and let* $\mathcal{A}$ *be the set of all possible assumptions. The set of all possible timed assumptions* $\mathcal{AT} \subseteq \mathcal{A} \times \mathcal{T} \times \mathcal{T}$ *is a set of triples of assumptions and two moments in time, the reference time and the validity time, such that* $(a, t, v) \in \mathcal{AT}$ *implies* $(a, u, w) \in \mathcal{AT}$ *for* $v \leq w$.

We write $\mathcal{A}_v = \{a \mid (a, t, v) \in \mathcal{AT}\}$ *and* $\mathcal{AT}_v = \{(a, t) \mid (a, t, v) \in \mathcal{AT}\}$ *for the projections of the possible assumptions at validity time* v. *For committed assumptions* $A \subseteq \mathcal{AT}$, *we write* $A_v = \{(a, r) \mid (a, r, v) \in A\}$ *for the projection of all assumptions holding at validity time* v, *and we write* a^r *for* (a, r), *the assumption with reference time* r.

The following example illustrates the notation. Note that assumption a_2^1 means assumption a_2 at reference time 1, in other words, the 2 is an index of the assumption and not a temporal reference.

Example 1. Consider the planning of robot Willie, represented abstractly in Fig. 2. $\mathcal{A}_0 = \{a_1, a_2, a_3, a_4, a_5\}$ represents the set of all possible assumptions in our model at time $t = 0$. $\mathcal{AT}_0 = \{a_1^0, a_2^0, ..., , a_1^1, a_2^1, ..., , ..., a_1^3, a_2^3, ...,\}$ represents the set of all possible assumptions at a moment in time, made at time $t = 0$. The subset $A_0 = \{a_1^0, a_2^1, a_3^1, a_4^0, a_5^1\}$ represents the set of assumptions committed to at validity time 0. The fact that Willie assumes at the moment of planning 0 that the bottle opener is on the table at reference time 1 is represented by the presence in the set A_0 of the element a_2^1.

Reasons are defined in precisely the same way as assumptions.

Definition 2 (Reasons). *Let $\mathcal{R}$ be the set of all possible reasons. The set of all possible timed reasons $\mathcal{RT} \subseteq \mathcal{R} \times \mathcal{T} \times \mathcal{T}$ is a set of triples of reasons and two moments in time, the reference time and the validity time, such that $(r, t, v) \in \mathcal{AT}$ implies $(r, u, w) \in \mathcal{AT}$ for $v \leq w$.*

We write $\mathcal{R}_v = \{r \mid (r, t, v) \in \mathcal{RT}\}$ and $\mathcal{RT}_v = \{(r, t) \mid (r, t, v) \in \mathcal{RT}\}$ for the projections of the possible reasons at validity time v. For committed reasons $R \subseteq \mathcal{RT}$, we write $R_v = \{(r, t) \mid (r, t, v) \in R\}$ for the projection of all reasons holding at validity time v, and we write r^t for (r, t), the reason with reference time t.

Reasons can be norms, goals, principles, or plans. We say that a reason is satisfied if and only if the norm is fulfilled, the goal is achieved, the principle is satisfied, or the plan is committed to.

Example 2. Continued from Example 1, we represent the set of reasons similar to the assumptions. For the abstract representation of Willie's plan we define the following sets: $\mathcal{R}_I = \{r_0, r_1, r_2, r_3, r_4, r_5\}$, $\mathcal{RT}_I = \{r_1^0, r_2^0, ...r_5^0, ..., r_1^3, r_2^3, ..., r_5^3\}$, $R = \{r_1^3, r_2^2, r_3^2, r_4^1, r_5^1\}$

The elements of R_t which do not have parents in the graph are called **root** reasons, and the elements of R_t which do not contain a child in the graph are called **leaf** reasons.

Definition 3 (Assumptions dependences). *We define assumptions dependences as a function $AoR : R \rightarrow 2^A$ that maps a reason to its underlying assumptions.*

Example 3. We illustrate assumptions dependences from Example 1 as follows: $AoR_0(r_2^2) = \{a_1^0\}$, equivalently written $AoR_0 = \{(r_2^2, a_1^0)\}$, maps at validity time 0 the assumption "owner is thirsty" with Willie's commitment to "get the beer." The reason has reference time 2, meaning it is expected to hold at time moment 2.

Definition 4 (Reasons dependences). *We define reasons dependences as a function $RoR : R \rightarrow 2^{2^R}$ that maps a reason to a subset of influenced reasons.*

For each reason there can be several sets of other reasons depending on it, such that committing to one of these sets of reasons is sufficient to satisfy the reason. This has the property that if S and T depend on the same reason, then S cannot be a strict subset of T. This property can be seen in the way we represent the "or" relation between reasons.

Example 4. Continued from Example 1, for the validity time moment 0 we define the function RoR as follows: $RoR_0(r_1^3) = \{\{r_2^2, r_3^2\}\}$. In our example, r_1^3 is the root. Notice that r_2^2 and r_3^2 are in an "and" relation in respect with the parent intention r_1^3. $RoR_0(r_2^2) = \{\{r_4^1\}, \{r_5^1\}\}$. In this case the commitments r_4^1 and r_5^1 are placed in an "or" relation in respect to their parent. For instance, using set notation, the "and" relation for the children of the root can be written as $\{(r_1^3, \{r_2^2, r_3^2\})\}$. The "or" relation for reason r_2^2 can be written equivalently $\{(r_2^2, r_4^1), (r_2^2, r_5^1)\}$. $RoR_0(r_4^1) = RoR(r_5^1) = RoR(r_3^2) = \{\}$. All three reasons are leaf nodes.

Definition 5 (Alternatives under discussion). *The alternatives under discussion are a tuple $Alt_t = \langle A_t, R_t, AoR_t, RoR_t \rangle$, where: $t \in T$ is the validity time, A_t is a set of assumptions, R_t is a set of reasons, $AoR_t \subset A_t$ is the set of assumptions of each reason $r \in R_t$, $RoR_t \subset 2_t^R$ is a set of set of reasons of each reason $r \in R_t$, such that RoR_t is acyclic, connected and the sets of reasons in RoR_t does not contain strict subsets.*

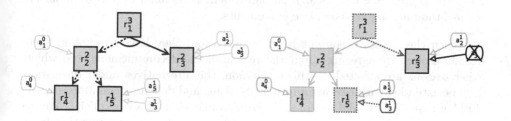

Fig. 3. Alternatives under discussion   **Fig. 4.** An explained event

Example 5. The following example illustrates the alternatives under discussion, as presented in Example 1. Considering the time moment 0, we say that the entire plan is part of the alternatives under discussion, Willie having both options being equally valid, being able to commit to either "get the beer from the fridge" or to "get the beer from the table." On the other hand, at time moment 2 it has to make a choice so the plan is divided in two independent alternatives, left and right side of the tree. The alternatives of the robot are represented abstractly in Fig 3.

Property 1 (Acyclic graph). We say that RoR is acyclic iff the graph $\{(x, y) \mid (Y) \in RoR(x), y \in Y\}$ is acyclic. A graph is acyclic if there is no path from a node to itself. We do not consider discussions with cyclic dependencies among reasons.

Property 2 (Connected graph). A graph is connected if there is a path from each node to each other one if we add the inverse to the graph, i.e. inverse of G is $\{(x, y) \mid (y, x) \in G\}$. We consider only single issue discussions, that is, in which the graph of reasons in the alternatives under discussion is connected.

Definition 6 (Agreement). *An agreement at moment t is a tuple $AG_t = \langle C_t, RoR_t(r) \rangle$, where: $C_t \subseteq R_t$ is set of reasons committed to, such that $RoR_t(r) \cap C_t \times C_t$ is connected.*

Example 6. Continued from Example 1, an agreement is a subset of the alternatives under discussion. At time moment 1 we can represent the choice of "bring the beer from the fridge" as follows: $C_1 = \{r_1^3, r_2^2, r_4^1, r_3^2\}$, meaning that Willie committed to "get the beer from the fridge" to "bring a bottle opener."

The reasons dependencies are defined for each reason in C_1. An agreement made at time moment 1 is a tuple $AG_1 = \langle C_1, RoR_1(r) \rangle$.

Property 3 (Complete agreement). An agreement is complete iff C_t contains all root reasons and for every reason r which is not a leaf, C_t contains all reasons of one of the elements of $RoR_t(r)$.

Property 4 (Minimal agreement). An agreement is minimal iff it is minimal for set inclusion among the complete agreements.

When the agents decommit from an intention, they have to explain their decommitment by agreeing about the reason of the decommitment, and which other reasons are affected. In this discussion, the alternatives under discussion may be extended with new assumptions, reasons, and dependencies among them (hidden assumptions and reasons, i.e. hidden agenda is made explicit). We do not introduce new names for alternatives under discussion, we assume that from now on A_t, R_t, AoR_t and RoR_t refer to the expanded sets.

Definition 7 (Explained event). *An explained event E_t is a tuple $\langle D_t, V_t \rangle$, where: $D_t \subseteq C_t$ is a set of reasons the agents decommit from and $V_t \subseteq A_t$ is a set of assumptions which are violated such that $\{r \mid \exists a \in AoR_t(r) \cup V_t\} \subseteq D_t$.*

Example 7. Continued from Example 1, in Fig. 4 we illustrate an explain event (plain black lines), composed by the assumption that Willie "can reach the table" and the reason "bring bottle opener." With dotted lines we marked the other reasons that are influenced by the failure of this assumption. More details follow in the algorithms presented in Sect. 6.

There can be two explanations of a decommitment: either an assumption is violated, or the agents decommitted from the reasons for the reason. Note that there can be several reasons why the agents committed to a reason, and therefore an explanation has to decommit from all these reasons.

Property 5 (Complete event). An explained event is complete iff for every $r \in D_t$, either there is an $(a \in V_t \cup AoR_t(r))$ or $(\{r' \mid \exists R \text{ s.t } r \in R \in RoR(r')\} \subseteq D_t)$.

This leads to new alternatives under discussion Alt_{t+1}. Violated assumptions and decommitted reasons are removed from the alternatives under discussion, and new assumptions and reasons may be added to it.

Finally we consider the new agreement. We assume that the agents stay committed to their reasons, i.e. they are persistent.

Definition 8 (Persistent decisions). *The agents decisions are persistent iff* $C_t \cup R_{t+1} \subseteq C_{t+1}$.

5.2 Intention Reconsideration Requirements, Part 1

In this section we discuss how our model satisfies 4 of the 10 requirements for the mechanism of intention reconsideration presented in Sect. 3.

Requirement 1. Inspired by Dung's abstract theory of argumentation [11], providing a graph based abstraction for non-monotonicity logics, our mechanism is expressed on a graph based representation of reasons and intentions. We can also instantiate our abstract model with logical formulas, along the lines of the aspic+ model [4].

Requirement 2. We can represent that an agent is not blindly committed, but drops its intentions once it believes that the intention is no longer achievable, by representing the belief as an assumption.

Requirement 3. Goals are a kind of reasons. The goal of an intention can be represented as a reason for the intention. Once the goal is dropped, the agent decommits from the reason and therefore also the intention is dropped. This is detailed in the algorithms presented in the next section.

Requirement 4. Beliefs revision leads to violation of assumptions, and consequently to decommitment of intentions. However, decommitment of intentions (or more generally, reasons) does not lead to violation of assumptions.

6 Algorithms and Requirements

6.1 Reconsideration Algorithms

In this section we introduce two revision algorithms: first, if the assumptions are violated we generate a reason revision; second, when we drop a commitment we generate a reason revision based on reasons.

Algorithm 1. Reason reconsideration based on assumptions

```
1: function      REVISEBASEDONASSUMP-
   TIONS(A'', R, AoR, RoR)
2:     define R'', uncommitted reasons
3:     for all ā ∈ A'' do
4:         for all r ∈ R do
5:             if (r, a) ∈ AoR then
6:                 r ← r̄
7:                 add r to R''
8:                 del (r, X) ∈ AoR
9:                 del (r, {X}) ∈ RoR
10:            end if
11:        end for
12:    end for
13:    reviseReasons(R'', R, RoR)
14: end function
```

Algorithm 2. Reasons reconsideration based on reasons

```
1: function REVISEREASONS(R'', R, RoR)
2:     while R'' is not empty do
3:         for all r_c ∈ R'' do
4:             for all r_p s.t r_p parent of r_c do
5:                 rel_1    ←    (r_p, {X})    s.t.
      (COND1)
6:                 rel_2 ← (r_p, {Y}) ∈ RoR
7:                 if rel_2 − rel_1 == empty then
8:                     r_p ← r̄_p
9:                     add r_p in R''
10:                end if
11:                RoR ← RoR − rel_1
12:            end for
13:            remove r_c from R''
14:        end for
15:    end while
16: end function
```

where $COND1 : (r_c \in X or X \equiv r_c) and ((r_p, \{X\}) \in RoR)$.

The first algorithm receives as its parameters the invalidated assumptions, together with the reasons and relations among them (all sets defined in previous sections). It constructs a set of all invalidated reasons (R'') given the assumptions that failed (lines 2, 6 and 7). It also revises the relations between reasons and assumptions (lines 8 and 9). For the set of invalid reasons it calls the function for revision based on reasons (line 13).

The second algorithm receives as its parameter the set of reasons that turned out to be invalid. For each reason r_c it iterates in the original tree of reasons and builds the relation function between reasons ($rel1$). By taking the original function RoR and making a difference between the elements ($rel2 − rel1$) we basically check if the parent node has more valid children or has to be invalidated also (lines 7–9). $COND1$ is checking that each element of RoR containing an invalid reason is added to the set rel_1. In the end, we update the relation RoR and remove the current invalid reason from the set R''. It repeats the same operations for each reason in R'', until the set becomes empty.

Example 8. Consider that Willie's assumption that he "can reach the table" fails. Using the first algorithm we iterate through the set of reasons and select all those affected ("get beer from the table" and "bring bottle opener"). We also remove all pairs of reasons and assumptions from the list of assumption dependencies (AoR). The first algorithm calls also the revision based on reasons. The second algorithm receives as its parameters the invalid reasons ("get beer from the table" and "bring bottle opener"). For each reason it iterates in the tree in order to find, respectively check the validity of the parent. In the case of reason "get beer from the table" the parent "get the beer" remains invalid, because there is one element left in the reasons dependencies. This is not the case for the reason "bring bottle opener", which also invalidates the parent "enable owner to drink beer."

6.2   Intention Reconsideration Requirements, Part 2

In this section we discuss how our model satisfies the last 6 requirements for the mechanism of intention reconsideration, presented in Sect. 3.

Requirement 5. The *AoR* function associates assumptions with reasons. Moreover, Algorithm 1 shows how intentions are reconsidered, when the assumptions do not become reality.

Requirement 6. Both goals and intentions are represented as reasons, such that the *RoR* function can associate goals as well as other concepts like norms, intentions and actions with intentions. Moreover, the Algorithm 2 shows how intentions are reconsidered, when goals are dropped, actions are impossible to perform or norms are no longer in force.

Requirement 7. Since intentions are reasons, the *RoR* function can also represent that intentions depend on other intentions. For example, abstract intentions can be decomposed into several more concrete intentions. As for Requirement 6, the same method ensures that if intentions are decommitted, also intentions depending on it are decommitted.

Requirement 8. Algorithm 1 illustrates how the invalidation/reconsideration of an assumption can affect intentions.

Requirement 9. Algorithm 2 illustrates how the reconsideration of an intention can affect other intentions.

Requirement 10. The model only introduces assumptions and reasons. Many concepts have been unified, such a goals, norms and intentions into a single class called reasons. The fact that even intentions are called reasons, is that an intention itself can be a reason for another intention in an extension of the model (see Requirement 7.) We cannot further unify assumptions and reasons, because they have to be treated differently following Requirement 4. Finally, we show in the previous section that the algorithms can be applied on these two abstract classes, without for example having to know whether a reason is actually a goal, norm or intention. The algorithms distinguish only assumptions from reasons, and do not have to distinguish types of reasons.

7   Related Work

Decisions are treated as plans, in which the assumptions about the world are represented in a variety of ways, depending on the nature of the assumptions. When a plan is executed in a real environment it can encounter differences between the expected and actual context of execution. Those differences can manifest as divergences between the expected and observed states of the world, or changes in goals to be achieved. In both cases, the old plan must be replaced with a new one [23]. Classical planning techniques are often not sufficient, and they have therefore been extended with the theory of intentions.

Wooldridge and Parsons [19,24] develop a simple formal model and investigate the behaviour of this model in different types of task environment. An agent's internal state is characterised by a set of beliefs and a set of intentions. In addition, an agent has a deliberation function, which allows it to reconsider and if necessary modify its intentions, and an action function, which allows it to act towards its current intentions. Shoham suggest viewing the plan as specifying an "intelligent database" [14,22] capturing the current beliefs of the agent while ensuring that the beliefs remain consistent at all times. Each action has associated an associated pre- and post- condition, with the property that if the preconditions are absent or invalid, the action can not be taken, but in case the action was taken then the postcondition hold. What is lacking in those BDI approaches are reasons for an intention, which may be another intention. We introduced an abstract framework that allows us to reason on relations between multiple goals, principles, actions (all called "reasons" for simplicity) and their assumptions. We developed a model of intention reconsideration inbetween the "single-minded" and "open-minded" revision, as described by Cohen and Levesque [8] or Rao and Georgeff [20]. We call this paradigm "assumption-minded" revision.

Mavromichalis and Vouros [18] propose a BDI approach for plan elaboration and reconsideration based on reasons for intentions (recorded as previous user inputs). In the case of a conflictual situation the user asks for the collaborative agent's help. The agent recognizes the cause of failure and initiate collaboration for an alternative action, that is defined based both on the erroneous action and an action that can resolve the conflict. Therefore, the agent communicates the actions that have to be performed and motivates their performance. We take a similar approach, formally defining an *explained event*, that contains both the set of violated assumptions and the reasons the agents decommits from (see Definition 7 and Example 7).

An alternative approach to belief revision for *updating existing information* is the use of Truth Maintenance Systems, as described by Doyle [10]. Both try to solve the same problem, but TMS can be seen as a way of storing proofs, while our approach is an abstract framework for intention reconsideration, therefore there is not a straight forward link to TMS.

We consider the work of Castelfranchi and Paglieri [7] complementary to ours. The authors created a constitutive theory of intentions and a taxonomy of beliefs, we, on the other hand, are not concerned on how intentions are formed, but rather on how they are triggered to change. The author's claim that "goals have to be supported by beliefs" is completely integrated in our framework by the *AoR* relation (see Definition 3). We go one step further and investigate also the regulative/supporting role of intentions over other intentions (see Definition 4).

Another important difference between our formalism and others mentioned above is the way we represent time. Rao and Georgeff use a CTL (Computation Tree Logic), meaning that the model of time is a tree-like structure in which the future is not determined; there are different paths in the future, any one of which might be an actual path that is realised. Cohen and Levesque define intentions as temporal sequences of the agents' beliefs and goals. We represent time modalities using LTL (Linear Temporal Logic), such that we can encode information about the future (a condition will eventually be true, a condition will be true until another fact becomes true). In TMSs time is not represented explicitly. Time steps can be deduced by the sequential tagging rules that feed the system.

Also, we mention that our framework is abstract, not instantiated, while Rao and Georgeff or Shoham use propositional logics. Some of TMSs use propositional logic, others are designed for predicate logics, others for only monotonic or non-monotonic logics [21].

8   "ArchiSurance" – Case Study

We illustrate our intention reconsideration model with an example from enterprise architecture driven by the fact that decisions (together with their associated commitments) in enterprise architecture typically change various times during their life span. Enterprises are in a constant state of change given by, e.g. the economic climate, companies merging or acquisitions, new technologies. Business performance depends on a balanced and integrated design of the organization, involving people, competences, structure, business processes, IT, finance, products, and services [12]. Our framework allows us to revise commitments, rather than creating them from scratch. The driving hypothesis of our work is that the resulting traceability between decisions and their underlying assumptions can enable a better underpinning of architectures, while at the same time triggering advanced impact analysis when confronted with changes. We are not interested in how decisions are taken in the first place, what cultural issues are involved (like norms, trust, organisation...), as we do not follow the contractual aspects. Instead, we focus on planning and on changes on the level of intentions, triggered by the change of assumptions or other intentions.

8.1   Description of the Case Study

In this section we briefly present the *ArchiSurance* case study. This case is inspired by a paper on the economic functions of insurance intermediaries [9], and is the running case used to illustrate the ArchiMate language specifications [15]. More details about the application of the current framework on the case study can be found in our related work [16,17].

ArchiSurance is the result of a merger of three previously independent insurance companies: *Home and Away*, specializing in home owner's insurance and travel insurance, *PRO-FIT*, specializing in auto insurance and *LegallyYours*, specializing in legal expense insurance. The company now consists of three divisions with the same names and headquarters as their independent predecessors.

The board's main driver (goal) is to increase its "Profit". Drivers motivate the development of specific business goals, as shown below in Fig. 5. Sub-goals such as "cost reduction" can be partitioned into the "reduction of maintenance costs" and the "reduction of personnel costs".

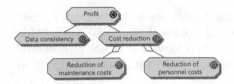

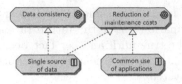

Fig. 5. "ArchiSurance"- business goals associated with "Profit" [15]

Fig. 6. "ArchiSurance" - refinement of business goals [15]

Business goals can be further refined, as presented in Fig. 6. The company needs to commit to realise a "single data source" in order to fulfil "data consistency", and commit either to "single data source" or "create common use application" to ensure the realization of the goal "reduction of maintenance costs".

8.2   Application of the Framework

In the original case study time is not present explicitly but implicitly, due the influence relations between commitments made. For example, it is pointless to commit to testing an application if chronologically you did not commit to creating the application beforehand. We use common sense reasoning and attach time points to the goals, principles, actions and assumptions. We describe below the reasons, assumptions and relations between them.

We consider that the board decides to commit to the strategic goal "profit" (r_1^5). This commitment appears at $t = 0$, the moment of initial planning and it means that at moment $t = 5$ the goal "profit" will be fulfilled. In order for this to happen, the board expects that the strategic principles "data consistency" (r_2^4) and "cost reduction" (r_3^4) will be fulfilled at time moment 4. Data consistency can be achieved by the acquisition of a new server (r_4^2) and/or merging of the databases (r_3^3). Notice that those actions have to be completed at an earlier time that the moment we expect data consistency to hold, here time moments 2 and 3. In order to validate the "cost reduction", the board commits to "creating a common use application" (r_6^3). This leads to a testing phase (r_7^4).

Notice that the time point associated with each commitment show a logical ordering of actions. For example we cannot plan at time moment 4 a testing phase (r_7^4) before committing to creating an application (r_6^3) at an earlier time point, here 3.

In a real world environment all commitments are made based on assumptions about the world. In our example the assumptions that were made are as follows: buying a new server was generated by the availability of the technology on the market (a_2^1); common application and merging of databases require the hiring of a new developer (a_4^2) and the acquisition of software licenses (a_5^1); testing phase is planned on the assumption that bugs might be introduced (a_7^3).

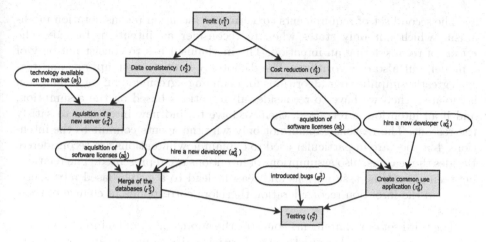

Fig. 7. Initial planning for the company "ArchiSurance"

Example 9. The planning of the merger of the three companies is presented in
Fig. 7. The time point of this planning is $t = 0$. We notice that the initial planning
contains also alternatives. We see that in order to obtain "profit" we need both
"data consistency" and "cost reduction", but for example "data consistency"
can be fulfilled with either a "merge of databases" ($\mathcal{AG}_2$) or "acquisition of a
new server" ($\mathcal{AG}_1$). The company can very well plan in the beginning to obtain
both, even if one is already sufficient:
$$\mathcal{AG}_1 = \langle \{r_1^5, r_2^4, r_3^3, r_4^4, r_6^3, r_7^4\}, \{(r_1^5, \{r_2^4, r_3^3\}), (r_2^4, \{r_3^3\}), (r_3^3, \{r_6^3\}), (r_6^3, \{r_7^4\})\}\rangle$$
$$\mathcal{AG}_2 = \langle \{r_1^5, r_2^4, r_4^2, r_3^4, r_6^3, r_7^4\}, \{(r_1^5, \{r_2^4, r_4^4\}), (r_2^4, \{r_4^2\}), (r_4^4, \{r_6^3\}), (r_6^3, \{r_7^4\})\}\rangle$$
Note that each time there is a "fork" in the plan the board has to get to a new
agreement.

9   Conclusions and Future Work

In this paper we introduced a mechanism of intention reconsideration based on
reasons and assumptions. Intention reconsideration is a central challenge in BDI
theory, but the models of the early nineties (e.g. Cohen and Levesque, Rao and
Georgeff) focus on *when* an intention may be reconsidered, for example when it
has been achieved, when it is no longer achievable, or when the associated goal
has been dropped. The first contribution of the paper is a list of ten requirements
for intention reconsideration mechanisms.

The first set of requirements concern the nature of the model, which must be
expressive enough to incorporate key concepts of existing models, for example to
express commitment strategies. The models of the early nineties focus on *when* an
intention may be reconsidered, for example when it has been achieved, when it is
no longer achievable, or when the associated goal has been dropped. In addition,
we require that intentions may be reconsidered too when the associated assumptions are violated, or when the reasons for the intention are no longer valid.

The second set of requirements concerns the intention reconsideration mechanism, which not only states when to reconsider an intention, but also the *effects* of reconsidering an intention. The mechanism has to consist not only of a model, but also of algorithms. The dichotomy between assumptions and reasons greatly simplifies our algorithms for changing agreements: if an assumption is violated, then we have to reconsider all intentions based on the assumption, and if an intention is retracted, then we have to find new intentions to satisfy the reasons. The reasons explain not only why the agents commit to the intentions, but they are in particular used to explain how intentions are reconsidered. Besides the reasons, also assumptions of intentions are represented. The relations between intentions, assumptions and reasons lead to a graph based representation, and the intention reconsideration therefore corresponds to change of these graphs.

The third set of requirements concerns the applicability of an intention reconsideration mechanism. Despite the popularity of existing models and formalisms, Shoham observes that due to their philosophical nature, they also tend to become relatively complicated. To make our mechanism widely applicable, we require an abstract approach. Here we are inspired by Dung's theory in the field of argumentation, which achieved a much wider public after existing work on non-monotonic logic and logic programming was abstracted to simple graph based notions. We would like to make an additional comparison with Dung's theory of abstract argumentation. The success of this formalism is partly due to the possibility to instantiate the abstract arguments with logical proofs. We intend to study the possibility of instantiating our abstract model with logical languages to relate it to logical models of intention reconsideration, such as Shoham's model which we used to represent assumptions as preconditions of actions.

We applied our framework of intention reconsideration with a case study from the field of enterprise architecture. Even if it presents a simplification of reality, it is a step further in assessing both the utility and the applicability of the framework. In practice it is often the case that we can not commit to more goals or actions at the same time. Another topic for future research is investigating the consequences of conflating intentions, norms and goals. It is easy for an agent to drop goals and intentions unilaterally (assuming no external commitment), but norms cannot be unilaterally changed (although one could choose to ignore them). We envision refining our model by distinguishing between norms and goals, but this is out of the scope of this paper. Furthermore, it is often the case that we can not commit to more goals or actions at the same time. It happens due to the lack of resources or due to the conflicting goals, to be forced to chose "exactly one" commitment. In order to describe those situations, we should introduce a relation of the type "xor" between reasons. We also believe that further investigations should be done on concurrent commitments and on the issues raised.

In this paper, we kept the formal details at a minimum, to make the paper as accessible as possible. We focused on the ideas and motivations rather than technical details. In the foreseen extension of this paper, these technical details will be developed further, and the mechanism will be illustrated with a larger case study.

We intend to continue with time manipulation in the structure. For example, at time moment 2 we realize the impossibility to fulfill a commitment. After revision the newly generated alternative should follow at a later time point. All commitments that depended on the invalid reason, their children, children of children, etc., should shift their time point.

References

1. IEEE guide for developing system requirements specifications. Technical report (1998)
2. Merriam Webster Dictionary, July 2013
3. Alchourrón, C.E., Gärdenfors, P., Makinson, D.: On the logic of theory change: partial meet contractions and revision functions. J. Symbolic Logic **50**(2), 510–530 (1985)
4. Bex, F., Prakken, H., Reed, C.: A formal analysis of the AIF in terms of the ASPIC framework. In: COMMA, pp. 99–110 (2010)
5. Boella, G., da Costa Pereira, C., Pigozzi, G., Tettamanzi, A., van der Torre, L.: The role of goals in belief selection. Logic J. IGPL **18**(4), 559–578 (2010)
6. Bulandran, S.: An exploration of assumptions in requirements engineering. Ph.D. thesis, The University of Western Australia (2012)
7. Castelfranchi, C., Paglieri, F.: The role of beliefs in goal dynamics: prolegomena to a constructive theory of intentions. Synthese **155**(2), 237–263 (2007)
8. Cohen, P.R., Levesque, H.J.: Intention is choice with commitment. Artif. Intell. **42**(2–3), 213–261 (1990)
9. Cummins, J., Doherty, N.: The economics of insurance intermediaries. J. Risk Insur. **73**(3), 359–396 (2006)
10. Doyle, J.: A truth maintenance system. Artif. Intell. **12**(3), 231–272 (1979)
11. Dung, P.M.: On the acceptability of arguments and its fundamental role in non-monotonic reasoning, logic programming and n-person games. Artif. Intell. **77**(2), 321–358 (1995)
12. Greefhorst, D., Proper, H.: Architecture Principles - The Cornerstones of Enterprise Architecture. Enterprise Engineering Series. Springer, Berlin (2011)
13. Grossi, D.: Designing invisible handcuffs - formal investigations in institutions and organizations for multi-agent systems. Ph.D. thesis, University of Utrecht (2007)
14. Icard, T.F., Pacuit, E., Shoham, Y.: Joint revision of beliefs and intention. In: KR (2010)
15. Jonkers, H., Band, I., Quartel, D.: The ArchiSurance Case Study. White paper, The Open Group, Spring (2012)
16. Marosin, D.: Changing enterprise architectures: abstract framework, revision procedures and algorithms. Master's thesis, University of Luxembourg (2012)
17. Marosin, D., Proper, H.A., van der Torre, L.: Changing agreements: intention reconsideration based on assumptions and reasons. In: Ossowski, S., Toni, F., Vouros, G.A. (eds.) AT. CEUR Workshop Proceedings, vol. 918, pp. 262–263. CEUR-WS.org. (2012)
18. Mavromichalis, V.K., Vouros, G.: Building intelligent collaborative interface agents with the icagent development framework. Auton. Agents Multi-Agent Syst. **13**(2), 155–195 (2006)

19. Parsons, S., Pettersson, O., Saffiotti, A., Wooldridge, M.: Intention reconsideration in theory and practice. In: ECAI, pp. 378–382 (2000)
20. Rao, A.S., Georgeff, M.P.: Intentions and rational commitment. In: Proceedings of the First Pacific Rim Conference on Artificial Intelligence (PRICAI-90) (1993)
21. Shapiro, S.C.: Belief revision and truth maintenance systems: an overview and a proposal. Technical report (1998)
22. Shoham, Y.: Logical theories of intention and the database perspective. J. Philos. Logic **38**, 633–647 (2009)
23. van der Krogt, R., de Weerdt, M.: Plan repair as an extension of planning. In: ICAPS, pp. 161–170 (2005)
24. Wooldridge, M., Parsons, S.: Intention reconsideration reconsidered. In: Papadimitriou, Ch., Singh, M.P., Müller, J.P. (eds.) ATAL 1998. LNCS (LNAI), vol. 1555, pp. 63–79. Springer, Heidelberg (1999)

Normative Conflicts that Depend on the Domain

Viviane Torres da Silva[✉] and Jean Zahn

Computer Science Department, Universidade Federal Fluminense (UFF),
Rua Passos da Pátria 156, Bloco E, Niterói 24210-240, Brazil
{viviane.silva, jzahn}@ic.uff.br

Abstract. Norms are being used in multi-agent systems as a powerful abstraction to capture social constraints. Norms regulate the behavior of the agents by describing the actions that can be performed, actions that must be performed, and actions that cannot be performed. One of the main challenges on design and implementation of normative systems is that norms may conflict with one another. Although there are several works that contribute to the checking and solving conflicts between norms, there is still a need for approaches able to check for conflicts when such conflicts are only detected when analyzing the application domain. Without considering the application domain it is not possible to identify conflicts that, for instance, regulate the execution of different, but related actions, executed by different, but related entities. In this paper we present an approach bases the checking for conflicts between the norms on the description of the application.

Keywords: Norms · Conflicts · Relationships · System specification

1 Introduction

Open multi-agent systems (MAS) are societies in which autonomous, heterogeneous and independently designed agents can work towards similar or different ends [14]. In order to cope with the heterogencity, autonomy and diversity of interests among the different members, norms have been used. In the scope of Sociology, norms are rules that a society or a group use to define appropriate and inappropriate values, beliefs, attitudes and behaviors [2]. In MAS, norms are being used to regulate the behavior of the agents by describing the actions that can be performed (permissions), actions that must be performed (obligations), and actions that cannot be performed (prohibitions). They represent a way for agents to understand their responsibilities and the responsibilities of the others.

One of the major challenges on the specification of norms is the identification of normative conflicts. Although there are several works that have proposed solutions for the checking of conflicts, the majority focus on the identification of simple conflicts that occurs when a given action is simultaneously prohibited and obliged (or permitted) for a particular entity. Those approaches are not able, for instance, to check for conflicts between two norms that regulate different, but related actions, and that govern the behavior of different, but related entities. In order to be able to identify those set of

T. Balke et al. (Eds.): COIN 2013, LNAI 8386, pp. 311–326, 2014.
DOI: 10.1007/978-3-319-07314-9_17, © Springer International Publishing Switzerland 2014

conflicts it is necessary to understand the application domain, i.e., it is important to figure out how the elements that compose a norm (for instance, the actions being regulated and the entities whose behavior is being regulated) are related to each other.

In this context, this paper presents an approach for checking the conflicts between norms that is based on the description of the elements and the relationships among the elements of the application. By using such description it is possible to figure out how the elements that constitute two norms are related and consider such information when checking for conflicts. The conflict checker is then able to identify conflicts between norms even though the elements identified in the norms are not the same.

This paper is organized as follows. In Sect. 2 we state the definition of norm being used in this paper. In Sect. 3 we describe the relationships to relate the elements that compose norms. Together with such relationships we describe a set of rules to be followed when checking for conflicts between the norms by taking into account how the entities are related. In Sect. 4 we detail how a norm that regulates the execution of an action influences on the execution of related actions by taking into account the deontic concept applied to the norm. Section 5 describes a motivational example and the Java program that implements the proposed conflict checker. Section 6 presents some related work and, finally, Sect. 7 states some conclusions and future work.

2 Norm Definition

In this section we introduce a simplified specification of norms by following our previous work on the normative modeling language NormML [4]. We consider that a norm prohibits or obliges an entity to execute an action in a given context during a certain period of time. We also assume that everything is permitted unless a prohibition is described. Therefore, we do not consider norms stating permission. Besides, we assume that agents (and organizations) play roles in organization and inhabit environment. Such relationships are defined in Sect. 3.

Several normative specifications, modeling languages, methodologies and organizational models define norm in similar ways. In all of them, a norm is always associated with a deontic concept, an entity and an action (or state) that is being regulated. In Definitions 1, 3 and 4 we present the definition of norm, entity and action.

Definition 1: (Norm) A norm n is a tuple of the form {deoC, c, e, a, ac, dc, s}, where *deoC* is a deontic concept from the set {obligation or prohibition}, $c \in C$ is the context (among a set of contexts) where the norm is defined, $e \in E$ is the entity whose behavior is being regulated, $a \in A$ is the action (from a set of actions) being regulated, $ac \in Cd$ indicates the condition (from a set of conditions) that activates the norm, $dc \in Cd$ is the condition that deactivates the norm and s indicates the state of the norm from the set {fulfilled, violated, none}. *None* indicates that the norm has not been fulfilled or violated yet.

The context of a norm indicates the scope where the norm is defined. A norm must be fulfilled only when the entity is executing in such context. Outside its context, the norm is not valid. Almost all approaches consider that a norm is defined in the context of an organization. Some of them consider that a context can be an interaction or a scene, for example.

Definition 2: (Context) A context c is a tuple of the form {name, cType} where *name* is the name of the context and *cType* is the type of the context from the set {organization, environment, none}. A norm can be defined in the scope of an organization or an environment. When a norm applies to an organization, the entity must only comply with the norm when it is executing in the scope of such organization. When a norm applies to an environment, the entity must only comply with the norm when it is executing in the context of such environment. If a norm does not specify the context, we consider that the norm applies to all contexts. In such case, the attribute name is not specified.

In this paper we consider that a norm can be defined to regulate the behavior of an agent itself, a role, an organization or all agents in a given context.

Definition 3: (Entity) An entity e is a tuple of the form {name, eType}, where *name* is the name of the entity and *eType* is the type of the entity from the set {agent, role, organization, all}. If a norm applies to all, it applies to all agents executing in a given context. In such case, the attribute name is not specified.

Definition 4: (Action) An action is a tuple of the form {name, setStates}, where name is the name of the action and setStates is the set of states that the action achieves when it is executed.

A norm restricts the execution of an action after the activation condition is fired and before the deactivation condition is trigged. The works analyzed present several ways to describe the period during while a norm is active. For simplicity, we are considering in this paper that the activation (and deactivation) condition of a norm is an, as in Definition 5.

Definition 5: (Condition) An activation condition *ac* and a deactivation condition *dc* state an event in time that can be a data, the execution of an action, the fulfillment of a norm, and so on.

3 Entities Relationships

The seven relationships presented in this section are based on the relationships stated in NormML and they are: inhabit, play, playin, ownership, inheritance, composition and refinement. Besides describing the relationships, we also point out a set of rules that should be followed when considering the conflicts between norms. Such rules state the consequences of applying a norm to an entity when such entity is related to others. The purpose of the rules is to state the transitive relationships of the norms applied to related entities. Therefore, the rules are described after presented each relationship.

It is important to stress that the set of relationships can be enlarged. The set of relationships were defined following our previous work [4] but is not limited to it. When defining new relationships it is also important to describe the rules that define the transitive relationships of the norms applied to different but related entities.

- **Inhabit:** it relates an entity to the environment that it inhabits. The relationship can be applied in the following cases: agent x environment; organization x environment.

Rule 1 states the relation between a norm defined in the context of the environment and the behavior of the entities executing in such environment.

Rule 1. If a norm applies in the scope of an environment, such norm applies to all entities that inhabit such environment.

For instance, if a norm N1 defined in the scope of the campus of a school prohibits the carry of guns, and the specification of the application states that the agent Mary executes in (or inhabits) that campus, she must fulfill N1: Mary is prohibited of carrying guns.

- **Play:** it relates an entity to the roles that it can play. Such relationship can be applied to the following entities: agent x role; organization x role. Rule 2 defines the consequences of defining a norm applied to an agent (or organization) when it is playing roles and a norm applied to a role played by agents (or organizations), respectively.

Rule 2. If a norm applies to a role, it applies to all agents (or organization) playing such role. When a norm applies to a role, it does not care about the entity that plays the role. Any entity playing such role must follow the norm.

For instance, let's suppose that Mary is a security guard and there is a norm N2 stating that security guards can carry guns in the scope of the school. In this example, we can clearly see that N1 and N2 are in conflict since the former norm prohibits every agent to carry guns and the latter permits security guards to carry guns.

- **Playin:** it relates an entity and the organization where it is playing the role. Such relationship is applied to the following entities: agent x organization; organization x organization. Rule 3 states what happens to the entities playing roles in an organization when a norm applies to such organization.

Rule 3. If a norm applies to an organization, it applies to any entity playing role in such organization. Any entity executing in an organization must comply with the norms applied to such organization.

For instance, if a norm N3 states that everyone in the school must use uniforms, Mary, as a security guard of such school, must use uniforms.

- **Ownership:** it states the roles defined in the scope of an organization. Such relationship is defined to the following entities: role x organization. Rule 4 relates a norm applied to an organization and the roles being played in the organization.

Rule 4. If a norm applies to an organization, it applies to all roles being played in such organization. If a role is being executed in such organization, the entity executing such role must comply with the norm.

Following our example, considering norm N3 and knowing that such school has secretaries and students, they all are obliged to use uniforms.

- **Hierarchy:** it defines that an element is the superelement of another called the subelement. Such relationship can be applied to the following entities: agent x agent; organization x organization; role x role; environment x environment. Rules 5, 6, 7, 8, and 9 state that a norm applied to a superentity also applies to its subentities.

Rule 5. If a norm is defined in the scope of an environment, the norm also applies in the scope of all its subenvironment.

Rule 6. If a norm is defined in the scope of a superorganization, the norm also applies in the scope of all its suborganizations.
Rule 7. If a norm applies to a superorganization, the norm also applies to all its suborganizations.
Rule 8. If a norm applies to a superagent, it also applies to all its descendent in a hierarchy of agents.
Rule 9. If a norm applies to a superrole, it also applies to all its descendent in a hierarchy of role.

For instance, following rule 7, if a norm is defined in the scope of the school, it also applies in the scope of all its departments. In the next section we detail the composition and the refinement relationships applied among actions since the analyses of such relationships depends on the deontic concepts indicated in the norms.

4   Actions Relationships

In this section we discuss how a norm that regulates the execution of a given action influences on the execution of the actions related to such action. Different relationships can be used to connect actions. Some examples of action relationships are: (i) refinement: an action is a refinement of another [1]; (ii) composition: an action is composed of other actions [7, 10, 16]; (iii) dependency: an action can only be executed after the execution of another action [16]; and (iv) orthogonal: two actions cannot be executed at the same time [13]. In this paper we discuss two action relationships: action refinement and action composition. In this paper we concentrate on these two. In order to exemplify such relationships, let's consider the two very simple examples below:

E.g.1: (refinement relationship) *to walk* and *to fly* are actions that specialize *to move*.
```
(supeaction, subaction, refinement)
(to move, to walk, refinement)
(to move, to fly, refinement)
```

E.g.2: (composition relationship) *to clean the house* is an action composed, in this example, of three other actions: *to do the laundry, to clean the floor and to wash the dishes.*
```
(wholeaction, partaction, composition)
(cleanHouse, doLaundry, composition)
(cleanHouse, cleanFloor, composition)
(cleanHouse, washDishes, composition)
```

4.1   Action Refinement

If the refinement relationship is defined between two actions, it means that there is an action called subaction that is more specific than another action called superaction and that the superaction is an abstract[1] action. Being more specific, the execution of the

---

[1] By abstract action we mean the action that cannot be executed since it does only define the goals to be achieved when it is executed but no implementation is provided.

subaction achieves the goal of executing the superaction, and may also achieve other goals. The states that should be achieved by executing the superaction are a subset of the states achieved by executing the subaction. If there is more than one subaction for a given superaction, it is necessary to execute only one subaction in order to achieve the goal of executing the superaction.

Definition 6: Let's consider *setStates(j)* the set of states achieved by executing an action *j* and *subActs(j)* the set of subactions of *j*. For all actions *i* being a subaction of *j*, the set of states achieved by *j* is a subset of the states achieved by executing *i*.

$$\forall i \in subActs(j) \rightarrow setStates(j) \subset setStates(i)$$

Obligation: If the norm applied to the superaction is an obligation, it means that the entity, whose behavior is being regulated by the norm, is obliged to execute the superaction and achieve its states. If such superaction has more than one subaction and knowing that the states achieved by the superaction are a subset of the states achieved by any subaction (Definition 6), when one of the subactions is executed (in the period during while the norm is active), the entity fulfills its obligation. In order to illustrate such case, let's consider that there is a norm obligating an entity to *move*. Thus, if it *walks* or if it *flies*, it will fulfill the norm. On the other hand, if the entity does not execute any of its subaction (in the period during while the norm is active), the entity will violate the obligation. The equations below formalize the fulfillment and violation of such norm.

$$\forall n \in N : n.dc = 'obligation' \wedge n.a = j$$
$$if(\exists i \in subActs(j) \wedge n.e.executed(i)) \quad (1)$$
$$\rightarrow n.s = 'fulfilled'$$

$$\forall n \in N : n.dc = 'obligation' \wedge n.a = j$$
$$if (\forall i \in subActs(j) \wedge n.e.notexecuted(i)) \quad (2)$$
$$\rightarrow n.s = 'violated'$$

where *n* is the norm, *n.e.executed(i)* means that the entity *e* whose behavior is being regulated by the norm *n* has executed action *i* in the period during while the norm was activated and *n.e.notexecuted(i)* means that the entity *e* has not executed the action *i* in the period during while the norm *n* was activated. The equations below formalize the fulfillment and violation of such norm and Rule 11 relates an obligation applies to a superaction and the norms apply to the subactions.

Rule 10. *If there is an obligation applied to a superaction (and knowing that such action is abstract), there must be at least one subaction that is not being prohibited for being executed at related contexts, by related entities in related periods of time.*

$$\forall n \in N : n.dc = 'obligation' \wedge n.a = j \wedge subActs(j)) \neq \emptyset$$
$$\exists i \in subActs(j), \exists m \in N : m.a = i \wedge m.dc \neq 'prohibition' \wedge n.c \approx m.c \wedge$$
$$n.e \approx m.e \wedge n.ac \approx m.ac \wedge n.dc \approx m.dc$$

Prohibition: If the norm applied to the superaction is a prohibition, it means that the entity, whose behavior is being regulated by the norm, is prohibited to execute the superaction and achieve any of its states. If such superaction has more than one sub-action and knowing that the states achieved by the superaction are a subset of the states achieved by any of its subactions (Definition 6), if the entity executes any subaction (in the period during while the norm is active), it will be violating its prohibition. For instance, let's assume that there is a norm prohibiting an entity to move. If it walks or if it flies it will be violating the norm. On the other hand, if the entity does not execute any subaction (in the period during while the norm is active), it will fulfill the norm. Equations 3 and 4 formalize the fulfillment and violation of such norm and Rule 11 relates a prohibition applies to a superaction and the norms applied to the subactions.

$$\forall n \in N: n.dc =' prohibition' \land n.a = j$$
$$if(\exists i \in subActs(j) \land n.e.executed(i))$$
$$\rightarrow n.s = 'violated' \tag{3}$$

$$\forall n \in N: n.dc = 'prohibition' \land n.a = j$$
$$if(\forall i \in subActs(j) \land n.e.notexecuted(i))$$
$$\rightarrow n.s = 'fulfilled' \tag{4}$$

Rule 11. *If there is a prohibition applied to a superaction (and knowing that such action is abstract), there must be no subaction being obligated for being executed at related contexts, by related entities in related periods of time.*

$$\forall n \in N: n.dc = 'prohibition' \land n.a = j \land subActs(j)) \neq \emptyset$$
$$\rightarrow \nexists i \in subActs(j), \exists m \in N : m.a = i \land m.dc = 'obligation' \land n.c \approx m.c \land$$
$$n.e \approx m.e \land n.ac \approx m.ac \land n.dc \approx m.dc$$

4.2 Action Composition

If the composition relationship is defined between two actions, it means that there is an action called part that is part of the action called whole and that the whole action is an abstract action. The states achieved by executing the whole action are the union of the states achieved by executing all its parts. Therefore, in order to achieve the goals of executing the whole action it is necessary to execute all its parts.

Definition 7: Let's consider *setStates(j)* the set of states achieved by executing an action *j*, *partAct(j)* the set of actions part of *j* and n the number of parts of j.

$$\forall i \in partActs(j) \rightarrow setStates(j) = \bigcup_{(i=1)}^{n} setStates(i)$$

Obligation: If the norm applied to the whole action is an obligation, it means that the entity is obliged to execute the whole action and achieve its states. If such whole action has more than one part and knowing that the states achieved by each part are a subset of the states achieved by the whole (Definition 7), the entity is obliged to execute all its parts (in the period during while the norm is active) in order to fulfill the obligation[2]. If one of the parts is not executed, the norm will be violated. Let's use the example of reviewing a paper in order to exemplify such normative condition. If there is a norm obligating an entity of *reviewing a paper*, in order to fulfill such norm the entity needs *to read the paper* and also *to send the revision*. Equations 5 and 6 formalize the fulfillment and violation of such norm and Rule 12 relates an obligation applies to the whole action and the norms applied to its parts.

$$\forall n \in N : n.dc = 'obligation' \land n.a = j$$
$$if\,(\forall i \in partActs(j) \land n.e.executed(i)) \quad (5)$$
$$\rightarrow n.s =' fulfilled'$$

$$\forall n \in N : n.dc = 'obligation' \land n.a = j$$
$$if\,(\exists i \in partActs(j) \land n.e.notexecuted(i)) \quad (6)$$
$$\rightarrow n.s = 'violated'$$

Rule 12. *If there is an obligation applied to a whole action, there must be no norm prohibiting the same entity to execute any of the parts of such whole action at related contexts, by related entities in related periods of time.*

$$\forall n \in N : n.dc = 'obligation' \land n.a = j \land partActs(j)) \neq \emptyset$$
$$\rightarrow \nexists i \in partActs(j), \nexists m \in N : \land m.a = i \land m.dc = 'prohibition' \land n.c \approx m.c \land$$
$$n.e \approx m.e \land n.ac \approx m.ac \land n.dc \approx m.dc$$

Prohibition: If the norm applied to the whole action is a prohibition, it means that the entity is prohibited to execute the whole action and achieve any of its states. If such whole action has more than one part, the agent will fulfill the prohibition if it does not execute one of the parts (in the period during while the norm is active). On the other hand, the agent will violate the prohibition if it executes all its parts (in the period during while the norm is active). The agent is only violating the prohibition if it executes all the parts. For instance, if there is a norm prohibiting an entity of *reviewing a paper*, the act of *reading the paper* does not violate the norm. Equations 7 and 8 formalize the fulfillment and violation of such norm and Rule 13 relates a prohibition applied to the whole action and the norms applied to its parts.

$$\forall n \in N : n.dc =' prohibition' \land n.a = j$$
$$if\,(\exists i \in partActs(j) \land n.e.notexecuted(i)) \quad (7)$$
$$\rightarrow n.s = 'fulfilled'$$

$$\forall n \in N : n.dc = 'prohibition' \land n.a = j$$
$$if\,(\forall i \in partActs(j) \land n.e.executed(i)) \quad (8)$$
$$\rightarrow n.s = 'violated'$$

Rule 13. *If there is a prohibition applied to a whole action, there must be no norms obligating the same entity to execute all parts of such whole action at related contexts, by related entities in related periods of time.*

---

[2] In this paper we are not dealing with partial fulfillment.

$$\forall n \in N : n.dc = \text{'prohibition'} \land n.a = j \land partActs(j)) \neq \emptyset$$
$$\rightarrow \forall i \in partActs(j), \forall m \in N: m.a = i \land m.dc \neq \text{'obligation'} \land n.c \approx m.c \land$$
$$n.e \approx m.e \land n.ac \approx m.ac \land n.dc \approx m.dc$$

5 Conflict Checker

Before presenting the program that checks for conflicts between norms taking into account the system specification, we present a motivational example. In this example, we demonstrate that two, apparently, not related norms can be in conflict.

5.1 Motivational Example

When a conflict between two norms occurs an agent is not able to comply with the conflicting norms since whatever it does or refrain from doing will violate one of the norms dealing to a social constraint being broken. If the agent fulfills one of the norms, it automatically violates the other and vice-versa. Having said that, this section presents a conflict checker that takes two norms and the system specification in order to figure out if the norms are in conflict.

The system specification is important when checking for conflicts because to answer the question "Are these two norms in conflict?" it is necessary to understand the relation between the contexts where the two norms are defined, the relationship between the refereed entities whose behaviors are being regulated, and the relationship between the actions regulated by the norms. Without considering the relationships between such elements, the conflict checker may conclude that the two norms are not in conflict since they are applied in different contexts, to different entities, and regulate different actions. However, if the elements and their relationships are provided the conflict checker may conclude the opposite.

In order to illustrate the need for considering the system specification when checking for conflicts let's take a look in the following example. Below we describe two norms by following Definition 1 and the part of the system specification applied to the example.

Norm1: In the university, professors are obliged to give talks.

```
norm1 = {obligation, {university, organization}, {professor, role},
                      {giveTalks, (talksGiven)} _, _, none}
```

Norm 2: In the computer science department, researchers are prohibited to teach.

```
norm2 = {prohibition, {depCS, organization}, {researcher, role},
        {teach, (talksGiven, classesGiven, classesPrepared)}, _, _, none}
```

System Specification:

"DepCS is a sub-organization of university". (depCS, university, compositon)
"Researcher is a descendent of professor". (professor, researcher, hierarchy)
"Teach is the subaction of giveTalks". (giveTalks, teach, hierarchy)

Without considering the information about the application domain, we may say that these two norms are not in conflict since they are not applied in the same context, to the same entity executing the same action. However, by taking into account the system specification, the rules and definitions above, we conclude the opposite. By applying Rule 7 (described in Sect. 3) to the example and considering that the Computer Science department is a sub-organization of University, we can say that norm 1 also applies to such department and, thus, such norm can be rewritten as follows:

```
norm1.a = {obligation, {depCS, organization}, {professor, role},
                          {giveTalks, (talksGiven)} _, _, none}
```

Following the system specification, researches are professors, i.e., the role research is a descendent of the role professor. Then, by applying rule 9, norm 1.a can be rewritten:

```
norm1.b = {obligation, {depCS, organization}, {researcher, role},
                          {giveTalks, (talksGiven)} _, _, none}
```

Finally, the specification states that *to teach* is a specialization of *to giveTalks* (that is a superaction). By applying Definition 6 to norm1.b we rewrite such norm as follows:

```
norm1.c = {obligation, {depCS, organization}, {researcher, role},
            {teach, (talksGiven, classesGiven, classesPrepared)} _, _, none}
```

After such analysis, we are able to conclude that norm 2 and the norm 1 are in conflict.

5.2 The Program

The program for the checking of conflicts is based on the rewriting of the norms in order to normalize them. If the scope of a norm includes the scope of another norm, the more general norm can be rewritten to comply with the more specific norm. Similar to unification [5], we rewrite the more general norm when the scopes of the norms overlap. Note that we *locally* rewrite the norm, i.e., the norm is rewritten only in the scope of the conflict checker and the system version of the norm is not modified.

The rules and definitions described in Sects. 3 and 4 are used when rewriting the norms. We explain the *conflictChecker* program (see Algorithm 1) by referencing such rules and definitions and also by pointing out the lines of the Java method presented below. In this paper the system specification is described as an object that stores a set of relationships between entities and a set of relationships between actions, by following definitions in Sects. 3 and 4.

Algorithm 1. Conflict Checker Main

Require: The *norm* base (represented by *norms*)
Require: The n_1 and n_2 from the *norm* base
if *contextsRelationship(n_1, n_2)* **then**
  if *entitiesRelationship(n_1, n_2)* **then**
    if *timeIntersect(n_1, n_2)* **then**
      if *actionsRelationship(n_1, n_2)* **then**
        return *Norms are in conflict!*
      end if
    end if
  end if
end if
return *Norms are not in conflict!*

The algorithm starts by checking if the contexts of the norms are related, as explained below and detailed in Algorithm 2:

(a) If the contexts are the same, it is not necessary to rewrite any norm;

(b) If the context of a norm is not defined, it means that the norm applies in any context. Therefore, the context of such norm is rewritten in order to comply with the context of the other norm (see Definition 2);

(c) If both contexts are organizations (or both are environment) and there is a hierarchy relationship between them, the norm whose context is the supercontext is rewritten in order to comply with the subcontext (see Rules 5 and 6);

(d) If the context of one norm is an organization and the other is an environment, and the organization inhabits the environment, the norm whose context is the environment is rewritten to comply with the organization (see Rule 1);

Algorithm 2. Function: Verifying Context Relationship

Require: n_1 and n_2 as parameter
function *contextsRelationship(n_1, n_2)*
  if $(n_1.c = n_2.c)$ **then**
    return true
  else
    if $(n_1.c.cType = organization)$ **and**
      $(n_2.c.cType = organization)$ **then**
      if $(n_1.c \sqsubseteq n_2.c)$ **or** $(n_2.c \sqsubseteq n_1.c)$ **then**
        return true
      end if
    end if
    if $(n_1.c.cType = environment)$ **and**
      $(n_2.c.cType = environment)$ **then**
      if $(n_1.c \sqsubseteq n_2.c)$ **or** $(n_2.c \sqsubseteq n_1.c)$ **then**
        return true
      end if
    end if
    if $(n_1.c.cType = organization)$ **and**
      $(n_2.c.cType = environment)$ **then**
      if $(n_1.c \sqsubseteq n_2.c)$ **then**
        return true
      end if
    end if
  end if
  return false
end function

If the contexts are related, the algorithm checks if the entities described in both norms are related, as shown in Algorithm 3 and detailed below:

(a) If the entities are the same, it is not necessary to rewrite the norms;
(b) If both entities are agents, roles or organizations, and there is a *hierarchy* relationship between them, the norm whose entity is the superentity is rewritten in order to comply with the subentity (see Rules 7, 8 and 9);
(c) If one of the norms applies to an agent (or organization) and the other to a role, and the entities are related by the *play* relationship, the norm whose entity is the role is rewritten in order to comply with the norm whose entity is the agent (or organization) (see Rule 2);
(d) If one of the norms applies to an agent (or organization) and the other to an organization, and these entities are related by the *playin* relationship, the norm whose entity is the organization where the role is being played is rewritten in order to comply with entity of the other norm (see Rule 3).
(e) If one norm is applied to a role and the other to an organization, and the role and organization are related to the *ownership* relationship, the norm whose entity is the organization is rewritten (see Rule 4).

Algorithm 3. Function: Verifying Entities Relationship

Require: n_1 and n_2 as parameter
function *entitiesRelationship(n_1, n_2)*
  if *($n_1.e = n_2.e$)* **then**
    return true
  else
    if *(checkEntitiesRelationship($n_1.e$, $n_2.e$) = hierarchy)*
      then return true
    end if
    if *(checkEntitiesRelationship($n_1.e$, $n_2.e$) = play)*
      then return true
    end if
    if *(checkEntitiesRelationship($n_1.e$, $n_2.e$) = playin)*
      then return true
    end if
    if *(checkEntitiesRelationship($n_1.e$, $n_2.e$) = ownership)*
      then return true
    end if
  end if
  return false
end function

If the entities are related, the program checks if the constraints intersect, i.e., if the period during while one norm is active intersects with the period during while the other norm is active. If it is the case, the program analyzes if the actions are related, as follows (see Algorithm 4):

(a) If the actions are the same, it is not necessary to rewrite the norms;
(b) If the actions are related by the refinement relationship:(i) If the supernorm is a prohibition and the subnorm an obligation, the norms are in conflict (see Rule 11); and (ii) If the supernorm is an obligation, the algorithm checks if there is a norm applied to the subnorm that is not being prohibited (see Rule 10);

(c) If the actions are related by the composition relationship: (i) If the wholenorm is an obligation, the norms are in conflict if there is a norm prohibiting the execution of a part (see Rule 12); and (ii) If the wholenorm is a prohibition, the algorithm checks if there is a norm applied to the partnorm that is not being obliged (see Rule 13);

Algorithm 4. Function: Verifying Actions Relationship

Require: n_1 and n_2 as parameter
function *actionsRelationship(n_1, n_2)*
  if *($n_1.a = n_2.a$)* **then**
    return true
  else
    if *(checkActRelationship($n_1.a$, $n_2.a$) = refinement)* **and**
      (($n_1.deoC$ = F **and** $n_2.deoC$ = (O) **or**
      ($n_1.deoC$ = O **and** *checkAllSubActions($n_1.a$*, F))) **then**
        return true
    end if
    if *(checkActRelationship($n_2.a$, $n_1.a$) = refinement)* **and**
      (($n_2.deoC$ = F **and** $n_1.deoC$ = (O) **or**
      ($n_2.deoC$ = O **and** *checkAllSubActions($n_2.a$*, F))) **then**
        return true
    end if
    if *(checkActRelationship($n_1.a$, $n_2.a$) = composition)* **and**
      (($n_1.deoC$ = O **and** *checkAnyPartActions($n_1.a$*, F)) **or**
      ($n_1.deoC$ = F **and** *checkAllPartActions($n_1.a$*, O))) **then**
        return true
    end if
    if *(checkActRelationship($n_2.a$, $n_1.a$) = composition)* **and**
      (($n_2.deoC$ = O **and** *checkAnyPartActions($n_2.a$*, F)) **or**
      ($n_2.deoC$ = F **and** *checkAllPartActions($n_2.a$*, O))) **then**
        return true
    end if
  end if
  return false
end function

---

6 Related Work

Although there are several approaches that propose solutions for the checking of conflicts between norms, the majority focuses on conflicts that occur when two norms simultaneously prohibit and obligate (or prohibit and permit) the execution of the same action by the same entity. The authors in [9, 14, 16, 17] propose mechanism not only to detect but also to resolve conflicts focusing on conflicting norms that regulate exactly the same behavior. In [15] the authors distinguish conflicts from inconsistences and propose solution for norms that regulate virtual organizations. Similar to our approach their mechanisms for the checking of conflicts use unification to find out if the norms overlap. However, it is out of the scope of those papers to figure out conflicts between norms that regulate the behavior of different entities executing different actions.

On the other hand, authors in [6, 7, 10] propose mechanisms for checking indirect conflicts. The approaches [6, 7] focus on the checking of conflicts by taking into account that normative positions of one activity are propagated to other activities. In [6] the authors present an approach dedicated to detect normative conflicts by considering that multiple, concurrent and related activities are executed by agents. The authors in [7] present an approach for detecting conflicts among norms that regulate composed actions. They state that an activity can be composed of several sub-activities and that the conflict-free normative positions of an activity propagate to its sub-activities. The conflicts occur when the normative position of a sub-activity contradicts the normative positions coming from the super-activity. Besides stating the conflict-cases, in our approach we also describe if the execution of a subaction (called in this paper part action) implies the fulfillment or violation of the norm applies to the superaction (called in this paper whole action). In [10] the authors propose mechanisms to address conflicts by taking into account the domain-specific relationships among actions. They propose the used of composition and delegation as possible relationships among actions.

There are other approaches that concern about detecting and resolving conflicts on legal environments. The works presented in [3, 11, 12] focuses on conflicts between norms defined in different jurisdictions. The authors in [3] claim that a particular situation can be judged by different legal systems and the norms of those systems can conflict. The authors [11, 12] claim that acting under several jurisdictions at the same time is becoming the norm, so, it is important to have a mechanism to find conflicts between them. In this paper we focus on conflicts between norms defined in the same legal systems. In [8] the authors present a new logic to formalize different operations for solving conflicts but they do not concern about the relationships among the entities of the system when checking for conflicts.

7 Conclusion and Related Work

The paper addresses one of the main problems when dealing with the specification of norms: the checking of normative conflicts. The proposed mechanism uses the system specification that describes the relationships among the systems elements when checking the conflicts. In Sect. 5 we exemplify the need for considering the system specification by checking for conflicts between two norms that, apparently, were not in conflict. After the analysis, we could demonstrate that the norms that applied at different context to different entities and regulates different actions were in fact in conflict.

Before presenting the algorithm for the checking of conflicts, we have described a set of definitions and rules. Since norm is an important concept in this paper we have formally defined such concept and its related concept in Sect. 2. In the sequence, we have presented the characteristics of the system by describing the relationships we have predefined and the related rules. The rules state the consequence of applying a norm to an entity when such entity is related to others. When describing the relationships between actions (refinement and composition) and the consequence of defining a norm to an action that is related to another, it was important to carefully analyze the deontic concept. It is out of the scope of this paper to detail how a norm described in English is mapped to our specification and how it is created.

It is our intention to extend our approach in order to be able to indicate the cases of conflicts between norms. By using the rewritten norms, it is possible to observe where the conflicting cases occur. Such rewritten norms could be used are a feedback to the one using our conflict checker and also used when proposing solutions for the conflicts.

References

1. Aldewereld, H., Alvarez-Napagao, S., Dignum, F., Vazquez-Salceda, J.: Making Norms Concrete. In: Proceedings of the 9th International Conference on Autonomous Agents and Multiagent Systems, pp. 807–814 (2010)
2. Deutch, M., Gerard, H.: A study of normative and informational social influence upon judgment. J. Abnorm. Soc. Psychol. **51**(3), 629–636 (1955)
3. Dung, P., Sartor, G.: The modular logic of private international law. Artif. Intell. Law **19**(2–3), 233–261 (2011)
4. da Silva Figueiredo, K., Torres da Silva, V., de Oliveira Braga, C.: Modeling norms in multi-agent systems with NormML. In: De Vos, M., Fornara, N., Pitt, J.V., Vouros, G. (eds.) COIN 2010. LNCS, vol. 6541, pp. 39–57. Springer, Heidelberg (2011)
5. Fitting, M.: First-Order Logic and Automated Theorem Proving. Springer, New York (1990)
6. Gaertner, D., Garcia-Camino, A., Noriega, P., Vasconcelos, W.: Distributed norm management in regulated multi-agent systems. In: 6th International Conference on Autonomous Agents and Multiagent Systems, pp. 624–631. ACM, Hawaii (2007)
7. García-Camino, A., Noriega, P., Rodríguez-Aguilar, J.-A.: An algorithm for conflict resolution in regulated compound activities. In: O'Hare, G.M., Ricci, A., O'Grady, M.J., Dikenelli, O. (eds.) ESAW 2006. LNCS (LNAI), vol. 4457, pp. 193–208. Springer, Heidelberg (2007)
8. Governatori, G.: Legal Contractions: A logical analysis. In: Proceedings of the 14th International Conference on Artificial Intelligence and Law, pp. 63–72 (2013)
9. Kollingbaum, M.J., Vasconcelos, W.W., García-Camino, A., Norman, T.J.: Managing conflict resolution in norm-regulated environments. In: Artikis, A., O'Hare, G.M., Stathis, K., Vouros, G.A. (eds.) ESAW 2007. LNCS (LNAI), vol. 4995, pp. 55–71. Springer, Heidelberg (2008)
10. Kollingbaum, M.J., Vasconcelos, W.W., García-Camino, A., Norman, T.J.: Conflict resolution in norm-regulated environments via unification and constraints. In: Baldoni, M., Son, T.C., van Riemsdijk, M., Winikoff, M. (eds.) DALT 2007. LNCS (LNAI), vol. 4897, pp. 158–174. Springer, Heidelberg (2008)
11. Li, T., Balke, T., De Vos, M., Satoh, K., Padget, J.: Detecting conflicts in legal systems. In: Motomura, Y., Butler, A., Bekki, D. (eds.) JSAI-isAI 2012. LNCS, vol. 7856, pp. 174–189. Springer, Heidelberg (2013)
12. Li, T., Balke, T., De Vos, M., Padget, J., Satoh, K.: Legal conflict detection in interacting legal systems. In: The 26th International Conference on Legal Knowledge and Information Systems (JURIX) (2013)
13. Oren, N., Luck, M., Miles, S., Norman, T.: An argumentation inspired heuristic for resolving normative conflict. In Proceedings of the International Workshop on Coordination, Organisations, Institutions and Norms in Agent Systems (COIN@AAMAS 2008) (2008)
14. Vasconcelos, W., Kollingbaum, M., García-camino, A., Norman, T.: Achieving conflict freedom in norm-based societies. In: Workshop on Coordination, Organizations, Institutions, and Norms in Agent Systems (2007)

15. Vasconcelos, W., Kollingbaum, M., Norman, T.: Resolving conflict and inconsistency in norm regulated virtual organizations. In: 6th International Joint Conference on Autonomous Agents and MultiAgent Systems, ACM (2007)
16. Vasconcelos, W., Kollingbaum, M., Norman, T.: Normative conflict resolution in multi-agent systems. Auton. Agent. Multi-Agent Syst. **19**(2), 124–152 (2009). ACM
17. Vasconcelos, W., Norman, T.: Contract formation through preemptive normative conflict resolution. In: 12th International Conference of the Catalan Association for Artificial Intelligence, pp. 179–188. IOS Press (2009)

Norm Aware Agents

A Value-Centric Model to Ground Norms and Requirements for ePartners of Children

Alex Kayal[1]([✉]), Willem-Paul Brinkman[1], Rianne Gouman[2],
Mark A. Neerincx[1], and M. Birna van Riemsdijk[1]

[1] Interactive Intelligence Group, Delft University of Technology,
Delft, The Netherlands
{a.kayal,w.p.brinkman,m.a.neerincx,m.b.vanriemsdijk}@tudelft.nl
[2] Thales Netherlands, Hengelo, The Netherlands
rianne.gouman@d-cis.nl

Abstract. Children as they grow up start to discover their neighborhood and surrounding areas and get increasingly involved in social interaction. We aim to support this process through a system of so-called electronic partners (ePartners) that function as teammates to their users. These ePartners should adapt their behavior to norms that govern the social contexts (e.g., the family or school) in which they are functioning. We argue that the envisaged normative framework for ePartners for children should be based on an understanding of the target domain that is grounded in user studies. It is the aim of this paper to provide such understanding, in particular answering the following questions: *(1) what are the main elements that make up the social context of the target domain (family life), and how are they related?*, and *(2) what are the relationships between these elements of the social context and the normative framework in which we envision the ePartners to operate?* To answer these questions we conducted focus groups sessions and a cultural probe study with parents and children. The transcripts from these sessions were analyzed using grounded theory, which has resulted in a grounded model that shows that (1) activities, concerns, and limitations related to family life are the main elements of the social context of this user group, and that all three elements are connected through the central concept of user *values*, and (2) norms can support these values by promoting activities, alleviating concerns and overcoming limitations. In this way the model provides the foundation for developing a normative framework to govern the behavior of ePartners for children, identifying user values as the starting point.

1 Introduction

Children as they grow up start to discover their neighborhood and surrounding areas (and more so unsupervised the older they are), and get increasingly involved in social interaction (e.g. at school or sports clubs). It is our aim to

This publication was supported by the national Dutch program COMMIT.

T. Balke et al. (Eds.): COIN 2013, LNAI 8386, pp. 329–345, 2014.
DOI: 10.1007/978-3-319-07314-9_18, © Springer International Publishing Switzerland 2014

support this process with intelligent technology to enable children to feel more socially connected, safe, and secure. We call this *socio-geographical support*. Such support can for example concern a child's safety as he/she is learning to explore its surroundings or learning to cycle to school, as well as the organization of children events in the community, birthday parties, and assistance in arranging play dates. We focus on *elementary school children* (between 6 and 12 years old) as our target group, as well as important people in their social environment such as their parents and teachers. We choose this target group as this is the age where they begin to explore their social and geographical environment on their own.

Our proposed solution for providing socio-geographical support is to create a system of so-called *electronic partners* (ePartners), that function as teammates to their human users as they navigate through their socio-geographical environment. ePartners in this setting may take the form of an application on a smartphone or another hand-held device. ePartners have already been investigated in various domains, e.g., within control systems [3], robots [18], and applications that promote positive lifestyle changes [17].

Existing work on ePartners focuses on the bilateral relation between a single human and his/her ePartner. We propose that for our target domain it is also important to take into account the *social context* in which ePartners are functioning to enable them to adapt their support accordingly. For example, if a family normally allows a child to wander around the neighbourhood alone, the ePartner of the child might only notify the parents in case the child has left the area considered familiar or secure. On the other hand, if a family lives in an unsafe area they might not allow the child to do this, in which case the ePartner of the child could send a warning to the parents if the distance between child and parents has crossed a certain limit. We propose to model these different requirements for the behavior of the ePartner as *norms* [2] that govern the respective social contexts. New norms may arise at run-time due to changing circumstances and social contexts. The idea is that the ePartner will be able to adapt its behavior accordingly to provide tailored support.

It is our view that development of interactive, human-centred automation such as ePartners for socio-geographical support should be built on empirical research to ensure that the provided support aligns with the context of use (see also [13,26]). Thus we argue that the development of the ePartner for socio-geographical support and the normative framework on which it is based should be *grounded in user studies* that provide an understanding of the target domain and the ePartner's supportive role in it in a systematic way. To achieve such understanding, in this paper we answer the following questions: *(1) what are the main elements that make up the social context of the target domain (family life) in relation to socio-geographical support, and how are they related?*, and *(2) what are the relationships between these elements of the social context and the normative framework in which we envision the ePartners to operate?* We aim for a grounded model that concisely describes these elements and their relations. This model is the main scientific contribution of this paper, and is anticipated to help guide future development of normative models suited for specifying behavioral requirements of an ePartner for socio-geographical support within a family life context.

To answer our research questions we applied a situated cognitive engineering methodology [25] (described in Sect. 3). In particular, we conducted focus group sessions [22] and a cultural probe study [15] with parents and children (Sect. 4). Transcripts from these sessions were analyzed using grounded theory [31] (Sect. 5). The resulting grounded model (Sect. 6) identifies the main elements and their relations in the social context of family life concerning socio-geographical support, and it shows how these are related to norms for the ePartner. In this way our model provides the foundation for developing a normative framework to govern the behavior of ePartners for children. We discuss related work that forms the background of our research in Sect. 2 and conclude the paper in Sect. 7. To the best of our knowledge, this is the first time that situated cognitive engineering has been used in normative systems research.

2 Background

In this section we give more background on important elements of our research, namely ePartners (Sect. 2.1) and normative and organisational frameworks (Sect. 2.2).

2.1 ePartners

ePartners are defined as computerized entities that partner with a human (development of a relationship) and share tasks, activities, and experiences [10]. In that sense, as automation becomes sophisticated, ePartners will function less like tools and more like teammates [7]. They follow a paradigm shift from automation extending human capabilities to automation partnering with a human [10]. Examples of ePartners can be seen in various domains: critical domains such as space missions [34], naval command and control [3], and virtual reality exposure therapy (VRET) [27], as well as other, less critical domains such as socio-cognitive robotics [18], and personal digital assistants [17,24].

The notion of ePartner fits very well with the role that we envisage intelligent technology to play in socio-geographical support, namely as an intelligent entity able to partner with people. ePartners can form individual agreements ("contracts") with their users and can take the initiative to act in specific situations. ePartners have not yet been investigated in the context of socio-geographical support nor with the emphasis on the social role that they are playing and the ensuing need for adaptation to norms in their social contexts.

2.2 Normative and Organizational Frameworks

In recent years, an increasing amount of research has proposed to assign an organization or a set of norms to a multi-agent system (MAS) with the aim of organizing and regulating it (see, e.g., [11,21,32,35,36] and the overview in [2]), similar to the way social norms and conventions organize and regulate people's behavior in society [36]. This should make agents more effective in attaining their purpose, or prevent undesired behavior from occurring. Organizational frameworks often incorporate norms as an element of the specification of an organization (see [11,20]). Research in this area has yielded a wide range of frameworks and languages for expressing organizations and norms.

We aim to build on this work by using norms to allow people to define requirements of social contexts in which ePartners should function. To ensure that the normative framework allows to express those aspects that are important for people in the context of socio-geographical support of children, we perform user studies to obtain an understanding of this social context and the role that norms could play in governing the ePartner's functioning.

The use of normative systems as the basis for supporting collaboration between humans and artificial teammates has been investigated only to a limited extent. KAoS [32], which is a framework that allows to specify policies for human-agent/robot teamwork, takes steps in this direction. To the best of our knowledge, the requirements for their policy framework are however not elicited based on user studies to understand the context in which these agents or robots should function, but rather on a general analysis of aspects of human-agent teamwork. The work in [1] proposes that software adaptation be achieved through allowing users to modify the system at runtime through feedback, though the work does not propose the use of norms.

3   Methodology

In this section we describe the methodology we are using to develop ePartners as socially supportive applications that understand and adapt to user's social contexts. In Sect. 3.1 we introduce *situated Cognitive Engineering* (sCE), the general framework we will use for development, and in Sect. 3.2, we describe the methods we used for data collection and analysis within the sCE framework.

3.1   Situated Cognitive Engineering

As a principle stance in the development of ePartner that can adapt to its social context, we reject the notion of a generic, context independent normative model, suitable for any social context. Instead we argue for the need of normative models specifically tailored for their social context, in our case family life. Situational dependency is also core to the situated cognition theory [8] which posits that cognition can not be separated from its context. Therefore, this study uses *situated Cognitive Engineering* (sCE) as the general framework for development [25]. sCE describes an iterative process based on *Cognitive Engineering* (CE) approaches [19] whereby practical theories and methods are developed that are *situated* in the domain. Using a situated approach allows for better addressing of the human factors (i.e. human characteristics that influence their behavior in a certain environment), which in turn leads to a better human-machine collaboration design. sCE is composed of three main phases:

1. *Foundation:* understanding the domain, human factors, and technology involved;
2. *Specification:* the specification of the requirements and the corresponding use cases (the steps that define the interaction between a user and a system) and claims (what the developer proposes the system to be capable of doing);
3. *Evaluation:* validating these claims through development of a prototype application that is tested in the field.

We use this methodology for the development of ePartners for socio-geographical support by instantiating the three phases in the following way (Fig. 1):

1. *Foundation:* understanding our users' social context;
2. *Specification:* developing an expressive normative framework tailored to the target domain of socio-geographical support, to allow users to communicate their social requirements to the ePartner;
3. *Evaluation:* creation of a prototype ePartner for socio-geographical support according to the specification and iteratively evaluating it in the field.

In this paper we address the first phase (understanding social context). That is, we leave development of a normative framework and a prototype application for future work.

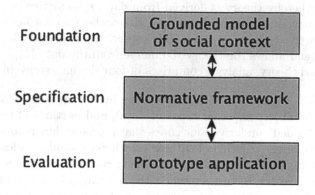

Fig. 1. The three phases of sCE and how they align with the phases of our research

3.2   Research Methods

As explained in the previous subsection, we aim in the first phase to get an understanding of the important elements in the social contexts in which the ePartner will function. Therefore we need to collect data that describes the attributes, properties, and characteristics of the content of these social contexts. That type of *descriptive* data is usually obtained using *qualitative* methods (as opposed to quantitative methods, that start with a pre-assumed concept or model of a phenomena, and set out to collect specific, often quantified data to study this concept or model).

Two established types of user studies can be used to collect such descriptive data from the target environment: the first type is *cultural probing* (CP), a methodology initiated by Gaver [15]. It consists of providing users with packages of postcards, maps, disposable cameras, post-it notes, and other material for them to use to record spontaneous data related to their lives. No explicit usage instructions on exactly how to use the material are provided. Users collect data over a period of several days or weeks (for examples on works involving cultural probes, see [5,6,29]). The aim of CP is not to reach a comprehensive view of the user's requirements, but rather to use the collected material to inspire design. The second type of user studies we have used is *focus groups*, which can be defined as "carefully planned series of discussions designed to obtain perceptions on a defined area of interest in a permissive, non-threatening environment" [22]. In a setting like focus groups, a small group (usually 5–10 participants) is gathered in one place, and then a discussion session is led by a moderator. The moderator proceeds to ask open ended questions, stimulating conversations between the participants relating to the subject of research.

We aim to obtain an understanding of the elements of the social context and the relationships among these elements, building a theoretical model on top of the collected data, or "grounded" in the data. This motivated the choice of *grounded theory* as our data analysis method: grounded theory is a bottom-up approach whereby theory is derived from data, systematically gathered and analyzed throughout the research process. Researchers do not begin the project with a preconceived theory in mind, but rather, the researcher begins with an area of study and allows the theory to emerge from the data [31].

In grounded theory, analysis comprises of four distinct steps [9]:

1. *Open coding*[1] where data is examined line by line in case of pieces of text (or object by object for other types of data), and portions of text and other media are "coded" under various codes that represent key points in the data.
2. *Axial coding* or the creation of categories, whereby similar codes are grouped together to highlight the presence (or emergence) of a theme or a concept.
3. *Selective coding* (or to further refine the existing set of codes), to identify themes central to the research questions and aims, and several iterations of coding and re-coding of the data may take place until a satisfactory level is reached.
4. *Theory building* or the discussion and linking of emergent themes, and visual portrayal of connections that build up themes into a theoretical model.

In future work we will use the model that results from step 4 to identify requirements for a normative framework to support ePartner functioning in

---

[1] Here, codes bear the meaning closer to tags in modern social applications. To code a piece of text is to tag it with a number of words or short phrases that relate to the content of that piece.

socio-geographical support (sCE's specification phase), which we will in turn use to build a first prototype (sCE's evaluation phase).

Grounded theory, as any qualitative analysis methods, is inherent subjective in nature and therefore vulnerable to validity threats such as researcher bias, interpretation bias, or respondent bias. This study therefore followed two strategies as proposed in the grounded theory literature [31] to minimize these intrusions. The first strategy applied was comparative thinking, i.e. comparing findings with reports in the literature, and with other data sets. In this study, we therefore collected data through both focus groups and cultural probes, noting the presence of similar themes in the analysis of both sets. Secondly, we applied a re-evaluation strategy [23], whereby an independent researcher was invited to re-evaluate the analysis of samples of the text, in order to investigate the degree of understandability, correctness, and completeness of the coding schema (details in Sect. 5.2).

4   User Studies

In this section we describe the user studies that we have performed to get an understanding of the contexts in which ePartners for socio-geographical support are expected to function.

We have conducted three focus group sessions and one cultural probe study to investigate user requirements. The participants in these studies were parents and (some of) their children in a town of approximately 30,000 inhabitants, located in the South-West of The Netherlands. Through a small 'snowball sample' [4] we requested a group of 6 parents and another group of 6 children to participate in the studies. "In snowball sampling you locate one or more key individuals and ask them to name others who would be likely candidates for your research" [4]. Our snowball sample started with a contact who participates in the school board, a youth centre and in a website for the local community.

The first focus group session included the six parents only. We introduced to them our project, research, and explained the aim of our user studies. To stimulate discussion, we displayed a few ePartner usage scenarios (created beforehand) and design claims (i.e. claims about a few positive and negative effects of the ePartner features within our scenarios) then asked the participants (individually) to rate to what extent they agree with our claims. After a short general discussion, we provided the parents with cultural probing kits (each kit contains a map, an instant camera, post it notes, post cards, pens, and some glue). The session ended with a brief explanation on the typical usage of the kit material.

The second session (three weeks later) included the same group as the first session. The parents brought back the material they (along with their children) collected during that period, and then proceeded (individually) to describe the data (e.g., pictures, map highlights, etc.) they collected with their kits. This process stimulated the discussion for a further 45 min in which many of the parents' and their children's life issues, values, and concerns were raised.

The third session included the six children only. The ages of the children ranged between six and eight years old. That session was led by an experienced elementary school teacher, and consisted of a discussion where the teacher asked the children a number of open ended questions related to their knowledge and usage of current technology, what activities they are allowed to do, how they connect with other children at school, sport clubs, and other places. All sessions were audio-taped.

5   Data Analysis and Evaluation

We transcribed the audio recordings from all three focus group sessions and imported these transcriptions and the scanned probe kit material into QSR NVivo[2] to perform qualitative analysis.

First, thorough reading of the transcriptions allowed us to derive the preliminary coding schema from the data material. In the second round of analysis, each passage of text was annotated with the appropriate codes, and the relevant codes were grouped together which resulted in a tree of codes. Afterwards, the tree of codes was further refined (e.g., codes with similar or close meaning were merged, codes under the same topic were grouped, infrequent codes were removed, etc.). Coding was then re-done according to the new tree, and portions of it were rated by another researcher.

5.1   Tree of Codes

In this section we describe the tree of codes that has resulted from our data analysis.

The tree can be seen in Fig. 2. The leaves of the tree represent the set of codes used in the analysis to mark relevant pieces of text in the transcriptions. Groups of codes represents the main "themes" or "elements" of the social context within our user group that we have identified in the data, created through grouping together codes that are similar or related. Two groups (limitations and concerns) were split into sub-groups (in italic) for further clarification.

Second level nodes represent groupings of codes that together represent a theme within the participants' social context. *Activities* includes codes relevant to activities participants engage in, such as playing with friends, church, or sports. *Concerns* represent issues raised by parents (and children) that are present in their current life or are a cause for a certain worry, such as "contact with strangers" and "misuse" of technology. *Limitations* covers a rather broad theme that consists of both *imposed* (overprotection, privacy) or *natural* (spatial, age) issues that present a specific barrier towards the performance of an action (whether related to technology or not). *Perceptions* include mental models formed by an individual or a group (parents or children) of their understanding of certain concepts such as technology or social media, and *use-cases/ideas* represent suggestions that were given directly by focus group participants about ePartner features they believe to be be useful.

---

[2] http://www.qsrinternational.com/products_nvivo.aspx

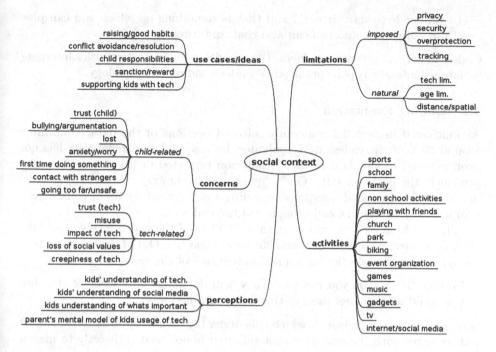

Fig. 2. Final tree of codes

To explain in more detail, a few passages and their related codes taken from the data are shown below[3]:

– A: I think safety and security is important, also for the family, how do you handle this? If they can hack such an "ePartner" system, they will know everything about your child: Where they go, where they play their sports, how the routes are, and that's a lot of data. When I drew these data for the probe kit, I realized: You now know how my kid goes to the football field. Security is extremely important.

Coded under (a) limitations:imposed:security, (b) limitations:imposed:privacy, and (c) activities:internet/social media.

– B: You know everything about it, and I don't feel like it, to be on something like Facebook, but I am forced to do this to follow the developments.
– C: We were wondering this week, do we have to make a Facebook account for ourselves to be prepared for when cC wants to have such an account?

Coded under (a) concerns:anxiety/worry, (b) concerns:trust:(child), (c) activities: internet/social-media, and (d) perceptions:parents' mental model of kids understanding of technology.

---

[3] Names of participants are anonymized. Adults are referred to with one capital letter (for example, A or B), and children are referred to with a small c before one capital letter (for example, cA means the child of adult participant A).

– cC: (about her smartphone)... and that is something on which you can play all sorts of games, and you can also chat and listen to music.

Coded under (a) activities:gadgets, (b) activities:music, (c) activities:internet/ social media, and (d) perceptions:kids' understanding of technology.

5.2   Coding Evaluation

As motivated in Sect. 3.2, randomly selected portions of the data (containing around 20 % of the codes) were evaluated by a second researcher who has not been exposed to the data before. Evaluation consisted of (a) rating the codes present in the passages with "OK", "questionable" or "reject", and (b) answering a set of open-ended questions regarding the terminology used, consistency, completeness, placement and grouping of the codes.

The result of part (a) was that roughly 60 % of the codes received an OK, 20 % were rated as questionable and 20 % were rejected. Out of the rejected 20 %, we agree with the rejection in approximately half of the cases, for example:

– Coding "D: Maybe you can say: They will do things on Facebook etc., but you could let them get used to this in a controlled way",

was classified under "misuse" (which falls under the theme concerns:tech-related), but we agree with the evaluator that this text is not related directly to misuse of technology. For these cases we have adapted our codings.

We disagree with the rejection in the rest of the cases, for example:

– Coding "So, where do you have to interfere? Maybe, do you have to give children their own responsibility not to do these kind of things?"

was coded under "overprotection" (which falls under the theme limitations: imposed), because the idea of overprotection is being discussed, especially considering the overall context of that part of the discussion.

The answers to the questions in part (b) were:

– The current coding schema represents the data fairly well.
– Adding codes such as "future plans" and "playing outside" was suggested, seen to be useful in the third session with the children in specific.
– A few changes to current codes were suggested, for example splitting "bullying/argumentation" into two separate codes, changing "trust (ePartner)" into the more specific "trust (social media)", and renaming "distance/spatial limitations" to become more specific.
– No changes were suggested for the grouping (themes) of the codes.

These suggestions were taken into account to the extent that they had implications for the final tree, though not strong enough to produce prominent changes to the hierarchy and placement of codes within the tree. This suggests that the tree of codes resulting from the analysis has a good level of comprehensibility. Analyzing the evaluation as well as applying many of the suggested modifications to the codes and the tree contributed to a joint-view tree of codes in the final form.

6   Grounded Model

With no more refining of the themes and codes in the tree to be done, the fourth and last step in grounded theory is theory building (the discussion and linking of emergent themes, and visual portrayal of connections that build up themes into a theoretical model, as discussed in Sect. 3.2).

6.1   Values as a Central Element

We queried the data material with various combinations of codes within the different themes in the tree of codes, especially codes with a high density in the text. We found that many of the passages of text that were returned as a result of queries of this type were statements from parents and children regarding certain elements that they believe to be "good" or "bad", "preferred to" or "not preferred to" a certain familial or societal issue they encounter.

Before we elaborate further on the possible significance of these types of statements, we need to briefly introduce the notion of "values" as discussed in across various academic domains. According to Cambridge Dictionary, a value is defined as "the importance or worth of something to someone".

Schroeder [30] shows that values can be represented as phrases containing a subject matter, and a claim of "good/better/best" or "bad/worse/worst", relating the subject matter to someone or something, or in general. Examples of that can be "too much cholesterol is bad for your health", "my new can opener is better than my old one" and "pleasure is good". Though the word "value" in itself seldom appears in a sentence of this form, the existence of the varieties of "good" and "bad" in the sentence signify how the value of the subject matter is seen. In his 1973 book [28], social-psychologist Milton Rokeach published a list of values (based on a survey he conducted) that has become popular and widely used. The list included 18 terminal values (end results, or what one seek to accomplish such as happiness, freedom, and a comfortable life) and 18 instrumental values (ways of seeking and accomplishing terminal values, such as ambition, self-control and honesty).

The statements of the the "good/bad" and "preferred to/not preferred to" form, which were returned as results of the queries discussed earlier, may then provide clues to the values of the person providing such statements. Often, the values they refer to align with some of the values in Rokeach's value survey.

To illustrate, querying the data for passages containing both the tree codes of "internet/social media" and "safety", would return several results, one of which is:

– "E: Often I get why-questions from children, and on the Internet you can get really strange things if you Google some words. Can you have a child-friendly Internet, that is safe and enclosed?"

Transforming this passage into the "good/bad" form returns the following value statement:

– "It is good to protect your children from the Internet's unsafe side".

Within Rokeach's value survey, we can arguably link the previous sentence to the value of "family security".

– "C: cC would really be happy if she could see that her best friend is available to play, but then I think they can already phone each other, but such a feature would be nice for children: to see each other's availability".

Transforming this passage into the "good/bad" form returns the following value statement:

– "It's good if children are able to use technology for coordinating their activities".

Within Rokeach's value survey, we may link the previous sentence to the values of "independence" and "social recognition".

We found that several of values in Rokeach's survey are important for this type of user groups, including family security, independence, inner harmony, true friendship and social recognition.

6.2   Relationship Between Social Context and Values

Highlighting values as a central concept in the user data brought forth the idea for a unifying link that can be established among three of the five themes in the social context through the values of our user group: Activities are driven by their values, concerns pose a threat to their values, and limitations obstruct fulfillment of their values (or in the case of imposed limitations, pose a threat to their values). This relationship is depicted in Fig. 3.

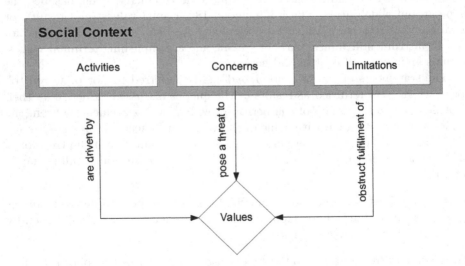

Fig. 3. Relationship between social context and values

6.3   Relationship Between Values and Norms

The second question we posed in the introduction highlighted the need to understand the relationship between the normative framework in which we envision the ePartner to operate, and the elements of the social context. Having seen how the elements of the social context are interconnected through user values, we proceeded by investigating the relationship between these values and norms. This relationship has been established in literature. For example, in [16] it is investigated to what extent norms (obligations, permissions, and prohibitions) can be expressed in terms of value predicates (good, bad, better, etc.). In [12], a method is proposed to identify conflicts between the values of an agent, and the norms to which it subscribes. In [33] norms represent the middle layer in a 3-layer hierarchy (Fig. 4) which shows how design requirements can be elicited from values. Social norms (as an intermediary step in this model), can thus be derived from (or to be more specific, created to support) values.

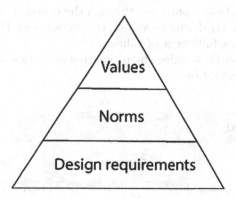

Fig. 4. A model that shows how to move from values to design requirements [33]

Based on the previous literature examples, we propose that norms that influence the behavior of an ePartner can be created to support the values of our user group. Consider our last example of a sentence expressing a value:

– "It is good to protect your children from the Internet's unsafe side".

This means that the user believes a specific concern (misuse of technology) poses a threat to one of their values (family security).
We identify ePartner norms can support this value, for example:

– ePartner is obliged to block websites that are considered unsafe, or
– ePartner is obliged to inform parent if child is accessing unsafe websites.

By adhering to either of these norms, the ePartner alleviates this instance of the concern "misuse of technology", thereby averting its possible threat to the value "family security".

To generalize from that example, the elements of the social context (activities, concerns, limitations) affect user values positively or negatively, and though adhering to norms, ePartners can enforce a positive effect or diminish a negative one.

6.4 Relationship Between Social Context, Values, and Norms

We have seen how the elements of the social context are related to the values of our user group, and that ePartner norms can be created to support these values. We can now "close the loop" and see how norms for the ePartner can support the elements of that social context. The resulting grounded model (Fig. 5) shows the relationship between social context, values, and norms, answering the two research questions that we posed in the introduction (Sect. 1):

1. *Activities* that families engage in, *concerns* about and *limitations* on family life form the main elements of the social context of this user group, and these three elements are connected through the central concept of user *values* (namely, activities are driven by values, concerns pose a threat to values, and limitations obstruct fulfilment of values).
2. *Norms* can support these values by promoting activities, alleviating concerns and overcoming limitations.

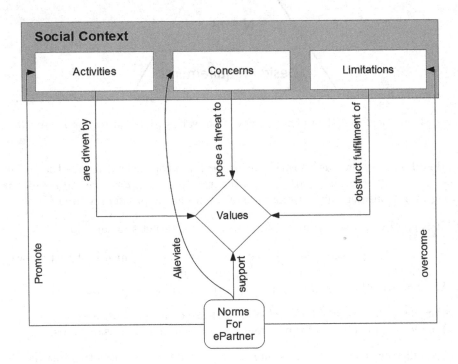

Fig. 5. A grounded model that shows the relationship between social context, values, and norms.

In this way the model provides the foundation for developing a normative framework to govern the behavior of ePartners for children. It shows that to develop a normative framework for ePartners for socio-geographic support, user values should form the starting point. It also provides guidance on the type of prototype application and corresponding norms to be developed in the next phases of sCE, since these should be aimed at promoting activities, alleviating concerns and overcoming limitations.

7   Conclusion and Discussion

Our contribution in this paper is a grounded model that shows the main elements of the social context of this user group, namely the (1) activities, concerns, and limitations related to family life, and that these three elements are connected through the central concept of user *values*, and that (2) norms can support these values. In this way the model provides the foundation for developing a normative framework to govern the behavior of ePartners for children, identifying user values as the starting point.

The model we presented is grounded, meaning that it was constructed on the basis of user studies and corresponding data analysis, and it provides a coherent and concise specification. We believe that taking users into account is crucial for developing this type of interactive technology, and having done so in this paper, the ePartner's support taken from this model onwards will align with this target group's context of use. This paper also forms an example of how one can use empirical methods as the basis for developing a normative framework.

In future research, we will continue with the next phase of the sCE framework, building on the findings we presented in this model. Relevant research at this stage is Value-Sensitive Design (VSD) [14], which is an approach that seeks to design technology that accounts for human values in a principled and comprehensive manner, and investigate how values are supported or diminished by particular technological designs.

Following the development of a normative framework for socio-geographic support we will create and evaluate a first prototype on top of a mobile phone sensing platform. The prototype should allow users to express express their requirements on ePartners' behavior, supported by a normative specification language. We will evaluate the prototype through user studies situated in the environment of the target group.

References

1. Ali, R., Solís, C., Omoronyia, I., Salehie, M., Nuseibeh, B.: Social adaptation - when software gives users a voice. In: ENASE, pp. 75–84 (2012)
2. Andrighetto, G., Governatori, G., Noriega, P., van der Torre, L. (eds.): Normative Multi-Agent Systems. Dagstuhl Follow-Ups, vol. 4. Schloss Dagstuhl–Leibniz-Zentrum für Informatik, Wadern (2013)

3. Arciszewski, H.F.R., de Greef, T.E., van Delft, J.H.: Adaptive automation in a naval combat management system. IEEE Trans. Syst. Man Cybern. A Syst. Humans **39**(6), 1188–1199 (2009)
4. Russell Bernard, H.: Research Methods in Anthropology. Qualitative and Quantitative Approaches. AltaMira Press, Walnut Creek (1995)
5. Bernhaupt, R., Obrist, M., Weiss, A., Beck, E., Tscheligi, M.: Trends in the living room and beyond: results from ethnographic studies using creative and playful probing. Comput. Entertain. **6**(1), 5:1–5:23 (2008)
6. Bernhaupt, R., Weiss, A., Obrist, M., Tscheligi, M.: Playful probing: making probing more fun. In: Baranauskas, C., Abascal, J., Barbosa, S.D.J. (eds.) INTERACT 2007. LNCS, vol. 4662, pp. 606–619. Springer, Heidelberg (2007)
7. Breazeal, C., Gray, J., Hoffman, G., Berlin, M.: Social robots: beyond tools to partners. In: 13th IEEE International Workshop on Robot and Human Interactive Communication, 2004. ROMAN 2004, pp. 551–556, Sept 2004
8. Brown, J.S., Collins, A., Duguid, P., Bolt Beranek and Newman, Inc., Cambridge, MA, University of Illinois at Urbana-Champaign, Center for the Study of Reading.: Situated cognition and the culture of learning. Report (Institute for Research on Learning), University of Illinois at Urbana-Champaign (1989)
9. Creswell, J.W.: Qualitative Inquiry and Research Design: Choosing Among Five Traditions, 1st edn. Sage Publications, London (1998)
10. de Greef, T.E.: ePartners for dynamic task allocation and coordination. Ph.D. Thesis, Delft University of Technology (2012)
11. Dignum, V.: A model for organizational interaction: based on agents, founded in logic. Ph.D. Thesis, Universiteit Utrecht (2004)
12. Figueiredo, K., Silva, V.: An algorithm to identify conflicts between norms and values. In: Balke, T., Dignum, F., van Riemsdijk, M.B., Chopra, A.K. (eds.) COIN 2013. LNCS (LNAI), vol. 8386, pp. 259–274. Springer, Heidelberg (2014)
13. Fogli, D., Guida, G.: Knowledge-centered design of decision support systems for emergency management. Decis. Support Syst. **55**(1), 336–347 (2013)
14. Friedman, B., Kahn Jr, P.H.: Human values, ethics, and design. In: Jacko, J., Sears, A. (eds.) The Human-Computer Interaction Handbook, pp. 1177–1201. L. Erlbaum Associates Inc., Hillsdale (2003)
15. Gaver, B., Dunne, T., Pacenti, E.: Design: cultural probes. Interactions **6**(1), 21–29 (1999)
16. Hansson, S.O.: Norms and values. Crítica **23**(67), 3–13 (1991)
17. Blanson Henkemans, O.A., van der Boog, P.J.M., Lindenberg, J., van der Mast, C.A.P.G., Neerincx, M.A., Zwetsloot-Schonk, B.J.H.M.: An online lifestyle diary with a persuasive computer assistant providing feedback on self-management. Technol. Health Care **17**, 253–257 (2009)
18. Hindriks, K., Neerincx, M.A., Vink, M.: The iCat as a natural interaction partner - playing go fish with a robot. In: Dechesne, F., Hattori, H., ter Mors, A., Such, J.M., Weyns, D., Dignum, F. (eds.) AAMAS 2011 Workshops. LNCS, vol. 7068, pp. 212–231. Springer, Heidelberg (2012)
19. Hollnagel, E., Woods, D.D.: Cognitive systems engineering: new wine in new bottles. Int. J. Man-Mach. Stud. **18**(6), 583–600 (1983)
20. Hübner, J.F., Boissier, O., Bordini, R.H.: From organisation specification to normative programming in multi-agent organisations. In: Dix, J., Leite, J., Governatori, G., Jamroga, W. (eds.) CLIMA XI. LNCS, vol. 6245, pp. 117–134. Springer, Heidelberg (2010)

21. Hübner, J.F., Sichman, J.S., Boissier, O.: Developing organised multi-agent systems using the MOISE+ model: programming issues at the system and agent levels. Int. J. Agent-Oriented Softw. Eng. 1, 370–395 (2007)
22. Kreuger, R.A., Casey, M.A.: Focus Groups: A Practical Guide for Applied Research, 4th edn. Pine Forge Press, Newbury Park (2008)
23. MacQueen, K., McLellan-Lemal, E., Bartholow, K., Milstein, B.: Team-based codebook development: structure, process, and agreement. In: Guest, G., MacQueen, K. (eds.) Handbook for Team-Based Qualitative Research. AltaMira, Lanham (2012)
24. Myers, K., Yorke-Smith, N.: A cognitive framework for delegation to an assistive user agent. In: Proceedings of AAAI 2005 Fall Symposium on Mixed-Initiative Problem Solving Assistants, pp. 94–99, Arlington, VA. AAAI Press, Nov 2005
25. Neerincx, M.A., Lindenberg, J.: Situated cognitive engineering for complex task environments. In: Schraagen, J.M.C., Militello, L., Ormerod, T., Lipshitz, R. (eds.) Naturalistic Decision Making and Macrocognition, pp. 373–390. Ashgate, Aldershot (2008)
26. Norman, D.A., Draper, S.W.: User Centered System Design: New Perspectives on Human-Computer Interaction. L. Erlbaum Associates Inc., Hillsdale (1986)
27. Paping, C., Brinkman, W.P., van der Mast, C.: An Explorative Study into a Tele-delivered Multi-patient Virtual Reality Exposure Therapy System, pp. 203–219. IOS press, Amsterdam (2010)
28. Rokeach, M.: The Nature of Human Values. The Free Press, New York (1973)
29. Schmehl, S., Deutsch, S., Schrammel, J., Paletta, L., Tscheligi, M.: Directed cultural probes: detecting barriers in the usage of public transportation. In: Campos, P., Graham, N., Jorge, J., Nunes, N., Palanque, P., Winckler, M. (eds.) INTERACT 2011, Part I. LNCS, vol. 6946, pp. 404–411. Springer, Heidelberg (2011)
30. Schroeder, M.: Value theory. In: Zalta, E.N. (ed.) The Stanford Encyclopedia of Philosophy, Summer 2012 edition, 2012th edn. CSLI, Stanford (2012)
31. Strauss, A.L., Corbin, J.M.: Basics of Qualitative Research: Techniques and Procedures for developing Grounded Theory. Sage Publications, Newbury Park (1998)
32. Uszok, A., Bradshaw, J.M., Jeffers, R.: KAoS: a policy and domain services framework for grid computing and semantic web services. In: Jensen, Ch., Poslad, S., Dimitrakos, T. (eds.) iTrust 2004. LNCS, vol. 2995, pp. 16–26. Springer, Heidelberg (2004)
33. van de Poel, I.: Translating Values Into Design Requirements. Springer, Dordrecht (forthcoming)
34. van Diggelen, J., Neerincx, M.A.: Electronic partners that diagnose and guide and mediate space crew's social and cognitive and affective processes. In: Proceedings of Measuring Behaviour 2010, pp. 73–76. Noldus Information Technology bv, Wageningen, The Netherlands (2010)
35. Vázquez-Salceda, J., Dignum, F.P.M.: Modelling electronic organizations. In: Mařík, V., Müller, J.P., Pěchouček, M. (eds.) CEEMAS 2003. LNCS (LNAI), vol. 2691, p. 584. Springer, Heidelberg (2003)
36. López, F.L.y., Luck, M., d'Inverno, M.: A normative framework for agent-based systems. Comput. Math. Organ. Theory 12(2–3), 227–250 (2006)

Towards the Norm-Aware Agent: Bridging the Gap Between Deontic Specifications and Practical Mechanisms for Norm Monitoring and Norm-Aware Planning

Sofia Panagiotidi$^{(\boxtimes)}$, Sergio Alvarez-Napagao, and Javier Vázquez-Salceda

Universitat Politècnica de Catalunya-BarcelonaTECH, Edifici Omega,
Despatx 206-207 C/ Jordi Girona Salgado 1-3, 08034 Barcelona, Spain
{panagiotidi,salvarez,jvazquez}@lsi.upc.edu

Abstract. In the agents' literature, norms have been studied from multiple perspectives, but while formalisations tend to be disconnected from possible implementations due to the lack of differentiation between abstract norm and norm instantiation, on the other hand implementations tend to be weak groundings of deontic logics, tightly coupled to one particular implementation domain. Furthermore, different formalisations are typically used for norm enforcement and norm reasoning. In this paper we report on our attempt to bridge this gap by reducing from deontic statements to structural operational semantics (for norm monitoring) and to planning control rules (for practical normative reasoning). We hint at the feasibility of the translation of these semantics to actual implementation languages (Clojure and Drools for norm monitoring and TLPlan for norm-aware planning). Finally we discuss the limitations of our approach and suggest some improvements and future lines of research.

Keywords: Deontic logics · Normative systems · Planning · Monitoring

1   Introduction

In literature the concept of *norms* has been defined from several perspectives [1]: as a rule or standard of behaviour shared by members of a social group, as an authoritative rule or standard by which something is judged, approved or disapproved, as standards of right and wrong, beauty and ugliness, and truth and falsehood, or even as a model of what should exist or be followed, or an average of what currently does exist in some context. Moreover, from the Artificial Intelligence community there has been a continuous effort on researching how to formalise norms from a logic perspective, on one hand, and how to make them feasibly computable, on the other hand.

In this work we will focus on the regulative aspects of sets of norms (that we will call normative specifications), seen as a way to model the governance of

T. Balke et al. (Eds.): COIN 2013, LNAI 8386, pp. 346–363, 2014.
DOI: 10.1007/978-3-319-07314-9_19, © Springer International Publishing Switzerland 2014

distributed, agent-oriented systems by explicitly specifying the agents' expected behaviour.

The main advantage of normative specifications over other governance mechanisms is that norms make explicit the (social) expectation about *what* is expected to happen, but not *how* the agents are supposed to bring it about. Therefore normative specifications allow the design of complex social setups while giving enough flexibility to give agents some level of autonomy to, e.g., react to unexpected states of the system.

In literature there is a lot of work on normative systems' formalisation (mainly focused in Deontic-like formalisms [2]) which is declarative in nature, focused on the expressiveness of the norms [3], the definition of formal semantics [4–7] and the verification of consistency of a given set [8,9]. There are some works that focus on norm compliance and norm monitoring [6,7,9–12] with varying degrees of covered abstraction level and allowed flexibility. Also there is some work on how agents might take norms into account when reasoning [5,13–16], but few practical implementations exist that cover the full BDI cycle, as many approaches do not include the *means-ends reasoning step* (that is, deciding *how* to achieve *what* the agent is aiming for). However, we have found no work in the literature that (1) formally connects the deontic aspects of norms with their operationalisation, (2) properly distinguishes between abstract norms and their (multiple) instantiations at run-time, (3) formalises the operational semantics in a way that ensures flexibility in their translation to actual implementations while ensuring unambiguous interpretations of the norms, and (4) covers both institutional-level norm monitoring and individual agent norm-aware reasoning to ensure that both are aligned.

In this paper, we present a proposal to bridge the gap between a single norm formalisation and the actual mechanisms used for both (rule-based) norm monitoring and norm-aware planning. Taking advantage of a recent trend in the Planning community to use Linear Temporal Logic (LTL) formulas as strong and soft constraints on plan trajectories (e.g., TLPlan [17] and PDDL 3.0 [18]), we have chosen LTL as a bridge from the norm specification to its implementation by reducing deontic-based norm definitions to temporal logic formulae which, in turn, can be translated into both rule-based and planning operational semantics.

The paper is organised as follows: Sect. 2 introduces the formalism of temporal logics to be used as basis in following sections. Section 3 focuses on the concepts of norm instance and norm lifecycle, and discusses how norm operationalisation is usually handled in literature. In Sect. 4 we focus on the semantics of norms and norm instances from the deontic statement level, while in Sect. 5 we focus on the operational semantics and how it can be used in practical implementations for monitoring and planning. Finally, in Sect. 6 we present some conclusions and future lines of work.

2   Linear Temporal Logic

LTL [19] is built up from a finite set of predicates $\mathscr{L}$, the logical operators $\neg$ and $\vee$ (logical operators $\wedge$, $\rightarrow$, $\leftrightarrow$, true, and false can be derived by the primitive ones), and the temporal modal operators $\mathbf{X}$ (next) and $\mathbf{U}$ (until). Formally, the set of LTL formulas over $\mathscr{L}$ is inductively defined as follows:

- if $p \in \mathscr{L}$ then p is a LTL formula;
- if ψ and ϕ are LTL formulas then $\neg\psi, \phi \vee \psi, \mathbf{X}\psi$ and $\phi\mathbf{U}\psi$ are LTL formulas.

We define a substitution (grounding) $\theta = \{x_1 \leftarrow t_1, x_2 \leftarrow t_2, ..., x_i \leftarrow t_i\}$ as the substitution of the terms $t_1, t_2, ..., t_i$ for variables $x_1, x_2, ..., x_i$ in a formula $f \in \mathscr{L}$. Thus, $\theta(f(x_1, x_2, ..., x_i)) \equiv f(t_1, t_2, ..., t_i)$. A *state of the world* s_t is a set of atomic predicates grounded by θ holding true at a specific moment. An LTL model $M = (S, \Re, \theta)$ consists of a non empty set S of states, an accessibility relation $\Re$ (connecting a state to another) and an substitution θ for predicates. A full path π in M is a sequence $\pi = < s_0, s_1, s_2, ... >$ such that for every $i \geq 0$, s_i is an element of S and $s_i \Re s_{i+1}$, and if π is finite with s_n its final state, then there is no state s_{n+1} in S such that $s_n \Re s_{n+1}$. Additionally, let π_i be the subpath of π starting from the i'th state of π, i.e. $\pi_i = < s_i, s_{i+1}, ... >$. Validity of an LTL formula ϕ on a model $M = (S, \Re, \theta)$ over a path π, written as $M, \pi \models \theta(\phi)$, is defined as:

- $M, \pi \models \theta(p)$ $\quad\quad \Leftrightarrow \theta(p) \in s_0$
- $M, \pi \models \neg\theta(\phi)$ $\quad\quad \Leftrightarrow$ not $M, \pi \models \theta(\phi)$
- $M, \pi \models \theta(\phi) \vee \theta(\psi) \Leftrightarrow M, \pi \models \theta(\phi)$ or $M, \pi \models \theta(\psi)$
- $M, \pi \models \mathbf{X}\theta(\phi)$ $\quad\quad \Leftrightarrow M, \pi_1 \models \theta(\phi)$
- $M, \pi \models \theta(\phi)\mathbf{U}\theta(\psi) \Leftrightarrow \exists n > 0$ such that:
  (1) $M, \pi_n \models \theta(\psi)$ and
  (2) $\forall i$ *with* $0 \leq i < n : M, \pi_i \models \theta(\phi)$

Additional temporal operators are $\mathbf{G}$ for always (globally), $\mathbf{F}$ for eventually (in the future), $\mathbf{R}$ for release and $\mathbf{W}$ for weakly until. Details about LTL can be found at [19].

3   Norms and Norm Instances

Searle [20] distinguishes between two types of norms: regulative rules, which describe ideal situations from an institutional perspective in terms of obligations, prohibitions and permissions, and constitutive rules, which allow to construct social reality by expliciting the relationship between brute facts and institutional events. The main difference between both types of norms is that while constitutive rules, by their very nature, are categorical, regulative rules are conditional, in the sense that they specify every applicable condition of each particular norm [4].

Although there have been recent attempts to make regulative rules concrete by the reduction to constitutive rules [21], in general regulative norms based on deontic statements have been the most common way to represent normative constraints in multi-agent systems. In such systems, thus, norms are expressed as computer-readable specifications based on deontic logics.

3.1 Norm Operationalisation and Levels of Abstraction

However, operationalisation of regulative norms[1] is not straightforward. Deontic statements express the existence of norms, rather than the consequences of following (or not following) them [22]. In order to implement agents and institutional frameworks capable of reasoning about norms, we need to complement deontic logics with semantics defining fulfilment and violation – among other operational normative concepts. Examples of work on this direction are abundant and for many different purposes, i.e., compliance [6,7,9,11,12,23], verification [8,10,24,25], or agent behaviour [5,13–16].

While it is true that most of them define semantics to interpret norms, there seems to be a disconnection between such semantics and either (1) the deontic logics they are supposed to be based upon; or (2) the operational level closer to the actual practical implementation. For instance, [9] defines a norm-operationalisation language that can be connected with higher level abstractions, but it is not clear whether it can be translated into generic rule-based languages. [6] presents a rule-based language with constraints, with an implementation on Prolog, on top of which other higher-level languages can be formalised, but with no direct relationship to deontic logics. On this line of work, approaches such as [7,13] define clear operational semantics by the use of syntax loosely inspired by, but not directly related to, deontic statements.

An approach that is close to bridge this gap is presented in [26] by specifying formal methods for the implementation of norm enforcement and the automatic creation of protocols based on constraints specified by the norms. However, this proposal focuses on norm modelling from an institutional point of view, not covering the agent perspective (i.e., how norms influence the agent behaviour). A second limitation is that it does not get to the implementation level and, in fact, there does not seem to be a straightforward way to achieve it. Furthermore, it includes no treatment of the consequences, i.e. norm reparation.

In summary, there are many approaches that tackle different parts of the formalisation of norm operationalisation. One of the purposes of this paper is, thus, to complement these approaches by filling the gaps that exist between the deontic statements and both rule-based and planning operationalisation by means of (1) additional predicates representing norm fulfilment and violation, and (2) an intermediate representation based on temporal logics (see Sect. 4).

3.2 Identification of Norm Instances

A related issue that is somehow missing in general in the literature is a clear separation between an abstract norm and a particular (contextual) instantiation of the norm. This problem was already discussed by Abrahams and Bacon in [27]: *"since propositions about norms are derived from the norms themselves, invalid or misleading inferences will result if we deal merely with the propositions rather*

---

[1] In the rest of the paper we will use the term *norms* or *regulative norms* to refer to Searle's *regulative rules*.

than with the identified norms[2] that make those propositions true or false". This issue is not banal, as it has implications on the operational level: in order to properly check norm compliance, norm instantiations have to be tracked in an individual manner, case by case.

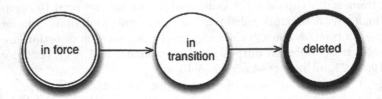

Fig. 1. Norm lifecycle

We find useful, at this point, to stress the fact that the lifecycles of a norm, and of a norm instance, should be differentiated because they are different in essence. The lifecycle of a norm (see Fig. 1) deals with its validity in the normative system: a norm is *in force* when it can be fully activated, monitored, and enforced; *in transition* when it is being removed and cannot be activated anymore, but the effects of past activations have to be tracked until their end; and *deleted* when the history of the norm is to be kept but it can have no further effect on the normative system. Therefore, such lifecycle is related to the concepts of promulgation, abrogation and derogation, out of the scope of this paper. On the other hand, the lifecycle of a norm instance deals with the fulfilment/violation of each particular instance.

The concept of norm instance life-cycle has been treated by different authors, e.g. [7, 27–29], but with no real consensus. Taking those interesting elements that would allow to manage norms with the concepts of activation, maintenance, fulfilment and reparation, a suitable norm life-cycle would be similar to the one based on the automata depicted in Fig. 2. A norm instance gets activated due to a certain activating condition and starts in an (A)ctive state, but if at some point a certain maintenance condition is not fulfilled, the norm instance gets into a (V)iolation state. If the norm instance is (A)ctive and a certain deactivation (or fulfilment) condition is achieved, the norm gets (D)eactivated[3]. Usually reparations are not treated explicitly, but in our proposal we add the concept for completeness. If a norm instance is (V)iolated, fulfilling a reparation condition can bring it back to the (A)ctive state, but if the deactivation condition occurs while violated, only by fulfilling the same reparation condition (VD state) the norm instance can be (D)eactivated. A (V)iolated norm instance could not ever get repaired, so for safety we use a *timeout* condition[4] to make sure the norm instance is not alive forever and thus mark those permanent violations as (F)ailures.

---

[2] In this paper, we will denote such identified norms as *norm instances*.

[3] Please note that we assume the deactivation condition to eventually happen.

[4] The timeout condition is evaluated as starting at the point of time of violation.

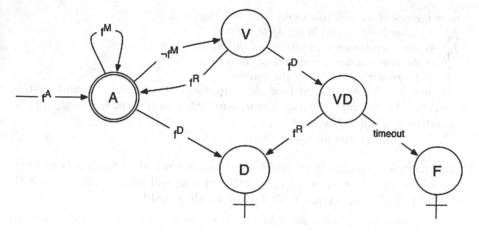

Fig. 2. Norm instance lifecycle with reparation and timeout handling

Once there is a norm life-cycle the question to answer is how to deal with it from an operational perspective. Abrahams and Bacon [27] solve this problem by means of *occurrences* of the predicates contained in the deontic operator, but there are cases in which this can be insufficient, e.g., when the obligation defines a deadline or its instantiation depends on contextual information. More recently, some works have been advancing in the direction of tackling this issue. For example, by treating instantiated deontic statements as first-class objects of a rule-based language [23,30]. However, as these deontic statements are already implicitly identifying the norm instance, there is no explicit tracking of which elements of the domain are involved in fulfilling or violating. Other approaches declare the norm only at the abstract level and the tracking of the norm instance, and implicitly of the norm instance lifecycle, is purely done at the operational level [7,11,12].

4   Formalisation

In this section, we present a proposal for a deontic logic for support for norm instantiation via obligations parametrized by three states (conditions). For the purpose of this formalisation, we assume the use of a predicate based propositional language $\mathscr{L}$ as in Sect. 2. We also adopt the notion of state from the same section.

4.1   Norms

In this paper we define a norm following a modified version of the *abstract norm* definition from [7], adding elements for tracking of reparation of violations:

Definition 1. *We define a norm n as a tuple $n = \langle \alpha, f_n^A, f_n^M, f_n^D, f_n^R, timeout \rangle$, where:*

- α is the agent obliged to comply with the norm,
- f_n^A is the activating condition of the norm,
- f_n^M is the maintenance condition of the norm,
- f_n^D is the deactivation condition of the norm,
- f_n^R is the repair condition of the norm,
- timeout is a fully-grounded formula that represents the upper-bound waiting condition for the reparation of a violation, taken into account of only after a violation and not before, and
- $f_n^A, f_n^M, f_n^D, f_n^R, timeout \in \mathcal{L}$.

If, for example, we wanted to model the following norm: "while Ag is driving, he is obliged to not cross in red light, otherwise he will have to pay a fine with cost 100^5 before time is equal to 500", the result would be:

$$n = \langle Ag, \{driving(Ag)\}, \{\neg crossed\text{-}red(Ag, L)\}, \{\neg driving(Ag)\}, \{fine\text{-}paid(100)\}, time(500)\rangle$$

The interpretation of the tuple in Definition 1 is done by means of the deontic formula:

Definition 2. *The deontic interpretation of a norm n, is:*

$$O_{f_n^R \leq timeout}([\alpha \; stit : f_n^M] \preceq f_n^D \mid f_n^A)$$

The syntax of the operator proposed is similar to the obligation operator from other deontic logics, such as dyadic deontic logic and semantics of deadlines, but with important differences. While the $\leq$ used for $f_n^R \leq timeout$ corresponds to the deadline semantics [3] (if *timeout* occurs, there is a permanent violation), the $\preceq$ used in $[\alpha \; stit : f_n^M] \preceq f_n^D$ should rather be read as "$[\alpha \; stit : f_n^M]$ should hold at all times at least until f_n^D". Also, the conditional notation | used in dyadic deontic logic, which not always has clear semantics in terms of temporality, in the case of the operator proposed $O(A|B)$ should be read as "starting the moment B happens, A should happen" rather than simply "given B, A should happen"[6].

Therefore, the expression shown in Definition 2 is informally read as: *if at some point f_n^A holds, agent α is obliged to see to it that f_n^M is maintained until, at least, f_n^D holds; otherwise, α is obliged to see to it that f_n^R before timeout.* Note that in this informal reading we are not dealing with norm instances yet. How we address this issue, along with the semantics of this obligation operator, will be explained in Subsect. 4.2. Following the example:

$$O_{fine\text{-}paid(100) \leq time(500)}([Ag \; stit : \neg crossed\text{-}red(Ag, L)] \preceq \neg driving(Ag) \mid driving(Ag))$$

informally read as: *if at some point Ag is driving, Ag is obliged to see to it that no red light is crossed until, at least, Ag is not driving anymore; otherwise,*

---

[5] Each time there is an infraction the fine has to be paid, still, for reasons of simplicity we use a predicate that keeps no track of the different violations

[6] In some works in the literature, this is interpreted as "given B and as long as B happens, A should happen", while in other works it is interpreted in a closer way to our reading

Ag has to pay a fine of 100 before the time is 500. The semantics of this operator are presented in the rest of this section.

4.2   Norm Instances

As previously discussed in Sect. 3, we have to take into account the following issues:

1. deontic statements do not express truth value related to a norm, but rather the existence of a norm [22]; and
2. to check the compliance of a norm, its particular instances must be tracked [27],

Therefore, we need to define the compliance of a norm based on the fulfilment of each of its instantiations. That is, a norm has been complied up to a certain time t if, and only if, each one of the instantiations triggered in times $t_i < t$ have not been violated, where violated means that there has been $\neg f_n^M$ before f_n^D ever happening.

A norm is defined in an abstract manner, affecting all possible participants enacting a given role. In order to work with instances, we need to define a norm instantiation. We consider a substitution θ (we denote it as *substitution instance* when referring to norms) as defined in Sect. 2. Whenever a norm is active, we will say that there is a *norm instance* n^θ for a particular norm n and a substitution instance θ.

Definition 3. *Given a norm n in force and a substitution set θ, we define a norm instance n^θ as $n^\theta = \langle \alpha, \theta(f_n^A), \theta(f_n^M), \theta(f_n^D), timeout \rangle$, where:*

- $\theta(f_n^A)$, *timeout are fully grounded, and*
- $\theta(f_n^M)$, $\theta(f_n^D)$ *may be fully or partially grounded.*

The reason that $\theta(f_n^M)$, $\theta(f_n^D)$ may be partially grounded is that the substitution instance that instantiates the norm – that is, θ such that $\theta(f_n^A)$ holds – is considered in our model to be the sufficient and necessary set of substitutions needed to fully ground f_n^A. It can be the case that the set of variables used in f_n^M and/or f_n^D is larger than the arity of θ. Let us suppose, for example, that the norm should be instantiated at all times while it is *in force*, regardless of any contextual condition: in that case, $f_n^A = \top$. Therefore, we have to assume that a substitution instance θ' for f_n^M or f_n^D should fulfil: $\theta \subseteq \theta'$.

4.3   Norm Lifecycle

Although LTL as a formalism is suitable enough in terms of complexity for reductions to monitoring and planning scenarios, and therefore for practical reasoning from an institutional or individual perspective, there are intrinsic constraints that limit the expressiveness of the framework.

More concretely, the norm instance lifecycle proposed in Fig. 2 cannot be expressed in LTL. As proved in [31], in order to reduce an automata to an LTL expression – and vice versa –, such automata has to be free of loops that involve more than one state, i.e. only cycles that start and finish in the same state and involve no second state are allowed.

This is an important constraint that prevents our model to have a loop between the (A)ctive and the (V)iolated states. In other words, if we want to use LTL, the lifecycle cannot have cycles that allow to go backwards. Therefore, for the purpose of our formalisation, we propose to adopt the more straightforward lifecycle shown in Fig. 3.

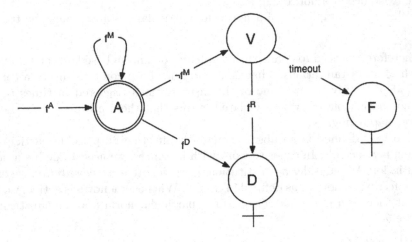

Fig. 3. Self-loop alternating automata-based norm instance lifecycle

The main difference with respect to the automata in Fig. 2 is the handling of violations. As there is no way back to an (A)ctive state anymore, from a (V)iolation state there are only two options: either to repair the norm instance and subsequently (D)eactivate it, or mark it as a (F)ailure if it has not been dealt with for a given amount of time. From an operational perspective, this issue can be worked around by allowing the norm-aware system to create more instances of the same norm if an instance is violated before a deactivation.

For an obligation to have a deontic effect, it is required that the activating condition actually happens at some future point. Additionally, either of the following three conditions should happen:

- The activating condition never occurs so the norm never gets activated.
- Always, between the activating and deactivation condition, the maintenance holds (reached "deactivated" state).
- Maintenance condition holds up to a point where it becomes false and then a violation is permanently raised. In addition, the repair condition occurs later (reached "deactivated" state) before timeout is reached.

In this way we approach most closely that the maintenance of $\theta(f_n^M)$ causes the $\neg viol(n^\theta)$. Thus, the deontic effect of an obligation can be described by the causal effect between the maintenance condition and a violation in Definition 4.

In order to give meaning to the fulfilment of a norm instance, we define a specific operator $\mathcal{O}$ with similar syntax to the abstract norm operator O. Let $M = \{S, \Re, \theta\}$ be an LTL model (using a predicate set $\mathscr{L}$ for the formation of LTL formulas and with θ as described in Subsect. 4.2), $\pi =< s_0, s_1, s_2, \ldots >$ a full path in M, and $viol(n^\theta)$ a predicate belonging to $\mathscr{L}$ representing the violation of a norm instance n^θ, we can establish the semantic relationship between the lifecycle of a norm instance and the fulfilment/violation of a norm as:

Definition 4. Causal semantics for the operator $\mathcal{O}$

$$M, \pi \models \mathcal{O}_{\theta(f_n^R) \leq timeout}([\alpha\ stit : \theta(f_n^M)] \preceq \theta(f_n^D) \mid \theta(f_n^A))$$
$$\equiv_{def}$$
$$M, \pi \models \mathbf{G}\big(\neg\theta(f_n^A) \wedge \neg viol(n^\theta)\big)\vee$$
$$\Big(\mathbf{F}\Big(\theta(f_n^A) \wedge [\forall\theta' : \theta'(\theta(f_n^M))\mathbf{U}\exists\theta'' : \theta''(\theta(f_n^D))]\Big) \wedge \mathbf{G}\neg viol(n^\theta)\Big)\vee$$
$$\mathbf{F}\Big(\theta(f_n^A) \wedge [\neg viol(n^\theta)\mathbf{U}\exists\theta' : \neg\theta'(\theta(f_n^M))]\wedge$$
$$[\theta'(\theta(f_n^M))\mathbf{U}\big(\neg\theta'(\theta(f_n^M)) \wedge \mathbf{G}viol(n^\theta)\wedge (\neg timeout\mathbf{U}\exists\theta'' : \theta''(\theta(f_n^R)))\big)]\Big)$$

The first line of the temporal formula says that the activating condition actually never happens and no violation is raised throughout the executional path. This case does not cause any change in the state of the system. The second line says that there exists some substitution for the activating condition in the future, and that always until a substitution raises an instance of the deactivation condition, the maintenance condition holds for all substitutions. No violation is raised throughout the executional path. This case terminates the norm in a state of *deactivation* (D). The rest of the lines in the formula imply that there exists some substitution for the activating condition in the future, and that at some later point a substitution makes the maintenance condition not hold, thus raising a violation (which remains thereafter). In addition, another substitution makes the repair condition happen at some future after the violation has occurred but before timeout occurs. The norm terminates in a state of *deactivation* (D).

The *failed* state (F), in which the timeout has occurred without the norm having realised the repair condition after a violation, is not described in the formula, since it is an "unwanted" state and should be avoided.

The lifecycle defined in Fig. 3 can be seen as an transition automaton. Transition properties that define how the norm changes its status while events (world changes that modify the predicates' truthness) are occurring can be easily extracted. We are interested in directly representing these transitions as it is useful when dealing with monitoring of norms' status (see Sect. 5.1). The four states *active* (A), *viol* (V), *deactivated* (D), *failed* (F) are described in Definition 5:

Definition 5. Norm lifecycle predicates

$$M, \pi \models \mathbf{X}active(n^\theta) \text{ iff } M, \pi \models (\mathbf{X}\theta(f_n^A) \vee active(n^\theta)) \wedge \mathbf{X} \nexists\theta' : \theta'(\theta(f_n^D))$$

$M, \pi \models \mathbf{X}viol(n^\theta)$ iff $M, \pi \models active(n^\theta) \wedge \mathbf{X} \not\exists \theta' : \theta'(\theta(f_n^M))$

$M, \pi \models \mathbf{X}deactivated(n^\theta)$ iff
$\quad (M, \pi \models active(n^\theta) \wedge \mathbf{X}\exists\theta' : \theta'(\theta(f_n^D))) \vee (M, \pi \models viol(n^\theta) \wedge \mathbf{X}\exists\theta' : \theta'(\theta(f_n^R)))$

$M, s \models \mathbf{X}failed(n^\theta)$ iff $M, s \models viol(n^\theta) \wedge \mathbf{X}timeout$

The first says that the norm remains in *active* status until there is no instance of deactivation condition occurring. The second says that the norm moves from the *active* to the *viol* state if there is no instance of the maintenance condition. The third says that the norm moves from the *active* to the *deactivated* state if there is an instance of the deactivation condition occurring and that the norm moves from the *viol* to the *deactivated* state if there is an instance of the repair condition occurring. The last says that the norm moves from the *viol* to the *failed* state if timeout occurs.

4.4   From Abstract Norm to Norm Instances

Now we have the apparatus needed to connect the fulfilment of an abstract norm and the fulfilment of its instances, and give semantic meaning to the operator proposed in Definition 2:

Definition 6. Fulfilment of a norm based on the fulfilment of its instances

$M, \pi \models O_{f_n^R \leq timeout}([\alpha\ stit : f_n^M] \preceq f_n^D \mid f_n^A) \equiv_{def}$
$\exists \theta : M, \pi \models \mathbf{F}(\theta(f_n^A)) \Leftrightarrow M, \pi \models \mathscr{O}_{\theta(f_n^R) \leq timeout}([\alpha\ stit : \theta(f_n^M)] \preceq \theta(f_n^D) \mid \theta(f_n^A))$

Informally: *the abstract norm is fulfilled if, and only if, for each possible instantiation of f_n^A through time, the obligations of the norm instances activated by f_n^A are fulfilled.*

5   Operational Semantics

In this section, we will show how the formalisation proposed in 4 can be reduced to operational semantics that will allow for norm reasoning for two different purposes: the monitoring of normative states from what occurred in the past, from an institutional perspective (see Subsect. 5.1); and the planning of actions in the future taking into account normative constraints, from an agent perspective (see Subsect. 5.2).

5.1   Monitoring Norms

In terms of institutional normative compliance, the detection of normative states is a passive procedure consisting in monitoring past events generated by agents' actions and checking them against a set of active norms. This type of reasoning can be covered by the declarative aspect of production systems. Using a forward-chaining rule engine, events can automatically trigger normative states – based on a given operational semantics – without requiring a design on how to do it.

Having (1) a direct syntactic translation from norms to rules and (2) a logic implemented in an engine consistent with the process we want to accomplish, allows us to decouple normative state monitoring from the agent reasoning. Our approach is based on creating an initial set of agent- and institutional-independent rules, which the agents – such as manager agents – will be able to transparently query the current normative state at any moment and reason upon it.

In order to achieve this initial set rules, we need to establish a grounding for our formalism. First of all, we will define the lifecycle of a norm instance according to the LTL formalisations of the previous section. We will show how to transform the paths into transition rules, translating the principles of change in normative states into transition rules, effectively reducing our formalisation to a rule-based operational semantics.

In order to track the normative state of an institution at any given point of time, we assume the existence of a knowledge base, in which we will define four sets representing each of the lifecycle states: an active set AS, a violated set VS, a deactivated set DS, and a failed set FS, each of them containing norm instances in the form of tuples: $\{\langle n_i, \theta_j \rangle, \langle n_{i'}, \theta_{j'} \rangle, ..., \langle n_{i''}, \theta_{j''} \rangle\}$.

Definition 7. *A Normative Monitor* M_N *for a set of norms* N *is a tuple* $M_N = \langle N, AS, VS, DS, FS, S \rangle$, *where:*

- *s is the current state of the world, which corresponds to the current path state.*
- *N is the set of norms,*
- $n \in N,\ \langle n, \theta \rangle \in AS \Leftrightarrow M, s \models active(n^\theta)$
- $n \in N,\ \langle n, \theta \rangle \in VS \Leftrightarrow M, s \models viol(n^\theta)$
- $n \in N,\ \langle n, \theta \rangle \in DS \Leftrightarrow M, s \models deactivated(n^\theta)$
- $n \in N,\ \langle n, \theta \rangle \in FS \Leftrightarrow M, s \models failed(n^\theta)$

We denote Γ_{M_N} as the set of all possible configurations of a Normative Monitor M_N.

Definition 8. *The* Transition System TS_{M_N} *for a Normative Monitor* M_N *is defined by* $TS_{M_N} = \langle \Gamma_{M_N}, \rhd \rangle$ *where*

- $\rhd$ *is a transition relation such that* $\rhd \subseteq \Gamma_{M_N} \times \Gamma_{M_N}$

The inference rules for the transition relation $\rhd$ are described in Fig. 4, where s_i stands for the current state and as, vs, ds, fs correspond to instances of the AS, VS, DS, FS sets of the Normative Monitor tuple.

$$\frac{\theta(f_n^A) \vee \langle n, \theta \rangle \in AS \qquad \neg \theta(f_n^D)}{M_N \rhd \langle N, AS \cup \{\langle n, \theta \rangle\}, VS, DS, FS, s_{i+1} \rangle} \tag{1}$$

$$\frac{\langle n, \theta \rangle \in AS \qquad \neg \theta(f_n^M)}{M_N \rhd \langle N, AS - \{\langle n, \theta \rangle\}, VS \cup \{\langle n, \theta \rangle\}, DS, FS, s_{i+1} \rangle} \tag{2}$$

$$\frac{\langle n, \theta \rangle \in AS \qquad \theta(f_n^D)}{M_N \rhd \langle N, AS - \{\langle n, \theta \rangle\}, VS, DS \cup \{\langle n, \theta \rangle\}, FS, s_{i+1} \rangle} \tag{3}$$

$$\frac{\langle n, \theta \rangle \in VS \qquad \theta(f_n^R)}{M_N \rhd \langle N, AS, VS - \{\langle n, \theta \rangle\}, DS \cup \{\langle n, \theta \rangle\}, FS, s_{i+1} \rangle} \tag{4}$$

$$\frac{\langle n, \theta \rangle \in VS \qquad timeout}{M_N \rhd \langle N, AS, VS - \{\langle n, \theta \rangle\}, DS, FS \cup \{\langle n, \theta \rangle\}, s_{i+1} \rangle} \tag{5}$$

For all cases, $n \in N \wedge n = \langle \alpha, f_n^A, f_n^M, f_n^D, f_n^R, timeout \rangle \wedge \theta \subseteq s_i$ is also part of the transition condition.

Fig. 4. Inference rules for the transition relation $\rhd$: *(1)* Norm instance activated, *(2)* Norm instance violated, *(3)* Norm instance deactivated by fulfilment, *(4)* Norm instance deactivated by reparation, and *(5)* Norm instance failed

By combining these transition rules with the semantics of production systems [32], and additionally transforming the norm condition formulas – normalised in DNF – into rules by means of automatic norm parsing, we obtain a rule-engine which is semantically compliant with our formalism.

Details on the actual implementation have been already presented in [12]. The system designed for this purpose is summarised in Fig. 5 (left). The prototype has been implemented using a combination of XML for norm representation, Java and Clojure for the parsing of the norms, and Drools for the rule engine.

5.2   Planning with Norms

Although the Definition 5 is sufficiently expressive while implementing a monitoring framework, it cannot be applied in a planning system. This is because most planners allow modelling the transitions between states (actions) in a way such that there is exclusive dependency on the values of the previous state's properties. In this way, for example the *active*() status of a norm cannot be easily expressed, since not only does it need to be aware of the activeness at the previous state, but it also needs to be aware of whether at the current state the deactivation condition occurs. The use of extra predicates such as *previous*() and *current* that provide such functionality, allowing to check whether formulas hold in current and previous states, is permitted in some planning frameworks such as TLPlan [17] but it proves to be costly when extensively used.

An alternative, on which we base our implementation is the use of languages that support the use of LTL formulas to restrict the plans produced. Such an attempt is PDDL 3.0 [18]. PDDL 3.0 specification extends PDDL[7] with strong and soft constraints (expressed in LTL formulas) which are imposed on plan

---

[7] http://planning.cis.strath.ac.uk/competition/

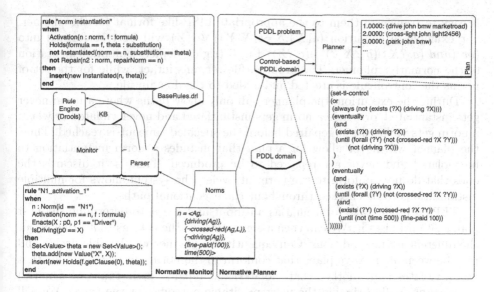

Fig. 5. Normative Monitor and Normative Planner

trajectories, as well as strong and soft problem goals, which are imposed on a plan. TLPlan [17] on the other hand, applies LTL formulas (called *control rules*) to a forward chaining search, reducing in this way the search path by pruning paths that do not comply to the rules. TLPlan is based on (STRIPS-like) semantics that can be easily reduced to PDDL. We choose TLPlan as it seems to contain a complete, robust and rather fast implementation, also allowing extra features such as existential and universal quantifiers. We explain below how the norms are introduced into the planning mechanism.

In order to implement the normative planner, the Definition 4 needs to be transformed into one of use to the planner. While the *viol()* predicate is useful to indicate semantical relation between the norm and its breach, it adds nothing when trying to apply it to a domain, since the violation is actually caused by the progress of the activating, deactivation, and maintenance condition. Therefore, we can eliminate the parts that contain it and create one that we can feed to the planner. The lifecycle then can be represented in Definition 9.

Definition 9. Formula producing norms that reach the deactivated state

$$M, \pi \models \mathbf{G}(\neg\theta(f_n^A)) \qquad\qquad\qquad \vee$$
$$\mathbf{F}(\theta(f_n^A) \wedge (\forall\theta' : \theta'(\theta(f_n^M))\mathbf{U}\exists\theta'' : \theta''(\theta(f_n^D)))) \quad \vee$$
$$\mathbf{F}(\theta(f_n^A) \wedge (\forall\theta' : \theta'(\theta(f_n^M))\mathbf{U}(\neg\theta'(\theta(f_n^M))\wedge (\neg timeout\mathbf{U}\exists\theta''' : \theta'''(\theta(f_n^R))))))$$

Thanks to Definition 9 we can represent the norms as control rules within the planning domain. This implies that, for every norm, we need to create such a control rule. The conjunction of all those rules will be the final control rule. We consider that since our norm conditions are defined in DNF form (see Sect. 4), it is easy to transform them to the appropriate LISP-like format for the planner. For example, a condition $(a(X) \wedge \neg b(X,Y)) \vee c(Z)$ will be transformed into (or (and (a ?X) (b ?X ?Y))(c ?Z)) Fig. 5 (right) depicts our implementation of the normative planner. The problem file remains intact, while for the set of norms the control rule is created and added to the domain file.

During the execution, the planner will only allow paths where a norm never gets instantiated, or where a norm gets instantiated and never violated or where a norm gets violated but repaired before the specified timeout is reached. Thus, the planner will never allow for a plan that includes a norm instantiation to be violated and never get repaired to be produced. That is, it discards the ones that do not conform to the norm lifecycle. The system allows for multiple instantiations to be checked throughout the executional paths.

TLPlan might take a formula as an input and use it to determine the best plan that optimises it. We can then assign values to the actions that bring about the different norm conditions. Consequently the planner will be able decide and pick between alternative plans that conform to the norm lifecycle (e.g. one that never violates and another that violates and repairs an instance of a norm) while additionally bringing the most profitable outcome for the agent. We will not enter into detail due to lack of space.

We have executed preliminary experiments with TLPlan [17] with up to three norms within a domain. The experiments were run on Mac OSX with Intel Core i7 2.9 Hz processor with 8 GB memory. The results seem promising as in almost all cases, where the outcome was a plan of up to 20 actions and up to 15 instances of norms were created throughout execution, the running time did not significantly increase and remained less than 1 second. This is due to the fact that branches of possible paths get rejected during the forward chaining search. On the other hand, small overhead could be added due to the check of the validity of the control rule on every state, still we have not had any noticeable change on the running time.

6   Conclusions

The resulting semantic framework presented in this paper directly tackles at the same time three important problems related to the practical materialisation of norm-aware systems: clear connection between the deontic level and the operational semantics, the formalisation of explicit norm instances, and the unambiguity of semantic interpretation across implementation domains. We have done so by building, upon diverse previous work, a connection between deontic statements and temporal logics, and between temporal logics to fluents and transition rules. Previous work also shows [12,16] that from the latter representations the translation to the implementation level is also clear. In our case this connection between a single normative specification and two different practical implementations allows us to have a norm monitoring mechanism (used for institutional enforcement) and a norm-aware planning mechanism (used for agent-oriented practical reasoning) that share exactly the same norm semantics (including the norm lifecycle). This result is vital to ensure that, for instance, the norm enforcement mechanism will state that there is a violation in a case the normative planner found legal and viceversa.

However, this is ongoing research that still needs improvement in several respects and we plan for immediate future work. First of all, we recognise that the constraints on the expressiveness of the norm life-cycle automata from Fig. 3 are quite limiting. We are looking into formalisms that may allow us to work with a version of the life-cycle closer to the one depicted in Fig. 2, probably in a logic framework different from LTL or CTG.

Also, we need to establish the properties of our obligation operator and compare them to the Standard Deontic Logics' properties. Moreover, we are especially interested in defining prohibitions and permissions keeping the syntax of Definition 1.

Section 3 states that there are already formalisations and/or languages that cover some parts of the issues we mention in the Introduction. It is our intention to connect our operational semantics with them.

Additionally, we have been testing our operational semantics with respect to run-time change of norms and normative contexts, and we will extend the norm lifecycle to include new states such as *abrogation* or *derogation*.

Finally, as mentioned in Sect. 3, Searle not only describes regulative rules but also constitutive. We intend to explore the possible implications of adding counts-as rules to our formalisation, following work from [21].

Acknowledgements. This work has been supported by the European funded projects IT-ALIVE (PF-215890) and SUPER HUB (PF-289067). The content of this paper however solely reflect the opinion of the authors, and does not necessarily represent the views of the European Commission.

References

1. Vázquez-Salceda, J.: The role of norms and electronic institutions in multi-agent systems applied to complex domains: the HarmonIA framework. Ph.D. Thesis, 218, January 2003
2. von Wright, G.H.: Deontic logic. Mind, New Series **60**(237), 1–15 (1951)
3. Dignum, F.P.M., Broersen, J., Dignum, V., Meyer, J.-J.: Meeting the deadline: why, when and how. In: Hinchey, M.G., Rash, J.L., Truszkowski, W.F., Rouff, C.A. (eds.) FAABS 2004. LNCS (LNAI), vol. 3228, pp. 30–40. Springer, Heidelberg (2004)
4. Boella, G., van der Torre, L.: Regulative and constitutive norms in normative multiagent systems. In: Proceedings of 10th International Conference on the Principles of Knowledge Representation and Reasoning, KR'04, pp. 255–265 (2004)
5. Aldewereld, H., Grossi, D., Vázquez-Salceda, J., Dignum, F.P.M.: Designing normative behaviour via landmarks. In: Boissier, O., Padget, J., Dignum, V., Lindemann, G., Matson, E., Ossowski, S., Sichman, J.S., Vázquez-Salceda, J. (eds.) ANIREM 2005 and OOOP 2005. LNCS (LNAI), vol. 3913, pp. 157–169. Springer, Heidelberg (2006)

6. García-Camino, A., Rodríguez-Aguilar, J.-A., Sierra, C., Vasconcelos, W.W.: Norm-oriented programming of electronic institutions: a rule-based approach. In: Noriega, P., Vázquez-Salceda, J., Boella, G., Boissier, O., Dignum, V., Fornara, N., Matson, E. (eds.) COIN 2006. LNCS (LNAI), vol. 4386, pp. 177–193. Springer, Heidelberg (2007)

7. Oren, N., Panagiotidi, S., Vázquez-Salceda, J., Modgil, S., Luck, M., Miles, S.: Towards a formalisation of electronic contracting environments. In: Hübner, J.F., Matson, E., Boissier, O., Dignum, V. (eds.) COIN@AAMAS 2008. LNCS, vol. 5428, pp. 156–171. Springer, Heidelberg (2009)

8. Lomuscio, A., Qu, H., Raimondi, F.: MCMAS: a model checker for the verification of multi-agent systems. In: Bouajjani, A., Maler, O. (eds.) CAV 2009. LNCS, vol. 5643, pp. 682–688. Springer, Heidelberg (2009)

9. Governatori, G., Rotolo, A.: Norm compliance in business process modeling. In: Dean, M., Hall, J., Rotolo, A., Tabet, S. (eds.) RuleML 2010. LNCS, vol. 6403, pp. 194–209. Springer, Heidelberg (2010)

10. Ågotnes, T., van der Hoek, W., Wooldridge, M.: Robust normative systems and a logic of norm compliance. Logic J. IGPL **18**(1), 4–30 (2010)

11. Criado, N., Argente, E., Noriega, P.: Towards a normative BDI architecture for norm compliance. COIN@ MALLOW2010 (2010)

12. Alvarez-Napagao, S., Aldewereld, H., Vázquez-Salceda, J., Dignum, F.: Normative monitoring: semantics and implementation. In: De Vos, M., Fornara, N., Pitt, J.V., Vouros, G. (eds.) COIN 2010. LNCS, vol. 6541, pp. 321–336. Springer, Heidelberg (2011)

13. López y López, F., Luck, M., d'Inverno, M.: Normative agent reasoning in dynamic societies. In: Third International Joint Conference on Autonomous Agents and Multiagent Systems, AAMAS '04, Washington, DC, USA, vol. 2, pp. 732–739 (2004)

14. Kollingbaum, M.J.: Norm-governed practical reasoning agents. Ph.D. Dissertation (2005)

15. Meneguzzi, F., Luck, M.: Norm-based behaviour modification in BDI agents. In: Proceedings of The 8th International Conference on Autonomous Agents and Multiagent Systems, AAMAS '09, vol. 1, pp. 177–184, Richland, SC. (International Foundation for Autonomous Agents and Multiagent Systems) (2009)

16. Panagiotidi, S., Vázquez-Salceda, J.: Norm-aware planning: semantics and implementation. In: 2011 IEEE/WIC/ACM International Joint Conferences on Web Intelligence (WI) and Intelligent Agent Technologies (IAT), pp. 33–36. IEEE, August 2011

17. Bacchus, F., Kabanza, F.: Using temporal logics to express search control knowledge for planning. Artif. Intell. **116**(1–2), 123–191 (2000)

18. Gerevini, A., Long, D.: Plan constraints and preferences in PDDL3: the language of the fifth international planning competition. Technical report R.T. 2005–08–07, August 2005

19. Huth, M., Ryan, M.: Logic in Computer Science: Modelling and Reasoning about Systems. Cambridge University Press, New York (2004)

20. Searle, J.: The Construction of Social Reality. Free Press, New York (1995)

21. Aldewereld, H., Alvarez-Napagao, S., Dignum, F., Vázquez-Salceda, J.: Making norms concrete. In: Proceedings of 9th International Conference on Autonomous Agents and Multiagent Systems (AAMAS 2010), pp. 807–814 (2010)

22. Walter, R.: Jörgensen's dilemma and how to face it. Ratio Juris **9**(2), 168–171 (1996)

23. Cardoso, H.L., Oliveira, E.: A context-based institutional normative environment. In: Hübner, J.F., Matson, E., Boissier, O., Dignum, V. (eds.) COIN@AAMAS 2008. LNCS, vol. 5428, pp. 140–155. Springer, Heidelberg (2009)
24. Koo, J.: A Study on the model checking for deontic logic. In: Convergence and Hybrid Information Technology, pp. 832–835 (2008)
25. Prisacariu, C., Schneider, G.: Abstract specification of legal contracts. In: Proceedings of the 12th International Conference on Artificial Intelligence and Law (ICAIL), ACM Request Permissions, pp. 218–219 (2009)
26. Aldewereld, H.: Autonomy vs. conformity: an institutional perspective on norms and protocols. Ph.D. Thesis, Utrecht University (2007)
27. Abrahams, A.S., Bacon, J.M.: The life and times of identified, situated, and conflicting norms. In: Sixth International Workshop on Deontic Logic in Computer, Science (DEON), pp. 3–20 (2002)
28. Fornara, N., Colombetti, M.: Specifying and enforcing norms in artificial institutions. In: Baldoni, M., Son, T.C., van Riemsdijk, M.B., Winikoff, M. (eds.) DALT 2008. LNCS (LNAI), vol. 5397, pp. 1–17. Springer, Heidelberg (2009)
29. Cardoso, H.L., Oliveira, E.: Directed deadline obligations in agent-based business contracts. In: Padget, J., Artikis, A., Vasconcelos, W., Stathis, K., da Silva, V.T., Matson, E., Polleres, A. (eds.) COIN@AAMAS 2009. LNCS, vol. 6069, pp. 225–240. Springer, Heidelberg (2010)
30. Governatori, G.: Representing business contracts in RuleML. Int. J. Coop. Inf. Syst. **14**(2–3), 181–216 (2005)
31. Tauriainen, H.: automata and linear temporal logic: translations with transition-based acceptance. Ph.D. Thesis, Helsinki University of Technology (2006)
32. Cirstea, H., Kirchner, C., Moossen, Michael, M., Moreau, P.E.: Production systems and rete algorithm formalisation. Research report inria-00280938, PROTHEO - INRIA Lorraine - LORIA (2004)

A Framework for Programming Norm-Aware Multi-agent Systems

Daniela Dybalova[1](✉), Bas Testerink[2], Mehdi Dastani[2], and Brian Logan[1]

[1] School of Computer Science, University of Nottingham, Nottingham, UK
{dxd,bsl}@cs.nott.ac.uk
[2] Department of Information and Computing Sciences, Universiteit Utrecht,
Utrecht, The Netherlands
{b.j.g.testerink,M.M.Dastani}@uu.nl

Abstract. We propose a programming framework for the implementation of *norm-aware multi-agent systems*. The framework integrates the N-2APL norm-aware agent programming language with the 2OPL organisation programming language. Integration of N-2APL and 2OPL is achieved using a tuple space which represents both the (brute) state of the multi-agent environment and the detached norms and sanctions comprising its normative state. To the best of our knowledge, this is the first implementation of an integrated framework for norm-aware MAS in which autonomous agents deliberate about whether to conform to the norms imposed by a normative organisation. The use of a tuple space makes it straightforward to integrate other system components. To illustrate the flexibility of our framework, we briefly describe its application in a novel normative application, a mixed reality game called GeoSense. We show how GeoSense game rules can be expressed as conditional norms with deadlines and sanctions, and how agents can deliberate about their individual goals and the norms imposed by the game.

1 Introduction

Norms can be viewed as defining standards of behaviour. They have been widely proposed as a means of coordinating and regulating the behaviours of individual agents to ensure global properties of a multi-agent system. For example, smart roads may be implemented as multi-agent systems, where autonomous cars are agents and the road infrastructure constitutes the agents' environment. Desirable properties of such a multi-agent system may include safety, road throughput, and minimal environmental damage. Such properties can be ensured by means of enforcement and regimentation of traffic norms such as speed limits, redirecting traffic, and closing road lanes [1]. Multi-agent systems that use norms to regulate agent behaviour are called normative multi-agent systems [2].

In building normative multi-agent systems, norms can be implemented either endogenously by integrating them into the programs of individual agents (e.g., an autonomous car may be programmed not to exceed the speed limit) or exogenously by additional components that observe and evaluate the agents' behaviours in order to check compliance or violation of norms (e.g., road cameras

T. Balke et al. (Eds.): COIN 2013, LNAI 8386, pp. 364–380, 2014.
DOI: 10.1007/978-3-319-07314-9_20, © Springer International Publishing Switzerland 2014

monitor cars' speed and register the identities of cars that violate speed limitations). In exogenous normative multi-agent systems, norms can regulate the behaviour of agents by means of regimentation or enforcement. Norm regimentation prevents agents from violating norms (e.g., closing lanes of a smart road) while norm enforcement allows agents to violate norms but imposes sanctions on violating agents to compensate for their violations (e.g., violating the speed limit incurs a sanction in the form of a fine) [1]. In multi-agent systems where norms are implemented exogenously, regulation is realized by processing norms at run time. The processing of norms in such systems requires creating and eliminating norms based on their conditions and deadlines, monitoring the activities of participating agents, evaluating their behaviour with respect to the specified norms and finally determining appropriate consequences for the participating agents. In multi-agent systems where norms are implemented endogenously, individual agents have internalized norms in the sense that their decision procedures are defined in terms of the norms. Although the agents' decisions in such systems do not necessarily need to be norm compliant, it is not clear how to cope with norm violations by self interested agents without an external entity that detects norm violations and compensates them by means of sanctions. It is also important to emphasize that not every norm can be regimented exogenously. In the smart road example, it is not clear how speed limits can be regimented in the highways since placing speed bumps is not a realistic option.

A number of programming frameworks have been proposed for the development of normative multi-agent systems, e.g., [3,4]. However in these frameworks, the agents do not deliberate about whether to comply with norms. In [5] an agent programming language N-2APL, for programming *norm-aware* agents was introduced. Norm-aware N-2APL agents are able to deliberate on their goals, norms and sanctions before deciding which plan to select and execute, and are able to violate norms if it is in their overall interest to do so, e.g., if meeting an obligation would result in an important goal of the agent becoming unachievable.[1]

In this paper we propose a framework for programming norm-aware multi-agent systems. The framework integrates the N-2APL agent programming language with the 2OPL language for programming normative organisations. The integration of N-2APL and 2OPL is achieved using a tuple space which represents both the (brute) state of the multi-agent environment and the detached norms and sanctions comprising its normative state. To the best of our knowledge, this is the first implementation of N-2APL and the first implementation of an integrated framework for norm-aware multi-agent systems in which autonomous agents deliberate about whether to conform to the norms imposed by a normative organisation. The use of a tuple space makes it straightforward to integrate other system components. To illustrate the flexibility of our framework, we briefly describe its application in a novel normative application, a mixed reality game called GeoSense [8]. We show how GeoSense game rules can be expressed as

---

[1] Norm-aware agents are related to the notion of *deliberate normative agents* in [6], and are capable of *behaving according to a role specification in a normative organization* and *reasoning about violations* in the sense of [7].

conditional norms with deadlines and sanctions, and how agents can deliberate about their individual goals and the norms imposed by the game.

The remainder of this paper is structured as follows. In Sect. 2 we introduce our programming framework. We briefly describe 2OPL and N-2APL and their implementations, and explain how they are integrated using the JavaSpaces tuple space. In Sect. 3 we briefly describe the application of our framework to allow norm-aware agents to play the mixed reality game GeoSense. We briefly outline the translation of game rules into 2OPL norms, how N-2APL agent programs encode the game play of the agents, and the integration of the resulting normative multi-agent system with the GeoSense game server. We discuss related work in Sect. 4 and conclude in Sect. 5.

2   Framework Description

In this section we describe our framework, which consists of three main parts: a 2OPL normative organization, a N-2APL multi-agent system and a Linda-like tuple space [9] which acts as a coordination mechanism.

2.1   2OPL Normative Organization

2OPL [3, 10] is a programming language designed to support the implementation of normative multi-agent systems where norms are implemented exogenously. 2OPL programs contain three types of data: facts, fact update rules, and norms. The facts and fact update rules are used to represent the state of the agents' environment and the effect of the agents' actions in the environment. For example, in the GeoSense game, a fact may represent the current location of an agent, while a fact update rule represents how the agent's location changes as a result of performing a 'move' action.

2OPL norms are state-based norms and are defined in terms of a unique label, an activation condition, and a deontic element.[2] The label functions as a name that can be used to refer to the norm and the precondition specifies when (i.e., in which states of the environment) the norm can be activated (detached). The deontic element of the norm is either an obligation or a prohibition. An obligation is defined by a subject (the agent to which incurs the obligation), a deadline, a state formula indicating the state of the environment that has to be brought about before the deadline, and a sanction formula indicating how the state is updated if the obligation is not discharged by the deadline. A prohibition is defined by a state formula indicating the state of the environment that must be avoided, and a sanction formula indicating how the state is updated if the prohibition is violated before the deadline. The subject and deadline are represented by atoms, and the state and sanction formulas are represented as conjunctions (lists) of atomic facts. For example, in the GeoSense game, a norm may prohibit the truck from entering a specific area, with violation of the norm resulting in the truck's score being reduced by 500 points.

---

[2] In what follows, we adopt the version of 2OPL described by Tinnemeier [10], which includes conditional norms with deadlines.

⟨*Norm*⟩   ::= "norm("⟨*label*⟩, ⟨*precond*⟩, ⟨*deontic*⟩")"
⟨*label*⟩   ::= ⟨*atom*⟩
⟨*precond*⟩   ::= "("⟨*atom*⟩("," ⟨*atom*⟩)*")"
⟨*deontic*⟩   ::= "obligation("⟨*subject*⟩, ⟨*state*⟩, ⟨*deadline*⟩, ⟨*sanction*⟩")" |
                  "prohibition("⟨*subject*⟩, ⟨*state*⟩, ⟨*deadline*⟩, ⟨*sanction*⟩")"
⟨*subject*⟩   ::= ⟨*atom*⟩
⟨*state*⟩   ::= "["⟨*atom*⟩("," ⟨*atom*⟩)* "]"
⟨*deadline*⟩ ::= ⟨*atom*⟩
⟨*sanction*⟩ ::= "["⟨*atom*⟩("," ⟨*atom*⟩)* "]"

Fig. 1. Syntax of 2OPL norms

The syntax of 2OPL norms is shown in Fig. 1 where the ⟨*atom*⟩ follows the Prolog syntax for atomic facts. All components of the norm must be ground when a norm instance is detached. For integration with N-2APL agents, we require that 2OPL norms conform to a more restrictive syntax than that shown in Fig. 1. In particular, we assume a global clock and require that deadlines are atoms denoting relative times after the time at which a norm is detached. We also require that prohibitions have a deadline of infinity. These restrictions are necessary to ensure that the normative reasoning of N-2APL agents remains tractable [5]. In addition, to simplify the mapping from sanctions to the priorities N-2APL agents assign to goals (see below), we assume that sanctions are single atoms.

2OPL programs are executed by means of an interpreter that consists of a loop in which agents' actions are observed, the effects of the actions are realized by means of the fact update rules, and norms are processed. Norms are processed as follows. If the precondition of a norm holds, then an instance of the corresponding obligation or prohibition is detached (comes into effect). For all obligations that are already in effect, the 2OPL interpreter checks if the deadline is reached while the obliged state of the environment is not realized. In such a case a violation has occurred, and the state of the environment is updated with the corresponding sanction. Moreover, for all prohibitions that are already in effect it is checked if the prohibited state is realized. In such a case a violation has occurred and the state of the environment is updated with the corresponding sanction.

To support the integration of 2OPL with the framework, the 2OPL interpreter was extended to interact via a tuple space as described in Sect. 2.3. Facts describing the current state of the environment and agent actions are read from the tuple space, and when the precondition of a norm becomes true in the current environment, a norm instance (an obligation or a prohibition with a specified subject, deadline and sanction) is written into the tuple space. The subject agent receives a notification from the tuple space and retrieves the new norm.

2.2   N-2APL Multi-agent System

N-2APL [5] is an extension of 2APL [11] with support for normative concepts including obligations, prohibitions, sanctions, deadlines and durations.

2APL is a BDI-based agent programming language that allows the implementation of agents in terms of cognitive concepts such as beliefs, goals and plans. A 2APL agent program specifies an agent's initial beliefs, goals, plans, and the reasoning rules it uses to select plans (PG-rules), to respond to messages and events (PC-rules), and to repair plans whose executions have failed (PR-rules). The initial beliefs of an agent includes the agent's information about itself and its surrounding environment. The initial goals of an agent consists of formulas each of which denotes a situation the agent wants to realize (not necessarily all at once). The initial plans of an agent consists of tasks that an agent should initially perform.

In order to achieve its goals, an 2APL agent adopts plans. A plan consists of basic actions composed by sequence, conditional choice, conditional iteration and non interleaving operators. The non interleaving operator, $[\pi]$ where π is a plan, indicates that π is an *atomic* plan, i.e., the execution of π should not be interleaved with the execution of any other plan. Basic actions include external actions (which change the state of the agent's environment); belief update and goal adopt actions (which change the agent's beliefs and goals), and abstract actions (which provide an abstraction mechanism similar to procedures in imperative programming).

Planning goal rules allow an agent to select an appropriate plan given its goals and beliefs. A planning goal rule ⟨*pgrule*⟩ consists of three parts: the head of the rule, the condition of the rule, and the body of the rule. The body of the rule is a plan that is generated when the head (a goal query) and the condition (a belief query) of the rule are entailed by the agent's goals and beliefs, respectively. Procedure call rules (PC-rules) are used to select plans to handle messages and external events and to select a plan for an abstract action. As with planning goal rules, a procedure call rule ⟨*pcrule*⟩ consists of three parts: a head, a belief condition, and a plan. The head of the rule is an atom ⟨*atom*⟩, which represents either a message, an event, or an abstract action. The belief condition indicates when a message, event or abstract action should result in the plan forming the body of the rule being added to the agent's plan base. Plan repair rules are used to revise plans whose execution has failed. A plan repair rule ⟨*prrule*⟩ consists of three parts: a head consisting of an abstract plan, a belief condition and a body which is also an abstract plan. A plan repair rule indicates that if the execution of the first action of a plan matching the head of the rule fails and the belief condition is true, then the failed plan may be replaced by an instance of the plan forming the body of the rule.

To support norm-aware agents, N-2APL extends some key constructs of 2APL and restricts or changes the semantics of others. We briefly summarise these changes below; for full details, including the operational semantics of N-2APL and how it supports norm-aware deliberation, see [5].

Beliefs, Goals and Events. Beliefs in N-2APL are the same as in 2APL and consist of Horn clause expressions. Goals in 2APL may be conjunctions of positive literals. In N-2APL we restrict goals to single atoms and extend their syntax to include optional deadlines. A *deadline* is a real time value (expressed in milliseconds) that specifies the time by which the goal should be achieved. If no deadline is specified for a goal as part of the agent's program, we assume a deadline of infinity. Norms are communicated to the agent in the form of events. An obligation event, represented as $obligation(\iota, o, d, s)$, specifies the time d by which the obligation o must be discharged, i.e., its deadline, and the sanction, s, that will be applied if the obligation is not discharged by the deadline. A prohibition event, represented as $prohibition(\iota, p, d, s)$, specifies a prohibition p that must not be violated and the sanction s that will be applied if execution of the agent's plans violates the prohibition. Obligations are adopted as goals with a deadline corresponding to the deadline of the obligation. In N-2APL it is assumed that prohibitions have a deadline of infinity. In addition we extend the state of the agent to include prohibitions, which are represented by single atoms, and the agent's initial state is extended to include its initial prohibitions. Lastly, we assume the programmer provides function $pref(x)$ where x is a goal or prohibition, that returns the priority of the goal or prohibition x. For non-normative goals, the priority corresponds to the importance of achieving the goal state. In the case of prohibitions and goals derived from obligations, the priority corresponds to the importance of avoiding the sanction that would be incurred if the corresponding norm is violated.

Actions & Plans. The syntax of external actions is extended to list the expected postconditions of the action, to allow the prohibitions violated by a plan to be determined. In N-2APL, non-atomic plans are the same as in 2APL. However in N-2APL we change the interpretation of the non interleaving operator: $[\pi]$ indicates that the execution of π should not be interleaved with the execution of other *atomic* plans (rather than not interleaved with the execution of *any* other plan as in 2APL). In N-2APL, atomic plans are assumed to contain basic actions that may interfere only with the basic actions in other atomic plans. For example, a plan that involves moving to a new location should not be interleaved with other plans that change the agent's location. However, external actions in different non-atomic plans are executed in parallel, rather than being interleaved as in 2APL. Lastly, we restrict the scope of the non interleaving operator such that non-atomic plans cannot contain atomic sub-plans, either directly or through the expansion of an abstract action, i.e., plans to achieve top-level goals are either wholly atomic or non-atomic.

PG-rules. We extend the syntax of plans in the body of a PG rule to include an optional field specifying the time required to execute the plan proposed by the PG rule. For simplicity, we assume that the time required to execute each plan π is fixed and known in advance.

The syntax of N-2APL is shown in Fig. 2 in EBNF notation. Programming constructs in bold are exactly the same as in 2APL. For details, please see [11].

Our implementation of N-2APL was based on the implementation of 2APL developed at the University of Utrecht.[3] The extensions to the 2APL interpreter can be split into three main parts: modification of parser, extension of

---

[3] The 2APL platform is available from http://apapl.sourceforge.net.

$$
\begin{array}{rcl}
\langle \textit{Agent\_Prog} \rangle & = & [\,"\texttt{Beliefs:"}\,\{\,\langle \textbf{belief} \rangle\,\}\,]\,, \\
& & [\,"\texttt{Goals:"}\,\langle \textit{goals} \rangle\,]\,, \\
& & [\,"\texttt{Prohibitions:"}\,\langle \textit{prohibitions} \rangle\,]\,, \\
& & [\,"\texttt{Plans:"}\,\langle \textit{plans} \rangle\,]\,, \\
& & [\,"\texttt{PG-rules:"}\,\{\,\langle \textit{pgrule} \rangle\,\}\,]\,, \\
& & [\,"\texttt{PC-rules:"}\,\{\,\langle \textbf{pcrule} \rangle\,\}\,] \\
& & [\,"\texttt{PR-rules:"}\,\{\,\langle \textbf{prrule} \rangle\,\}\,] \\
& & [\,"\texttt{Preferences:"}\,\langle \textit{prefs} \rangle\,] \\
\langle \textit{goals} \rangle & = & \langle \textit{goal} \rangle\,\{\,","\,\langle \textit{goal} \rangle\,\}\,; \\
\langle \textit{goal} \rangle & = & \langle \textit{atom} \rangle\,":"\,\langle \textit{deadline} \rangle\,; \\
\langle \textit{prohibitions} \rangle & = & \langle \textit{prohibition} \rangle\,\{\,","\,\langle \textit{prohibition} \rangle\,\}\,; \\
\langle \textit{prohibition} \rangle & = & \langle \textit{atom} \rangle\,; \\
\langle \textit{pgrule} \rangle & = & \langle \textit{goalquery} \rangle\,"<-"\,\langle \textit{belquery} \rangle\,"|"\,\langle \textit{plan} \rangle\,":"\,\langle \textit{duration} \rangle\,; \\
\langle \textit{goalquery} \rangle & = & \langle \textit{goalquery} \rangle\,"\texttt{and}"\,\langle \textit{goalquery} \rangle\,|\,\langle \textit{goalquery} \rangle \\
& & "\texttt{or}"\,\langle \textit{goalquery} \rangle\,|\,"("\,\langle \textit{goalquery} \rangle\,")"\,|\,\langle \textit{atom} \rangle\,; \\
\langle \textit{belquery} \rangle & = & \langle \textit{belquery} \rangle\,"\texttt{and}"\,\langle \textit{belquery} \rangle\,|\,\langle \textit{belquery} \rangle\,"\texttt{or}"\,\langle \textit{belquery} \rangle \\
& & |\,"("\,\langle \textit{belquery} \rangle\,")"\,|\,\langle \textit{literal} \rangle\,; \\
\langle \textit{plan} \rangle & = & \langle \textit{atomic-plan} \rangle\,|\,\langle \textbf{non-atomic-plan} \rangle\,; \\
\langle \textit{atomic-plan} \rangle & = & "["\,\langle \textbf{non-atomic-plan} \rangle\,"]"\,; \\
\langle \textit{prefs} \rangle & = & \langle \textit{pref} \rangle\,\{\,","\,\langle \textit{pref} \rangle\,\}\,; \\
\langle \textit{pref} \rangle & = & (\langle \textit{goal} \rangle\,|\,\langle \textit{sanction} \rangle)\,"->"\,\langle \textit{priority} \rangle\,; \\
\langle \textit{sanction} \rangle & = & \langle \textit{atom} \rangle\,; \\
\langle \textit{deadline} \rangle & = & \langle \textit{time} \rangle\,; \\
\langle \textit{duration} \rangle & = & \langle \textit{int} \rangle\,; \\
\langle \textit{priority} \rangle & = & \langle \textit{int} \rangle\,;
\end{array}
$$

Fig. 2. EBNF syntax of N-2APL

the agent's state to include obligations and prohibitions, and changes to agent's deliberation strategy. The 2APL parser is implemented using JavaCC, and the modifications necessary to accommodate the extended N-2APL syntax simply required changing the grammar specification. Obligation goals are stored in the existing 2APL goal base, and the original 2APL Goal class was extended to incorporate a deadline and a priority. Obligation deadlines are treated as relative times in milliseconds and transformed to goal deadlines (clock times) when the program in parsed (in the case of initial obligations) or when the obligation event is received from the normative organization. Prohibitions do not map to existing 2APL intentional attitudes. A prohibition base (set of states) was therefore added to record the agent's current prohibitions. The prohibition base is used by the N-2APL deliberation strategy (see below) to check whether execution of an intention will violate a prohibition.

Significant changes to the 2APL deliberation strategy were required to take the priorities and deadlines of goals and prohibitions into account when deliberating about which plan to adopt for a goal and when to execute the plans to which it currently committed. The N-2APL deliberation strategy returns a schedule. A schedule is an assignment of a start or next execution time to a set of plans which ensures that: all plans complete by their deadlines, at most one atomic plan executes at any given time, and where the goals achieved and the prohibitions avoided are of the highest priority. Scheduling in N-2APL is pre-emptive in that the adoption of a new plan π may prevent previously scheduled plans with priority lower than π (including currently executing plans) being added to the new schedule. Plans that would exceed their deadline are dropped. In the case of obligations, a sanction will necessarily be incurred, so it is not rational for the agent to continue to attempt to discharge the obligation. In the case of goals, it is assumed that the deadline is hard, and there is no value in attempting to achieve the goal after the deadline. Plan which violate a prohibition of higher priority than the intention of the plan are dropped. The deliberation strategy was modified so that after application of `PG-rules`, the set of previously scheduled and newly generated plans are scheduled, and plans with a scheduled next execution time of 'now' are then executed.

Changes were also required to the execution of atomic plans. To allow the interleaved execution of an atomic plan with non-atomic plans (rather than executing all the steps of an atomic plan in a single step as in 2APL), atomic plans are transformed into sequence plans during parsing of the agent's program code and flagged as being atomic. The plan execution module was also changed so that external actions in non-atomic plans are executed in parallel.

2.3 Tuple Space

Interaction between the 2OPL normative organization and the N-2APL agents is via a tuple space [9]. We choose a tuple space rather than message-based interaction primarily to facilitate the integration of non-agent-based components such as the GeoSense game server (see Sect. 3). Our primary aim was to support programming with norm-aware agents with the stress on interoperability and preservation of history of the state space, therefore JavaSpaces paradigm has been chosen despite its possible performance issues. The facts recording the current (brute) state of the multi-agent environment and the detached norms and sanctions comprising its normative state are represented as tuples. The agents are connected to the tuple space through an extension of the N-2APL `Environment` class and in an agent program the tuple space is accessed in the same way as any other external environment.[4] The normative organisation accesses the tuple space through Prolog queries that wrap native Java method calls to the 'Prolog to Java' middleware used by both the N-2APL `Environment` class and 2OPL (see Fig. 6).

The tuple space implementation is based on Jini JavaSpaces (Apache River). We choose JavaSpaces because of its simplicity and versatility [12], and because, like 2OPL and N-2APL, it is implemented in Java. JavaSpaces supports following primitive operations:

---

[4] To simplify the implementation, in the current prototype the effects (postcondition) of agent actions are written directly to the tuplespace, and 2OPL fact update rules are not used. However it would be straightforward to delegate action execution to 2OPL.

- `write` - writes a new entry into the tuple space.
- `read` - reads any matching entry from the space, blocking until one exists. Returns null if the timeout expires.
- `readIfExists` - reads any matching entry from the space, returning null if there is currently is none. Matching and timeouts are done as in read, except that blocking in this call is done only if necessary to wait for transactional state to settle.
- `notify` - when entries are written that match this template notify the given listener with a `RemoteEvent` that includes a handback object.
- `take` - take a matching entry from the space, waiting until one exists.

Both the normative organization and the multi-agent system synchronize with the tuple space. Using the `notify` method, the organization and the agents register to be notified when new a tuple matching a template is inserted in tuple space. For example, agents register to receive notifications about all new obligation and prohibition entries assigned to them, and the normative organization registers to receive notifications when a new agent location tuple is created in the tuple space. As the agents and the normative organisation receive only those updates that are relevant to them, the overhead of the tuple space relative to a message passing implementation is minimal.

Tuples are stored as serialized Java `Entry` objects. Each type of tuple is defined as a class that implements the `Entry` interface, and we defined a simple mapping from the Prolog terms used by 2OPL and N-2APL to `Entry` objects. JavaSpaces is non-deterministic and therefore all tuples need to be timestamped. Timestamps are implemented using a clock process which writes the current system time as a clock tuple in the tuple space. (In the example application described in the next section, the clock process is provided by the gameserver middleware, which writes a new clock tuple once a second.)

3   Example Application

To illustrate the flexibility of our framework, in this section we briefly describe its application in a novel normative application, a mixed reality game called GeoSense [8]. A mixed reality game is a useful test application because the game rules define the expected behaviour of the players rather than legal moves as in chess—violation of a rule results in a player incurring a penalty rather than termination of the game. The game rules thus give rise to a variety of obligations and prohibitions on the players (and corresponding sanctions for violation) that can be used to assess the expressiveness of the normative representative language. The shared game environment allows monitoring and enforcement of norms, and the (soft) real time requirements and scalability of the game in terms of number of players allow testing of the non-functional aspects of the framework.

GeoSense is a real-time location-based game based on the MapAttack! game framework.[5] The game involves the use of GPS enabled smart phones to record

---
[5] http://mapattack.org

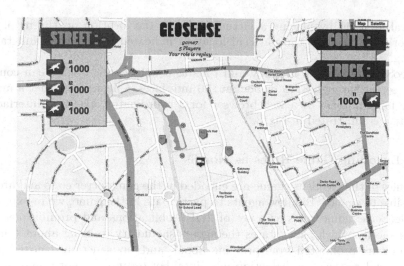

Fig. 3. GeoSense web interface

the locations of players and display it on a game map. Players must reach specific physical locations within the game area to complete tasks and win the game. GeoSense is normally played by teams of human players. The long term objective of integrating our normative programming framework with the game is to investigate the use of norms as means of coordinating human-agent interaction in human agent collectives—systems which involve both human and agent participants. We envisage a system in which mixed teams of humans and agents play the game and the expected and prohibited behaviors of both human and agent participants are expressed in terms of norms. However the version of the application described below involves only software agents.

The GeoSense game is played on a map of a physical location (typically part of a city such as a park) and has three kinds of players: a truck, pursuers and coordinators. The truck carries a load of radioactive waste, and attempts to avoid detection. The pursuers, assisted by the coordinator(s), attempt to determine the location of the truck. The physical (GPS) locations of the pursuers are shown on the map and updated as the players move in the real environment. The pursuers' locations are visible to each other and to the coordinator(s). The truck is a virtual player, and its location is not visible on the map. However its radioactive load leaves a virtual 'trace' that can be measured by taking a 'reading' at a pursuer's current physical location. The reading ranges from 0 to 100, with higher readings indicating a smaller distance to the truck. In an attempt to avoid detection, the truck may drop some of its load as it moves through the game area. Such dropped waste also gives a positive reading, making it more difficult for the pursuers to determine the location of truck. The coordinator(s) have a global view of the positions of all the pursuers and of all recent readings. The role of the coordinator is to aid the pursuers by directing them to promising areas of the map. The coordinator can request that a pursuer takes reading at a particular physical location by placing a virtual 'coin' at the location on the map. The pursuer must then go the physical location indicated by the coin and take a reading.

GeoSense is written in Ruby and runs as a web server. Clients can connect to the server through HTTP or Socket.IO interfaces. Clients are either a mobile device for a pursuer or a web browser for a coordinator. The web interface of the game is illustrated in Fig. 3.

3.1   Encoding Game Rules as Norms

The rules of the GeoSense game are encoded in the gameserver code and are not accessible to agents. To allow agents to participate in the game, we re-expressed the GeoSense game rules as a set of 2OPL obligations and prohibitions. The norms specify which game states the agents should try to bring about (and by when) or are prohibited from bringing about, and any sanction incurred if the norm is violated, e.g., a deduction in points. For example, a norm may specify that the truck is prohibited from entering a particular area of the map, and that violation of the norm results in the loss of 500 points. (Note that a norm-aware agent may still choose to violate a norm e.g., the agent may enter a prohibited area if doing so allows it to win the game.) Updates to the game state resulting from agent actions may trigger norms that apply to the agent that performed the action or another agent. For example, when a coordinator places a coin for a pursuer, the normative organisation creates an obligation that the pursuer must take a reading at the location of the coin within a specified time, and a prohibition specifying that the coordinator cannot place another coin at the same location. Example 2OPL game norms are illustrated in Fig. 4.

```
norm(forbidden_area(Agent),
     (truck(Agent), forbidden(X,Y)),
     prohibition(Agent, [at(X,Y,Agent)],
                 [reduce_score(Agent,500)])
).

norm(take_reading(Agent),
     (pursuer(Agent), coin(X,Y,Agent), clock(Now)),
     obligation(Agent, [reading(X,Y,Agent)],
                Now + 15000, [reduce_score(Agent,300)])
).
```

Fig. 4. Example GeoSense game norms

3.2   Agent Programs

We also developed N-2APL programs to allow the agents to play the game and achieve the goals resulting from the game norms. As an example, a program for

```
Beliefs:
  points(1000).
  position(19,19).
  clock(0).

Goals:
  at(2,2) : 120000,
  dropLoad : 60000

Preferences:
  at(2,2) -> 3,
  reduce_score(truck, 500) -> 4,
  dropLoad -> 5

PG-rules:

at(X,Y) <- true | { moveTo(X,Y); } : 60000
dropLoad <- position(10,10) | { drop(X,Y); } : 1000
```

Fig. 5. N-2APL program for the truck agent

a simple truck agent is shown in Fig. 5. The truck has two goals. The first goal
at(2,2) : 120000 is to reach position (2,2) in 2 min (120,000 ms) from the
start of the game and has a priority of 3. The second goal dropLoad : 60000 is
to drop (part of) its load within one minute of the start of the game, and has a
priority of 5. When the agent adopts a goal it executes the matching PG-rule.
For example, the rule to achieve the at(X,Y) goal specifies a plan that involves
moving to the required position. The PG-rule also includes an estimate of the
time required to execute the plan (one minute in this case).

The obligations and prohibitions the agent receives as a result of the game
rules may conflict with its own goals in the game. For example, the agent's goals
to be at(2,2) or to drop part of its load when at position (10,10) may require
visiting a prohibited area of the map. In such a situation, a norm-aware agent
must choose between its existing goals and the norms imposed by the game.
Critically, a N-2APL agent is able to violate norms (accepting the resulting
sanctions) if it is in the agent's overall interests to do so. For example, the
truck agent assigns a higher priority to achieving the goal at(2,2) than to the
sanction resulting from entering the prohibited area (losing 500 points), which
in turn has a higher priority than the dropLoad goal. The agent will therefore
enter the prohibited area if it necessary to reach (2,2) but would not violate
the norm to drop part of its load.

3.3   Gameserver Integration

To maintain the game state (and allow future participation by human players
using the GeoSense mobile and web browser clients), we integrated the GeoSense

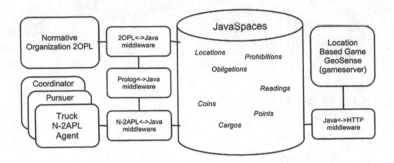

Fig. 6. Overall system architecture

gameserver with our normative programming framework consisting of 2OPL, N-2APL and JavaSpaces. GeoSense is connected to the framework through the tuple space as shown in Fig. 6. Updates to the tuple space corresponding to player actions are converted to HTTP POST requests to the game server. For example when a pursuer agent updates its location, the move action adds a new tuple to the tuple space, which is sent as a POST request to the gameserver. Similarly, the JSON updates generated by the gameserver used by the smart phone mobile clients are converted into tuples in the tuple space.

To simplify development of the agent programs, the tuple space to HTTP middleware discretises some aspects of the game state. For example, the locations of the players are represented as longitude and latitude pairs by the gameserver, while the agents see the game environment as a grid and move one cell at a time. Similarly, the real-time clock used by the gameserver to record the progress of the game is seen as a series of one second ticks by the agents. However these simplifications do not affect game play and are not inherent in the normative programming framework itself.

The agents' beliefs and actions are synchronized with the game state via the tuple space, allowing them to participate in the game. Moreover the actions of the agents are coordinated and regulated through the norms that implement the game rules.

4   Related Work

There has been considerable work on normative programming frameworks and middleware to support the development of normative multi-agent organisations, and such frameworks are often designed to inter-operate with existing BDI-based agent programming languages. However in these frameworks, the agents do not deliberate about whether to comply with norms.

For example, $\mathcal{J}$-$\mathcal{M}$OISE$^+$ [13] is designed to inter-operate with the $\mathcal{S}$-$\mathcal{M}$OISE$^+$ [14] middleware and allows Jason [15] agents to access and update the state of an $\mathcal{S}$-$\mathcal{M}$OISE$^+$ organization. Similarly, the JaCaMo programming framework combines the Jason, Cartago [16], and $\mathcal{S}$-$\mathcal{M}$OISE$^+$ platforms.

In JaCaMo, the organisational infrastructure of a multiagent system consists of organisational artefacts and agents that together are responsible for the management and enactment of the organisation. JaCaMo provides similar functionality to $\mathcal{J}$-$\mathcal{MOISE}^+$ in allowing Jason agents to interact with organisational artefacts, e.g., to take on a certain role. However while these approaches allow a developer to program e.g., when an agent should adopt a role, the Jason agents have no explicit mechanisms to reason about norms and their deadlines and sanctions in order to adapt their behaviour at run time. Another approach that integrates norms in a BDI-based agent programming architecture is proposed in [17]. This extends the AgentSpeak(L) architecture with a mechanism that allows agents to behave in accordance with a set of non-conflicting norms. As in N-2APL, the agents can adopt obligations and prohibitions with deadlines, after which plans are selected to fulfil the obligations or existing plans are suppressed to avoid violating prohibitions. However, unlike N-2APL, [17] does not consider scheduling of plans with respect to their deadlines or possible sanctions.

In contrast to frameworks such as $\mathcal{S}$-$\mathcal{MOISE}^+$ [14] which regulate behaviour by norm regimentation, our approach is based on norm enforcement and sanctions. Frameworks such as ORA4MAS [18] provide support for both norm regimentation and enforcement, however monitoring must be explicitly coded in organizational artifacts. An advantage of using a tuple space to represent both the brute and normative state of the agent's environment is monitoring of norm compliance and violation by the 2OPL interpreter is greatly simplified. On the other hand, approaches such as ORA4MAS allow decentralized (and arguably more flexible) decision making about the appropriate sanction for a violation.

A number of normative programming languages have recently been proposed that are similar in spirit to the 2OPL language used in our framework. NPL/NOPL [19] allows the expression of norms with conditions, obligations and deadlines, and norms may be regimented or enforced. However sanctions are represented as an obligation that an agent apply the sanction to the agent that violated the norm, whereas in our framework sanctions are applied by the organization. The norm-oriented language proposed in [20] is rule based like 2OPL. However, their norms relate to actions the agents should or should not perform while 2OPL norms relate to a state of the environment that should (or should not) be brought about. The normative language of the THOMAS multi-agent architecture [21] supports conditional norms with deadlines, sanctions and rewards. Conditions refer to actions (and optionally states). Norms are enforced rather than regulated, and sanctions may be applied by agents rather than the organization. As in our approach, the normative infrastructure does not restrict interactions between agents. A rule-based system implemented in Jess maintains a fact base representing the organizational state, detects norm activation and monitors violations. While these approaches offer similar functionality to 2OPL and the tuple space in our framework, they have not been integrated with a norm-aware agent programming language.

There has been relatively little work on applying norms to games. In [22] the authors describe the use of expectation monitoring by agents in the Second Life virtual environment. An expectation monitoring component integrated into the Jason interpreter allows agents to detect fulfilment and violation of their expectations. Expectations have some similarities to norms in specifying conditional constraints on future states. However, they are local to an agent rather than generated by a normative organization and there is no centralized monitoring or sanctioning of agents that violate expectations. Moreover, while the approach described in [22] allows agents to detect violations of expectations without recourse to a normative organization, the issues of how expectations are generated and what to do when they are fulfilled or violated are left to the agent developer. Perhaps the work that is most similar to ours is [23], in which the $\mathcal{MOISE}^{inst}$ normative organisation meta-model is used to control an interactive TV game show in which the avatars are implemented as agents. The purpose of the norms is to constrain players and their avatars to adopt team behaviour and to respect rules, while allowing some autonomy.

5   Conclusions and Future Work

We described a framework for programming norm-aware multi-agent systems which integrates the N-2APL norm-aware agent programming language with the 2OPL language for programming normative organisations. To the best of our knowledge, this is the first implementation of N-2APL and the first implementation of an integrated framework for norm-aware multi-agent systems in which autonomous agents deliberate about whether to conform to the norms imposed by a normative organisation. To illustrate the flexibility of our framework, we described its application in a location-based mixed reality game called GeoSense. We showed how the game rules can be expressed as conditional norms with deadlines and sanctions, and how agents can deliberate about their individual goals and the norms imposed by the game.

The GeoSense game is normally played by teams of human players. In future work, we plan to use the integration of norm-aware agents and the GeoSense game to investigate the use of norms for coordinating interaction and achieving adjustable autonomy in systems involving both human and agent participants. We also plan to address some of the limitations of our current implementation. For example, our approach currently assumes that the normative organisation assigns norms and sanctions to individual agents. While this is appropriate for many applications, there are situations where it would be more natural to address norms and sanctions to a group of agents. For example, a coordinator agent may create an obligation that some pursuer agent take a reading at a particular location without specifying which agent should do so; if none of the agents discharge the obligation by the deadline, the normative organisation applies a sanction to the pursuers as a group. In future work we plan to look at extending our framework to incorporate group norms and sanctions.

Acknowledgements. We would like to thank the reviewers for their helpful comments and Wenchao Jiang for making the code of the GeoSense game available and for assistance in developing the gameserver middleware. This work was partially supported by EPSRC grant EP/I011587/1.

References

1. Boella, G., Torre, L.V.D.: Introduction to normative multiagent systems. Comput. Math. Organ. Theory **12**, 71–79 (2006)
2. Andrighetto, G., Governatori, G., Noriega, P., van der Torre, L.W.N. (eds.): Normative Multi-Agent Systems, vol. 4 of Dagstuhl Follow-Ups. Schloss Dagstuhl - Leibniz-Zentrum fuer Informatik (2013)
3. Dastani, M., Grossi, D., Meyer, J.J.C., Tinnemeier, N.: Normative multi-agent programs and their logics. In: Meyer, J.J.C., Broersen, J. (eds.) Knowledge Representation for Agents and Multi-Agent Systems, pp. 16–31. Springer, Heidelberg (2009)
4. Hübner, J.F., Boissier, O., Bordini, R.H.: From organisation specification to normative programming in multi-agent organisations. In: Dix, J., Leite, J., Governatori, G., Jamroga, W. (eds.) CLIMA XI. LNCS, vol. 6245, pp. 117–134. Springer, Heidelberg (2010)
5. Alechina, N., Dastani, M., Logan, B.: Programming norm-aware agents. In: Conitzer, V., Winikoff, M., Padgham, L., van der Hoek, W. (eds.) Proceedings of the 11th International Conference on Autonomous Agents and Multiagent Systems (AAMAS 2012), Valencia, Spain, vol. 2, pp. 1057–1064. IFAAMAS, June 2012
6. Castelfranchi, C., Dignum, F., Jonker, C.M., Treur, J.: Deliberative normative agents: principles and architecture. In: Jennings, N.R., Lespérance, Y. (eds.) ATAL 1999. LNCS (LNAI), vol. 1757, pp. 364–378. Springer, Heidelberg (2000)
7. van Riemsdijk, M.B., Hindriks, K., Jonker, C.: Programming organization-aware agents. In: Aldewereld, H., Dignum, V., Picard, G. (eds.) ESAW 2009. LNCS (LNAI), vol. 5881, pp. 98–112. Springer, Heidelberg (2009)
8. Fischer, J.E., Jiang, W., Moran, S.: AtomicOrchid: a mixed reality game to investigate coordination in disaster response. In: Herrlich, M., Malaka, R., Masuch, M. (eds.) ICEC 2012. LNCS, vol. 7522, pp. 572–577. Springer, Heidelberg (2012)
9. Carriero, N., Gelernter, D.: Linda in context. Commun. ACM **32**(4), 444–458 (1989)
10. Tinnemeier, N.: Organizing agent organizations: syntax and operational semantics of an organization-oriented programming language. Ph.D. thesis, Utrecht University, SIKS (2011)
11. Dastani, M.: 2APL: a practical agent programming language. Auton. Agent. Multi-Agent Syst. **16**(3), 214–248 (2008)
12. Oaks, S., Wong, H.: Jini in a Nutshell - A Desktop Quick Reference. O'Reilly, Sebastopol (2000)
13. Hübner, J.F., Sichman, J.S., Boissier, O.: Developing organised multi-agent systems using the $\mathcal{MOISE}^+$ model: programming issues at the system and agent levels. Int. J. Agent-Oriented Softw. Eng. **1**(3/4), 370–395 (2007)
14. Hübner, J.F., Sichman, J.S., Boissier, O.: $\mathcal{S}$-$\mathcal{MOISE}^+$: a middleware for developing organised multi-agent systems. In: Boissier, O., Padget, J., Dignum, V., Lindemann, G., Matson, E., Ossowski, S., Sichman, J.S., Vázquez-Salceda, J. (eds.) ANIREM 2005 and OOOP 2005. LNCS (LNAI), vol. 3913, pp. 64–78. Springer, Heidelberg (2006)
15. Bordini, R.H., Hübner, J.F., Wooldridge, M.: Programming Multi-agent Systems in AgentSpeak using Jason. Wiley Series in Agent Technology. Wiley, Chichester (2007)

16. Ricci, A., Viroli, M., Omicini, A.: Give agents their artifacts: the A&A approach for engineering working environments in MAS. In: Durfee, E.H., Yokoo, M., Huhns, M.N., Shehory, O. (eds.): Proceedings of the Sixth International Joint Conference on Autonomous Agents and Multiagent Systems (AAMAS 2007), pp. 601–603. IFAAMAS (2007)

17. Meneguzzi, F.R., Luck, M.: Norm-based behaviour modification in BDI agents. In: Sierra, C., Castelfranchi, C., Decker, K.S., Sichman, J.S. (eds.): 8th International Joint Conference on Autonomous Agents and Multiagent Systems (AAMAS 2009), pp. 177–184. IFAAMAS (2009)

18. Hübner, J., Boissier, O., Kitio, R., Ricci, A.: Instrumenting multi-agent organisations with organisational artifacts and agents. Auton. Agent. Multi-Agent Syst. **20**, 369–400 (2010)

19. Hübner, J., Boissier, O., Bordini, R.: A normative programming language for multi-agent organisations. Ann. Math. Artif. Intell. **62**, 27–53 (2011)

20. García-Camino, A., Rodríguez-Aguilar, J., Sierra, C., Vasconcelos, W.: Constraint rule-based programming of norms for electronic institutions. Auton. Agent. Multi-Agent Syst. **18**, 186–217 (2009)

21. Criado, N., Julián, V., Botti, V., Argente, E.: A norm-based organization management system. In: Padget, J., Artikis, A., Vasconcelos, W., Stathis, K., da Silva, V.T., Matson, E., Polleres, A. (eds.) COIN@AAMAS 2009. LNCS, vol. 6069, pp. 19–35. Springer, Heidelberg (2010)

22. Ranathunga, S., Cranefield, S., Purvis, M.: Integrating expectation monitoring into BDI agents. In: Dennis, L., Boissier, O., Bordini, R.H. (eds.) ProMAS 2011. LNCS, vol. 7217, pp. 74–91. Springer, Heidelberg (2012)

23. Gâteau, B., Boissier, O., Khadraoui, D., Martinez, F.H.: Controlling an interactive game with a multi-agent based normative organisational model. In: Noriega, P., Vázquez-Salceda, J., Boella, G., Boissier, O., Dignum, V., Fornara, N., Matson, E. (eds.) COIN 2006. LNCS (LNAI), vol. 4386, pp. 86–100. Springer, Heidelberg (2007)

Author Index

Printed in the United States
By Bookmasters